The Geography of Movement

The Geography of Movement

John C. Lowe
Associate Professor of Geography
George Washington University

S. Moryadas
Formerly Assistant Professor of Geography
George Washington University

Houghton Mifflin Company Boston
Atlanta Dallas Geneva, Illinois
Hopewell, New Jersey Palo Alto London

Printed in the United States of America.

Library of Congress Catalog Card Number: 74-15401

ISBN: 0-395-18584-X

Contents

Preface

As an excuse to write a book, most professors bemoan the lack of a "suitable" text. In our case, when we conceived of this book in the fall of 1970, no comparable text was in fact available. In 1973 and 1974, two paperbacks and a selection of readings were published, indicating a congruent identification of a need in the textbook repertoire in geography.

There is no such thing as an objective or value-free social science, and attempts at such objectivity may be pretense and self-delusion. For this reason, Myrdal emphasizes that social scientists have an obligation to recognize and attempt to identify their value premises and the concomitant biases. We have chosen to be strictly "spatial," emphasizing the roles of distance and relative location in human interaction. As explanatory factors, we have concentrated largely on economic variables to the exclusion of social, behavioral, political, historical, institutional, and other factors. Therefore, we may be accused of overdoing the "spatial separatist" theme. To this charge we plead guilty since our individual and combined interests happen to be largely in the spatial tradition and we have derived intellectual satisfaction from what we have done.

The Geography of Movement provides a partial rather than a comprehensive view of the subject matter. The following topics are some of those included by other writers but ignored by us: railroad gauges; seaports and airports; containerization of freight; freight rates, their regulations, and their impact on flows; engineering factors associated with route construction; the role of railroad barons and other influential individuals in leading to route alignment; the political shenanigans behind many decisions impinging on transport development; the concatenation of subproblems that go under the rubric of "the urban transportation problem"; and a whole host of other considerations which, undoubtedly, do have relevance for transportation broadly conceived. Obviously, students interested in fully understanding transport in all its ramifications should pursue their interests in many disciplines besides geography.

The paradigm we have chosen is one that has developed over the last fifteen years or so, starting with the pioneering work of William Garrison and his associates at Northwestern University. By now, the contents have become standard in professional journals, but we believe that this is the first comprehensive textbook to treat movement or *circulation* broadly rather than transportation *sensu stricto.* Accordingly, we have taken a very general approach and have endeavored to incorporate within one framework all forms of human movement: commuting, shopping trips, migration, commodity flow, telephone message flows, and the movement of ideas and innovations. Therefore, there are no chapters entitled "Migration" or "Intrametropolitan Commuting." These topics, however, are treated under more general headings such as "The propensity for interaction" and "The modeling of flows."

Our approach is oriented toward an elucidation of concepts rather than techniques, although the latter is given some attention. For those interested in the operational aspects of techniques, various manuals on transportation planning and quantitative techniques in geography may be consulted. Further, we have tried to provide an exposition of the underlying regularities and processes that may lead to an understanding of the nature of human movement. For this reason, we have excluded modes and regions. Movement in both Asia and North America can be adequately treated in the same framework. Our examples are taken mostly from the American context, but alternatives can be rather easily substituted. In any event, this point may be irrelevant since examples are meant to support generalizations; hence whether a trip for medical attention, for example, is to a witch doctor or to a medical complex is totally immaterial.

Both of us spent a great deal of time at the outset developing an overall structure that would enable us to fit together the many pieces. The final shape of the book bears a striking resemblance to the initial outline despite three years of work and several revisions. This structure consists of the following major modules: (1) The basis of interaction, the nature of distance, and the costs of overcoming distance are all preliminary considerations that are discussed in the first three chapters. (2) The spatial structure of movement, or its geometry, consists of nodes, routes, networks, and their development. These constitute the topics of Chapters 4 through 6. (3) The propensity for movement (i.e., the generation of flows) and the economic, cultural, and other influences that have a bearing on movement propensities are treated in Chapter 7, which is a precursor to an extensive discussion of a variety of flow-modeling strategies and the structure of flows (Chapters 8 to 10). While these chapters are devoted largely to the movement of tangible objects, the place-to-place movement of innovations, both hierarchical and contagious, is elaborated upon in Chapter 11. Each of Chapters 1 through 11 is concerned with an explanation of how much moves from where to where and why. A description of how much *ought* to move from where to where and along what paths (i.e., a consideration of optimization problems) is briefly outlined in Chapter 12. Finally, the consequences of circulation for socioeconomic development of nations and regions are viewed from the vantage point of complex systems.

We have used the structure and major content of this book in courses at the George Washington University over a period of four years, and, therefore, we are able to make some suggestions about its use in a classroom situation.

In a one-semester course where only a nonformal approach to the subject matter is desired, the following materials can be easily eliminated: in Chapter 5, Multistep connections, Gross vertex connectivity and redundant paths, and Network regionalization; in Chapter 6, Simulation of alternative links; in Chapter 8, Stochastic approaches; in Chapter 9, A derivation of the gravity model and its operational version, Modeling intrametropolitan consumer shopping trips, Some operational problems, and Entropy-maximizing model: A new departure; in Chapter 10, Regionalization of flows; in Chapter 11, Epidemiology models; in Chapter 12, Paths between pairs of nodes and all material following it.

A deeper understanding of many of the models discussed can come about only if students work out example problems. While many of the models are suitable for manual calculations, some, such as the gravity model, require the facility of a computer.

In our experience, given a thirteen-week semester, the following schema is quite feasible:

Week 1	Chapter 1
Week 2	Chapter 2
Week 3	Chapter 3
Week 4	Chapter 4
Week 5	Chapter 5
Week 6	Chapter 6
Week 7	Chapter 7
Week 8	Chapter 8
Week 9	Chapter 9
Week 10	Chapter 9
Week 11	Chapters 10 and 11
Week 12	Chapter 11
Week 13	Chapters 12 and 13

Even ten years ago, a book such as this would have been impossible because adequate research had not yet been accomplished in the paradigm to which this book belongs. Consequently, we owe a big debt of gratitude to the many writers in several disciplines, but especially in geography and regional science, who have produced the raw materials upon which this book is based. They have been acknowledged in the bibliography. Additionally, we specifically thank the many individuals who, in various ways, have made a contribution: Prof. R. H. T. Smith of Monash University, Australia, who from the outset made many constructive comments; our own colleague Prof. Eldor Pederson, who on numerous occasions acted as arbiter and spotted goofs before drafts were sent out; Prof. Stephen Birdsall, University of North Carolina, who was responsible for a very detailed and painstaking check of the penultimate draft; Prof. James Davis, University of Western Kentucky, who also made useful comments; many of our students who have cheerfully functioned as guinea pigs over the many years, but especially Judy Conny and Eileen Barrett Anderson who undertook some bibliographic research and computational work for us; the succession of typists in the Department of Geography at George Washington University who undertook the repeated typing of extremely messy drafts — Irene Jones, Tanya Pshevlozky, Olga Pshevlozky, and Nicole Greene; Prof. Marvin Gordon, chairman of the Department of Geography, who presides over an unusually happy-go-lucky department which freed large blocks of time; our respective wives, Shirley and Virginia, and children, Tamara and Denise, and Yashy, George, and Anita, who kept asking us when we were going to finish the book.

Most books which have coauthors are actually the result of combining individually written chapters. *The Geography of Movement* is probably an exception in that each chapter has been written jointly. We both have greatly enjoyed the experience and benefited from mutual intellectual stimulation. As always, despite the help we have received from many individuals, the remaining sins of omission and commission are solely our own.

John Lowe

S. Moryadas

The Geography of Movement

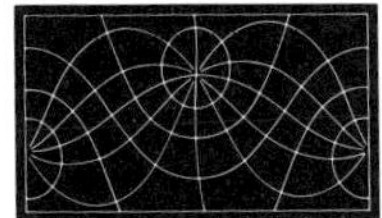

1 The Causes of Movement

A critical event in the life of any animate species is the acquisition of mobility, as when a baby learns to crawl or a bird to fly. All forms of animate movement involve certain common elements. A particularly interesting example is the waggle dance of the honeybee. This dance is performed by a worker bee when it returns to its home base (hive), after having discovered a new location of food or a potential new site for a hive. The waggle dance, in the form of a figure 8, is actually a sophisticated mode of communication. The straight run, that is to say, the middle of the figure 8, points to the direction of the newly discovered location from the hive. The length of the straight line indicates the distance to the destination. Apparently, a straight run lasting 1 second means that the target is 500 meters away from the hive, while one lasting 2 seconds indicates a distance of 2 kilometers. Subsequent to the transmission of this information, many other bees begin to commute, as it were, to the newly found employment opportunity, and the great majority alight within 20 percent of the correct distance to the intended destination.

This event in the animal world illustrates a number of elements common to all forms of movement. There is a specific *origin* in geographic space, in this case the home or hive, as well as a specific *destination* some distance away from the origin. There is a path connecting these two points. Movement between origin and destination requires the expenditure of both time and effort. Movement is purposeful: there is one location of supply and another of demand. The volume of movement (flow) is a function of both the number of bees in the hive (population) and the potential supply at the other end (natural resources or raw materials). The move may constitute a temporary flight with a return to home base or a more permanent one in which a swarm establishes a new home (migration) in virgin territory. Like human communities, beehives are agglomerations, and when a hive becomes too full (high population density), migration occurs to specific destinations where desired wants can be satisfied.

Since this is not a text in zoology, the conceptualization of movement used in this book incorporates primarily the movement of people, goods, information, and ideas. This conceptualization is sometimes regarded as "spatial interaction," referring broadly to all forms of movement between two or more places (Ullman, 1956). Without conscious decisions and actions on the part of individuals there can be no interaction, and, therefore, it is appropriate to refer to spatial interaction as human interaction in space.

The major purpose of this chapter is to introduce, in a preliminary and nonformal manner, some fundamental reasons for interaction. In the strictest sense, people's wants with respect to goods, contacts, information, etc., cannot be satisfied at any one given location. Therefore, it follows that their wants must be met from other locations. Movement occurs to the extent that people have the ability to satisfy their desires with respect to goods, services, information, or experience at some location other than their present one, and to the extent that these other locations are capable of satisfying such desires.

Since all phenomena can be viewed in a spatial context, we begin by examining the influence of their spatial separation.

THE INFLUENCE OF THE SPATIAL SEPARATION OF PHENOMENA

All phenomena can be referred to by means of a specific address in geographic space, i.e., the surface of the earth as differentiated from the subsurface and from outer space. Even underground oil deposits can be identified by a location on the surface of the earth. Clearly, it is a physical impossibility for two objects to occupy the same location simultaneously. Therefore, people and things are "spread out" in geographic space, even in the crowded parts of this planet.

Each point in geographic space is unique with respect to other points in that space even though some points may have similar characteristics. Despite the existence of an infinite number of points in geographic space, only a finite number are occupied or used by people for the satisfaction of their physical and psychological wants. Such facilities as grocery stores, churches, and police stations are located at specific points, and these are, of necessity, both origins and destinations of all movement.

There are, of course, billions of people on the earth's surface, millions of villages, and thousands of towns, all of which could generate vast amounts of pairwise potential interaction. The actual number of place-to-place interactions is much less than the potential, owing to a variety of constraints.

THE INFLUENCE OF SPECIALIZATION, AGGLOMERATION, AND SCALE ECONOMIES

Human beings organize themselves in different forms in order to obtain a greater level of satisfaction than would be possible if they operated as lone individuals. There are political, economic, social, and other types of organizations, each of which has a spatial component also. As a cause of movement, we have chosen to emphasize here differing modes of economic organization.

As one considers the many groups of people inhabiting the earth's surface, it is evident that they are engaged in many different ways of making a livelihood, ranging from food gathering to postindustrial economies. Although many of these ways are still in existence, it appears that there has been a process of cultural evolution. A most significant aspect of this evolution has been an increasing level of occupational specialization and a concomitant increasing level of spatial specialization. Simultaneously, the role of movement has been increasing secularly.

In food-gathering tribal economies, the most significant division of labor is within the most elemental unit of society, the family. Each unit tends to be self-sufficient since most of the wants of the group can be satisfied by its members. In addition, the field or territory of a group engaged in food gathering tends to be sharply circumscribed by limits imposed by both nature and culture. One consequence of the circumscribed field is that individual trips are likely to be of limited distance and duration, while the low level of technology necessitates repeated single-purpose trips.

In the case of sedentary agriculture the nature of social organization is more complex, its needs are more diverse, and, as a result, the division of labor is finer than in the case of the food gatherers. As a result of full-time work in a particular occupation, individuals can produce a surplus. Generally these surpluses create an outbound movement of certain farm goods and an inbound movement comprising both farm and nonfarm products. Furthermore, people in an agricultural society operate in a broader field than their food-gathering counterparts and are likely to have greater opportunity to come into contact with locations far outside their immediate environment.

In industrial societies, social organization is even more complex; basic needs have now proliferated into wants to such a point that an extremely fine division of labor is required for the satisfaction of these wants. The multifarious products and services required by an industrial society are made by specialists working singly or in groups. The export surplus of such a society is much greater and more varied than that of an agricultural society, just as the quantity and the variety of imports are also greater. This being the case, the number and range of contacts between settlements are greatly increased, and the resulting volume of movement is large.

Finally, in the postindustrial economies, which are characterized by high mass consumption and the increasing dominance of service activities, the division of labor and resulting specialization reach extremes. In such a society, the needs for products of other specialists are greatly amplified simply because any one individual can produce only a minute fraction of his or her own total needs. Most individuals are specialists in particular activities. The satisfaction of the diverse and enormous needs of a postindustrial society generates a great deal of movement. Simultaneously, the means by which interaction occurs have proliferated into a multitude of alternative modes.

The multiplicity of minutely specialized occupations in complex societies has had two profound consequences: (1) the increasing role of agglomeration economies and (2) the increasing importance of scale economies.

The initial establishment and continued maintenance of any activity in geographic space are predicated upon the existence of a threshold population. Translated into a spatial context, low threshold activities can survive in a relatively small trade area and, consequently, tend to be located close together.

On the other hand, activities that require a high threshold will be dispersed in geographic space. Thus, in a given area, for example, there will be many supermarkets, which are located a short distance apart, and few regional hospitals, which are separated by long distances. There are characteristic relationships among threshold, number, spacing, and size of activities, and these relationships have been generalized in central place theory.

Given a certain population distribution and certain threshold requirements for a variety of activities, the geographic distribution of activities may necessitate a large number of single-purpose trips. A more convenient spatial organization stems from agglomeration of groups of activities at a small number of locations. Shopping centers, industrial parks, and cities represent such agglomerations, all of which enable multipurpose trips, thus reducing overall volume of movements. The underlying reason for the existence of agglomerations is the realization of what are called "agglomeration economies." There are cost advantages, in both production and marketing, which ensue from the concentration of production at one location (Weber, 1929, 126; Isard, 1956, 172–187). The unit cost of production for a particular enterprise is lower because other firms or institutions located in the same area can share certain costs, such as those associated with police protection, trash removal, tax consulting firms, and telephone answering services. The spatial juxtaposition of a number of activities enables the development of interindustry linkages at relatively low movement costs. Large industrial agglomerations are part of major urban areas which have a concentration of population that provides a ready market for a variety of products. Therefore, distribution costs are minimized. *Agglomerations* are both the origins and the destinations of massive amounts of movement, or, alternatively, they represent the basic elements in spatial interaction.

The second consequence of specialization in complex societies is the critical role played by economies of scale. *Economies of scale* refer to the differences in unit cost of production due solely to the differences in aggregate volume of output. These can be realized through the creation of increasingly larger establishments. In this process, the smaller establishments either disappear from the cultural landscape or are merged. In the locational context, this means that the overall number of production or service locations is reduced in a given area unless the market demand increases in such a manner as to create new opportunities for smaller establishments.

In a number of industries, especially in primary metals, metal fabricating, and transportation equipment manufacturing, and in electric power generation, the initial capital costs related to plant and equipment are of such magnitude as to compel production at large volume. Thus, the aggregate demand for such products can be met from a small number of production locations, even in large and affluent economies such as that of the United States. Thus, agglomeration and scale economies can be realized by locating many large activities at a given location simultaneously. Just as the needs of a country for various industrial products can be supplied from a small number of plants, similarly the economic and cultural needs of a country can also be supplied from a small number of large cities, each of which can be considered to be an agglomeration of firms.

Most cities, although multifunctional in the sense that they perform manufacturing, retailing, wholesaling, and other such functions, are, nevertheless, different from one another. Thus, while one city's manufacturing activities may consist largely of apparel manufacturing, another's may consist of electronic design and assembly. Not only are specialized manufacturing activities located in particular cities, but the cities themselves are also concentrated in particular regions. For example, Kalamazoo, Lansing, Ypsilanti, Pontiac, and Detroit, all of which have a heavy concentration of the automobile assembly industry, are located in a relatively small area of southern Michigan that constitutes an automobile production region. In the same manner, there are textile regions, shoe manufacturing regions, and petrochemical complexes, facilitating the realization of agglomeration and scale economies.

There emerges a national space-economy in which productive activities are differentiated from place to place. In the richer nations of the world consumer preferences, tastes, habits, and budgets are relatively uniform, and consequently consumers, regardless of their location, demand a standardized "market basket of goods." What, then, are the implications of these ideas for movement? Berry (1964) suggests that the smooth and orderly functioning of the space-economy requires that the specialized products and services from each region of a country be moved in some manner to the locations where consumers live.

Figure 1-1 shows the location of five specialized "production regions," two of which specialize in two products. All consume one another's products, resulting in a complex pattern of interaction flows (commodity movements) among the several locations.

A convenient way to recapitulate the ideas expressed in this section is to make a comparison between simple and complex societies. Table 1-1 enumerates the attributes having implications for movement as they vary between the two types of societies.

In spite of the list of sixteen attributes in Table 1-1, it must be emphasized that once occupational division of labor is assumed to be at a certain level, all the rest of the attributes follow automatically as necessary conditions and logical end results. The most important consequence of the differences in level of division of labor between the two types of societies is the difference in intensity of human interaction in space. Figure 1-2, showing low levels of interaction, is offered in contrast to Figure 1-1. Without movement, the space-economy of complex societies cannot function at all. Major transportation routes are sometimes referred to as arteries, an appropriate analogy. Just as the arteries in the physiological context carry the life-sustaining substances to the entire organism, the transportation system keeps a complex space-

Figure 1-1
Interaction flows in a complex society

R_i = the ith production region

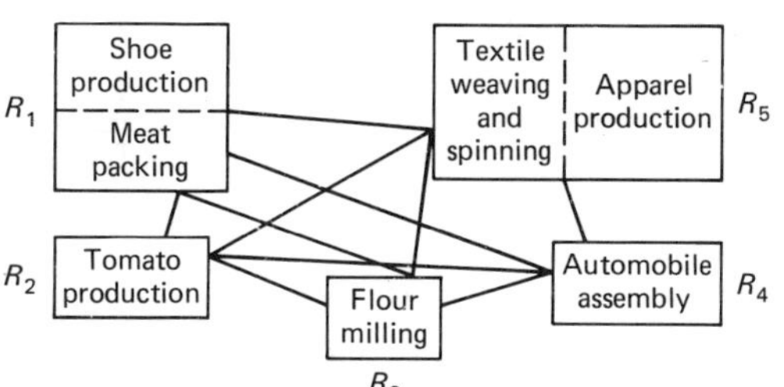

Table 1-1
Selected Attributes of Simple and Complex Societies

Social and economic organizational attributes	Simple	Complex
1. Population density	Very low	High
2. Division of labor	Coarse	Fine
3. Functional role of the individual	Multifunctional	Highly specialized
4. Ratio of fixed costs to variable costs of productive activities	Mostly variable costs	Increasing role of fixed costs
5. Role of economies of scale	Unimportant	Critical
6. Role of agglomeration economies	Unimportant	Critical
7. Productivity of the individual	Low	High
8. Extent of export surplus	None	Large
9. Range of goods produced	Limited	High
10. Demand for products of others	Limited	Very high
11. Level of interdependency of an individual with others	Low	Extremely high
Consequences for interaction	**Simple**	**Complex**
1. Mean number of essential journeys	Low	Very high
2. Nature of journeys	Many single-purpose	Many multipurpose
3. Number of journey origins	Low	High
4. Number of potential destinations	Low	Very high
5. Intensity of human interaction, per capita	Very low	Extremely high

economy functioning. Therefore, any disruption of the transportation system has paralytic effects.

THE INFLUENCE OF THE SPATIAL SEPARATION OF RESOURCE ENDOWMENTS

Even without the occupational division of labor, there would be broad differences in the nature and characteristics of activities in geographic space. These are due to significant place-to-place variations in the distribution of

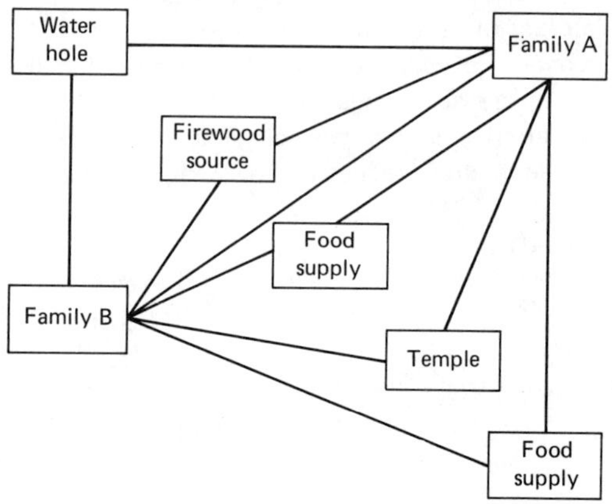

Figure 1-2
Interaction flows in a simple society

natural and human resource endowments on the earth's surface. Such variations enable particular areas to enjoy differential or "comparative cost" advantages with respect to the production of certain goods and services, giving those areas a certain leverage in interregional and international trade.

Natural resources are not uniformly distributed on the earth's surface. There are both quantitative and qualitative variations. Most resources are spatially concentrated in a few locations so that we have the Corn Belt in the American Midwest, the rubber plantations of Malaysia, the paper and pulp production regions of Scandinavia, oil fields at the head of the Persian Gulf, and Appalachian coal fields. If all natural resources were available everywhere, they would not have to be transported anywhere else, since there would be no deficit areas. Air, as a natural resource, does not enter interregional or international trade. A fundamental cause of movement, therefore, is the existence of spatially concentrated resources which, in turn, leads to surplus and deficit areas. Each region exchanges its surplus for other surplus commodities produced in other specialized regions.

The distribution of people also varies greatly at the macroscale. Of the estimated 1970 world population of 3.619 billion, 57.5 percent was distributed among the seven largest countries (Davis, 1970). Furthermore, even within these countries — in China and India, for example — the preponderant share of the population is concentrated in a few river basins and mineral-rich regions.

If too many people are competing for two few resources within a nation or region, *population pressures* are said to exist. These pressures may be alleviated by international or interregional population transfers. In the context of resource constraints, migration would occur from areas of high population density to those of low density, until some overall equilibrium was reached. In times past, there have been great migrant streams between regions and continents. One of the last big streams was from Europe to the United States, from 1840 to 1930, a period during which 37 million persons emigrated to the United States.

Given the existence of areas of surpluses (of people, products, money) and also of deficits, other things being equal, we may expect that there would be large-scale flows between the areas of greatest surplus and those of largest deficit. But, of course, other things are not equal; otherwise spatial interaction would be a trivial concept. There is a variety of constraints to "free flow" of people, things, and information, whose movements are channeled between particular pairs of origins and destinations. The major constraints we wish to emphasize at this juncture are the relative accessibility of resources (distance constraints), political considerations, and the impact of economic space.

Relative Accessibility of Resources

Accessibility may be defined as the ease with which a specific location can be reached from a given point. When a number of similar locations (e.g., towns) are considered simultaneously, the accessibility concept is a comparative one which is referred to as *relative accessibility*. For example, Berlin is more accessible to Paris than to Vienna, while Vienna is more accessible to Berlin than to Paris.

The influence of relative accessibility in converting potential interaction among regions into actual flows stems from at least three considerations:

1. The cost of transportation in relation to unit cost of production. High-quality resources can be exploited at a lower unit cost, and since producers are interested in minimizing total costs, it may be preferable, under certain circumstances, to pay higher transport costs for high-quality resources at a great distance rather than to use a nearer, lower-quality resource. "Carrying coal to Newcastle" is, in certain cases, possible and desirable. If, however, the transport cost from a high-quality source of supply is prohibitively expensive, and if a feasible but lower-quality alternative exists close to the region of demand, the latter will be utilized and therefore there is a trade-off between the unit cost of transportation and the unit cost of production.

2. The existence or the absence of transportation facilities. Transport facilities make resources accessible and, therefore, available as a good. Unless there exist organized transportation facilities, including networks, warehouses, and a variety of institutional arrangements, resources cannot be exploited on a massive scale at the supply location, and despite the spatial variation in resource endowments, there can be no large-scale movement. An example of this situation is the Turk-Sib railroad in the Soviet Union, which connects the previously existing Siberian railroad with the Turkestan region and makes that region's resources accessible to the major markets of the U.S.S.R. Of course, small-scale movements in simple societies can function quite adequately using minimum facilities, such as a network of trails.

3. Substitution among resources. If a certain resource is too far away from the region of demand, or if traditional sources of supply are cut off for some reason, the search for substitution is encouraged. Substitution can occur between products, between locations, or both. During World War II, the rice-eating population of India was forced to use grain sorghum and millets, because the traditional suppliers of imported rice, Burma and Thailand, were occupied by the Japanese.

Political Considerations

Earth space is fragmented into about 140 bounded political-territorial entities, each of which can be referred to as a *political space.* Crossing a national boundary usually requires the permission of the respective national governments which control the territory on either side of the boundary. Governments have at their disposal a variety of policy instruments to modify and channel movement, including tariffs, quotas, currency and exchange regulations, total embargoes, and quarantines. In the case of international movement, government policies can presumably be enforced since borders are controlled by customhouses and check posts. The ways in which political considerations play a role in structuring the flow of goods include the topics discussed in the following paragraphs.

The imperial preference system, practiced by member nations of the British Commonwealth, is designed to accord "most favored nation" treatment to Commonwealth countries. Preferential tariffs stimulate intra-Commonwealth trade and restrict the supply from other nations for comparable goods.

Political considerations both encourage and inhibit the movement of people. Most countries have stringent regulations about who may enter. Even the United States, which claims to offer a home for the world's huddled masses, had a national-origins quota system for a long time. Under the Alien and Sedition Acts, Chinese immigration was virtually prohibited. At the other extreme, we also have the example of Israel, to which any Jew born anywhere in the world has a legal right of citizenship. Not only is entry controlled, but so is exit. The current cause célèbre in this regard is the emigration policy in the Soviet Union with respect to Jews, but even from the United States, it is difficult to travel to Cuba and Albania because of the policies of our State Department.

Economic Space and Corporate Considerations

Economic space is that area over which a certain economic activity or activities prevail. Unlike political space, economic space is more amorphous in that its boundaries tend to be fuzzy and permeable. The Corn Belt in the United States and the retail trade area of a store are examples of economic space.

Economic space and political space overlap, but in some cases, because of the existence of tariffs and quotas, a political boundary may also be considered the boundary of an economic space. Economic space can also incorporate more than one complete political space, as, for example, the European Economic Community or the European Free Trade Association.

Movement is particularly significant in the context of the economic space of a modern, multiplant corporate organization. The particular territory over which a nation's corporate organizations function is affected by and may affect in turn the "sphere of influence" of the country. While British rubber manufacturing companies obtain much of their natural rubber from Malaya, until recently French companies obtained theirs from Indochina. The choice of a specific area in the tropics from which rubber will be imported is a function of the "spheres of influence" and of the concomitant spatial behavior of the various corporations. Ties forged between countries during the period of active colonial expansion still exist despite the rapid breakup of colonial empires since the end of World War II. In general, geographical habits of trading, once cultivated, tend to remain stable because patterns of corporate behavior become institutionalized and their importance transcends changes in political relationships among nations.

Given the existence of a number of alternate supply locations, the selection of a specific location is made by corporate organizations in their effort to satisfy existing demands.

THE CAUSES OF MOVEMENT: A CONCEPTUAL FRAMEWORK

We have analyzed in concrete terms and in some detail the causes of movement, and we can synthesize these many causes in terms of a few simple, abstract concepts which, together, constitute the basis of human interaction in space.

Place and Time Utility

Utility is the capacity of a commodity or a service to satisfy some human want.

Place Utility

"*Place utility* is the added economic value of a commodity created by transporting it from the place or area in which it has little or no usefulness or value to a place or places in which it has greater usefulness or utility" (Wilson, 1954, 5). For example, the fact that there is a lot of coal in Wales is of little use to an electric power generating station in London until that coal has been transported to the plant. Although the price paid by the power plant is higher than the pithead cost of coal, the value of coal has been enhanced as a direct result of its transportation. Similarly, there are very few automobile owners in Kuwait, and, therefore, the 13 percent of the world's petroleum reserves located there has no place utility unless transported to Western Europe, where the number of automobiles is high.

In some instances, a product may have a negative place utility or a *disutility* in the sense that we are interested in removal of the product and are willing to pay to have it taken away. The obvious examples are sewage and trash removal, as well as the disposal of industrial and mining wastes. Place utility and place disutility can be viewed as fundamental causes for movement in space.

Time Utility

"Transportation enhances the ability of goods to satisfy human wants by making goods available not only *where* they are needed but *when* they are needed. This results in time utility" (Wilson, 1954, 7). Many products have a short shelf life, and fresh inventories must be obtained periodically. In order to save on warehousing and storage charges, there is a need for regular and periodic fresh supplies of produce, as and when old stocks are depleted. Food products are particularly susceptible to the influence of time utility, especially in poor countries where most homes are not equipped with refrigeration.

Complementarity

The concepts of complementarity, intervening opportunities, and transferability were initially introduced in the geography literature by Ullman (1956). We elaborated earlier on the influence of the spatial variations of resource endowments on movement. Mere differentiation, however, does not automatically generate movement. If that were the case, much movement might occur between the arctic and equatorial regions since they represent the most highly contrasted natural environments. In order for movement to occur between two places, there must be a demand for a particular product in one region, and another region must be capable of supplying that particular product. This is known as *specific complementarity*.

The reciprocal relations between urban industrial regions and rural agricultural regions are based on mutual complementarity, as are the relations between industrialized nations and underdeveloped countries specializing in agricultural production and mineral resource extraction. Thus, cacao beans move from Ghana to the Cadbury chocolate manufacturing plants in the United Kingdom, and manufactured goods move in the opposite direction. Vacationers prefer environments which are in sharp contrast to their own homes; for example, many Swedes vacation in Gabon. Complementarity is a fundamental reason for international trade and human movement.

Intervening Opportunities

Just as mere spatial differentiation will not result in movement, mere complementarity will not of itself result in movement either. The question revolves around the availability of an alternative, closer, and more accessible source of supply. For example, many people in the United Kingdom vacation on the relatively warmer southwestern coast known as the Cornish and Kentish Rivieras rather than travel to the more distant Côte d'Azur.

"Intervening opportunities" is a negative concept in that it may prevent movement from occurring even where there is specific complementarity. It also encourages suboptimization and motivates people to select a lesser but still adequate alternative rather than the more distant but best location.

Transferability

A good that is involved in interaction between two places must be capable of being *transferred.* Different goods have different degrees of transferability, measured by the real cost of transfer. Transfer costs include all the costs associated with movement, such as the price of transportation, insurance in transit, storage charges (if any), pickup and delivery charges, as well as the time lost in transportation. It is evident that transferability is related to the price of the good before the good obtains place utility. Diamonds are precious and therefore are capable of bearing extravagant transfer costs in the form of very high transport and insurance premiums as they move by air freight over long distances. Conversely, sand and gravel have very low transferability.

Despite specific complementarity, transfer will not occur in the absence of a transportation facility. For example, the fantastic scenic wonders that exist in the Pamirs are enjoyed by very few tourists because that region is inaccessible to much of the world.

The four concepts just discussed are mainly applicable to the movement of goods between places and, to a lesser extent, to the movement of people and ideas. Most movements can be understood and explained in terms of these four concepts, which should all be taken into consideration simultaneously in order to provide a parsimonious explanation of why place-to-place movement occurs.

Pursuant to the discussion of the causes of movement in this chapter, the next six chapters constitute building blocks, as it were. Bricks and cement blocks are necessary for the construction of a structure, but in the absence of an architectural design the blocks, by themselves, have no utility. Therefore, it would be well to lay out here the format of the design employed in the next several chapters.

At the end of this chapter, we are left with a world in which there are a number of locations where demand is generated. These locations are separated by distance from other places that can supply the products demanded. In Chapter 2, the nature of intervening distance is considered, emphasizing its conceptual aspects and ways of measuring. Chapter 3 is concerned with some of the more important economic considerations of movement. Regardless of the distance traveled or the amount transported, there is no such thing as free movement. The cost of overcoming distance is one price that we pay to satisfy our wants.

The elements of the spatial structure of movement include nodes, routes, and networks. These constitute the subject matter of Chapters 4 through 6. All movement originates or terminates at particular points in geographic space which we shall term "nodes." Their characteristics and functions and geographic patterning are treated in Chapter 4. All flows between nodes, whether passenger movement, commodity shipments, mail flows, telephone messages, or whatever, are channeled along discrete route segments. Their nature, functions, and impacts are also explored in Chapter 4. Nodes and routes together constitute a network as is explained in Chapter 5. In recent years, networks have been viewed from a geometric perspective using the notions of graph theory. In Chapter 5 we summarize various ways of studying networks, and attention is paid to their classification, levels of accessibility, and hierarchical characteristics. Networks, of course, do not remain constant through time. Nodes become larger or smaller, some disappear, new ones emerge on the landscape. Equally, new route segments are added, and older ones are enlarged, straightened, or deleted. Changes in the structure of networks through time are considered in Chapter 6 by using a variety of models.

All of us as individuals and as members of groups have varying tendencies to interact with other people at other places. That certain systematic regularities have, however, been uncovered with reference to propensity for interaction is shown in Chapter 7.

It is only after we have considered these various "building blocks" that we can proceed to an analysis of flows — how much of what moves from where to where and why.

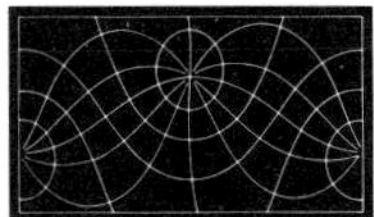

2 Distance: Concepts, Measures, and Transformations

In this chapter, we elaborate on a variety of theoretical and operational aspects of distance, as well as on alternative ways of measuring and transforming it.

CONCEPTS OF DISTANCE

We are all familiar with statements such as "New York City is 225 miles from Washington, D.C.," "Staten Island is 5 cents away from Manhattan," "the White House is sixteen blocks from the Capitol," "the airport is a half-hour away," and "gee, that seemed a lot farther away than it really is!" All these statements refer essentially to the distance between two locations in geographic space. The varied yardsticks underscore the point that distance is a rather sophisticated and complex concept and that, indeed, there may be more than one concept applicable to it. Since all movement entails the overcoming of distance, we need to obtain an appreciation of these concepts.

Harvey (1969, 191–229), in a chapter entitled "Geometry — The Language of Spatial Form," provides an excellent discussion of the various spatial languages in which many geographical problems could be couched and summarizes an extensive literature from the fields of mathematics and the philosophy of science. A spatial language is a conceptual framework that enables one to describe and analyze the distribution of objects in space. Harvey notes that people's concepts of space and therefore of distance are dependent upon both culture and experience. Formal geometries with elaborate syntaxes have been developed, and many of these provide useful "model-languages for discussing geographic problems" (Harvey, 1969, 228). In this and the following sections on measures of distance, we limit ourselves to euclidean geometry primarily because geographical tradition has regarded space as a framework for things and events. Harvey refers to this as the "container view of space" which postulates an absolute space (Harvey, 1969, 208). In this space, the axiomatic statements of Euclid are valid. In euclidean space, the distance between two points is the intervening spatial interval between their absolute locations, defined by the intersection of cartesian coordinates, such that on a two-dimensional surface the north-south direction is referenced by Y and the east-west direction by X. If these two points are located at X_1Y_1 and X_2Y_2 respectively, then the distance between them is given by the Pythagorean theorem as $d = \sqrt{(X_1 - X_2)^2 + (Y_1 - Y_2)^2}$.

Distance can be measured only in terms of process and activity, and it appears that different notions of space and distance are appropriate for each. Thus, "economic distance" and "perceptual distance" must be measured with different yardsticks, as we shall see later. The difficulties encountered by geographers in empirically verifying location theory are stimulating an exploration of alternative geometries.

Riemann was the first to show that there are many surfaces and, therefore, that many geometries exist. In each of them, different distance measurements are appropriate. While there are many commentaries available on Riemann geometry, one of the best is by Aleksandrov et al. (1963, 164–178). The properties of a particular space could be adequately defined in terms of the form of *geodesics* (the path of shortest distance between two points) embedded in that space. Therefore, economic space has a different geodesic than social space. Further, space has many dimensions, such as the three dimensions of physical space, a time dimension, a cost dimension, and so on.

Riemann space is more applicable than euclidean space to the spherical earth and the universe, which are characterized by constant positive curvature. In Riemann space, the shortest distance is *not* a straight line but a curved one, as, for example, the great circle routes used in navigation. In contrast to euclidean geometry, in Riemann geometry and on the spherical earth, parallel lines are not possible since all great circles intersect.

Harvey notes a possible application of Minkowski space (a special case of Riemann space applied to four dimensions) to the geography of movement. Consider an individual moving about in a two-dimensional euclidean space, changing his (X,Y) coordinate location over a time dimension T, with varying amounts of money to spend, so that money is the fourth, or Z, dimension (Harvey, 1969, 226). This is a space, time, and cost conceptualization of movement for which some noneuclidean geometry is perhaps more appropriate; but these spatial languages are strange in that space may be curved and the angles of a triangle may add up to more or less than 180°.

Progress in the use of noneuclidean geometries has been somewhat inhibited in geography because most of us have been indoctrinated into thinking in terms of euclidean space, superseding the child's conception of a flexible space where distances are elastic. Consequently, we tend to translate noneuclidean geometries into a euclidean framework, which can sometimes be misleading. This ambiguity arises because each of the different geometries, although pertaining to the same universe, is a different abstract construct. Unlike the case of international monetary units, there are no standard conversions between the various geometries, so that a question such as What is the Minkowski distance between the White House and the Capitol? does not have any ready answer. Why, then, should we introduce novel geometries here?

Basically, we do so to suggest the existence of other ways of conceptualizing space and distance that someday may become both powerful and practical languages to describe spatial form and spatial interaction. At present, none of these various geometries has been used in geography in an operational situation; nevertheless, they could provide important insights. An engineer, after all, does not denigrate pure mathematics simply because it cannot help him design a bridge.

A fundamental aspect of the distance concept is that distance depends upon the relative location of points. An elementary dichotomy may be established as between the distance between any two points and the distance in a set of *n* points viewed as a whole.

Point-to-point Distances

We can conceptualize absolute or point-to-point distances as being either straight-line short paths or non-straight-line short paths. Both of these may be referred to as "geodesic paths" regardless of the type of surface or the unit of measurement (Nystuen, 1963).

The basic difference between the two types of point-to-point distance is caused by variations in the quality and characteristics of the geographic space (surface) which separates the points. Among the different types of surfaces utilized in the following discussion are (1) isotropic surfaces, on which the movement effort is the same in all directions from every point, and (2) anisotropic surfaces, on which the movement effort may vary with direction from any point.

Straight-line Short Paths

The simplest way of viewing distance is to think of it as the shortest path along a straight line between two points. Highway networks in the Great Plains of North America consist of a series of straight lines (Figure 2-1). When a crow flies from tree *A* to tree *B* and back again, it is probably traveling the same distance both ways. This assumption arises from the metric property of euclidean space which states that the distance between two points *i* and *j* is reciprocal. Frequently, however, this is not the case, and the distance d_{ij} may not be equal to d_{ji}; a familiar example of this discrepancy is the driving distance on a network of one-way streets (Figure 2-2).

Non-straight-line Short Paths

Under certain circumstances, the shortest absolute distance between two points may be not one straight line, but rather a series of straight lines with different directional orientations. The need for changing direction arises from the existence of one or more obstacles lying athwart the most direct path between these points. Familiar examples of non-straight-line short paths include a hike through the woods (Figure 2-3*a*) and running an errand in a city with a gridiron pattern of streets. The latter is an example of what is sometimes referred to as "Manhattan geometry" (Figure 2-3*b*).

Nordbeck (1964) has studied variations in point-to-point distances in a town, using, on the one hand, airline distance and, on the other, rectangular

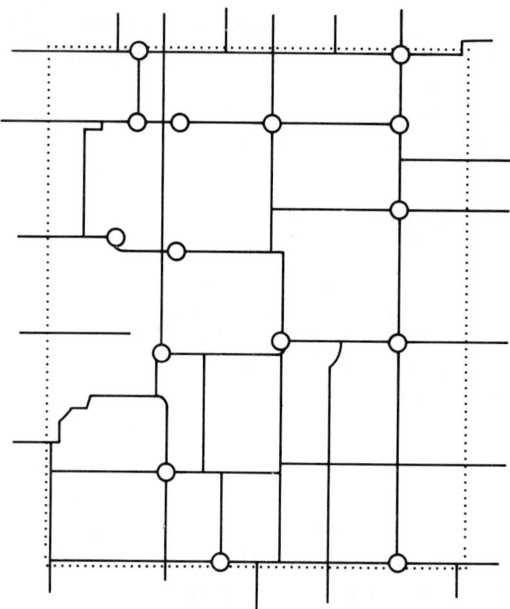

Figure 2-1
Route network of Spink County, South Dakota

distance along city streets. He concluded that the variations may be large in a relative sense. For short distances, the value of rectangular distance may be 1.43 times larger than the euclidean distance. For longer distances, however, the rectangular-euclidean ratio diminishes. Whereas Nordbeck's study pertained to the comparison of distances within a town, Timbers studied variations in the ratio of real distance along the roads to airline distance between cities in the United Kingdom and found the ratio to be 1.17 on the average

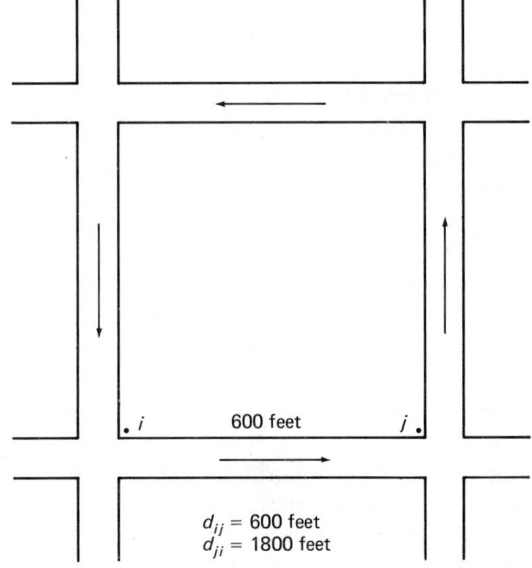

Figure 2-2
Point-to-point distance in a system of one-way streets

Figure 2-3 Non-straight-line short paths: (*a*) a hike through the woods; (*b*) running an errand in the city.

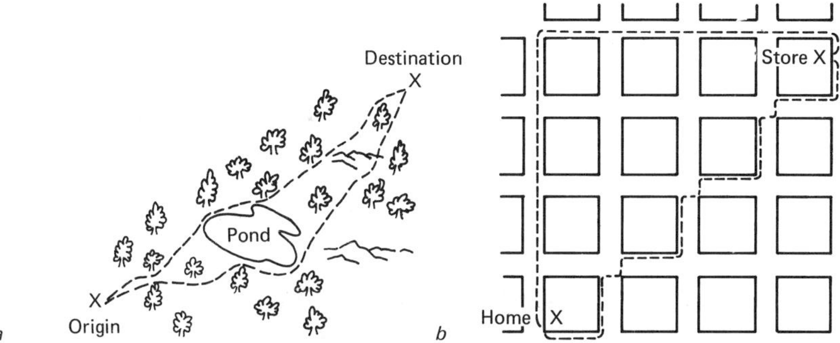

(Timbers, 1967, 401). This ratio seems to suggest that as the size of the area under consideration increases, the difference between airline distances and actual distances along existing routes tends to diminish.

A crucial difference between isotropic and anisotropic surfaces is that while on the former the shortest distance between two points is along a straight line, on the latter it need not be so, and, in fact, it could be a curved line.

An example of a non-straight-line short path is the shortest time-distance between two points on the edge of a large metropolitan area. The intervening surface is anisotropic with reference to the amount of traffic congestion at various intersections along the straight line between the two points. The geodesic path would not be a straight line through the congested portions of downtown; rather, it would be a curved path skirting the relatively continuous built-up area along a beltway, if one exists.

At a macroscale, Warntz (1965) has constructed land-acquisition isocost maps of the United States from several points. He derived these maps from a map of population potential or accessibility. He found that the land values in dollars per acre were strongly related to population-potential figures, and thus he approximated a continuous land-value surface for the United States by transforming the population-potential surface by a factor of proportionality. One result is an isocost surface in hundreds of thousands of dollars integrated about Lewiston, Montana (Figure 2-4). A least-acquisition-cost, or geodesic, path on this surface takes on an orthogonal trajectory, which intersects each contour at a right angle. The resulting paths are curved lines. Only six paths are shown on Figure 2-4, although an infinite number are possible.

Warntz's work on geodesic paths on anisotropic surfaces has been widely referenced in the geography literature, but a question may be raised as to its utility. The meaning of a "least cost path on a surface of land acquisition costs" is not clear. Perhaps, if we hold everything else constant, we could consider these paths as potential highway or railroad routes from Lewiston to selected points. Warntz himself agrees that a "literal application of it [geodesic path] to the real earth and especially the various conceptual surfaces covering it" (1965, 18) needs to be intensively studied.

It is interesting to note that in order to minimize time, DC-8 aircraft flying across the North Atlantic employ a curved path computed from variable tail-

Figure 2-4 Geodesic paths on an isocost surface from Lewiston, Montana. (Isolines are shown in hundreds of thousands of dollars.)

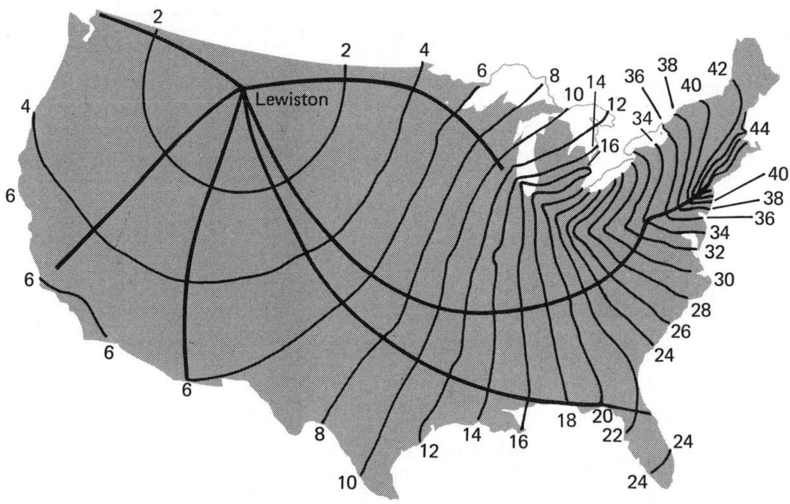

wind or headwind components at various points along the route (Warntz, 1961, 205).

Geodesic paths of Warntz's genre deal with a single anisotropic surface such as that of the United States or of the air above the North Atlantic Ocean. Let us examine the case of two adjacent isotropic surfaces characterized by sharply differing movement costs, such as one might find along a coastline. A well-known example is that provided by Lösch (1954, 184–185) in which an analogy is made to the law of refraction in physics.

On Figure 2-5, points *A* and *B* are located on water and land respectively. It is assumed that transport costs over water are significantly lower than those over land, and one may ponder the alternate ways of moving between the two points. One way might be to move along a straight-line short path through point *F*, splitting evenly the total travel between water and land. Costwise, this method would be inefficient, due to the differential transport costs over the two surfaces. Another alternative might be to move the shortest distance possible on water and the longest distance possible over land, such as that represented by path *ADB*, which would also be the most expensive under our transport-cost assumptions. Path *AEB* maximizes the distance over water and minimizes that over land. The least-cost path, the geodesic path, can be evaluated as a function of $(\sin \alpha)/(\sin \beta) = k$ (land)/k (water), in which k is the cost per unit distance. This path could be anywhere between *AEB* and *AFB* depending upon (1) the value of k over water and land respectively and (2) the absolute locations of both *A* and *B*. In our hypothetical example, the geodesic path is represented by *ACB*. The reader will note that the path is deflected at sea in this instance, hence the analogy to the law of refraction, which was identified by Lösch (1954, 184) as the principle of least resistance or as the "hypothesis that natural events reach their goals by the shortest route."

A numerical example will perhaps serve to make the point in Figure 2-5 clearer. The values on the figure refer to distance units. If we assume seaborne transportation costs to be \$1 per unit weight per unit distance (for example, 100 tons/kilometer) and the overland cost to be \$2, the total transportation costs over several routings are as follows:

1. Minimum distance over water and maximum over land

$ADB = (15 \times \$1) + (43 \times \$2) = \$101$

2. Equal distances over land and water

$AFB = (25 \times \$1) + (25 \times \$2) = \$75$

3. Maximum distance over water and minimum distance over land

$AEB = (43 \times \$1) + (15 \times \$2) = \$73$

4. The geodesic path

$ACB = (36 \times \$1) + (16 \times \$2) = \$68$

Note that even though sea-transport cost is half that of land transport, maximizing the distance traveled over water, as in *AEB*, does not necessarily minimize the overall transport cost. Given the assumed routes, the optimal solution is a compromise between the two extremes of *ADB* and *AEB* and lies along *ACB*.

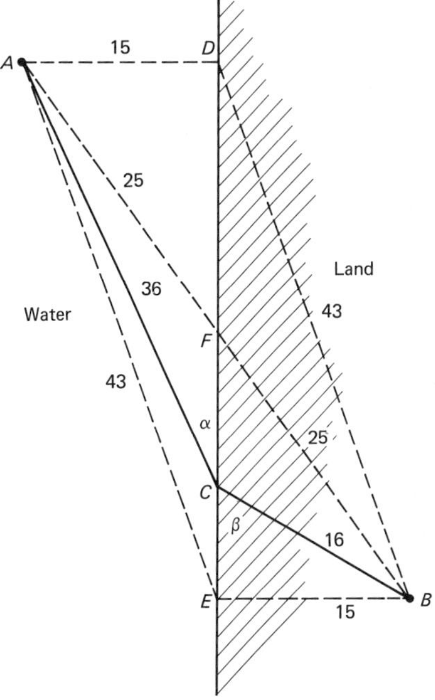

Figure 2-5
Alternative paths over two different surfaces, illustrating the applicability of the law of refraction to geodesics

Distance in a Group of Points

In considering a group of points, it is not appropriate to think of distance in terms of discrete measurements such as kilometers, travel time per kilometer or monetary cost per kilometer. Instead, it is necessary to introduce aggregate measures in order to describe the totality.

Consider a set of *n* points in euclidean space, each of which has a specific location on cartesian coordinates. It is possible to describe the dispersion of the set by means of the "standard distance." The statistician Bachi (1963) has developed a variety of standard distance measures.

Broadly, *standard distance* represents the average of all distances d_{ij} between all possible pairs of points in a spatial distribution. Thus, it is an aggregative measure of the distribution. The observations may represent any phenomena such as individuals, houses, or settlements.

Bachi (1963, 86–88) suggests three alternative definitions of standard distance, summarized as follows:

1. The quadratic average of distance from the center of gravity:

$$d = \left(\sum_{i=1}^{n} \frac{d_{ic}^2}{n} \right)^{1/2} \tag{2.1}$$

2. The square root of the sum of variances of longitudes and latitudes:

$$d = (\sigma_x^2 + \sigma_y^2)^{1/2} \tag{2.2}$$

3. The mean quadratic distance with repetition between any pair of cases, divided by $\sqrt{2}$:

$$^2{}_rD = \left(\sum_{i=1}^{n} \sum_{j=1}^{n} \frac{d_{ij}^2}{n^2} \right)^{1/2} \tag{2.3}$$

or

$$^2{}_rD = \left(2 \sum_{i=1}^{n} \frac{d_{ic}^2}{n} \right)^{1/2} \tag{2.4}$$

In the above expressions, *d* and $^2{}_rD$ are standard distances, d_{ic} is the distance between any observation *i* and the mean center of all observations *c*, *n* refers to the number of observations, σ_x^2 is the variance of *x*, $\sqrt{\sigma_x^2}$ is the standard deviation* of *x*, and *x* and *y* are coordinate locations.

In Figure 2-6*a* and *b*, two alternative arrangements of points are shown. These are hypothetical patterns; Figure 2-6*a* may be conceived of as representing dwelling units in an Appalachian "hollow," and *b*, farmsteads in the Great Plains. The standard distance of each of these has been computed as the square root of the sum of variances of the *x* and *y* coordinates of the points [Equation (2.2)]. It may be noted that the value of the standard distance can be regarded as an index of dispersion for which the minimum value approaches zero. As a spatial distribution becomes increasingly more dispersed, the value

* Remember that for any term *x*, $x^{1/2} = \sqrt{x}$. Likewise, $(\sigma_x^2)^{1/2} = \sqrt{\sigma_x^2}$.

Figure 2-6 Point patterns with a standard distance (*a*) equal to 1.82, (*b*) equal to 3.61.

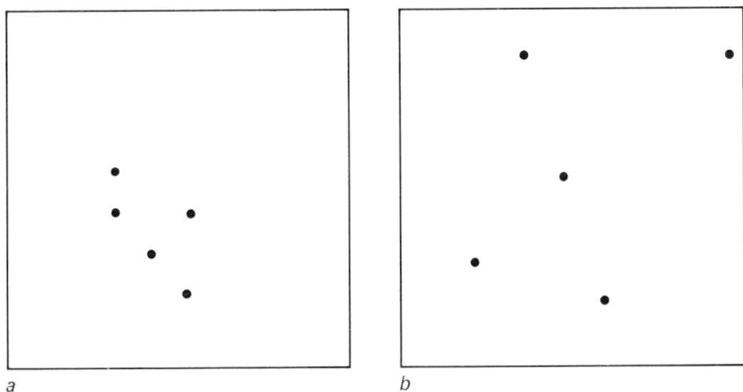

of the standard distance increases, as can be seen by comparing values in Figure 2-6*a* and *b*.

Assuming an isotropic surface and equal interaction propensities regardless of distance, it may be presumed that a greater aggregate amount of movement would occur when the standard distance is large since pairwise distances are great. On the other hand, if we recognize that the propensity for interaction is inversely related to distance, then a more logical result would be that the total volume of interaction will increase as the standard distance decreases.

Just as measures of central tendency can be biased if the distribution is not normal, similarly standard distance can be biased by extreme locations. However, standard distance is only one of a number of techniques used to describe distances in point patterns. King (1969, 89–113) reviews a number of other such techniques. We have chosen to highlight standard distance here because, unlike some of the other techniques, it seems to focus directly on distance qua distance. Specifically, the value of the standard distance is not affected by the alignment and size of the boundaries or by the size of the area included by the boundaries. This is not true, for example, of the "nearest-neighbor" statistic, which is frequently used to describe patterns such as cluster, random, and regular and which is a function both of relative locations of pairs of points and of the size of the region under consideration.

MEASURES OF DISTANCE

Given two points *i* and *j*, each with an (*x*,*y*) coordinate location, how can we measure d_{ij}? There are many measures, each of which is appropriate under certain circumstances. In this section, we review briefly some of these.

Physical Measures

Physical distance is the spatial interval between two points. As a euclidean measurement, it is calibrated according to some standard system. The metric system is most widely used, and its fundamental unit, the meter, is measured as 1,650,763.73 wavelengths of the orange-red radiation of krypton 86 under specified conditions. The metric system is unusually precise, a sharp contrast to the measurement of distance in some cultural and temporal contexts. In ancient India the standard unit, the *yojana*, was the distance that an elephant, the royal mode of transportation, could travel from dawn to dusk. Other units of the metric system, such as millimeters and kilometers, are base-10 fractions and multiples of the meter. The British system of measurement, on the other hand, does not have such a base: its fundamental unit is the foot, and other units consist of fractions and multiples of the foot. (It may be noted, however, that the British are gradually adopting the metric system.)

Not all physical measures of distance are standardized. For example, in American cities the most popular measurement of physical distance is the block, whose length varies from city to city and within any one city. The intersections between city blocks are easy to count so that one knows how much farther one has to go to reach a particular destination.

Time Measures

Individuals tend to place a greater value on time in certain societies than in others. The distance between two places is frequently measured by the amount of time required to move from point to point. Unlike the movement of goods, the movement of people is generally affected more by time considerations. However, there are some goods, particularly perishables, that also need to move rapidly between points.

In contrast to physical distance, which is invariant, *time-distance* is a function of the mode of movement, the density of traffic on the route, the physical environment or characteristics of the surface over which movement occurs, the manmade regulations concerning movement, and, finally, the state of the art with reference to movement technology.

For example, if we were to join all places 5 miles distant from a certain point, we would draw a circle, with a radius of 5 miles, centered at that point. A series of concentric circles with differing radii would locate equidistant points from the same center. If the points were located on an isotropic surface, time contours, or isochrones, similarly would be concentric. However, owing to the factors mentioned earlier, the time required for movement varies from point to point over any one surface, and, as a result, isochrones typically are

Figure 2-7 Isochrones in 5-minute intervals from the CBD (central business district) of a hypothetical city: (*a*) at rush hour; (*b*) not at rush hour.

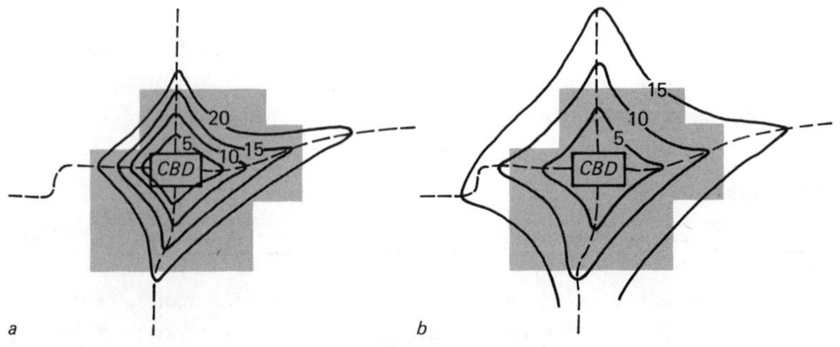

not concentric. Figure 2-7 shows isochrones for a hypothetical city, illustrating the stretching and shrinking of time-distance as a function of rush-hour and non-rush-hour traffic conditions, respectively. It is possible to combine time and physical distance so that on a modern superhighway 60 miles may be equal to 1 hour of travel.

The time required to move over a given distance has been decreasing secularly, as we shall see in Chapter 3. Warntz (1967, 16) dreams of the day when "everyplace on earth would be forty-two minutes from Broadway." Whether this day is to be a dream or a nightmare remains to be seen.

Economic Measures

Economic distance is a budgetary notion incorporating the amount of energy required to move between two points. Movement is seldom costless even though the cost of movement may not involve money directly. In considering a monetary measure of distance, it is evident that the cost of moving depends upon the price of inputs required to make movement possible over a given physical distance. These input prices vary between modes as well as between countries. For example, the bus fare for a distance of 100 miles in the United States is about 30 times greater than the equivalent in Ceylon, and the air fare from Washington to New York is twice as much as the bus fare. The physical distance between i and j may also be equated to a 40-cent bus ride in which case 40 cents is the measure of the economic distance between i and j.

Generally, the monetary costs of movement increase with physical distance. However, the nature of the relationship between the two is complex, as we shall see in Chapter 3.

Perceptual Measures

Many studies by psychologists have shown that the human mind functions as a filter as it accepts, rejects, and modifies various bits of information. The result of this process is that certain subjective mental images of reality are synthetically created from the welter of information at our disposal. These mental images are our individually perceived versions of reality, and while they may be subjective, they are the only basis we have for decisionmaking.

Spatial perception refers to our varying individual ability to be precise with respect to locations and their attributes. Spatial perception is a class within the overall subject of perception and, as such, is affected by the same biases, prejudices, and irrationalities affecting perception in general. Most people's terra cognita consists of a relatively small area within which they can specify relative locations more or less accurately, while relative locations outside this area tend to be perceived fuzzily. In addition, locations are judged according to whether we like or dislike what we associate with them.

Thus, spatial perception affects our measure of distance in at least two ways: (1) directional preference and (2) stimulus along the route. The pioneering geographic work on directional preference and mental maps is that of Gould (1966, 1967, 1969a), who generalized the residential preferences of groups of individuals from four different locations in the United States. The preferences vary with the location of the respondents; further, there seems to be a consistent directional "bias": Northerners prefer the West to the South, Southerners also prefer the West to the North, while Westerners prefer their own area but like the North better than the South.

A caveat is appropriate here. Directional preference is frequently due to real or imagined qualities associated with a location rather than with a direction as such. California is preferable not because it is in the West but because it is California. Since many people seem to prefer California as a place in which to live, they think of it as being nearer than other locations which may actually be closer when measured in physical, temporal, and economic terms.

Perception also affects our measure of distance through the visual stimulus offered by a particular route. The monotonous scenery observed along many an American freeway (the "Green Subway") frequently makes distance appear longer than it actually is. Quickly changing vistas, on the other hand, especially those that please the eye, generate a kaleidoscope of colorful images and seem to abbreviate physical distance. However, even the most stimulating route can wither with age and stale with custom. People have a great capacity for becoming jaded.

A bodily manifestation of the perception of distance is our physiological response to travel. Experiments have been conducted to measure the amount of driver stress under varying road and traffic conditions. With experience, people learn which routes are more stressful than others and, if possible, will try to avoid them. Thus, for example, a long and pleasant country ride along quiet roads may be perceived as being of a shorter distance than a short trip downtown during rush hour, owing strictly to the differential stress involved.

Golledge et al. (1969), in a study designed to test the effect of both familiarity and directional preference on distance perception, derived certain conclusions that are relevant here. They selected a sample of beginning graduate students (group 1) who were unfamiliar with Columbus, Ohio, and third-year graduate students (group 2) who had had the opportunity to become acquainted with where things are. The perceived distances to certain specified locations were compared with the actual distances for each of the samples. The members of group 1 had few common perceptions, suggesting that these individuals had very different spatial habits (different residential locations and highly varied travel paths). They were able to perceive distances rather accurately along a north-south orientation mainly because the major commercial center in Columbus lies athwart a major north-south arterial running through the university campus. In contrast, the third-year students apparently had accurate perceptions of distance in the north-south as well as east-west directions.

However, it was found that both groups systematically overestimated distances toward the south (downtown). This may be due to the existence of increased congestion and travel time. Conversely, in the northward direction (going out of town), the discrepancies between the perceived and the actual distances were much less. It must be emphasized that distance perception in the sense treated here may be applicable only to highly industrialized and urbanized regions of the world since it is in such areas that congestion is a major problem.

MAP TRANSFORMATIONS

In the foregoing section, we discussed a number of ways of measuring distance, many of which can be equated. For example, a map showing isochrones is simply a way of measuring distance using time as a basic unit. This map represents a transformation of physical distance into time-distance. In this section, we consider some additional transformations of distance.

All transformations use certain definite rules according to which one coordinate system can be changed into another. Using projective geometry, cartographers have long transformed the spherical surface of the earth onto a plane. On such a transformation, the continuity of space is violated: the world ends at the end of the page of the atlas. There are other transformations where surfaces can be bent, contracted, or stretched, and we provide some examples below.

Geographers are interested in map transformations for a number of reasons, including:

1. Most location theory models or constructs assume certain properties of geographic space, such as the isotropic plane, and consequently these models can be verified only in terms of a geographic space that has analogous properties. Even if the "real" world contained many examples of the isotropic plane, it would be much easier to modify it into the language of the theory rather than vice versa. Thus, map transformations may be useful in the verification of theory.

2. Perceived distances differ from distances in the "real" world. Nevertheless, people's spatial behavior is conditioned by their perception rather than by actual distances. Thus, it would seem that spatial behavior may be more readily explained by maps compiled from distance transformations rather than by conventional maps. Despite the important advantages to be derived from map transformations, little work has been done on this topic with the exceptions of the outstanding studies of Tobler (1961, 1963) and Getis (1963).

Logarithmic Transformations

Hägerstrand (1957) was the first geographer to make use of a logarithmic map transformation. Rather than employing an arithmetic scale, he plotted distances from Asby, Sweden, to certain other points, using the logarithms of those distances. The result is shown in Figure 2-8. Note that distances to places close to Asby are exaggerated while those to places far away are shrunk. This map is useful in plotting data on movement whose intensity decreases sharply with increasing distance from the point of origin. Many types of human interaction in space, such as telephone calls and automobile traffic, exhibit a strong negative relationship with distance. This relationship between the level of interaction and distance can be generalized with a regression line which is often referred to as a *distance-decay function*. (See Chapter 7.)

A logarithmic transformation may be an appropriate representation of perceived distances. For example, Stea (1969, 242) asked a group of students to estimate distances from New York City to certain other cities and vice versa. The responses were compared with the actual distances, and it was concluded

Figure 2-8 Logarithmic transformation of distances from Asby, Sweden

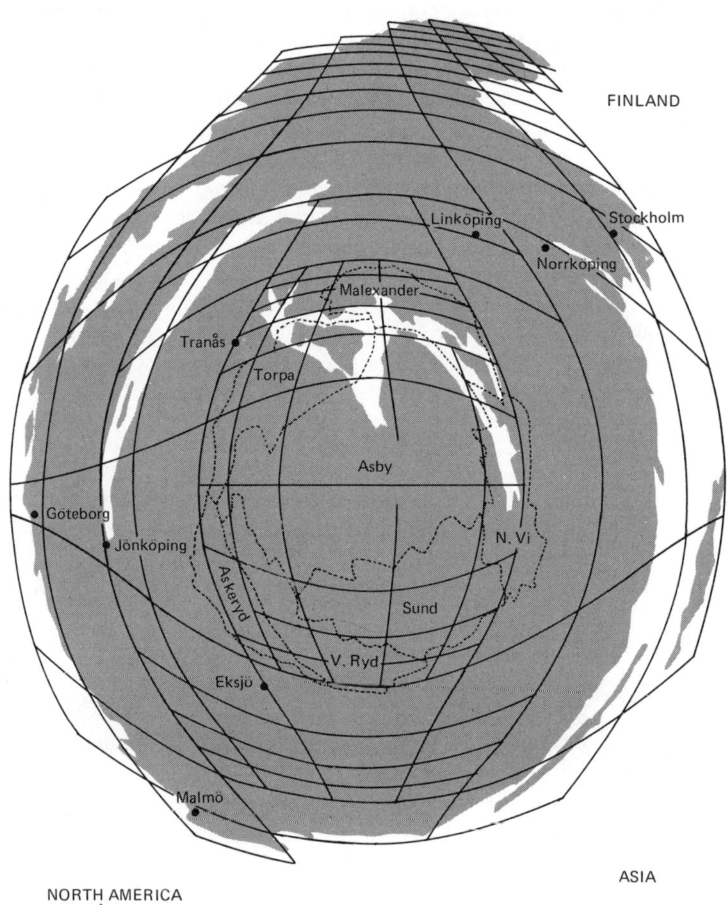

that distances to places within 4000 miles were consistently overestimated, while distances to places more than 4000 miles away were systematically underestimated. It is possible that our mental map of distances between points on the globe is indeed a logarithmic transformation of the "real" world.

Additionally, a cartographic advantage is that a logarithmically transformed map provides more space to plot data near the point of origin, where much of the interaction occurs, and comparatively less space at greater distances from the point of origin, where interaction is weak.

Topological Transformations

In euclidean space distances are defined by recourse to the Pythagorean theorem, whereas in topological space this is not the case. Topology is qualitative geometry. It is concerned only with "the continuous connectedness between the points of a figure" (Hilbert and Cohn-Vossen, 1952, 289, as cited by Harvey, 1969, 217). Topological space is elastic, and within it the spatial order, or sequence and contiguity of points, lines, and areas, is maintained. However, a topological map does not have a scale, and linear distances between points do not correspond to those on the surface of the earth. Most bus, railroad, and airline maps are examples of what are known as *graphs*.

Graph theory, a topic in topology, has its own special nomenclature. For example, a route or path is termed an *arc*, or an *edge*, while an intersection or the endpoint of an edge is a *node*, or *vertex*. The relationships between edges and vertices, as well as measures of networks, i.e., a series of edges and vertices, are considered in graph theory, aspects of which are summarized in Chapter 5.

Figure 2-9*a* shows the routing of a bus company system that operates between Washington, D.C., and Ocean City, Maryland. This is a representation of euclidean space because the directional relationships between places are accurate, the specific sinuosity of the routing is shown in detail, and the map is drawn to scale. Figure 2-9*b*, on the other hand, is a topological representation of the same bus route. Note that the directional relationships have been distorted. Contiguity and spatial ordering are preserved, and for a user of the bus system these are the key properties. On departing from Washington, a passenger needs to know whether the stop for Queenstown is before or after

Figure 2-9 Map of bus company routing showing (*a*) euclidean representation, (*b*) topological representation.

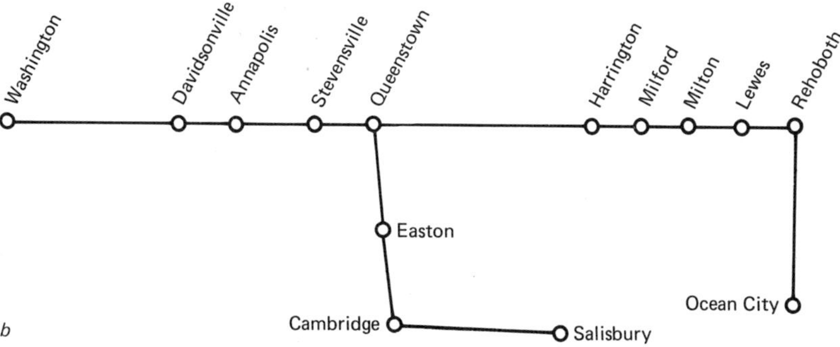

Stevensville. For the user, euclidean distance as such is not very relevant nor are the sinuosities of the route, and thus all edges are straight lines.

Since the distance perception of most individuals does not correspond to linear distance but rather is ordinal (more than, less than), it would seem that a topological view of space is more appropriate to the geography of movement than a euclidean one.

For many operational problems concerned with movement, distance is far more important than direction. The crucial question is, How far? not, Where? Rate-making agencies are typically concerned with setting rates by mileage blocks from points of origin rather than by direction of freight movement, although there are directional variations in freight rates. One example, initially from the work of Tobler as cited by Bunge (1966), illustrates the role of map transformations in highlighting the range of distances separating places. Figure 2-10 shows the distances and direction from Seattle measured by parcel-post rates. The rates apply to groups of points, and the zonal boundaries are circular in shape. Note that Galveston, Miami, Atlanta, Cleveland, Buffalo, and Boston are all on the same zonal boundary, and in this sense they are all the same cost-distance away from Seattle.

A final example of a map transformation is that provided by Flaherty concerning the Belcher Islands in the Hudson Bay (Raisz, 1948, 4). Figure 2-11*a*

Figure 2-10 Postal-zone rates from Seattle, Washington

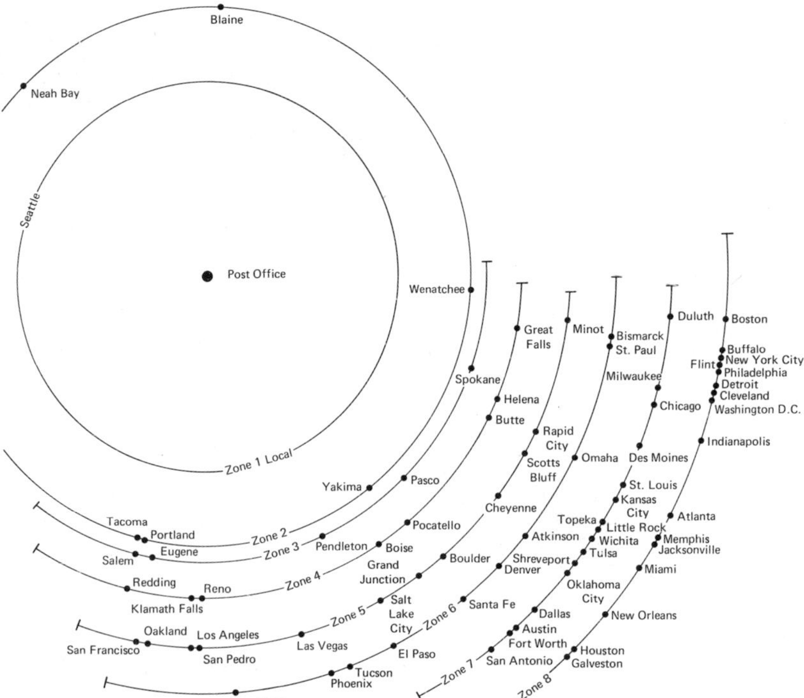

Figure 2-11 The Belcher Islands as drawn by (*a*) the Islanders, (*b*) the British Admiralty.

From *General Cartography* by Erwin Raisz. Copyright 1938, 1948, McGraw-Hill Book Company. Used with permission of McGraw-Hill Book Company. Adapted from p. 4, Fig. 2.

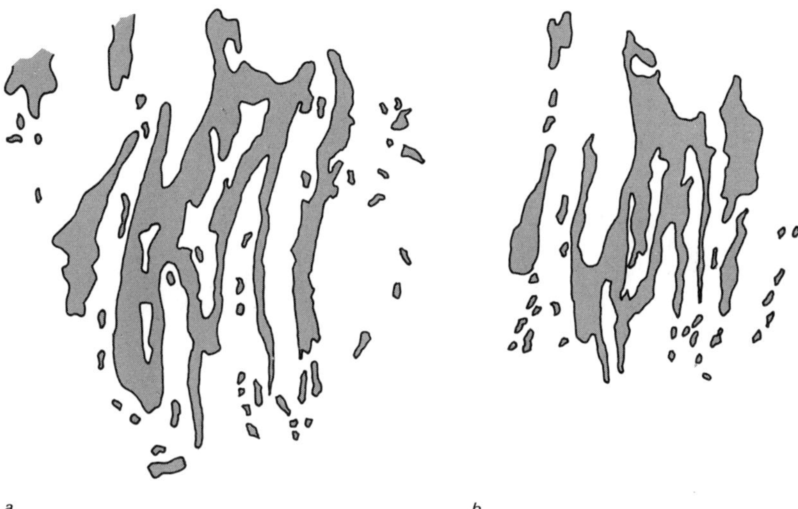

is a map of the Belcher Islands drawn by the Islanders, while Figure 2-11*b* is a map of the same area constructed by surveyors of the British Admiralty. It should be noted that the indigenous people were ignorant of the principles of surveying and lacked surveying equipment. Nevertheless, the Islanders' map of these several thousand square miles is remarkably accurate. The discrepancies between Figure 2-11*a* and *b* can be understood in terms of those variables that are more significant to the indigenous peoples of the region. Steffanson, as cited by Raisz, observes that Eskimos generally deemphasize the scale property of a map, but, on the other hand, are likely to be quite precise about the number and shape of the curves in a meandering river. The location of portages is likely to be shown quite precisely while that of mountains alongside a river may be forgotten. Apparently, time-distance is more important than physical distance. It is in light of such considerations that the discrepancies between the two maps must be interpreted.

In concluding this section on map transformations, one may fairly ask, Who is transforming what? To survive in their natural environment, the Islanders' map is more practical and is undoubtedly the correct transformation inasmuch as the relevant variables are emphasized while unnecessary details are ignored. Information theorists would call this procedure the elimination of "random noise" which is one of the prime purposes of mapping. In contrast, the Admiralty chart is precise and preserves the properties of euclidean space. However, in order to be most useful for survival, this map must perhaps be transformed into the cartographic idiom of the Belcher Islanders.

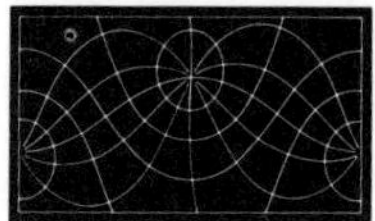

3 Costs of Overcoming Distance

Regardless of the different ways of conceptualizing, measuring, and transforming distance, overcoming it is never costless. Distance impedes the level of spatial interaction largely because of the cost involved in traversing it. Sometimes, we speak of a distance deterrence function and measure it in monetary units. All individuals, however rich, operate under some budget constraint. Transportation is just one of the many needs that have to be satisfied from a finite supply of money. In the American context, expenditure on transportation is a necessary adjunct to the satisfaction of most needs. Thus, Fox and Kumar (1965, 59) comment that, "in the modal case, the male traverses the habitat to exchange labor for money, and the female traverses it to exchange this money for food and other objects of value." In either case, an expenditure is involved which, in turn, curtails individual propensity for movement (Chapter 7). This being the case, at this stage we need to obtain a broad understanding of the nature of transport cost and transport price.

At the outset we must be clear about the distinction between cost and price. In a bookkeeping sense, these two appear on opposite sides of a ledger, and one man's cost is another man's price. The money you paid to purchase this book is part of your cost of education, while it is the price that the bookstore charged you, just as it was a cost to the bookstore to obtain it from the publisher. Accordingly, cost and price are sequential notions.

It is not always necessary that transport cost be a monetary one. A walk to the bakery for a loaf of bread entails the expenditure of effort which can be measured in caloric units and labeled as a cost. In contrast, taking a bus, a train, or a plane involves a monetary transaction. We all know that the prices charged by the carrier to transport us from one location to another vary greatly. This is because the cost of providing the service also varies greatly by mode.

It is not our intention to treat the elements of transport economics in any great detail, but rather to convey an understanding of the economic factors that constrain different types of movement.

TRANSPORT COST

The cost of producing any good or service includes a number of elements, such as the payment of wages and salaries (to bus drivers, airline pilots, telephone operators, and maintenance crews), taxes, depreciation (wear and tear of equipment), capital (interest payments to lenders), and so on.

The cost structure among alternative modes of movement varies widely as a function of the differing proportions of the two major cost components: (1) fixed costs and (2) variable costs. Fixed costs refer specifically to the terminal costs incurred in maintaining such facilities as ports, railroad stations, and airports. These costs are largely fixed since they are not directly related to the level of movement and cannot be allocated readily to specific users. An increasing use of terminal facilities as well as of capital equipment (trucks, railroad cars, etc.) results in decreased average fixed costs.

Variable transportation costs are over-the-road costs which increase with the level of movement and can be allocated specifically to users. Some examples include wages, fuel, wear and tear of capital equipment, and tolls, which generally increase with distance. Route maintenance costs may also be regarded as variable costs since these are directly related to traffic volume.

Total transport costs — the combination of fixed and variable costs — are curvilinear rather than linear functions of distance, as is shown in Figure 3-1. This curvilinearity is caused by scale economies in long-haul transport which make it possible to average fixed costs over longer distances. Figure 3-1 illustrates the differences in movement cost between truck, railroad, and barge. Note that the fixed-cost component for each mode varies greatly: the maintenance of the port of London is far more expensive than the maintenance of the loading dock of a trucking firm. Note also the different slopes of the three curves and the fact that they intersect. The near linearity of the cost curve for trucking is caused by the lower fixed costs which prevail in this mode. For very long distances, transportation by barge costs less than by either truck or rail. Thus, if there were no transshipment costs, overall transport optimization would be achieved by shipping goods from 0 to α by truck, from α to β by railroad, and finally from β onward by barge.

Figure 3-1
Relationship between cost of movement and distance, by mode

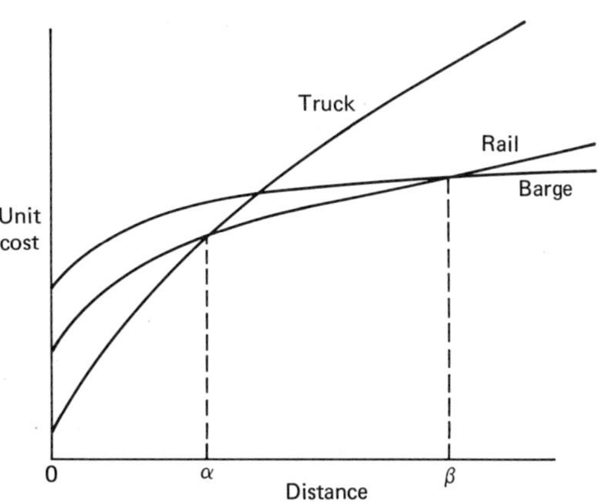

For liquid goods, pipelines offer the cheapest cost of transportation although only petroleum products, natural gas, coal slurry, and water have been transported in this manner over long distances.

Movement costs on airlines are the highest among all modes, owing mainly to the high cost of the vehicle (e.g., about $17 million for a jumbo jet) in comparison to its capacity. Further, since passenger airlines have to operate on regular schedules, their movement cost per passenger depends on their load factor. This is generally true of all carriers of people: airlines, buses, trains, ships, etc. Therefore, the unit cost of passenger movement is likely to vary highly within a mode in relation to the load factor of the specific trip. This and other considerations offset to some extent the impact of distance upon the cost of movement.

The cost of movement is influenced by factors other than distance, such as the "trafficability" of the terrain, the nature of the good being transported, and the size of the individual shipment. The relationships between volume of shipment, length of haul, and movement cost are shown in Figure 3-2. In contrast to Figure 3-1, Figure 3-2 makes use of a logarithmic scale along the vertical axis. This scale enables a comparison of the three different modes, in which the absolute costs are very different. The costs pertain to the lower Mississippi valley, and the wide differentials are readily apparent. For example,

Figure 3-2
Relationship between volume of shipments, mode of shipment, length of haul, and cost

From *The Location of Economic Activity* by Edgar M. Hoover. Copyright 1948 by McGraw-Hill, Inc. Used with permission of McGraw-Hill Book Company. Adapted from p. 4, Table 2.2.

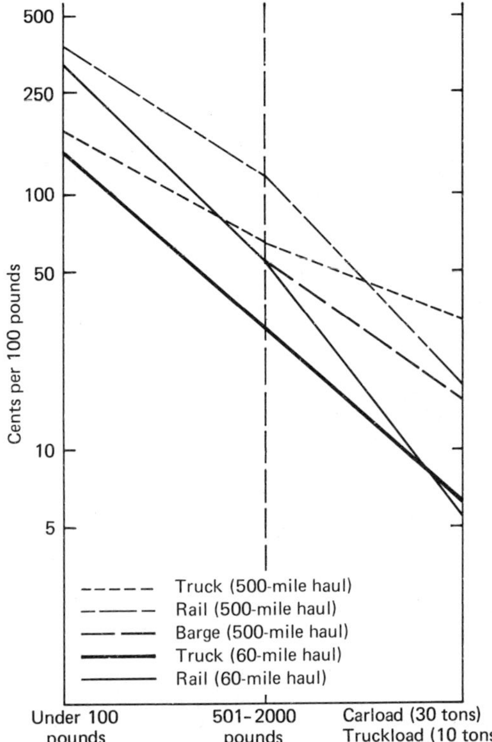

the cost of shipping 100 pounds by rail over a distance of 60 miles is 301 cents if the size of shipment is small and only 5.5 cents if a carload lot is involved. For large-volume, long-distance (500-mile haul) movement, barge transport is the least expensive, followed by rail and truck in that order. On the other hand, for short-distance movement (60-mile haul), rail offers the cheapest mode, followed by truck and barge.

The movement of people in an urban area occurs via a number of modes, each of which has a different per-mile cost. For example, in 1966 the total cost of operating an automobile in the United States, according to figures from the Bureau of Public Roads as cited by Smith (1966, 378), was 9.6 cents/mile. This figure included operation, maintenance, taxes, tolls, and depreciation-cost components. The equivalent cost figure of operating a bus was computed for a sample of American cities and was found to vary from 47.6 cents in Salt Lake City to 74.1 cents in Philadelphia (Smith, 1966, 337). However, assuming a load of, say, 50 persons, the cost per passenger-mile in Philadelphia is 1.48 cents, which, superficially, appears to compare favorably with the automobile, even if it is assumed that four passengers occupy the automobile.

The cost of the spatial transfer of information is related to distance although it is difficult to compute the specific cost of moving one unit of information, such as a single letter or one newspaper, over a given distance. The organizations which perform these services operate as highly complex systems in which the cost of performance of an individual service cannot be isolated. Many enterprises that perform a transportation service are licensed or regulated in one way or another by some public authority. In the United States, railroads are regulated by the Interstate Commerce Commission, airlines by the Civil Aeronautics Board, and bus lines by local authorities such as the Washington Metropolitan Area Transit Authority. One of the conditions under which operating licenses are granted is that satisfactory service shall be provided on a regular basis. In turn, this means that the amount of capital equipment put in place must be sufficient to cope with peak demands, even though during nonpeak hours the equipment is grossly underutilized. In terms of economics, the riders of bus lines during rush hour, for example, are subsidizing those in the early hours of the morning. Thus, the real cost of movement to the carrier varies by the hour, even though the price charged to the user is constant. It will be noted, that many airlines, on the other hand, do vary their prices by time and day of the week, not only to reflect their costs, but also to even out their load factor.

TRANSPORT PRICE AND RATE STRUCTURE

Price is a rate at which a commodity or service is exchanged for money. Thus, we may refer to the price of a taxicab ride or the price of a long-distance call to Los Angeles from Boston. In either case, this is a monetary payment (rate) charged by the cab driver or the telephone company. Over and above the cost elements identified earlier, this price includes something extra that may be labeled as profit. In some instances, the price of movement is specifically related to the cost of the particular bit of movement as, for example, in the case of a taxicab ride while, in other instances, the price is related to the cost of operating the system as a whole.

Generally, transport price varies with distance in a relationship which is largely curvilinear, as is shown in Figure 3-3. Because of the impossibility of developing rate schedules applicable to all movement between numerous origins and destinations, the rate-making organizations find it necessary to establish different rate structures for the movement of goods, people, and information.

Pricing of Goods Movement

There are, in general, three alternative methods of rate construction: distance scale, grouping of points, and the basing-point system.

Distance Scale

The distance between two points, such as the 900 miles between Chicago and New York, is disaggregated into mileage blocks. There may be 20 blocks of 5 miles each, 14 blocks of 10 miles each, 28 blocks of 20 miles each, and the balance may be in 25-mile blocks. Since movement costs are partly related to urban congestion, the 5-mile blocks may be in and around New York and Chicago, whereas the 25-mile blocks may cover sparsely populated portions of the route over which movement costs are comparatively low. Because rates are charged on the basis of distance blocks or fractions thereof, if a certain destination is 2 miles within a 20-mile block, the rate charged assumes that movement had occurred over the range of the whole block. Mileage blocks

Figure 3-3 Relationship between price and distance, by region, for railroad movement in the United States

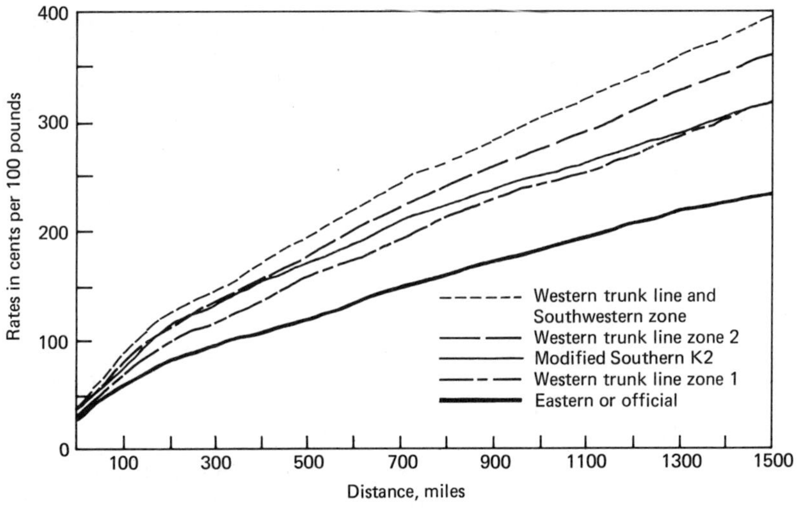

blanket the entire United States in an intricate manner so that most of the commodity flow is priced according to the distance-scale principle.

Grouping of Points

A number of points are grouped together, and a common rate is applicable to all movement originating from or destined to any one of the points in the group. For example, most points in Illinois are grouped together, and all movement is assumed either to have originated from or to be destined to Chicago, the largest city in the group. This system nullifies, to some extent, the impact of distance on the price of movement.

The Basing-point System

This system, which was a widely used method of pricing goods movement in the United States until the thirties, is mentioned here mainly for its historical role in influencing the concentration of manufacturing industries in the Northeast. For each commodity, one or more basing points were regarded as the origin of all movement of that commodity, regardless of its actual origin. Thus, at one time, Pittsburgh was the basing point for steel, and consumers of steel in Huntsville, Alabama, for example, who bought steel in Birmingham, Alabama, paid the transport cost from Pittsburgh to Huntsville. Lösch (1954, 165) notes that this price arrangement curtailed the possibility of a rational spatial arrangement of economic activities. In the United States today, basing-point pricing is illegal, although "phantom-freight" is widespread in the automobile industry and European Common Market steel movements are priced according to basing points (Chisholm, 1966, 181).

Among the different kinds of movement, that of goods is the most significant in a quantitative sense, and its pricing structure is more complex than that for people and information.

Pricing of People Movement

The price of movement of people varies between modes and as a function of distance. In an interesting empirical study, Snyder (1962) compared the travel rates between railroads, bus lines, and airlines to Montevideo. Figure 3-4 shows the relationship between distance from Montevideo and travel rates. He found that for a distance of 40 kilometers from Montevideo, bus fares were lower than rail fares, because as the town is approached, traffic congestion on highways increases and slows down the service. In contrast, trains have their own roadbeds and are not adversely affected by traffic congestion. In a competitive situation, therefore, railroads can demand a higher fare. Beyond the 50-kilometer zone, buses in Uruguay are able to maintain faster speeds than railroads, and thus the price charged to the passenger was higher.

There are two methods of pricing taxi service. In the case of metered pricing, the charge is specifically related to distance as well as to any waiting time. Many cities are divided into uniform taxi zones that are both origins and destinations. Figure 3-5 is a taxi zone map of Washington, D.C., on which three landmarks are located. The reader will note that although the White House is farther from the Capitol than from the Lincoln Memorial, the fare is

Figure 3-4
Travel cost to Montevideo, Uruguay, in pesos

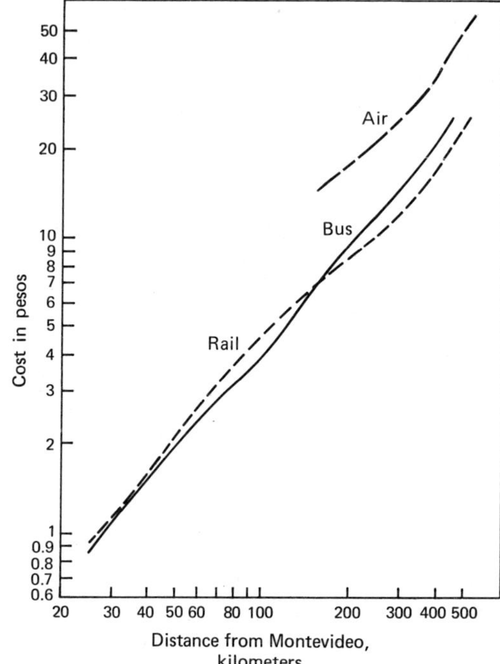

Figure 3-5
Taxi zones in Washington, D.C.

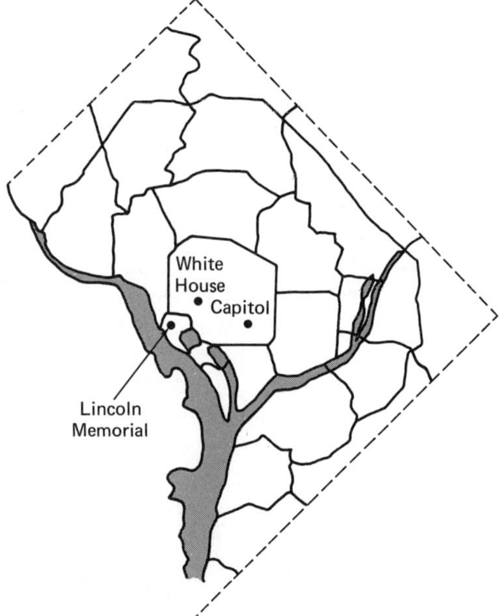

less to the Capitol because a zonal boundary is not crossed. Within any particular zone, no matter how distant the origin and destination are, the fare is standard and does not vary from zone to zone.

Intercity bus and train systems typically use station-to-station rates that are related to distance. In contrast, intracity bus and train fares in many cities in the United States tend to be uniform, regardless of distance traveled. If intercity rates were allowed to vary with distance, there would have to be an elaborate point-to-point rate schedule based on costs, and the logistics of issuing tickets and controlling the operation would be very complex.

In the developed countries of the world, the airplane has become a popular mode of movement in which distance is the main determinant of pricing, as is seen in Figure 3-6, which shows the relationship between fares and distance from London to selected points in the world.

While distance is a major determinant of pricing in the rail, intercity bus, and air transport industries, it is not the only one. Excursion rates, Eurailpass types of arrangements, charter rates, student rates, promotional rates designed to augment traffic between particular points, special rates to fly on weekdays and at night, and other similar practices modify the role of distance in the pricing of people movement.

Pricing of Information Movement

Complex societies cannot survive without the movement of very large quantities of information. The movement of information via the air waves is not destined to specific addresses. The cost in this case is a transmission cost

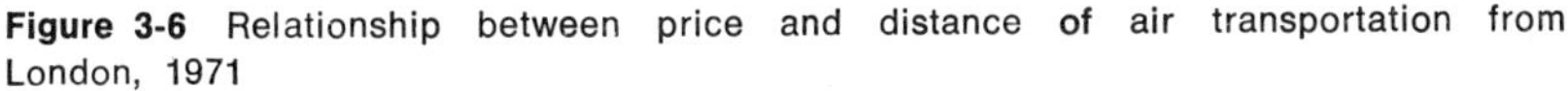

Figure 3-6 Relationship between price and distance of air transportation from London, 1971

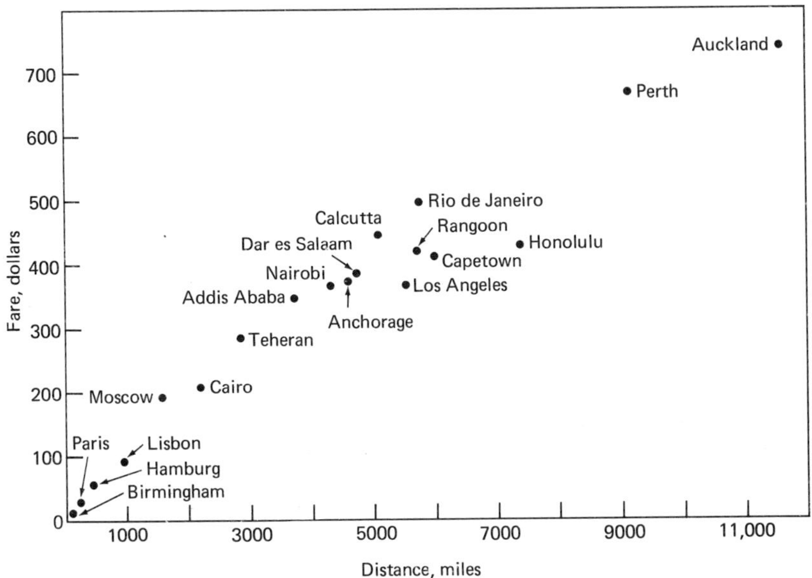

which, insofar as commercial broadcasting is concerned, is not charged directly to the consumer of information. In the case of publicly owned broadcasting media, the license fee is uniform throughout the nation and does not reflect the amount of viewing or listening on the part of the licensee. It is representative of the total cost of operating the system as a whole, averaged among the total number of licenses. Similarly, throughout the world, postal systems estimate the total cost of carrying different kinds of mail, and these are averaged. The result is the standard price of mailing a letter anywhere within a country regardless of distance. When we consider the relationship between the volume of mail and distance, we find that the largest flows are generally intracity short-distance movements which subsidize the lower-volume but longer-distance intercity mail flows.

The movement of telegraphed information is also priced by distance, but rates are not developed between each point of origin and destination. Instead, there are origin and destination zones. The pricing of telephonic communications varies with distance in the case of long-distance calls, as can be seen in Figure 3-7, which shows the price of telephone calls between Washington, D.C., and selected cities in the United States and Canada. Two points that emerge from Figure 3-7 should be highlighted. Within the United States, there is a curvilinear relationship between distance and the price of long-distance calls: New Orleans which is about 1000 miles from Washington is $1.15 away, while the cost-distance to Pittsburgh, 200 miles away, is a comparatively large 75 cents. The cost-distance from Washington increases at a decreasing rate. Again, short-distance calls (less expensive to provide) subsidize calls over

Figure 3-7 Relationship between price and distance of a telephone call from Washington, D.C., to selected cities in the United States and Canada

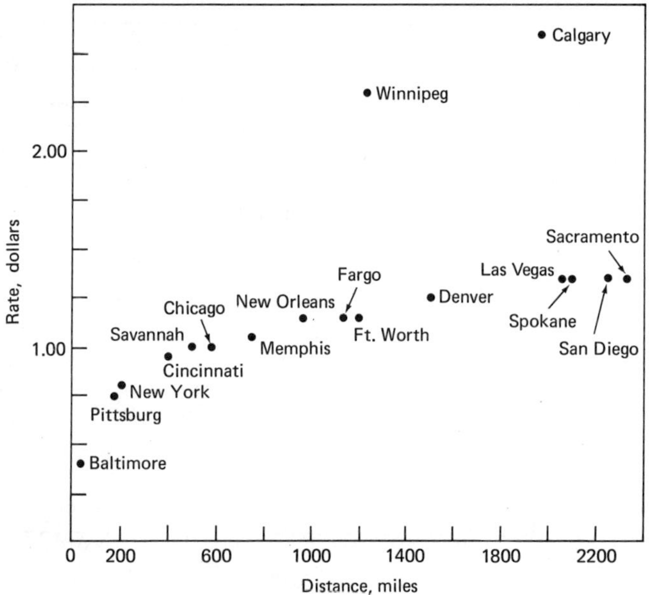

longer distances. The telephone companies, which are also regulated, operate on a systemwide basis. In order to obtain an "adequate" rate of return, they take into account their overall costs and adjust their revenues accordingly. Therefore, it is not possible to relate the pricing of telephone communications strictly to distance.

In Chapter 1, we considered the role of political boundaries in inhibiting human interaction in space. The agencies that approve rate increases in the United States and Canada are different. One consequence is that although Winnipeg is about the distance of Fargo, North Dakota, from Washington, D.C., the price of a long-distance call from Washington to Winnipeg is approximately double the price from Washington to Fargo. This factor undoubtedly decreases the level of interaction between Washington and Winnipeg.

The grouping of points around exchanges eliminates the logistical problems that would result if point-to-point long-distance rates were established for all possible pairwise combinations of telephones. In contrast, local telephone calls are subject to a flat charge.

The delivery cost of newspapers is not specifically allocable to consumers living at varying distances from the publisher although out-of-town newspapers have a specific extra charge for movement. National newsmagazines are sold at a uniform delivered price so that a consumer living next door to the publisher does not benefit from such proximity.

The costs of movement generally are passed on to the consumer. In some cases there is a direct price while in others it is difficult to identify explicitly and is "hidden." Transport cost, an element of total cost, can be regarded as an input (i.e., a purchased service) to the production process.

TRANSPORT COSTS AS A FACTOR OF PRODUCTION

In economic theory, except perhaps in the case of economic rent, location and therefore distance have been consistently and consciously neglected. Adam Smith's *Wealth of Nations* contains an exhaustive index which does not include references to transport, movement, distance, or location. Marshall (1930, 496) states: "The difficulties of the problem depend chiefly on variations in the area of space, and the period of time over which the market in question extends; *the influence of time being more fundamental than that of space*" (our italics).

Economic theory has traditionally focused on value, prices, and returns to factors. Equilibrium of price is determined by assuming that all resources are freely mobile both sectorally and spatially and that all transactions take place at one point in space. Furthermore, transport costs are usually considered to be an element of production costs, and with perfect competition in which everyone is seeking to maximize profits, it follows that optimal spatial patterns emerge automatically. Therefore, most economists have not considered location as a problem worthy of investigation.

Isard refers to what he calls the "Anglo-Saxon bias" in theoretical economics, explicit in Marshall's statement, in which time is important but space is not and the world is a wonderland of no spatial dimensions (1956, 25–26). In contrast, he stresses the importance of transport costs in an attempt to incorporate location in the mainstream of economic thought, treating transport as a necessary input to the production process.

Transport input may be initially defined as the movement of a unit of weight over a unit distance (Isard, 1956, 79) as for example, ton-miles and passenger-miles. It may be argued that transport is really an output derived from the use of inputs such as labor and capital. For our purposes, however, it is convenient to think of it as an input to production in order to comprehend the intensity and configuration of movement and the resulting geographical distribution of human activities.

All inputs involve a cost which is paid by the user: the price of labor is wages, that of capital is interest, that of land is rent, and, finally, that of transport is the rate. For most economic activities the input mix can be allowed to vary so that, for example, there can be capital-intensive forms of production where the use of capital is maximized while labor is minimized. Marginal and substitution analyses enable one to consider trade-offs among inputs for specific activities with a view to optimizing the choice of input or factor combinations. Isard has successfully integrated the concept of transport inputs into conventional economic theory by equating the effort required to overcome distance with the effort required to utilize other inputs.

The transport input is different from other factors of production. It has an ephemeral character in that there is no stock of transport inputs, in contrast to stock of capital, labor, or of a natural resource. An aircraft is not a stock of transport inputs unless it is used in combination with other inputs and is contributing to the production process simultaneously. In this sense, the transport input is a service input and may be redefined as "the composite of services needed to move raw materials, equipment, labor, and finished product to the appropriate places" (Isard, 1956, 90). Under this definition we should include the price of all kinds of movement.

Relative Importance of Transport Inputs

All production processes and other economic activities involve the use of a combination of inputs which vary from industry to industry. The word "industry" is used here as a generic term which incorporates all productive human activities. The combination of inputs required for any industry is reflected in an input-output transactions matrix. This matrix shows the monetary value of transactions between each industry and every other industry. An interindustry matrix has an equal number of rows and columns with identical headings. Table 3-1 is a hypothetical transactions matrix of an economy with six industrial sectors. Reading down a column, one obtains data on the amount of purchases of that industry from each of the industries listed along the rows. An input profile is thus obtained. Reading along a row, one obtains data on sales of that industry to each of the industries across the column headings. For example, the column total of industry *C*(78) represents the sum of the purchases from each of the six sectors.

An individual cell entry, expressed as a percentage of the column total, is called a *direct input coefficient.* When all the cell entries of the transaction matrix have been similarly converted into percentages, the result is called the

Table 3-1
Input-Output Analysis: Transactions Matrix (Values in millions of dollars)

		Industry purchasing						
		A	*B*	*C*	*D*	*E*	*F*	Final demand
Industry	*A*	2	12	20	4	10	30	78
producing	*B*	14	16	10	2	6	8	56
	C	16	6	14	2	10	4	52
	D	4	8	22	16	12	2	64
	E	2	4	8	28	6	0	48
	F	14	12	4	12	4	12	58
Total inputs		52	58	78	64	48	56	356

direct or technical coefficient matrix. The study of such a matrix yields information on the relative importance of specific inputs to any one industry. In order to obtain an idea of the proportionate importance of movement-related activities to an economy and to its individual sectors, one has only to look at the cell entries along the appropriate rows.

Input-output matrices of the United States economy have been constructed for the years 1947, 1958, and 1963. By summing the monetary values of all outputs of all movement-related industries and relating the result to the gross national product, we can obtain a quantitative measure of the relative importance of movement to the national economy, as is done in the following tabulation:

	1947	1958	1963
Movement Industries Output (Millions of dollars)	25,272	44,960	88,034
Gross National Product (Millions of dollars)	220,474	447,344	590,389
Percent of Gross National Product	11.46%	10.05%	14.91%

The dollar volumes of movement-related industries in the foregoing tabulation represent the total transport inputs that were required by the United States economy during those years.

In the most recent matrix, prices represent amounts charged by the producers and exclude distribution costs. This is unfortunate because the full impact of movement costs is grossly underestimated. For example, the costs of moving automobiles to the dealers' showrooms are not separately identified. From the latest input-output matrix, one can identify a number of industries for which the transport input is at least 4 percent of all direct inputs and which may be referred to as transport-oriented. These include cottonseed oil mills, soybean oil mills, processed textile wastes, wood preserving, wooden containers, paperboard mills, hydraulic cement, concrete blocks, lime, secondary and nonferrous metals, artificial flowers, insurance agents, post office, federal electric utilities, and business travel.

A detailed study of the 1963 input-output matrices for the United States allows one to obtain an indication of the price of transport inputs by eight different modes of movement for any one industry. Table 3-2 lists percentages derived from the direct coefficients for four selected industries.

Table 3-2
Relative Price of Transport Inputs in Four Selected U.S. Industries, 1963 (Values in cents)

	Iron ore mining	Ready-mix concrete	Motor vehicles and parts	Stock and commodity brokers
Railroad and related services	0.984	3.388	0.718	0.045
Local highway passenger transportation	0.000	0.000	0.000	0.000
Motor freight and warehousing	0.355	6.033	0.806	0.043
Water transportation	7.452	0.329	0.040	0.008
Air transportation	0.007	0.002	0.021	0.005
Pipeline	0.005	0.019	0.001	0.003
Transportation services	0.007	0.001	0.000	0.000
Communications	0.091	0.536	0.159	6.750
Total	8.901	10.308	1.745	6.854

Source: U.S. Department of Commerce (1969). Office of Business Economics, *Input-Output Structure of the U.S. Economy: 1963,* vol. 2. Direct Requirements for Detailed Industries, Washington, D.C., Government Printing Office.

In spite of the wealth of information available in input-output tables, a consideration of the relative importance of transport costs does not enable one to make statements concerning the reasons for either the locations of activities or the volume and direction of flows. Unfortunately, national input-output matrices, like the gross national product, are aggregated accounting systems in which space is ignored, and interregional input-output data for the United States are unavailable.

Locational Implications of Transport Inputs

From the perspective of the student of economic geography, the locational implications of the amounts of transport inputs (in comparison with other kinds of inputs) are crucial. Consequently, we wish to emphasize the role of transport costs in the location of economic activities here, and possibly the most direct way is to consider a couple of theoretical models. As illustrative examples, let us consider the location of one node, given the location of a set of nodes (the Weber problem), and the use of area, given the location of a central node (the Thünen problem).

Before we describe the essential features of these models, we need to make some preliminary assumptions of what may be called "classical location theory."

In classical location theory, the decision-making individual, that is to say, the actor, is viewed as a rational being. His sole goal is profit maximization or cost minimization (although these two are not quite the same). He is not bothered by conflict among multiple goals (e.g., searching for residential amenities versus minimizing the journey to work). He is endowed with perfect powers of perception, i.e., he is able to see the real world for what it is rather than through distorting perceptual filters, which is another way of saying that his mental map is highly accurate.

Further, our actor is a very rational individual who is endowed with reasoning powers that allow him to compute costs and benefits and thus evaluate alternative courses of action. He is not subject to prejudices, biases, irrationalities, and other frailties of normal human behavior. Moreover, the future is completely predictable, since he has the ability to gaze at crystal balls and outguess both nature and human competitors. Information availability is not a problem, in the sense that relevant information is readily available in usable form, and the actor knows what to do with it. Finally, he is flexible in that his behavior is unhampered by any constraints.

Rational economic man is a model, and, as with any model, some elements are selected for emphasis. In this way, while the model of the profit maximizer is, of course, not a faithful representation of any of us, it can be asserted that in capitalistic societies at least, the pursuit of money is a widely shared societal goal, save for some mavericks and dropouts. At the very least, there is in most of us some intended rationality.

Geographic space is assumed to be an isotropic plane, meaning that it is flat and featureless. From any location, transport effort is the same in all directions for the same distance. Thus, for example, isochrones will tend to be perfectly concentric circles. Further, because transport costs are assumed to be a linear function of distance, the effort required to travel 100 kilometers is exactly 10 times that required to travel 10 kilometers.

The isotropic plane is continuous and unbounded. Specifically, there are neither political boundary lines to impede movement nor political-institutional arrangements to regulate flows. On this isotropic plane, the location of some nodes is given; that is, we know where some things are and where, in consequence, others ought to be.

These simplifying assumptions do not necessarily render location theory models invalid or unrealistic. They can be relaxed without undermining the models. Such a procedure, however, will only make them more complex, as can be seen in the writings of Hoover (1948), Isard (1956), and others.

The Weber Problem

Let us first consider a few situations where there is a punctiform market, the transportation costs are borne by the producer, and the location of natural resources is given. This is the basic location problem, analyzed initially by Weber (1929), which is particularly relevant to the location of manufacturing industries.

The cost elements in any manufacturing industry can be divided into three categories: (1) assembly costs, or the expenditures resulting from bringing the raw materials and fuel to the site of production; (2) processing costs, including labor, taxes, depreciation, utilities, etc.; (3) distribution costs, or the expenses incurred in transporting the finished product to the market from the plant site. Among these elements, both assembly and distribution costs are associated with movement. Since the interest here is in focusing upon the role of transport inputs in the location of industries, we can assume, as did Weber, that initially, there is no spatial differentiation in processing costs.

Before proceeding further, however, it is necessary to establish a pair of dichotomies concerning the nature of materials:

1. Ubiquitous versus localized materials. Ubiquitous materials are available everywhere — air and water are familiar examples. Localized materials are available only in certain places — most mineral resources are localized.

2. Pure versus gross materials. Pure materials are those whose entire weight is part of the weight of the finished product. Most assembly types of manufacturing use pure materials (parts) as inputs. For example, in an automobile, the entire initial weight of tires, glass, shock absorbers, etc., as well as steel, is part of the finished automobile. Gross materials, on the other hand, are those that lose weight in the production process. In blast furnaces, coal is burned up and does not enter into the weight of the pig iron. Most mineral resources contain "gangue" material, that is, the waste product which is discarded early in the chain of production. Given this categorization of materials, we are now in a position to make certain generalizations regarding the location of manufacturing production.

If only ubiquities are used, the plant will be located at the market, because the costs of assembly and distribution are eliminated at that location. (We assume that there are no local pickup and delivery costs.)

If one or more ubiquities are used in conjunction with one or more localized pure materials, then the optimal production location will also be at the market.

If localized pure materials are used with or without ubiquities, then the question of location depends on the *material index*. This index is the ratio of the weight of the localized materials divided by the weight of the finished product. For pure materials the index is 1, and for gross materials it is greater than 1.

With one pure material ($MI = 1$) the industry is "footloose" and, therefore, three situations can be envisaged:

1. The material can be transformed into a manufactured good at the material site and transported to the market so that only distribution costs must be paid.

2. Identical assembly costs will be engendered if the pure material is transported from the material site to the manufacturing site at the market.

3. Alternatively, the production site could be at some point along a straight line connecting the site of the raw material and the market. In this case, the total transport inputs will be partitioned between assembly and distribution, although the sum will be the same as in situations (1) and (2) above.

If one pure raw material is used in conjunction with one or more ubiquities, the production site will be at the market, because ubiquities are available there too, and therefore a portion of the assembly costs (transporting the ubiquities to the market) is eliminated.

If two or more pure materials are used without ubiquities, then the location of production will be at the market site. It is cheaper to assemble the diverse pure materials from each of their respective origins than to locate the production site at one of the resource locations, which would involve extra distribution costs. If ubiquities are used in conjunction with two or more pure materials, then the "pull" of the market upon the location of production is all the stronger.

If weight-losing (gross) materials are used, the following situations obtain:

1. If the *MI* is greater than 1, the location of production will be at the source of the material since it is cheaper to get rid of the waste material at the source, process it, and transport the finished product to the market than to ship the raw material to the market location.

2. If weight-losing materials are used in conjunction with ubiquities, two situations obtain: as long as *MI* is greater than 1, production will be at the materials site; if *MI* is less than 1, the production site will be at the market.

3. If weight-losing materials are used in conjunction with pure materials, the *MI* is less than 1. As long as ubiquitous materials are not used and the proportion of pure materials used is not large, the location of production will be at the site of that weight-losing material which is the largest input (i.e., gross weight *before* purification or refining) in the production process. The objective is to minimize movement as measured by ton-miles. Specifically, the largest profits will be obtained at that location which will require the least total transport inputs or at which total ton-miles are minimized.

To recapitulate the major elements of Weberian analysis, in the case of ubiquities, transport inputs do not enter into the picture. Whenever the *MI* is greater than 1, regardless of whether pure or gross materials are used, production should occur at the source of materials. Thus, copper-refining plants are located in Montana and Arizona, even though the markets are on the East Coast. As the *MI* decreases, the "pull" of the market becomes stronger. This is especially true in the case of weight-gaining types of production where ubiquities are added. The most dispersed manufacturing industry in the U.S. is soft-drink bottling, which has almost a one-to-one correlation with the distribution of population. Syrup-manufacturing plants are agglomerated in the materials-producing regions (the Sorghum Belt). From there, syrup is transported to numerous destinations where water is added (i.e., weight gain) and from which the finished product is distributed locally.

In this manner, purely on the basis of transport inputs, manufacturing industries can be classified as being either market-oriented or material-oriented. If the assembly costs are greater than the distribution costs, then the industry is material-oriented. If, on the other hand, distribution costs are greater than assembly costs, then the industry is market-oriented (Figure 3-8*a* and *b*).

Although Weber considered the role of factors other than transportation, he insisted that transport orientation was fundamental in the location of industries and that other orientations were "distortions." Consequently, the influence of other factors must be understood as deviations from the minimum transport-cost location. Industries will seek low labor-cost locations only if the extra assembly and distribution costs engendered by so doing make it worthwhile. Specifically, the savings in labor cost per unit weight of product must be greater than the additional ton-miles of transport. Of course, the assumption is that cheap labor is not available at the point of minimum transport costs.

During the most important formative stage in U.S. economic history, when

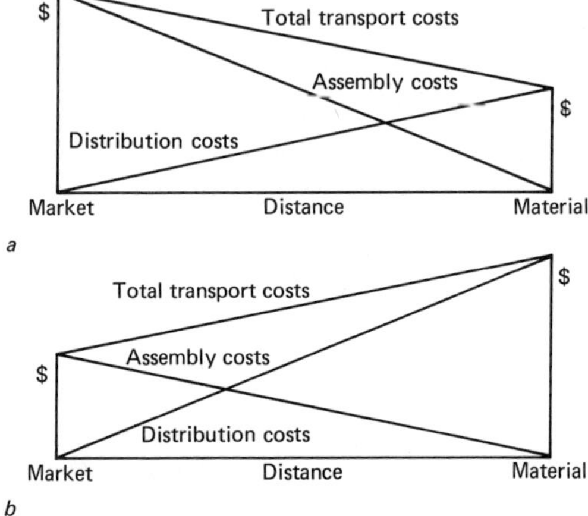

Figure 3-8
Least-cost location along a line. (*a*) Locate at the source of material; (*b*) locate at the market.

the basic "ground plan" of the locational pattern of manufacturing industries was established, the role of transport costs was paramount. Pred (1966) identifies this period as lasting from 1860 to 1900 and shows that concentration of manufacturing industries in the Northeast was, in part, due to lower transport costs. Later, as transport costs decreased, producers took advantage of low labor-cost locations, but as a result, the average length of commodity haul increased sharply. Therefore, manufacturers were substituting transport inputs for labor inputs. It is in this sense that other orientations, such as labor, are "distortions" of transport orientation.

The Thünen Problem

Agricultural activities are space-consuming or area-occupying ones. It is possible to conceive of the specific use of a parcel of land as being a function of its distance from markets. To simplify the problem, assume, as Von Thünen did, that there is one market located at the center of a featureless plain. The specific use of the land, at any location, will depend upon its potential rent. Accordingly, the land rent (L) equation is

$$L = E(p - a) - Efk$$

where E = yield per unit of land
p = market price per unit of commodity
a = production cost per unit of commodity
f = transport rate per unit of commodity per unit of distance
k = distance to market

In this equation, k is the only variable, as there is no place-to-place difference in prices, production costs, or output per unit of land.

The land rent, which represents the profit to be derived from the use of land, declines outward for each commodity with increasing distance from the market. The term Efk is the total transport cost incurred to move the production per unit of land to market. Obviously, this value is higher with increasing distance. The term $E(p - a)$, where $p - a$ is the difference between production cost and market price, is a constant for a particular crop. At some distance from the market, the transport cost will equal $p - a$. This is said to be the *zero-rent margin*, at which place the exploitation of the land for this particular crop is not economically worthwhile, unless there is an increase in the market price.

Since crops can be differentiated as to their yields, production costs, market prices, and transport costs, the resulting land rent or profit will vary from crop to crop at any distance from the market. Figure 3-9 shows the resulting land-rent curves for three hypothetical crops. The curve for crop *a* is the steepest, i.e., it is the most sensitive to transport inputs, and the commodity is probably bulky or perishable. Consequently, it cannot be produced economically at great distances from the market. Crop *c*, on the other hand, is easy to transport; therefore profits from its exploitation may be obtained at great distances from the market.

In this model, farmers are optimizers whose location is given. They will select that crop whose profitability is the highest for their location. Assuming that crops *a*, *b*, and *c* are the only ones that may be planted in a particular area, the choice of a specific crop at any location is then identified by the uppermost curve. The land-rent curves for crops *a* and *b* intersect at distance *x*. This means that although all three crops can be grown to the left of x_1, the profits to be obtained by growing crop *a* are the highest. Therefore, Mx_1 becomes the radius of a circle in which crop *a* is cultivated. To the right of x_1, crop *a* can still be grown at some profit. However, the uppermost curve is that for crop *b*. Therefore, within distance band x_1y_1, crop *b* is cultivated,

Figure 3-9
Land-use competition and land-use zones

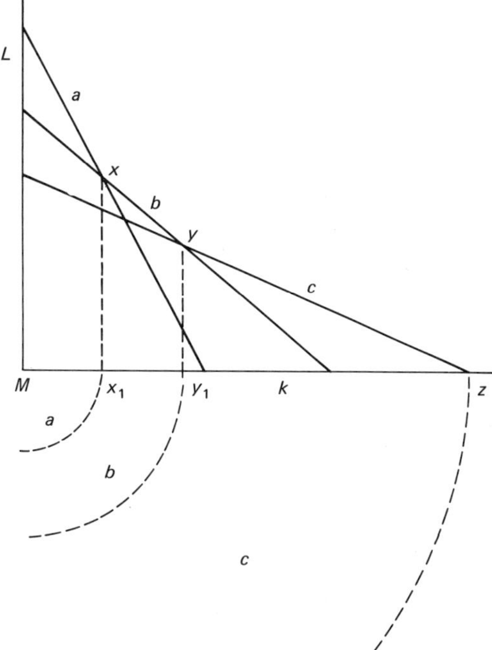

while crop *c* is cultivated at distances y_1z. In this way concentric zones of agricultural production emerge.

In the real world, vegetables and milk (perishable commodities) are produced close to urban markets. In some countries, bulky commodities like firewood are also "cultivated" close to urban markets, while grain production is carried on at relatively great distances.

In countries where agricultural land holdings are fragmented, a farmer may have several fields at varying distances from the village. The use of the individual parcels will be, in part, a response to distance. Accordingly, nearer parcels may be irrigated or used intensively, while farther ones are used for grazing or other extensive forms of agriculture. Chisholm (1967) has empirically corroborated these ideas with reference to the Canicatti area of Sicily.

The pair of models described above is narrowly focused, but at a larger scale an important implication of transport inputs is the emergence of strong interregional contrasts in the level of economic activity.

Economic Regionalization

Owing to initial advantage and circular and cumulative causation (Myrdal, 1957; Pred, 1966), in most countries there are regional concentrations of productive activities, population, markets, and transport facilities. These concentrations become attractive places in which to do business, partly because the distances between production and consumption locations are relatively small, and partly because scale economies in the movement industries enable them to charge lower rates. As a result, the movement industries acquire a self-perpetuating momentum (Ullman, 1958, 180).

The distribution of population outside the core areas of most countries also represents markets for goods and services. However, the predominantly dispersed population pattern in the periphery does not enable the realization of scale economies in the movement industries. Therefore, the price of the transport input is comparatively high, especially if the markets of the core region are at a great distance. If the natural-resource endowments are favorable, resource-based activities will develop, and the products will flow to the core regions. One result is a relatively permanent inequality in the level of activity between core areas and periphery.

The foregoing pertains to the impact of regional transport costs. At the local scale, transport costs are important also. Businesses tend to locate at points of maximum accessibility to their potential market, a key consideration in personal-service and retail-trade activities such as barbershops and cocktail lounges. These activities have assembly costs, while the distribution costs are borne directly by the customers. Consequently, the volume of their business is a direct function of their location.

Whether we look at the spatial distribution of manufacturing activities or agricultural land use in a narrow sense or at broad interregional contrasts in economic activity, we see that a powerful variable is distance and the cost required to overcome it. Consequently, distance minimization may be one principle that lends order to the human organization of space. However, there is no such thing as a permanent order; yesterday's order is today's chaos. The locational system is constantly undergoing a process of reorganization, partly in response to the relative importance and prices of transport inputs.

TIME, TRANSPORT COSTS, AND LOCATION

According to Keynes, in the long run we will all be dead. An operational definition of *long run* that is relevant to economic activities is the average life of the depreciable assets in an industry. Among different industries, this statistic is highly variable. In major capital-intensive industries, the life of depreciable assets may be as high as 40 years, and, in some cases, production may be carried on long after the assets have been entirely depreciated. Some activities use little capital equipment, and then rapid depreciation enables them to shift location frequently as and when conditions change. The former types of industries, which constitute the foundations of a complex modern economy, are relatively immobile. Rodgers (1952) has called this phenomenon "inertia" and has described it as a causative factor leading to the locational persistence of the steel industry in the core area of the United States.

As Birdsall (1971) has noted, the original location of industries characterized by inertia ignored supply-and-demand location factors. For example, the Oldsmobile plant was located in Lansing, owing to the personal preference of Mr. Olds. Subsequently, the improvements of and reductions in cost of materials transport allowed the suppliers of inputs to locate throughout the Manufacturing Belt of the northeastern United States. In recent decades, the locational pattern of demand has shifted, precipitating a need for the dispersal of assembly operations. Nevertheless, inertia has prevented spatial reorganization. Birdsall computed inertia costs as the difference in physical distance between the current location of the plant and the hypothetical median center location (taking into account the combined supply-demand patterns). This was found to be as follows: 1935, 89 miles; 1940, 94 miles; 1953, 95 miles; and 1963, 99 miles — that is, the Lansing location has progressively become more eccentric, owing to inertia.

Cost-space Convergence

In the previous chapter we observed that transport costs and physical distance can be equated in the sense that, for a given physical distance, such as that between New York and Bombay (about 10,000 miles), the cost distance is $475. This cost distance has decreased through time, especially in recent years. As recently as 1960, the equivalent fare was a little over $1200.

Data on changes in transportation costs and prices through time must be interpreted carefully because of the number of variables involved: cutthroat competition among modes and among carriers at a time when the transportation revolution was under way, seasonal rate fluctuations, impact of bargaining between shipper and carrier in the preregulation era, and the severe and short-duration fluctuations in the value of money. Therefore, such data must be regarded only as approximate indicators of the direction, not amount, of the cost of movement throughout time.

Taylor (1951, 132–152) has summarized the changes in transportation rates in the United States during the period 1815 to 1860, during which transportation was revolutionized. Before 1819, freight rates by wagon train westward from Philadelphia and Baltimore ranged from 30 to 60 cents/ton-mile, and after 1822, a rate of 12 to 17 cents was typical. While railroad freight rates varied widely, interregionally, among railroads and between commodities, a marked downward trend during the Civil War was clearly evident. In New York State, the average ton-mile rates were 9.04 cents in 1848, 4.05 cents in 1851, and 2.2 cents in 1860. The same was true of rates on canal barge transportation. On the Hudson River, the ton-mile rate was 6.2 cents in 1814 and dropped to 0.7 cents by 1854.

Striking changes in the prices charged for the transportation of persons have occurred also. An interesting example deals with the changes which occurred between 1816 and 1860 in the fares charged for people traveling between Philadelphia and Quebec. In 1816, the trip via a series of steamboats and stagecoaches cost $47 and took 5½ days. By 1860, the same trip by railroad alone cost $18.69 and took about 50 hours. Trans-Atlantic passenger rates in 1838 were $140, with wine included, while by 1852 the comparable rate was about $100.

In the early part of the last century in the United States, postal rates were high and zonal. In 1812, a letter written on a single sheet of paper cost 6 cents to mail to a point 30 miles distant. By 1851, to mail a letter up to 300 miles cost only 3 cents to the sender.

These trends, although most dramatic in the middle part of the last century, have continued into the present. Abler (1971) has noted that by 1863 postal rates were uniform throughout the country. "Complete cost-space convergence," a phrase used to denote places approaching each other in cost-space as a result of the decline in movement costs, had been accomplished. The result is a form of homogeneous cost surface on which the impact of distance on the cost of movement has been eliminated. Long-distance telephone rates have also been going down while intracity rates have been increasing, leading to a cost-space convergence of 29.5 cents/year for telephone communication between 1920 and 1970 in America.

The across-the-board reduction in movement costs and in prices has been mainly a function of improvements in transport and communications technology, including the expansion and intensification of railroads, the utilization of cheaper and more efficient sources of energy, the standardization of gauges, the elimination of circuity (the distance from New York to San Francisco with respect to large-scale freight movement decreased from 6100 to 3400 miles after the direct Trans-Continental railroad was completed in 1869), the utilization of automatic signals and controls, and later, the electrification of urban transportation (e.g., streetcars and subways).

These varied technological improvements in the movement and communications industries have had significant impact on the reduction of time required for human interaction in space. In turn, this impact has made "distance" a time-biased concept. How much "distance" is too far away has varied through time.

Time-Space Convergence

The concept of "shrinking world" suggests that places are coming together as a result of a decrease in the time required to move between them. Ellsworth Huntington (1952, 529) noted that the time required to travel from Portland, Maine, to San Diego, California, would have been 2 years on foot in the 16th century, 8 months on horseback in the 17th century, 4 months by stagecoach and wagon in 1840, 4 days by rail in 1910, and today 10 hours by "fast plane." Since then, air travel time has decreased to about 5 hours. Assuming a walking speed of 3 miles/hour, the improvements in transport technology through time in effect have brought San Diego to a point only 15 miles from Portland. The physical distance between those two points is and always has been about 2600 miles. Thus, during a period of more than 400 years, the time-distance has shrunk by 2585 miles.

Figure 3-10 is a striking illustration of the magnitude by which the United States has "shrunk" from 1912 to 1970. At least in terms of transcontinental or intermetropolitan area travel time, the United States of 1970 corresponds to the physical size of the Delmarva Peninsula. However, the notion of the shrinking world must not be exaggerated. Air transport has bypassed many small communities, and passenger rail service to and from small communities has been virtually eliminated. If these communities are not athwart new highways, for them time-space divergence rather than convergence has occurred.

Janelle (1968, 1969) has elaborated on the notion of the shrinking world and introduced the term "time-space convergence," another example of which is shown in Figure 3-11. Note that the travel time between London and Edinburgh has decreased from 20,000 minutes by stagecoach in 1658 to less than 200 minutes by airplane in 1966. Over the 300-year period, the annual rate of convergence has been 29.3 minutes. However, this rate is but an average rate. With the introduction of every new transportation innovation, locations approach each other in time-distance but at a decreasing rate. The rate of time-space convergence is the greatest during a period of transportation revolution: change from stagecoach to railroad or railroad to air line. Thus, it can be noted in Figure 3-11 that while in the 1840s the travel time from London to Edinburgh

Figure 3-10 The "shrinking" United States, 1912–1970

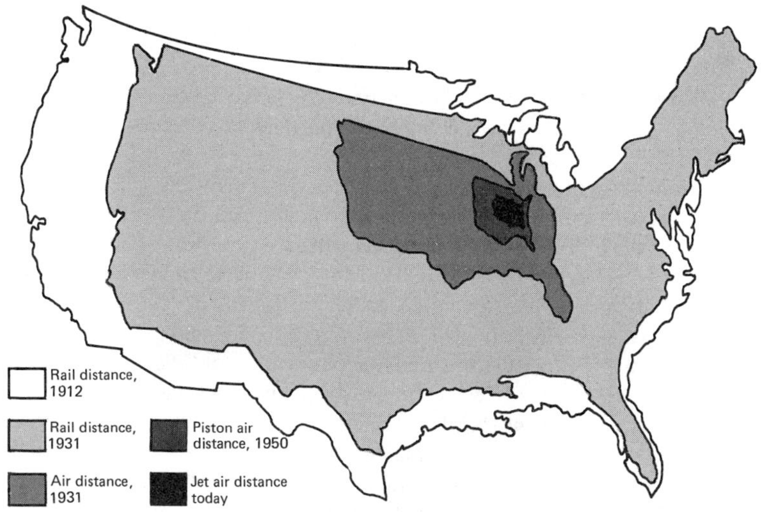

Figure 3-11
Time-space convergence between Edinburgh and London, 1658–1966

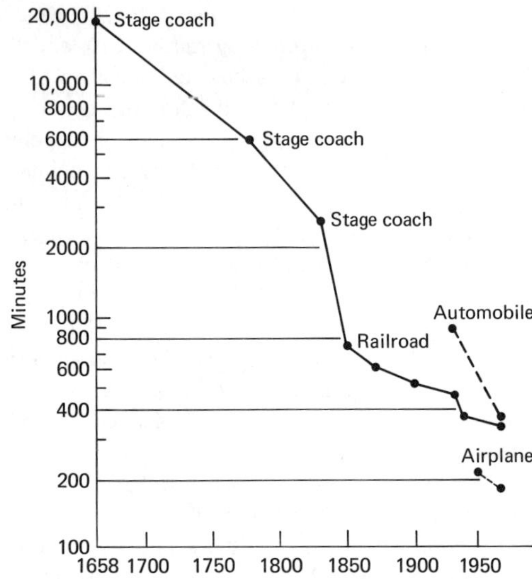

by stagecoach was about 2500 minutes, within 10 years it had declined by two-thirds to 800 minutes. Subsequently, the rate of time-space convergence leveled off so that by 1950, via railroad, the time-distance was still about 400 minutes.

Moreover, time-space convergence cannot continue indefinitely insofar as the movement of people and goods is concerned. Innovations appear to have marginal decreasing utility and also, owing to traffic congestion, it would appear that there is a practical limit to the reduction of time-distance between locations in space.

Time-space convergence in the case of information movement has also been phenomenal. In 1920, establishing a trans-United States telephone connection required 14 minutes (Abler, 1971, 1–2). In 1950 the time had shrunk to 1 minute, and in 1970, it was only 30 seconds. The rate of time-space convergence between 1920 and 1970 has been 16.2 seconds/year. Today, there is very little difference in connection time between a local call and a cross-country call.

The shrinking of cost and time distances have provided increasing flexibility of choice in the location of human activities. Looking to the future, Abler (1971), extrapolating from past trends, visualizes a time when increasing numbers of locational decisions will be made on the basis of noneconomic considerations. If there is no friction of distance, traditional spatial theory loses much of its validity. How people perceive distance and time and how they evaluate the quality of space in various locations may then become the primary considerations in locational choice rather than how long it takes and how much it costs to interact between points in geographic space. Ullman's (1954) early statement on the importance of amenity resources in locational choice may have been a portent of the future. Increasingly, natural beauty, the quality of the environment, and the recreational opportunities, rather than coal and iron ore, are becoming key resources because of cost and time-space convergence.

A gradual withering away of the "tyranny of space" (Warntz, 1967) implies that euclidean concepts of space are slowly becoming irrelevant and should be replaced by other geometries which will enable spatial analysts to deal more realistically with how man behaves in space.

Finally, it must be observed that the pace of cost-space and time-space convergence is extremely slow in most of the countries of the non-Western world, with the possible exception of Japan. Space continues to tyrannize, and ties to space are forged with iron, not a rubber band.

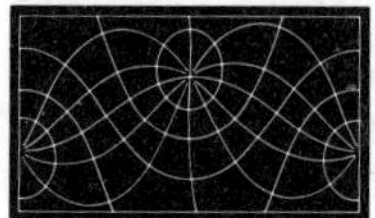

4 Nodes and Routes

It has been suggested previously that (1) geographic space consists of points; (2) a variety of human activities is conducted at some of these; (3) since human wants cannot be satisfied at any one point, there is a continuous need for interaction between locations; and (4) the cost of interaction is largely a function of the distance between points or nodes.

As a working definition of a *node*, we offer the following: a locational origin and/or destination of any form of interaction. People and objects occupy nodes which have specific coordinate locations in geographic space. We shall use nodes as the basic building blocks and develop a structure consisting of nodes connected by routes in this chapter. Subsequently, these will be synthesized into networks (Chapter 5), and eventually we shall proceed to a consideration of flows between the nodes over the entire network (Chapters 8, 9, and 10). Thus, the sequence is nodes, routes, networks, and flows.

An alternative schema, used by Haggett in his well-known *Locational Analysis in Human Geography* (1966), begins with movement and is shown in Figure 4-1. He developed a schema in which movement is the starting point as well as the source of energy sustaining and propelling the system. Beginning with movement, he developed a sequence of networks, nodes, and nodal hierarchies. However, an examination of Figure 4-1 prompts the question, Without nodes, why is there movement and where is it consigned?

In our view, all movement is purposive (the causes of movement have been elaborated on earlier), and each bit of movement has a specific origin and destination. Therefore, both in a logical and chronological sense, our schema is predicated on the existence of nodes prior to the development of networks and movement. These two different structures, used for the study of the geography of movement, are really two different ways of model conceptualization. Despite their differences in starting point, there is no inherent contradiction between them.

Figure 4-1 Stages in the development of movement: routes, nodes, and nodal hierarchies

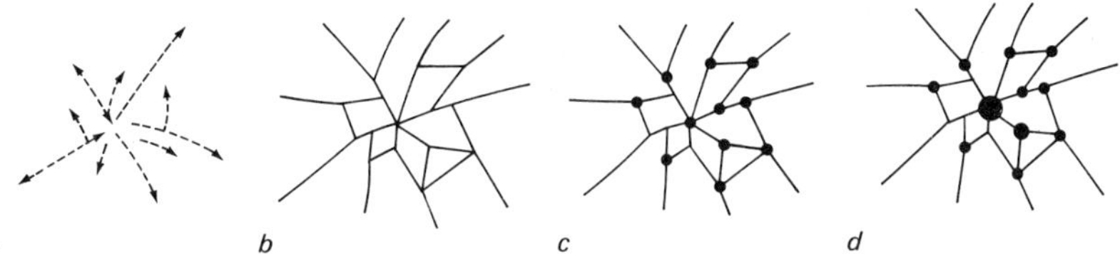

NODES

Human interaction in space involves people at certain places interacting with people at other places. Without either people or places, there is no interaction. Nodes are both sources and "sinks" (destinations) of all types of interaction. There are many types of nodes, each one with its own particular type of interaction, but certain common themes may be recognized. One possible way of classifying nodes is to place them into one of three categories: individuals, establishments, and settlements.

Types and Characteristics of Nodes

The individual is the foundation for the other two types of nodes in that groups of individuals constitute establishments, and groups of establishments make up settlements. At the outset it must be recognized that all nodes, regardless of the category to which they belong, are involved in spatial interaction processes as a necessary part of their overall functions. Thus, the individual is a node when receiving or transmitting something. An *establishment* is a collection of two or more individuals engaged in the supply or demand of any good or service at a specific location: churches provide salvation, bars provide liquor, and in either case there is both inbound and outbound movement. A *settlement* is a spatially juxtaposed collection of establishments engaged in diverse want-satisfying activities for a population.

While it may be possible to develop a lengthy list of nodal characteristics, two basic facets have been chosen for emphasis here because of their direct relevance to spatial interaction: (1) functional specialization of the different types of nodes, and (2) time discreteness in their functioning.

From an economic perspective, human society can be viewed as an occupational pyramid with unskilled individuals at the bottom and highly trained professionals at the top. There is a rough correlation between an individual's functional role in society and the degree to which that role depends upon movement. While a day laborer may travel less than 10,000 miles/year in the course of obtaining a livelihood, a distinguished brain surgeon not only may travel well over 100,000 miles/year but also may have come into contact with people who have traveled long distances specifically to see a doctor.

Most establishments have fixed locations and are engaged in specific functions. There is a pyramid of establishments in which there are numerous low-order business types at the bottom and a few highly specialized ones at the top. Corner drugstores and gas stations are ubiquitously located in contrast to stock exchanges and national administrative functions. Consequently, drugstores attract a small number of individuals from relatively short distances. Settlements can also be arranged along a functional continuum in which diversified places provide services whose demand is localized, while highly specialized ones may provide products or services nationally or internationally.

Each node has a "field" or "action space" within which most of its interactions occur. The size of fields varies according to the level of specialization of the node. Webber (1964) observes that intellectual elites have contacts with distant places via journals, books, mail, telephone, personal visits, and mutual contacts; such individuals form "communities without propinquity." In contrast, members of the working class exhibit an intense localism, with contacts largely being within their neighborhood. His surveys have shown that family ties are so strong that in working-class communities, married daughters live within walking distance of parents. The action space of specialized establishments, such as the White House and the United Nations, is quite literally worldwide, while the neighborhood barbershop's market area is restricted. In much the same way, Atlanta, Georgia, is a regional capital of the South, shipping products to other nodes within its region, while steel from Pittsburgh and automobiles from Detroit move nationwide.

Not all nodes are fixed in space. In particular, individuals are mobile nodes. Some establishments such as traveling circuses and mobile libraries, as well as settlements such as periodic markets in Third World nations, are mobile, owing to the need for demand accumulation at specific locations. Hodder (1965, 50) estimated that in southeastern Nigeria, for example, a population of 50 per square mile is the minimum density necessary to support a permanent market system. When densities are less than this, in order to avoid "dead time," groups of sellers move in a rhythmic pattern, substituting the tyranny of time for that of space. In Nigeria, traders travel long distances, frequently on foot, carrying up to 80 pounds/day and covering as much as 50 miles/week (Hodder, 1961, 154). And, as Eighmy observes, "where the cost of overcoming distance is high and profit margins are low, periodic market meetings serve to concentrate both supply and demand in time and place" (1972, 301).

The occurrence of interaction between nodes is also time-discrete. Individuals operate according to biological clocks so that some number of hours of sleep is required. Most individuals work and shop during daylight hours, and some "night persons," such as nightclub singers and some policemen and utility workers, function at night. Establishments, also, operate with specific periodicities: most operate from 9 to 5, but the CIA, hospitals, police stations, newspapers, and the telephone company operate around the clock. Many churches function on Sundays and special days, music festivals function during the summer, and ski resorts operate during the winter. Thus, interaction with a specific establishment requires the selection of an appropriate time band.

This discussion of mobile nodes and time bands leads us to the more general issue of time-space convergence, referred to in the last chapter, as well as the trade-off between time and space occasioned by periodic markets. In the language of the economist, we may say that time and space are two commodities that are mutually substitutable. Different individuals have different trade-off values which influence their spatial behavior.

Not only are there short-term fluctuations in the nature of nodes, but there are also long-term trends, in which there may be growth or decline. The growth-decline syndrome may be observed at a variety of scales and applies, *mutatis mutandis*, to all categories of nodes — individuals, establishments, and settlements. Individuals have a life cycle in which the requirements and the ability for interaction, as measured by the mean number of contacts and the field, change. A baby's action space is the crib, that of the school-age child is the neighborhood, and in working years the field is the maximum beyond which, at retirement, action space is once again curtailed.

Establishments also have their phases of change. A corner grocery store may graduate into a supermarket which, in turn, becomes the locus of a shopping center. Some central-city businesses decline because of a reduction in the number of customers and create conditions of commercial blight. As settlements compete with one another, some gain preeminence as a result of a winning combination of locational assets attracting diverse kinds of economic activities. There are also cases of settlements which have suffered a decline in their functional importance, followed by a contraction of their fields. The legendary transportation centers along the caravan routes of central Asia, such as Bokhara and Samarkand, both major nodes at one time, are pale shadows of their former selves today. At the height of the Ottoman Empire, Constantinople was the largest city in the world, but by 1970 it ranked forty-third in population among the world's cities.

The Functions of Nodes in a Movement-related Context

The "functional approach" is a well-recognized mode of study in geography, in which the basic question is, What is the role of the locational entity under investigation? Nodes may have a variety of functional specialties, such as the production of manufactured goods, the provision of retail trade or professional services, the administration of public services, and so on. All these types of nodes, regardless of their level of specialization, generate movement. For our purpose, we can therefore limit the consideration of the functional role of nodes to (1) the origin and reception of movement, and (2) the relay of movement.

Nodes as Origins and Destinations of Movement

In most cases, originating and receiving movement is a sequential process which cannot be disaggregated without violating the concept of spatial interaction, as can be seen from the following sequence of events. Let us illustrate the process of interaction between individuals, establishments, and settlements by observing the movement behavior of a specific individual traveling in geographic space to satisfy fairly common needs. He makes, initially, a decision to get a haircut at a particular place which is followed by a trip to the chosen barbershop, an establishment and the destination of this particular trip. At the barbershop a transaction occurs, whose two essential components are that a personal service is provided by the barber and that a sum of money is exchanged. We may regard the preceding as one complete interaction, consisting of an origin, a trip to a destination, and a transaction at that destination. Upon completion of the first interaction, the individual decides to eat a hamburger at a particular place which now becomes the receiving node or destination, while the barbershop is the origin of this second interaction. In this manner, each of us initiates many interactions with many nodes, although not all need involve physical travel.

Establishments also originate and receive flows, and just as the individual traveled to the barbershop, coal moves from the mines to steel mills, wheat is shipped from farms to grain elevators, devotees drive from houses to churches, and tax payments are sent to the Internal Revenue Service. In turn, these destinations originate movement themselves so that construction beams are shipped from steel mills, contributions for earthquake victims are sent from churches, and dunning letters or refunds are mailed by the IRS. In this manner, establishments interact with other establishments as well as with individuals.

The amount of movement originated and received by any particular node is related to its size and hierarchical position. All the individuals and establishments within a settlement can be conceptualized as composing a single entity ("mass") originating or receiving movement, even though in a real sense it is the establishments and individuals that are actually the specific origins and destinations of all movement.

In 1970, the personal consumption expenditures in the United States amounted to $615.8 billion. The spending of this much money was undoubtedly associated with an extremely large number of separate interactions. These consisted of the movement of people, goods, and information between millions of nodes comprised of 203,235,000 individuals and 11,672,000 business organizations, many with multiple locations agglomerated in 20,768 settlements. Moreover, such a large number of transactions required a highly complex system of routes and facilities which can be properly articulated only by a series of relay facilities.

Nodes as Relays of Movement

The second function of nodes is to relay movement, in which case the node is neither the ultimate origin nor the destination of the interactive process, although it is an important proximate origin or destination. The primary purpose of relay nodes is to receive flows in order to transmit them to another node with minimum delay or cost. In general, relay nodes enable the articulation of flows through (1) the amplification of signals, (2) the elimination or reduction of "noise" or irrelevancies in the incoming information, and (3) the provision of temporary storage.

In complex societies, the role of relay nodes is crucial both because of the multiplicity of origins, destinations, routes, and modes of movements on the one hand, and because of the sophisticated nature of production and the massive volumes that are transported from node to node on the other. In contrast, in simple societies, most transactions can occur at a face-to-face level which minimizes the need for intermediary nodes.

Some familiar examples of individuals as relay nodes are telephone operators, diplomatic intermediaries, and stockbrokers. Their role is essential to the completion of spatial interaction, but they are neither ultimate origins nor destinations in the ordinary course of events. They receive information from other nodes, the content of which is not altered in the transmission process. Indeed, one way to evaluate their function as relay nodes is to examine their veracity and fidelity in transmitting information in its pure form. Especially in diplomatic contacts, as, for example, in the case of a translator at high-level summit talks, nuances are important. Language is a sufficient barrier to interaction so that even if face-to-face propinquity exists, communication cannot occur without the presence of a relay node.

Establishments that specialize in relaying movement transfer not only information from place to place, but also people and goods. There is no change in the nature of the object being moved as it passes through a relay node. Thus, a major difference between a warehouse (a relay node) and a manufacturing plant (an ultimate node) is that in the former, value is added to a commodity by storage, while in the latter, it is added by transforming the nature of some material. Telephone exchanges may be regarded as relay nodes also. They receive information from a number of locations, amplify it, and pass it on. Amplification in this instance does not involve change in a structural or syntactical sense but only in magnitude. Even libraries may be regarded as storage houses of accumulated human knowledge where the producer and the consumer of ideas and information interact. Employment agencies bring job-seekers and potential employers together. When two nations do not have diplomatic relations, they use the embassy of a third as a relay. For example, Swiss embassies, because of the traditional neutrality of Switzerland, are frequently used for this purpose. American diplomatic contacts with China in the sixties were routed through Warsaw. Indeed, the notion of "routing through" is the essential quality of a relay node.

Some settlements, notably port cities, specialize in relaying movement. Every port has a hinterland, which is the area from which exports are routed and to which imports are destined. Patton (1958) made a detailed empirical study of the cargo hinterlands of New York, Philadelphia, Baltimore, and New Orleans. Figure 4-2 shows the location of the nodes from which at least one carload lot of freight was sent through the relay node of Baltimore. This port is in competition with Philadelphia, New York, and Hampton Roads. It has been able to compete successfully because of three factors. The first advantage was that the transport rate, on the average, was 1 cent/100 pounds below that of Philadelphia and 3 cents below that of New York on freight moving from the eastern part of the Middle West. Consequently, it may be noted that nodes along Lake Erie shipped via Baltimore rather than New York. During the sample period, Johnstown, Pennsylvania, dispatched more than 100 carloads through Baltimore but fewer than 10 carloads through Philadelphia. Second, the extensive Baltimore and Ohio railroad system has its principal terminals in Baltimore, enabling Baltimore to move commodities from widely separated origins. Third, the Sparrows Point steel plant is, by itself, a massive origin and destination. The arcane mysteries of freight rate-making are too complex to unravel here. Suffice it to note that rate differentials between alternative modes do have important consequences for the magnitude of both inbound and outbound movement.

Figure 4-2 General cargo hinterland of the port of Baltimore, as shown by origin of at least one carload exported

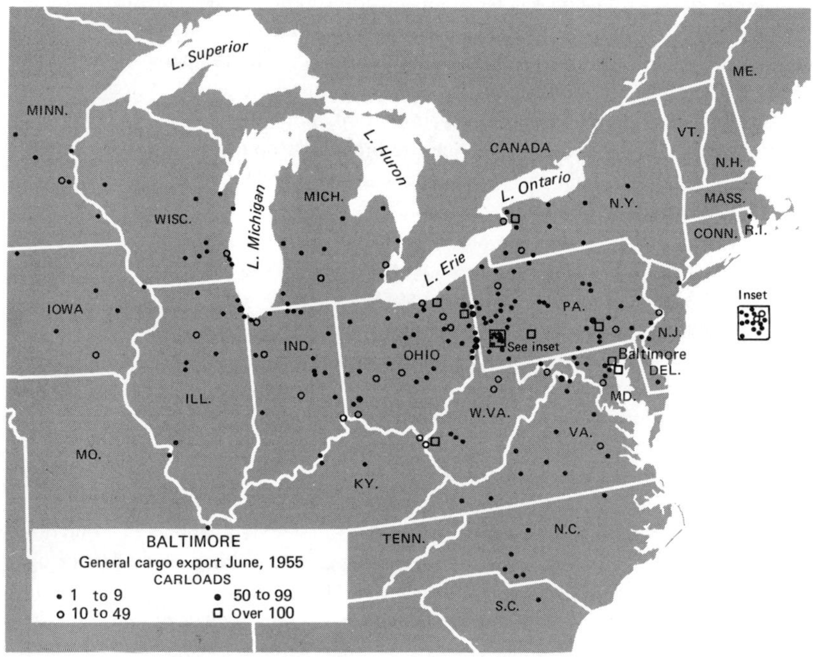

Railroad junctions also collect and redistribute people and goods. St. Louis, near the confluence of the Mississippi and Missouri Rivers, is appropriately labeled the Gateway City. In countries where there is complex point-to-point flow of large volumes of commodities, it is necessary to locate many switching yards. These are relay nodes where freight cars are disassembled and reassembled. Figure 4-3 shows the switching yards and the associated railroad network in France. Note the closer spacing of the nodes in the densely populated and heavily industrialized north and northeast (Alsace-Lorraine).

In complex societies, the rational location of relay facilities is an important problem. Rationality is achieved by organizing the pattern of location in such a manner as to yield movement minimization. Given the location of certain ultimate origins and destinations, the specified volumes of movement between them, and the cost of movement, it is possible to compute a solution which specifies the location, capacity, and internodal assignment of each relay facility. This type of problem is frequently referred to as the warehouse of transshipment problem, an important topic in operations research. While we will consider it more fully in Chapter 12, a simple example of a feasible solution is provided here. This is usually the starting point for the development of the optimal flow pattern.

Given four supply locations ($S_1, \ldots, S_4$), each with a given volume of production (10, 30, 20, 40 units, respectively), and three demand locations ($D_1, \ldots, D_3$), each with a specified volume of demand (20, 50, and 30, respectively), we can locate two relay facilities (R_1 and R_2) with capacities of 65 and 35, respectively. The volume of movement between the S_i and the two relays, as well as that between the relays and the various D_i, is indicated in Figure 4-4. The flows diagramed are arbitrary and are not necessarily the optimal ones. All that has been done is to assign the quantity supplied from various locations to that demanded at others. However, formally, the problems of allocation of flows is one of mathematical permutations and combinations in which the matching of supply and demand locations can be done via a number of alternative flow patterns, and for which a comparison of alternative cost yields the optimal solution.

Finally, it must be pointed out that the location of relay nodes is a dependent variable in a chronological sense. They are located subsequent to and are dependent upon a previously existing pattern of nodes. Thus, we find that warehouses are located in accordance with the spatial pattern of manufacturing industries and retailers, not the other way around; and the optimal location of a multilingual translator is New York City or Geneva, owing to the concentration of major international agencies in those cities.

The Locational Characteristics of Nodes

Thus far, this chapter has been couched largely in aspatial terms, despite the mentioning of place names. Place names are identification labels which, in the absence of locational specification, lack a geographical context.

Figure 4-3 Switching yards and associated railroad network in France

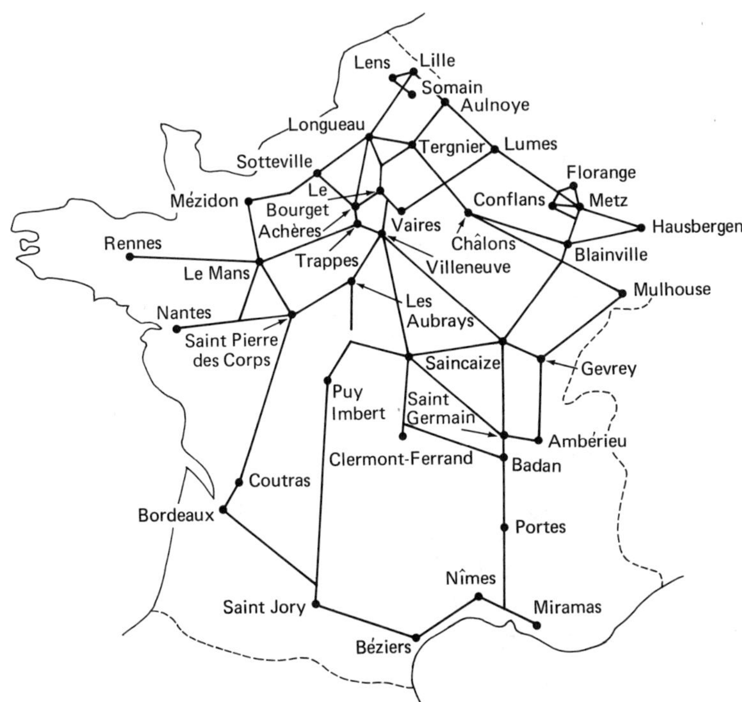

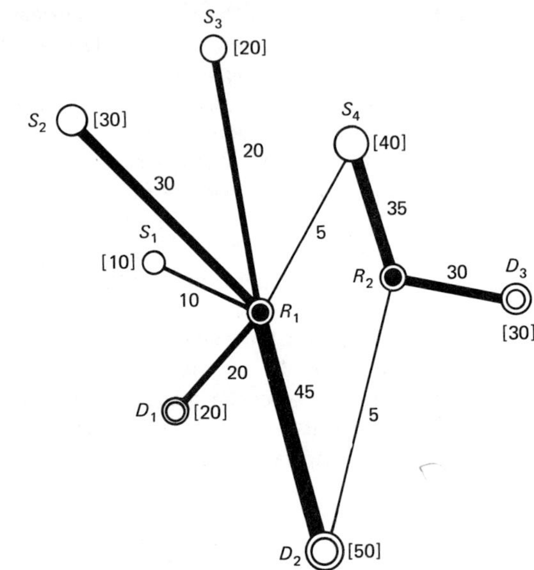

Figure 4-4
Feasible flows between supply locations and demand locations via relay nodes

Relative Location of a Node in a System of Nodes

When there is only one node in an area, there is neither a nodal system nor any interaction. Robinson Crusoe, as an individual, was not a node until his man Friday arrived on the scene, and provided an origin and destination for the transfer of information. An integral property of a system is that there is interaction between its various elements. While it is true that two nodes could constitute a system as long as there is interaction between them, the focus of this section on relative location necessitates the consideration of systems made up of at least three nodes.

One way to understand relative location is to consider sequencing. When the months of the year are arranged in alphabetical order — April, August, December, February, January, July, June, March, May, November, October, and September — it is evident that the alphabetical order imposed has destroyed the chronological order. In the same manner, alphabetizing places distorts spatial order. Thus, on a transit from Atlanta to Denver on the interstate highway system, the alphabetical sequence of the nodes that are part of the same highway system is: Atlanta, Cairo, Chattanooga, Denver, Kansas City, Nashville, St. Louis, and Topeka. Such an ordering ignores relative location, and we do not know which nodes come first and which come later. A more useful ordering is Atlanta, Chattanooga, Nashville, Cairo, St. Louis, Kansas City, Topeka, and Denver, because we are thereby informed that Kansas City is reached after St. Louis but before Topeka.

The identification of the specific location of a node depends on our ability to relate it to two or more other nodes in terms of time, distance, cost, spatial sequence, and so on. Additionally, relationships between nodes may be expressed in such terms as "closer than," "cheaper than," "it takes longer to get to . . . than to . . . ," etc.

On an isotropic plane, the node at the center of the system of nodes is the most accessible in that more nodes can be reached from it, at a lesser overall distance or cost, than from any other. In contrast, in the context of the same system, peripheral locations cannot be reached as readily from all others, although once we introduce other systems, the value of relative location changes. While New York City is somewhat at the periphery of the United States, it is central with respect to U.S.–West European commodity and other movements.

All nodes have a level of accessibility which can be measured and compared with the use of graph-theoretic indices (Chapter 5). On a global scale, treating areas as nodes and the land hemisphere as a system of such nodes, it is evident that the United Kingdom has the most central location with regard to distance to the world's land masses and, indeed, is at the crossroads of major oceanic and airline routes.

Nodal Distributions

Given an area in which nodes are located at various places, one could map the distribution, examine it, and then conclude that the overall distribution is "dense" or "sparse," "concentrated" or "dispersed." One might go one step further and compute certain critical indices and ratios such as the number of nodes per square kilometer of area, or the number of manufacturing plants per county, or other political subdivision. Such measurements yield somewhat more precise results than just a visual inspection. However, these indices do not give explicit consideration to distance between the nodes, nor do they lend themselves to comparative analysis and generalizations concerning the nature of nodal distributions.

In recent years, techniques developed by plant ecologists, who were concerned with the spatial distribution of plant species conceptualized as point patterns, have been borrowed by geographers in their study of spatial distributions. While the range of possible point distributions is a continuum, certain characteristic ones can be recognized. A widely used typology is that shown in Figure 4-5 which illustrates clustered, random, and uniform hypothetical nodal distributions. The points on these diagrams could represent any type of node classified earlier. For example, these distributions may represent the location of crimes in a city, poor persons, establishments such as pizza parlors,

Figure 4-5 Point distributions showing (*a*) a clustered pattern; (*b*) a random pattern; (*c*) a uniform pattern.

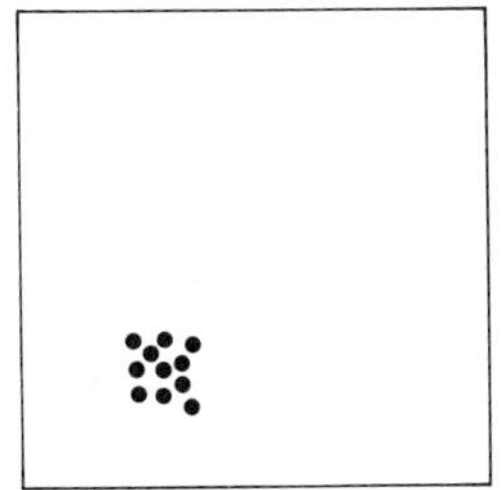

a

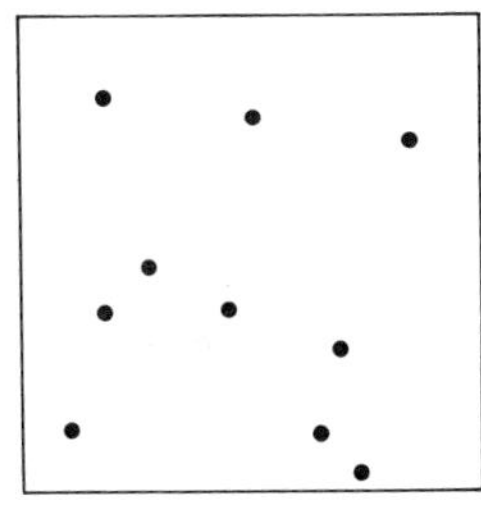

b

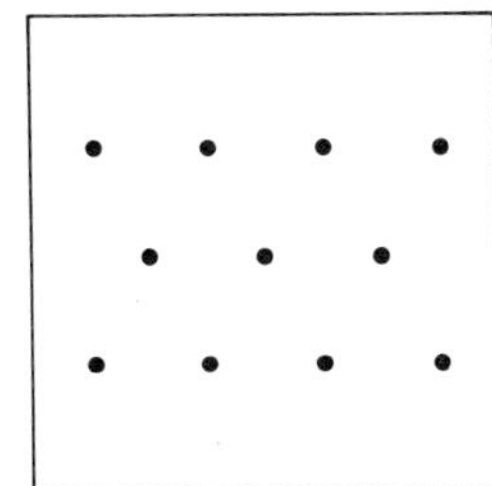

c

bowling alleys, fire stations, and hospitals, or settlements of various sizes. However, since the object of analysis in the study of point patterns is a distance relationship between the nodes, size can be ignored.

In a uniform pattern, there is maximum spacing between adjacent points resulting in a hexagonal-lattice network, an arrangement that is basic to central place theory. Real-world examples of this pattern are understandably scarce, although it is approximated by the gridiron pattern of street intersections in American cities and the distribution of farms in Iowa.

Many nodal distributions at a variety of scales in the real world may be described as being clustered, including department stores, banks, and shoe stores, in most cities; theaters in New York City; hotels on Collins Avenue in Miami Beach; and federal government offices in Washington, D.C.

The notions of uniformness and cluster as well as their spatial manifestations shown in Figure 4-5 are perhaps intuitively obvious. Spatial randomness is a more difficult concept to grasp. Therefore, it is necessary to define a *random distribution of points* as "a set of points on a given area (for which) it is assumed that any point has had the same chance of occurring on any sub-area as any other point; that any sub-area of specified size has had the same chance of receiving a point as any other sub-area of that size, and that the placement of each point has not been influenced by that of any other point" (Clark and Evans, 1954, 446).

Given various point patterns, it may be asked, Which one of these results in distance minimization and which one in distance maximization? Certain preliminary assumptions are necessary before attempting to answer these questions. (1) The points represent nodes of the same size, and consequently there is no nodal hierarchy. (2) Movement effort is strictly a linear function of distance. (3) Interaction probabilities are equal between each point and every other point. (4) All individuals and establishments in each of these nodes have equal propensities for interaction. (5) There are no topographic or other barriers to inhibit interaction.

It is first necessary to convert the maps of point patterns in Figure 4-5 to matrices of distance (Table 4-1) in which the element D_{ij} is the distance between point i and point j. These matrices are mathematical translations of the maps in which the essential locational information has been preserved but has been converted to a form more amenable to numerical analysis. The reader will note that the sum of distances in a clustered pattern approaches zero and that it is 972 for a uniform pattern. Among the three patterns compared, the sum of distances is the maximum for the uniform pattern, indicating that the latter represents inefficient spatial organization.

Since the cost of interaction between two points in a system of nodes is evidently the least in an agglomerated system, it would seem logical to conclude that there would be a greater volume of interaction in such a situation. However, given the possibility of congestion, ignored here so far, the added time-cost may erode the impact of total minimization of physical distance.

One of the assumptions made above was that all nodes were of equal size. Let us relax this assumption now, and assume instead a pattern such as those in Figure 4-6*a* and *b* which shows a uniform nodal distribution in which one settlement is 5 times larger than the others. The difference between the

Table 4-1
Distance Matrix for Clustered, Random, and Uniform Point Patterns

(*a*) Clustered

	To *A*	*B*	*C*	*D*	*E*	*F*	*G*	*H*	*I*	*J*	*K*	
From *A*	—	2	4	1	2	2	4	3	4	4	4	
B	2	—	2	1	2	2	2	3	4	4	4	
C	4	2	—	3	4	2	2	3	4	4	4	
D	1	1	3	—	1	1	3	2	3	3	3	
E	2	2	4	1	—	2	4	3	2	3	4	
F	2	2	2	1	2	—	2	1	2	2	2	
G	4	2	2	3	4	2	—	1	4	2	2	
H	3	3	3	2	3	1	1	—	3	1	1	
I	4	4	4	3	2	2	4	3	—	2	4	
J	4	4	4	3	3	2	2	1	2	—	2	
K	4	4	4	3	4	2	2	1	4	2	—	
Sum	30	26	32	21	27	18	26	21	32	27	30	290

(*b*) Random

	To *A*	*B*	*C*	*D*	*E*	*F*	*G*	*H*	*I*	*J*	*K*	
From *A*	—	8	3	6	6	8	10	11	11	13	14	
B	8	—	9	11	10	7	7	16	15	10	11	
C	3	9	—	3	3	6	9	8	8	10	12	
D	6	11	3	—	1	5	8	5	5	9	10	
E	6	10	3	1	—	3	7	6	6	8	10	
F	8	7	6	5	3	—	3	9	9	5	7	
G	10	7	9	8	7	3	—	12	10	3	5	
H	11	16	8	5	6	9	12	—	2	11	12	
I	11	15	8	5	6	9	10	2	—	9	10	
J	13	10	10	9	8	5	3	11	9	—	2	
K	14	11	12	10	10	7	5	12	10	2	—	
Sum	90	104	71	63	60	62	74	92	85	80	93	874

(*c*) Uniform

	To *A*	*B*	*C*	*D*	*E*	*F*	*G*	*H*	*I*	*J*	*K*	
From *A*	—	5	10	15	5	9	13	9	10	13	17	
B	5	—	5	10	5	5	9	10	9	10	13	
C	10	5	—	5	9	5	5	13	10	9	10	
D	15	10	5	—	13	9	5	17	13	10	9	
E	5	5	9	13	—	5	10	5	5	9	13	
F	9	5	5	9	5	—	5	9	5	5	9	
G	13	9	5	5	10	5	—	13	9	5	5	
H	9	10	13	17	5	9	13	—	5	10	15	
I	10	9	10	13	5	5	9	5	—	5	10	
J	13	10	9	10	9	5	5	10	5	—	5	
K	17	13	10	9	13	9	5	15	10	5	—	
Sum	106	81	81	106	79	66	79	106	81	81	106	972

two distributions arises solely from the location of the larger node. In the former case (Figure 4-6*a*) it is at the periphery, while in the latter (Figure 4-6*b*) the large node is at the center. Because of these variations in size, it is assumed that the amount of movement originating from the large node to each of the smaller ones is 5 times greater than that between any pair of the smaller nodes. The total volume of movement is the same whether the large node is at the center or at the periphery, as is shown in Table 4-2*a* and *b* which rep-

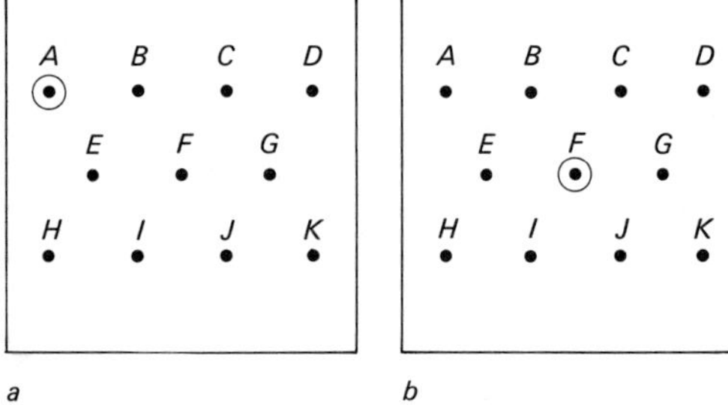

Figure 4-6
Uniform point distributions. (*a*) Point *A* is 5 times larger than the others; (*b*) point *F* is 5 times larger than the others.

Table 4-2
Internodal Flow Matrices for Uniform Point Patterns

(*a*) Peripheral Point *A* Is 5 Times Larger

From \ To	*A*	*B*	*C*	*D*	*E*	*F*	*G*	*H*	*I*	*J*	*K*	
A	—	25	50	75	25	45	65	45	50	65	85	
B	5	—	5	10	5	5	9	10	9	10	13	
C	10	5	—	5	9	5	5	13	10	9	10	
D	15	10	5	—	13	9	5	17	13	10	9	
E	5	5	9	13	—	5	10	5	5	9	13	
F	9	5	5	9	5	—	5	9	5	5	9	
G	13	9	5	5	10	5	—	13	9	5	5	
H	9	10	13	17	5	9	13	—	5	10	5	
I	10	9	10	13	5	5	9	5	—	5	10	
J	13	10	9	10	9	5	5	10	5	—	5	
K	17	13	10	9	13	9	5	15	10	5	—	
Sum	106	101	121	166	99	102	131	142	121	133	174	1396

(*b*) Central Point *F* Is 5 Times Larger

From \ To	*A*	*B*	*C*	*D*	*E*	*F*	*G*	*H*	*I*	*J*	*K*	
A	—	5	10	15	5	9	13	9	10	13	17	
B	5	—	5	10	5	5	9	10	9	10	13	
C	10	5	—	5	9	5	5	13	10	9	10	
D	15	10	5	—	13	9	5	17	13	10	9	
E	5	5	9	13	—	5	10	5	5	9	13	
F	45	25	25	45	25	—	25	45	25	25	45	
G	13	9	5	5	10	5	—	13	9	5	5	
H	9	10	13	17	5	9	13	—	5	10	15	
I	10	9	10	13	5	5	9	5	—	5	10	
J	13	10	9	10	9	5	5	10	5	—	5	
K	17	13	10	9	13	9	5	15	10	5	—	
Sum	142	101	101	142	99	66	99	142	101	101	142	1236

resents the matrices of internodal flows. However, since there is a greater amount of movement originating from the larger node, the number of trips originating from it is multiplied by the distance traveled and is entered in the appropriate cell. Thus, for example, in the cell at the intersection of row *C* and column *B*, the value represents the flow originating at *C* and destined for *B*. The values entered in each of the cells in Table 4-2 are in weight-distance units, such as "ton-miles" and "passenger-miles": that is, 100 ton-miles can be interpreted as either 100 tons moving over 1 mile or 1 ton moving 100 miles. Since all the cell entries are in the same unit of measurement, they may be compared directly.

A comparison of the summed weighted distances in both the hypothetical distributions (Figure 4-6) shows that the distribution in which the larger node is located in the center produces a lower aggregate distance (weight times distance) than that in which the larger node is located in the periphery.

A consideration of the nature of nodes, their hierarchical structures, the rationale for greater or lesser flows to or from particular nodes, and the spatial pattern of nodes enables one to understand two of the essential components of human spatial interaction: origins and destinations. Flows between these occur over certain routes, be they roads, telephone lines, or canals, all of which facilitate the process of interaction.

ROUTES

Routes are channels along which interaction occurs between any two nodes. There are both wandering and fixed routes or paths. Within limits, an airplane and a ship have a degree of flexibility in moving from point *A* to point *B*, establishing their paths as they move along. On the other hand, railroad tracks, highways, and canals are fixed paths that are important elements of the cultural landscape.

Route Capacity and Route Location

The locational configuration of a route and its capacity to handle traffic are partially a function of the characteristics of the environment. The nature of different physical environments varies, of course, as does their capacity to accommodate movement. While it is true that some form of movement is possible on land, sea, and air, the existence of ocean currents, prevailing winds, ice packs, jet streams, mountain ranges, mountain passes, and rivers facilitates or inhibits movement, as the case may be. These various phenomena tend to force the location of a particular route along certain trajectories which may be considered as geodesic paths. Thus, in the case of railroad route location, it is cheaper to follow the banks of a river than to cut a straight-line path between a pair of nodes.

At one time, the oceans were regarded as trackless wastes, as indeed were the North American prairies. The "prairie schooner" conjures up an image of a solitary ship traveling across a sea of grass. Although the vehicular size of the "schooner" enabled it to travel almost any path, such is not the case with a 10-ton truck which requires a roadbed with an easy grade. Such a roadbed cannot be built just anywhere without engendering exorbitant construction costs.

The configuration of a route and its capacity to handle movement are interrelated. A footpath can go uphill and downhill, following very steep gradients, but its capacity is severely limited. An interstate highway which can accommodate three lanes of traffic each way, however, is somewhat constrained with respect to its specific layout.

The Capacity of Routes to Accommodate Movement

Route capacity has been defined by traffic engineers in the context of highway passenger movement as "the maximum number of people that can pass a given location during a given time period under assumed service levels and conditions of operation, without unreasonable delay, hazard, or restriction" (Smith, 1966, 100). This definition, however, is not precise since capacity is a subjective notion. It is not constant, but rather variable, depending not only on width and design characteristics, but also on such things as rules concerning U-turns, other turning movements, adjacent land uses, and so on. With these qualifications in mind, highway capacity can be seen to be a function of vehicle size, design speed versus actual speeds at a given time, vehicles' peak passenger-carrying value (buses versus compact cars), the number of vehicles entering and leaving a particular route segment, and the spacing between adjacent vehicles. In the last three or four decades, the United States has experienced increasing spatial separation between place of work and place of residence, mass ownership of automobiles, and severe traffic congestion on a periodic basis.

Among the standard fares of American life are the five-o'clock rush hour, the Friday "airport syndrome," the summer weekend traffic jam on the way to the beach, the long lines at the post office at Christmas time, and the inability to get the long-distance operator on New Year's Eve.

Without prohibitive expense it is not possible to design movement facilities (both routes and terminals) so as to eliminate congestion altogether. In designing highways to accommodate a certain volume of traffic, American highway engineers use a rule of thumb in which the top dozen peak hourly volumes are not provided for. A certain measure of congestion is assumed to be tolerable.

One measure of congestion is the difference between design capacity and actual travel. This measure is both time- and space-specific. Over a 24-hour period in the entire Chicago metropolitan region, it was found that the capacity of the highway system was 36,473,000 vehicle-miles, while the demand was 36,200,000 vehicle-miles. Any Chicago resident would testify that this difference is a misleading statistic since, although a small surplus may exist on a systemwide basis, traffic moves in clumps both spatially and temporally. Thus, for example, Creighton (1970, 105) shows that in the band 3 to 14 miles from the Loop, demand exceeded supply and caused congestion, while at distances of less than 3 and greater than 14 miles, the reverse was the case. The apparent lack of congestion downtown reflects, in part, the fact that his data represent averages over many city streets at particular distances from the Loop which mask the existence of congested conditions at specific intersections.

The gap between design capacity and actual traffic leads to congestion in the case of not only highways but also other modes of movement. Pipelines would crack if the capacities were exceeded in the absence of emergency mechanisms; the Bell Telephone System at a certain level of demand responds with busy signals; and railroad trains wait on sidings until the tracks are clear. In some cases, however, congestion is the result not of inadequate route capacity per se but rather of the lack of adequate facilities at a terminal, and so planes are kept in holding patterns, ships anchor outside the port, and the bus terminal telephone answers with a recording.

Finally, in evaluating the performance of a route with respect to its ability to provide a service, we must be aware that both short- and long-term adjustments are possible in which the magnitude and velocity of flows change in accordance with certain conditions.

In the short run, each one of us has to seek a personal solution to the problem of congestion, perhaps by working late, by making long-distance calls on Sunday mornings, and by mailing Christmas packages after Thanksgiving.

In the long run, systemic adjustments are possible. The use of routes and their capacities change in response to shifts in demand for transportation, people's behavioral patterns, life-styles, the current state of the art in transport technology, and the spatial distribution of activities. Thus, individuals shop in a suburban shopping mall rather than in the central business district, go to the movies on midweek nights rather than on Friday, substitute a telephone call for a social visit, resulting in the movement of information rather than that of people, and, through time, have given up the streetcar for the automobile which they may trade someday, perhaps for the bicycle!

The Location of Routes between Two Nodes

In the real world, a route between any two settlements may have some intervening nodes of a different nature. In the strictest sense, a road between any two nodes, such as a gas station and an adjoining fast-food-service establishment, is a single route. However, such a definition, although logically proper, would entail much inconvenience in a pedagogical context; therefore our sole concern here is with routes between settlement nodes.

Configuration of links. The configuration of the link is an important spatial property. Given two nodes, one may well ask, Where should a link between them be located? Links can be relatively permanent and fixed or temporary and flexible, as dictated by differences in modes of movement. Most overland routes are fixed, i.e., highways, railroads, canals, and telephone and telegraph cables. Even in large deserts, caravan routes are fixed by the location of water holes as well as by tradition. Capot-Rey (1946, 45–46) notes that while each succeeding caravan does not follow the precise path of the preceding one, the overall pattern is one of a route, whose oscillations may wander over a width of 1 kilometer. Likewise, in a flood plain, at any one time a stream occupies only a relatively small portion, but there are transportation corridors.

Such corridors contain abandoned routes so that often there are abandoned streetcar tracks next to a new highway, evidencing the evolutionary nature of a transportation corridor.

Airline and oceanic navigation do not require fixed routes. The notion of a route over an ocean presupposes first that travelers know both *where* they are going and *how* to get there and then that given perfect knowledge of alternative routes, they are capable of selecting the optimal one. Thus, Columbus thought that the best way to get to India was to go west although both his assumptions and his perceptions were flawed. Vasco da Gama got there by traveling south and northeast. Generally, the route taken by early overland explorers was also the end product of a trial-and-error process, as was shown by the journeys of Marco Polo, Sven Hedin, and many others.

Normally, airline and oceanic navigation is along sea lanes and air corridors, which, in the context of the wide ocean and atmosphere, are relatively narrow channels. Lest the reader get the impression that the seas are so vast that vessels have great flexibility of movement, it must be noted that many of the major sea lanes are becoming rapidly congested. This congestion is due to such factors as the phenomenal increase in oceanic traffic, which amounted to 2 billion tons in 1971, and the use of larger and faster tankers with capacity in excess of 200,000 tons. Consequently, on the average, one ship sinks every day as a result of collision. The U.S. Coast Guard has reported that in the year ending June 30, 1971, there were 579 collisions off the coasts of the United States. In the English Channel, it has been found necessary to establish traffic lanes, marked with buoys from one end to the other.

Regardless of whether routes are fixed paths or not, we can treat their locations as being geodesic, with physical configurations ranging between the straight and the circuitous. Whatever configuration is manifested, it is probably in response to a fundamental process common to both nature and man: *effort minimization.* Thus, streams move downhill, crows fly more or less a straight line, and swimmers follow the current and not a straight line. Zipf (1949) lists a number of examples chosen from many fields of human activities that substantiate the hypothesis that man is basically a lazy animal exhibiting rational behavior insofar as it represents a choice between the easy and the hard way. On an isotropic plane, the establishment of straight links between various nodes is a manifestation of effort minimization.

The same desire to minimize effort can sometimes result in circuitous routes. To deliberately change scale, consider two nodes: the living room and the bathroom. Assume that a link needs to be established between these two nodes. Its configuration may not be that of a straight line because of the existence of intervening objects. Effort minimization will be achieved by going around furniture. This is a microscale example of a geodesic path whose physical configuration is circuitous. The same principle is valid at a variety of larger scales. Thus, rivers are bridged at their narrowest points, although this choice might cause deviation from the shortest path between two nodes. However, Thrower (1966, 99–101) suggests that the underlying cadastral survey has had a profound impact upon the alignment of roads. By comparing two areas in Ohio — one systematically surveyed according to the rectangular land survey, another the product of the more traditional "metes and bounds"

— he concluded that within the systematically surveyed area the survey itself "directed" the road alignment, creating more bridges than might otherwise have been necessary, while forcing the construction of bridges at usually costlier sites. Thus, human behavior, when evaluated strictly in monetary terms, is sometimes suboptimal.

In most cases, the degree of departure from a straight-line short path is determined by an examination of the relative costs of alternative routings. An interesting empirical study of the relationship between atmospheric pressure patterns and trans-Atlantic flight paths, undertaken by Warntz (1961), sheds some light on the problem of deviation from straight-line short paths. Generally flight paths oscillate in order to take advantage of tailwinds and to minimize the impact of headwinds and crosswinds.

Figure 4-7 is a cartographic portrayal of flight paths between New York and London. Using a procedure known as pressure pattern navigation, pilots endeavor to follow the least-time route, which frequently involves a deviation from the great circle. The problem of selecting this path is a three-dimensional one since wind velocities and directions vary with both altitude and coordinate location. Thus, rather than maintaining a constant altitude, the flight is adjusted in order to make use of a specific pressure surface, e.g., the DC-8 utilized the 300-millibar surface. Eastbound routes lie south of the great circle route, while westbound routes deviate in a northerly direction. Together, the oscillations amount to as much as 500 miles on either side of the 3339-mile great circle route, as can be seen in Figure 4-7. On September 1, 1960, the DC-8 westbound great circle route would have taken 7 hours 50 minutes, while the least-time path took 7 hours 35 minutes. The timesaving was even greater for the DC-7, for which the respective figures were 14 hours 58 minutes and 13 hours 5 minutes.

Alternative links. One of the distinguishing characteristics of a developed

Figure 4-7 Flight trajectories between New York and London, during December 1946

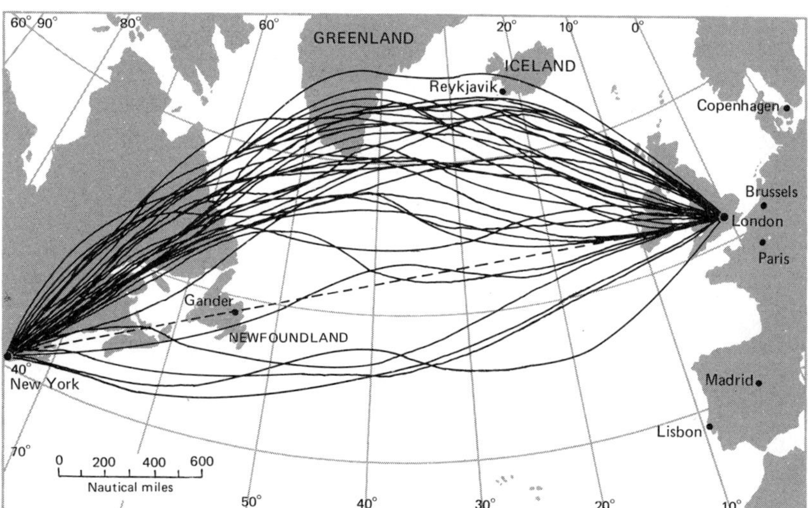

country, in contrast to an underdeveloped one, is that the number of routes as well as modes of transportation between any two nodes is much greater. This is not only a measure of the level of development but also a part of the developmental process itself, since routes cause development and are, in turn, caused by development.

The same contrast in the number of links between two nodes may be observed within a nation by comparing its richer and poorer regions. In many areas of Appalachia there is only one small country road between two adjoining hamlets. In addition, even if there is a railroad track, the passenger service between the hamlets probably has been curtailed, and the through train, if one exists, does not stop at either node. Thus, the choice of routes is severely restricted, and there is no alternative to the country road which has one narrow lane in each direction. An example of the paucity of routes is shown in Figure 4-8, where the only available route from Wolf Pen to Welch, West Virginia, is state road 16, a hard-surface but medium-duty two-lane road that goes by Indian Creek and then down Trailfork and Browns Creek. There are no alternatives, and the high-level circuity of the road is imposed by topographic constraints.

Contrast this situation with Figure 4-9, which shows direct routes between the beltways of Washington and Baltimore. There are four major direct routes located in a 6-mile-wide corridor, each of which is an alternative route for road travel between the two metropolitan areas. Further, the four highways together consist of 18 lanes or roadbeds, 9 each way. Thus, individuals in Wash-

Figure 4-8
Accessibility between Welch and Wolf Pen, West Virginia

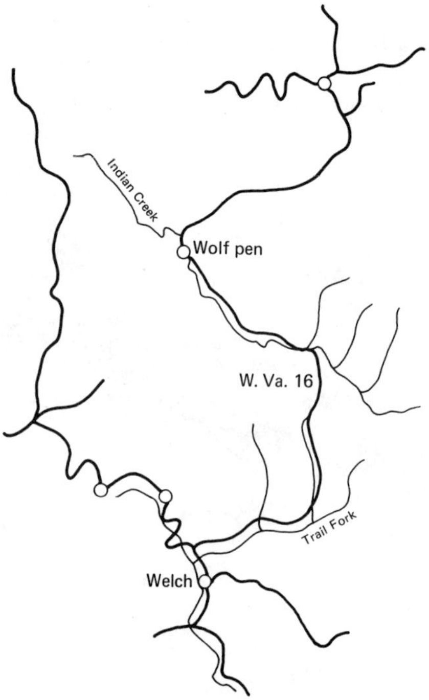

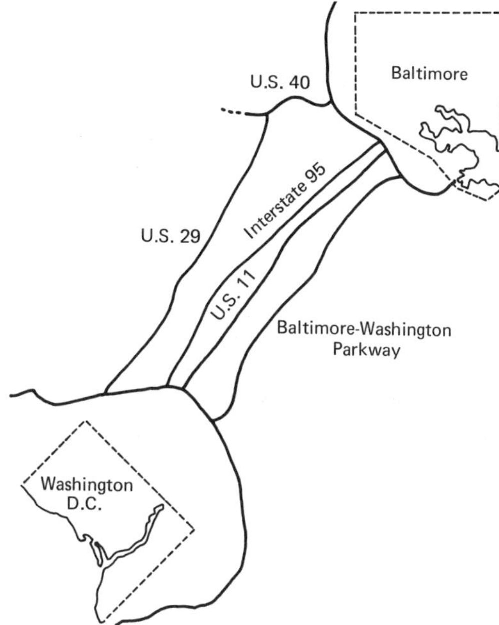

Figure 4-9
Major routes between the Baltimore and Washington beltways

ington and Baltimore face a number of route choices when they wish to travel from one city to the other, in contrast to people traveling between Wolf Pen and Welch.

The number of alternative routes between Washington and Baltimore is perhaps somewhat extraordinary and may be due to the relatively large size and short intervening distance of these agglomerations. Generally, most metropolitan areas in the United States have at least two direct highway links with their larger neighbors, one a freeway and the other an ordinary highway.

The flexibility in route selection between Washington and Baltimore is further enhanced by the existence of multimodal linkages; not only are there four highways, but there is also a railroad, as well as an airline service. An extreme example of multimodal routes between two nodes is that between Schenectady and Utica, New York, which are connected by the New York State Thruway, New York Highway 5, the old New York Central and the Pennsylvania railroads (now merged into the Penn-Central), the Erie Canal (now the New York State Barge Canal), airline services, telephone lines, telegraph lines, and mail service.

The Functions of Routes

Routes perform a variety of functions, and among these perhaps the most important are (1) contribution to movement efficiency by structuring flows, (2) accommodation of multipurpose movement, (3) maximization of space use, and (4) identification of portions of space.

In the absence of routes, individuals have to undertake a search procedure in order to determine how to come into contact with other individuals or travel to other locations. This method is obviously inefficient because one may get lost on the way, confront unforeseen hazards, or finally arrive at an unwanted destination.

Once they are established, routes direct and agglomerate movement between nodes so that the aggregate distance over which movement occurs tends to be minimized. This situation is in contrast to amorphous movement which consists of flows going hither and yon. In addition, routes accommodate different types and modes of movement simultaneously. Thus, for example, a typical city street in Calcutta or New Delhi accommodates pedestrians, bicycles, bullock carts, cows, pedicabs, automobiles, trucks, motorcycles, horse-drawn wagons, buses, and streetcars (Breese, 1966, 55). Such a miscellaneous array along one route is characteristic of city streets in the Third World. In contrast, American freeways are so specialized that pedestrians, bicycles, and carts are rigidly excluded. Further, minimum speed limits may deny the use of a certain road facility to vehicles which cannot maintain standard speeds. This restriction is a form of functional specialization in route design. Just as occupational division of labor was shown to be an efficient process earlier (Chapter 1), the neat partitioning of different routes, each with its own specialized use, is more efficient than the chaos found in a Calcutta street. Specialization at still another level is manifested by the designation of special bus lanes at particular times.

Routes also accommodate movement whose purposes are quite varied. For example, any major highway in a metropolitan area at ten o'clock in the morning may channel diverse kinds of movement simultaneously: someone is going late to work, a truck is carrying cake, another is carrying ale, a schoolboy is playing truant, a long-distance vacationer is passing through, a young man is going to visit his girl friend, and a bank robber is looking for a place with which to "interact." It may be observed that these are examples of different purposes, origins, and destinations. Nevertheless, they all occupy the same channel, and in the vocabulary of modern American young people, "each is doing his or her own thing." We can see, therefore, that one of the important functions of a route is its ability to promote spatial interaction by simultaneously accommodating diverse types of movement.

Routes induce the maximization of space use in that they facilitate the use of nonchanneled portions of space for other purposes. This process can be illustrated at a variety of scales. Thus, for example, if random movement in a park were allowed to occur, initially certain paths would be created, and, in turn, the random paths would make it possible for courting couples and children playing ball to use the rest of the park. Within a metropolitan area, intersecting city streets and sidewalks funnel movement along particular directions, thus marking up city space and creating blocks. In turn, this grid makes it possible to identify parcels of land and buildings, such as, the RCA building in New York, which is at the intersection of Sixth Avenue and West 49th Street, while the address of the White House is 1600 Pennsylvania Avenue. A street address of a building, couched in these terms, is a distinguishing hallmark of movement-oriented Western societies, particularly the United States. In contrast, in peasant societies, land parcels are identified with reference to other land parcels or with reference to the owner's name, e.g., Appuhamy's field. In fact, in such societies, a route may even be identified as being that "next to Appuhamy's farm."

The Impact of Routes

Thus far in this chapter, we have considered the nature and location of routes and the reasons for the location of routes. A remaining consideration is, What are the consequences of the existence of routes on human activities?

Since transportation plays a central role in technologically advanced societies, it is rather easy to show that many aspects of human endeavor in such societies are, in one way or another, related to transport development. Thus, for example, a chain of causation somewhat like the following is easily verifiable in the everyday experience of millions of Americans. A new highway is built between downtown and the land beyond the urban fringe, making it possible for farmland to be converted to residential uses. A family leaves downtown to buy one of the newly built houses. Since the convenience of a corner grocery store is no longer available, a second car is now required by the family. In turn, the purchase of the second car leads to increased production in the automobile industry and greater gas purchases by the same family, both of which swell the GNP. When many families similarly establish residence in the suburbs, regional shopping centers emerge and siphon business from downtown stores, eroding the tax base of the central city. As a result, the quantity and quality of municipal services decline, and as a result more people move to yet newer subdivisions farther out of the central city. In this way, pursuing the chain of causation just a little further amounts to a rendition of the litany of the familiar "urban problem" of which an integral part is obviously transportation. A convenient way to cut through the Gordian knot of impacts which lead to still more impacts ad infinitum is to take a rigidly spatial viewpoint.

The essential impact of a route is that the accessibility of some points (nodes) is enhanced, in contrast to points not located on that route. All points on the earth's surface are, literally, accessible to each other. However, the degree of accessibility between any two points is always enhanced by the presence of a formal route, whether it is a railroad or a scheduled air route. Accessibility is a relative, not absolute, concept in that it denotes the relative position of individual nodes vis-à-vis other nodes.

Consider a nodal pattern in a certain region as shown in Figure 4-10*a*. Neither the nature of the pattern, be it random, regular, or nucleated, nor the sizes of the nodes are pertinent here. Even in the absence of an established route, it may be expected that there would still be movement, either on foot or on horseback, between the nodes. The lines in Figure 4-10*a* are hypothetical accessibility contours. The central node is the most readily accessible, while the peripheral nodes are characterized by a low level of accessibility. All locations lying along any accessibility contour have the same level of accessibility to the other nodes identified in this figure. Thus, *A* and *B* are both in a highly accessible zone, making them, in turn, good locations for business activities of various sorts, especially retail trade and services. If the

Figure 4-10 Hypothetical accessibility contours for a system of points (*a*) without any route; (*b*) with a major route.

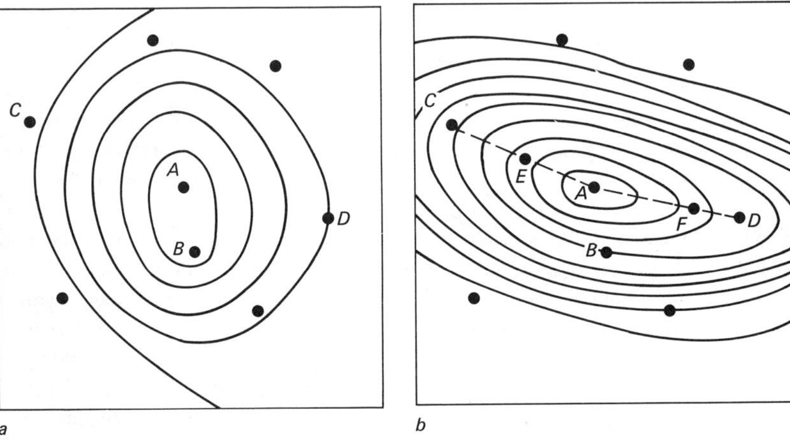

region under consideration were an agricultural one, these two locations would emerge as market towns. Indeed, in peasant societies, where most of the movement is on foot or by the use of animal power, Figure 4-10*a* may be visualized as a representation of the real world.

It must be emphasized that the concept of accessibility illustrated in Figure 4-10*a* is strictly a distance-based one in which the cost, time, or effort required to travel from *A* to *D* is one-half that required to travel from *C* to *D*, simply because the physical distance from *A* to *D* is one-half that from *C* to *D*. If we had a distance matrix, like those shown in Table 4-1, it would be possible to compute a specific measure of accessibility for each node.

When a route is introduced on the landscape, as in Figure 4-10*b* between points *C*, *A*, and *D*, the accessibility of the nodes is changed significantly. This change occurs because the route enables the utilization of more advanced technology and reduces the cost of movement (by one-fourth in this example). Nodes that are not on the route are relatively farther apart in cost- or time-distance than those which are on the route. *A* is now somewhat more accessible from *D* than from *B*. Despite *B*'s near geometric centrality, it no longer has functional centrality in this new economic space. The shape of the accessibility contours has been radically altered, and *B* has been bypassed by the route. As a consequence, existing businesses at *B* may shift their location to *A*, while *D* may become a new boom town. The overall process is known as spatial reorganization.

In the geography literature a well-known example of the impact on a node by changes in routing is that by Garrison et al. (1959) of Marysville, Washington. A new, divided, four-lane, limited-access highway was built in 1954, bypassing the town. Consequently, the traffic through downtown Marysville decreased to one-third its previous level. The reduction in traffic congestion, however, made it a more attractive residential and commercial center for low-order businesses, the sales of which increased 121 percent over that of pre-bypass volume. Part of the high-order functions, previously performed by

Marysville, was captured by the neighboring larger node of Everett. Land values of undeveloped sites suitable for residential development escalated, and Garrison et al. foresaw a residential boom.

Not only is the accessibility of the existing nodes along the route improved, but so is that of the points located between these nodes. Consequently, in Figure 4-10*b*, new nodes are created, such as those at *E* and *F*. In time, a business strip from *C* to *D* may become a prime-activity corridor. This phenomenon is sometimes known as ribbon development, which is made up of transport-oriented businesses such as gas stations, motels, grain elevators, and many manufacturing industries. At a widely divergent scale, the same process occurs so that, for example, Aden and Singapore developed on the lifeline of the Commonwealth from London to Sydney.

Place-to-place variations in land values and land uses are further direct consequences of the existence of routes. In fact, land-value contours and accessibility contours are approximately congruent. A parcel of land immediately adjacent to a route has a high value. This parcel will thus be occupied only by activities which have the ability to pay the high price because they require the corresponding level of accessibility. These activities include manufacturing industries, warehouses, shopping centers, etc. In contrast, activities that do not depend upon adjacency to routes avoid them and their associated noise and unaesthetic characteristics. Thus, high-income residences are seldom located next to freeways or railroad tracks.

The route between *C* and *D* in Figure 4-10*b* is just that, a route. If another route is built from *A* to *B*, the two together constitute a network. Although nodes and routes have been treated separately, these are elements of a system or network.

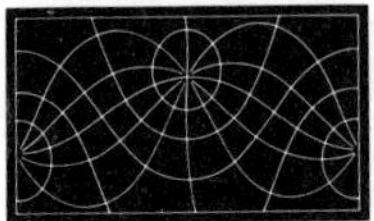

5 Transportation Networks

Even a little reflection will show us that "networks of friends and acquaintances," "transport networks," "telephone networks," and "drainage networks" are rather elusive concepts, though many of them physically exist on the earth's surface. In ordinary parlance, the term "network" seems to have a rather loose and catholic connotation. One way to obtain a somewhat sophisticated understanding of networks is to recognize a certain isomorphism, as between different types of networks, and to focus our attention upon their fundamental characteristics, such as their configuration, connectivity, and structure, ignoring such nitty-gritty questions as whether a highway is a divided one with U-turns prohibited. While for practical purposes these details are important, in a more fundamental sense a country road and the widest highway both connect and foster movement between a pair of nodes. Therefore, in this chapter we shall filter out the real world "noise" and use a restricted, model-based definition of networks.

WHAT ARE MODELS AND WHY MODELS?

A model is a simplified version of a slice of reality. There are many types of models and many ways of classifying them. A widely used typology divides them into three groups:

1. *Iconic models* are those in which all the properties and relationships of the original phenomenon are represented at a reduced scale. Examples are model trains and aerial photographs.

2. *Analog models* are those in which only those characteristics of the real world considered to be significant are incorporated. There is a certain level of abstraction in that certain things are eliminated and others are shown in stylized manner. When an analogy is drawn between phenomena in apparently disparate fields, such as Lösch's comparison of route-bending and Snell's law of light refraction, it is an analog model (see Figure 2-5). A topographic

map and a globe are analog models in which there have been scale reductions.

3. *Symbolic models* are those in which relationships are expressed usually by mathematical symbols in equation form, for example, $E = MC^2$. The gravity model, to be discussed in a subsequent chapter, is one of the most familiar examples of a symbolic model in geography.

Models are the building blocks of theories, the foundations of a science. There are more developed and less developed sciences, and a fundamental difference between them may be conceived of as the degree to which they possess interlocking models. In geography's current state of development, there are no grand architectural model designs, nor is there a general theory of movement. However, transportation research in geography has made use of a number of models which are useful for several reasons. (1) Models make it possible to deliberately eliminate a number of real world complexities, enabling greater comprehension. (2) They enable abstraction by allowing the analyst to stand, so to speak, above the subject and obtain a wider perspective. (3) They make it possible to manipulate data and test relationships among the components of a problem. (4) They allow generalizations, and once a general and holistic understanding is gained by the analyst, predictions are more likely. (5) They constitute a common language of scientific discourse, so that concepts and approaches from one discipline can be borrowed and used by workers in another. Indeed, much of the pioneering work in network analysis originated in the field of electrical engineering and was subsequently borrowed by geographers. The above-mentioned advantages of the use of models of course pertain generally to all models, and not just to those in transportation geography. A variety of model-based approaches has been applied in a number of subfields of geography. These approaches are elucidated in a useful compendium edited by Chorley and Haggett (1967).

NETWORKS AS MODELS

Figure 5-1*a* is a map of Martinique, a mountainous island whose road network is quite circuitous. An extremely complex mathematical specification would be required to describe this network. Additionally, there is wide variation in the sizes of the different nodes in that the capital city, Fort-de-France, is about 15 times larger than the next largest town, while the remaining towns are all small and roughly the same size. The road network of Martinique has been converted to a graph in Figure 5-1*b*. A graph may be defined as a set of systematically organized points and lines (Kansky, 1963, 7). "Graph theory," although so named, is not really a theory. It is a branch of combinatorial topology and is a powerful, versatile language which allows us to disentangle the basic structure of transportation networks. Excellent introductory presentations of the nomenclature and applications of graph theory are contained in Ore (1963), Berge (1962), and Avondo-Bodino (1962). Haggett and Chorley (1969) have made extensive and imaginative use of graph theory in their attempt to fuse some of the material from transportation geography and hydrology.

The graph of the Martinique network is a model which entails a certain amount of abstraction, simplification, and generalization. At the outset, it may

Figure 5-1
Representation of the roads of Martinique showing (*a*) the topographic network; (*b*) the network as a graph.

a

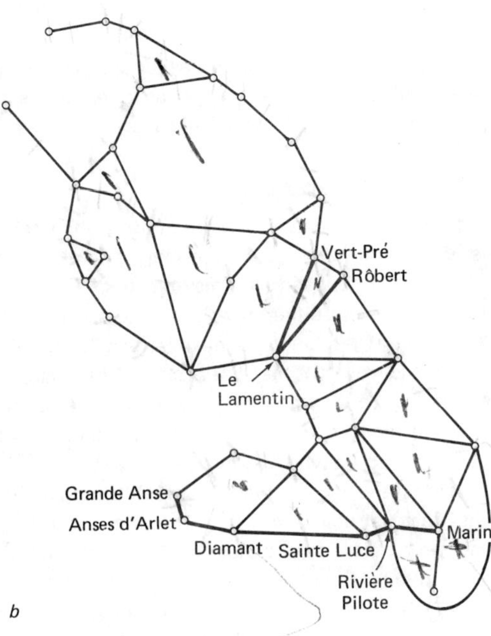

b

be noted that the island boundary of Martinique has been eliminated; further, the graph is not drawn to scale. Spatial sequence is maintained, so that from Grande Anse to Marin the order of nodes is Anses d'Arlet, Diamant, Sainte Luce, Rivière Pilote, and Marin, both on the map of the real world and on the graph. The existence of direct links between nodes is shown, but forks in the road network where settlement nodes do not exist have been eliminated, for example, from Le Lamentin to Vert-Pré and Rôbert. Thus, a Y-shaped road connecting three points is reduced to a triangle. As is true of all model-based approaches, there is obviously some information loss in the graph when compared to the real world, but the gains in generality would seem to outweigh this loss. This trade-off is acceptable because what has been eliminated is not important since our interest here is strictly in connections between places. The criteria for elimination or retention depend upon the purposes. The graph of the Martinique network cannot be used as a road map since a motorist would be interested in the very sinuosities of the roads that have been ignored.

The graph eliminates the flesh and blood, as represented by the sinuosities and the flows, although they will be reintroduced in subsequent chapters, for now what is left is the skeleton. As in any skeleton, there are links joined at specific places. Skeletal structures have definite arrangements, although the specific arrangements may differ somewhat among different species and over time. By reducing the complex transportation network to its fundamental elements of nodes and links, it is possible to evaluate alternative structures. Such an evaluation is conveniently done by using some elementary mathematics from graph theory.

Graph-theoretic Descriptions of Networks

Although the study of transportation networks, in terms of their topological properties, dates back to Euler's classical problem of the seven bridges of Königsberg in 1736, a subject which we shall consider in Chapter 12, it was not until 1936 that the first text on network topology, entitled *Theorie der Endlichen und Unendlichen Graphen,* appeared. It was not until 1960 that William Garrison, a pioneer in theoretical geography, introduced graph theory to the study of transportation networks in the literature of geography and of regional science. He modeled a portion of the U.S. Interstate Highway System as an ordinary graph and obtained several measures regarding relative location and accessibility of the nodes and the connectivity of the entire network (Garrison, 1960a). The major properties of ordinary graphs may be formally specified (Garrison, 1960a, 127):

1. A network has a finite number of places.
2. Each route is a set consisting of two places.
3. Each route joins two different places.
4. At the most, only one route may join a pair of places.
5. No distinctions are made between the "initial" and the "terminal" places or routes; in other words, routes are "two-way."

There are two types of ordinary graphs: *planar* and *nonplanar*. In a planar graph, the intersection of two edges is always a vertex, while this is not necessarily so in a nonplanar graph. An example of the former is the interstate highway system. An airline network is a nonplanar graph in which the routes from Seattle, for example, to New Orleans on the one hand and from Toronto to Los Angeles on the other intersect on the map, although there may not be a place or node at the intersection on the landscape.

When there is a link (road, railroad, or whatever) between two nodes, the nodes are said to be "connected." The degree of connection between all nodes in a system may be defined as the *connectivity* of the network. This structural property is an index of the relative simplicity or complexity of the network.

Given the Sri Lanka (Ceylon) railroad network, shown in Figure 5-2, how can we measure its connectivity? In this figure, $V_1, \ldots, V_{17}$ represent vertices and $E_{13}, \ldots, E_{1517}$ represent edges. Note that Figure 5-2 is not a map but a graph, and that it is not to scale. The varying lengths of the edges do not have significance since each edge is considered to be of unit length and since the distance between any pair of vertices is measured by counting the number of edges separating them. There are at least two aspects to connectivity: that which relates to any individual vertex, and that which relates to fineness or coarseness of the network as a whole.

Evaluating Vertex Connectivity

A variety of graph-theoretic measures is useful in evaluating the connectivity of nodes, and some are considered below.

The König index. The associated number or *König index* (K_i) is defined as

$$K_i = \max d_{ij}$$

122

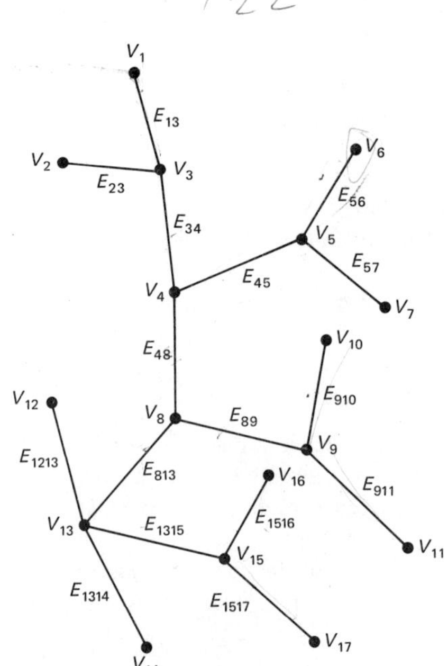

Figure 5-2
Graph of the railroad network of Sri Lanka (Ceylon)

that is, the maximum of the distances from vertex *i* to each of the other vertices. *Distance* in this context is the number of intervening edges between two vertices, measured along the shortest path, regardless of the actual mileage involved. With reference to the Sri Lanka (Ceylon) railroad network (Figure 5-2), the distance from V_1 to V_6 is 4, and that from V_{16} to V_{17} is 2. The associated numbers of the Sri Lanka railroad network are as follows: $V_1 = 6$; $V_2 = 6$; $V_3 = 5$; $V_4 = 4$; $V_5 = 5$; $V_6 = 6$; $V_7 = 6$; $V_8 = 3$; $V_9 = 4$; $V_{10} = 5$; $V_{11} = 5$; $V_{12} = 5$; $V_{13} = 4$; $V_{14} = 5$; $V_{15} = 5$; $V_{16} = 6$; and $V_{17} = 6$. It will be noted that six of the vertices have high associated numbers, a value of 6 being the maximum, which indicates that these are the least connected and most peripheral of the locations in the graph. By contrast, V_8 (Polgahawela) is said to be the central place of the network because its associated number is the minimum; it has a high degree of accessibility to the whole system of places. It could be considered to be an optimal location which would attract a variety of businesses and from which markets at all other vertices would be served better than from any of the other vertices in the Sri Lanka (Ceylon) railroad network.

Any graph can be converted to a matrix *C*, where $c_{ij} = 1$ if an edge exists between vertices *i* and *j*, and $c_{ij} = 0$ otherwise. Table 5-1, a matrix representation of the graph in Figure 5-2, is sometimes known as an *incidence* or a *binary connectivity matrix.* Column sums indicate the number of vertices that can be reached directly from the *i*th vertex. Thus, from V_3 it is possible to go directly to V_1, V_2, and V_4, but it is not possible to go from V_3 to V_5 without going via V_4. Incidence matrices provide us with another way of studying connectivity among places in a network. Vertex 13, Colombo, the capital of Sri Lanka (Ceylon), is the best connected, with a column sum of 4, which

Table 5-1
Connectivity Matrix of the Sri Lanka (Ceylon) Railroad Network

		To 1	2	3	4	5	6	7	8	9	10	11	12	13	14	15	16	17
From	1	0	0	1	0	0	0	0	0	0	0	0	0	0	0	0	0	0
	2	0	0	1	0	0	0	0	0	0	0	0	0	0	0	0	0	0
	3	1	1	0	1	0	0	0	0	0	0	0	0	0	0	0	0	0
	4	0	0	1	0	1	0	0	1	0	0	0	0	0	0	0	0	0
	5	0	0	0	1	0	1	1	0	0	0	0	0	0	0	0	0	0
	6	0	0	0	0	1	0	0	0	0	0	0	0	0	0	0	0	0
	7	0	0	0	0	1	0	0	0	0	0	0	0	0	0	0	0	0
	8	0	0	0	1	0	0	0	0	1	0	0	0	1	0	0	0	0
	9	0	0	0	0	0	0	0	1	0	1	1	0	0	0	0	0	0
	10	0	0	0	0	0	0	0	0	1	0	0	0	0	0	0	0	0
	11	0	0	0	0	0	0	0	0	1	0	0	0	0	0	0	0	0
	12	0	0	0	0	0	0	0	0	0	0	0	0	1	0	0	0	0
	13	0	0	0	0	0	0	0	1	0	0	0	1	0	1	1	0	0
	14	0	0	0	0	0	0	0	0	0	0	0	0	1	0	0	0	0
	15	0	0	0	0	0	0	0	0	0	0	0	0	1	0	0	1	1
	16	0	0	0	0	0	0	0	0	0	0	0	0	0	0	1	0	0
	17	0	0	0	0	0	0	0	0	0	0	0	0	0	0	1	0	0
Column sums		1	1	3	3	3	1	1	3	3	1	1	1	4	1	3	1	1

indicates that four other vertices may be reached directly from it. There are six other places that belong to the second order of connectivity with column sums of 3, while the rest are all peripheral or terminal places.

Accessibility index. The "reachability" of a vertex can be evaluated by means of the *accessibility index.* The accessibility of a node to the *i*th place is

$$A_i = \sum_{i=1}^{n} d_{ij}$$

where d_{ij} is the distance between the *i*th and the *j*th places.

Thus, in Figure 5-2, the accessibility index of vertex 1 (Kankesenturai) is 64, which represents the number of edges which must be traveled in order to reach each vertex from V_1. The value of the accessibility index is inversely related to the accessibility of that place to the network as a whole; that is, all other nodes can be reached from the most accessible place by a shorter total topological distance than from any other node. It seems reasonable to suggest that within the United States, Chicago and St. Louis have low accessibility indices in comparison to New York and Seattle, both of which are peripheral.

Since the accessibility index measures "reachability" of one node from all other nodes on the basis of the presence or absence of actual links, it does not follow that the geometric center of a region or nation is the most accessible node. While Wichita, Kansas, a node on the U.S. highway and railroad networks, is located at the approximate geometric center of these networks, Chicago, which is the major railroad terminal in the United States, is more accessible because more places can be reached directly from Chicago than from Wichita. Reciprocally, Chicago can be approached directly from a larger number of nodes. The phrase "you can't get there from here" denotes a low degree of accessibility, in marked contrast to the phrase "all roads lead to Rome."

Multistep connections. Suppose that one wishes to find out the number of ways in which the *i*th node in a network can be reached from the *j*th node in *n* number of steps, assuming that there is no direct connection between *i* and *j*. Since there is no direct commercial flight between Washington, D.C., and Hanoi, a trip between these places will involve subjourneys with connecting flights at certain nodes. Some of the possible routes are (1) Washington–Paris–Hanoi, a two-step connection, discounting intermediate refueling stops; (2) Washington–New York–Moscow–Hanoi, a three-step flight; (3) Washington–London–Singapore–Vientiane–Hanoi, a four-step flight. Undoubtedly, there are many other ways of traveling between these two locations which involve a large number of steps.

The total number of two-, three-, four-, and *n*-step connections to each node from any other node can be obtained by computing a series of powered connectivity matrices: C^2, C^3, C^4, . . . , C^n. Powering matrices and obtaining multistep connections are, of course, not meaningful unless there are alternative links between one or more nodes. Figure 5-2 is a tree graph of the Sri Lanka (Ceylon) railroad network. On it, there is only one way to go from V_8 to V_9, as indeed is the case from any vertex to any other vertex.

Squaring a matrix *C*, that is, raising it to its second power, involves the summing of the cross products of the elements:

$$C^2 = \begin{bmatrix} a & b \\ c & d \end{bmatrix} \times \begin{bmatrix} a & b \\ c & d \end{bmatrix} = \begin{bmatrix} aa + bc & ab + bd \\ ca + dc & cb + dd \end{bmatrix}$$

The above is a second-order matrix, and successively higher-order matrices can be obtained similarly.

A simple numerical example will make the procedure clear. Consider the following binary matrix, which indicates the presence or absence of connections between four vertices:

		To *A*	*B*	*C*	*D*
From	*A*	0	1	0	0
	B	1	0	1	0
	C	0	1	0	1
	D	0	0	1	0

Note that the cells along the principal diagonal contain zeros, indicating that a place is not connected to itself. The number of two-step connections between any pair of vertices may be determined by squaring the matrix. The number of two-step connections from *A* to *B* is

$$(0 \times 1) + (1 \times 0) + (0 \times 1) + (0 \times 0) = 0$$

This result is obtained by multiplying the corresponding cell entries of row *A* and column *B*. Thus, the first value (0) in row *A* is multiplied by the first value (1) in column *B*, and the product is added to that of the second value (1) in row *A* times the second value (0) in column *B*. This process is repeated until the entire row and column have been cross-multiplied. The result indicates the absence of any two-step connections from *A* to *B*; that is, there is only one way to get from *A* to *B*. If the procedure is repeated 16 times, the resulting 4×4 squared matrix will identify the number of two-step connections between each pair of nodes.

Although the procedure is simple, the powering of, for example, an intermetropolitan matrix of the United States with 247 rows and 247 columns would be tedious. The electronic computer, however, facilitates the rapid computation of relatively high-order matrices. At some stage in the powering process, the last remaining 0 in the off-diagonal cells in the matrix will be replaced by a nonzero element. In any network, the highest König index value is also said to be the "diameter" of the graph, or the span of the network. Matrix powering can be terminated at that step in which the order of the matrix is equal to the diameter of the graph. Operationally, at that step we can establish a connection between even the most remote pair of nodes identified in the initial incidence matrix.

However, not all networks can be powered to the diameter of the network thereby establishing an *n*-step connection between a pair of remote nodes. It may be necessary to continue powering beyond the diameter of the network in order to establish some connections. First, if there are one or more independent subgraphs in the initial network, it is of course impossible to establish a connection, no matter the level of powering used. Second, even assuming that we began with an integrated network, certain conditions have to be met initially, and these have been specified by Alao (1970). Nevertheless, in most cases, the powering of the matrix can be terminated at the diameter of the network.

In the context of international airline connectivity, London and New York are the most connected, since more places on the earth's surface can be reached directly from these two locations than from any others. Timbuktu may have a rather unjustified reputation, but assuming that it and Alice Springs are the two most remote spots on earth, an international airline connectivity matrix powered to that order which is the diameter of the international airline network would identify the number of n-step paths between these two locations. In terms of the successive-order matrices, a link would be established between Timbuktu and Alice Springs for the first time in some high-order matrix. But what of New York and London in such a matrix? A number of redundant paths would now be included, and the absolute value in the cell connecting London and New York would be very high. Thus, while there are a number of direct flights between these two vertices, our high-order matrix could indicate that there are, perhaps, 688 ways of making six-step connections between London and New York (if 6 is the diameter of the international airline network). One of these six-step paths might be London–Paris–Rome–Capetown–Buenos Aires–Santiago–New York.

Despite the disadvantages of redundancies, powered matrices enable us to obtain the maximum number of alternative routings in a given network. Such a finding can be of practical utility in such diverse areas as telephone networks and defense logistics planning. On New Year's Eve and at other busy times, the telephone network has to accommodate a very heavy volume of traffic. Particular line segments become filled to capacity, and hence a message from Washington to Chicago may have to be routed, say, via San Juan, Puerto Rico, New Orleans, and St. Louis, obviously not a very direct connection but a connection nevertheless.

Gross vertex connectivity and redundant paths. In the geography literature one example of the use of powered matrices is the study by Pitts (1965), which is concerned with the river connectivity between 39 settlements in 12th- and 13th-century Russia. Figure 5-3 shows a graph of the nodes and trade routes along the rivers of European Russia. On page 87 is a portion of the graph's first-order connectivity matrix applicable to the five settlements identified. While it was possible to go from Novgorod to Vitebsk directly, it was not pos-

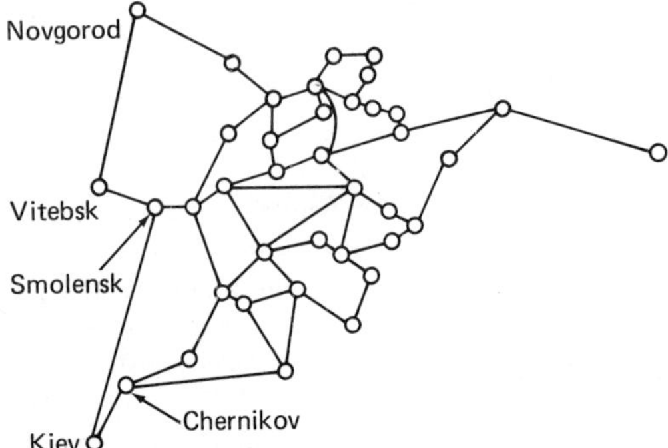

Figure 5-3
Graph of the 12th- and 13th-century Russian river network

sible to reach Smolensk directly; but since Vitebsk and Smolensk had a direct connection, there was a two-step connection between Novgorod and Smolensk.

	Novgorod	Vitebsk	Smolensk	Kiev	Chernikov
Novgorod	0	1	0	0	0
Vitebsk	1	0	1	0	0
Smolensk	0	1	0	1	0
Kiev	0	0	1	0	1
Chernikov	0	0	0	1	0

Source: Pitts (1965, 17, Fig. 3). Reproduced by permission from *The Professional Geographer* of the Association of American Geographers, Volume 17, 1965.

The whole 39 $\times$ 39 matrix, of which the above is a submatrix, was powered to the diameter (8) of the graph, resulting in the following matrix:

	Novgorod	Vitebsk	Smolensk	Kiev	Chernikov
Novgorod	110	15	143	16	71
Vitebsk	15	155	21	167	27
Smolensk	143	21	580	32	418
Kiev	16	167	32	257	84
Chernikov	71	27	418	84	513

Source: Pitts (1965, 17, Fig. 4). Reproduced by permission from *The Professional Geographer* of the Association of American Geographers, Volume 17, 1965.

The diagonal elements in this eighth-order matrix represent the number of eight-step routes going "out and back," i.e., the number of eight-step round-trips possible. Powered connectivity matrices, such as those computed by Pitts, enable us to obtain yet another measure of connectivity: the *gross vertex connectivity*. This measure is found by cumulatively adding the row sums of each of the powered matrices, up to and including the *n*th-order one. Thus, in Pitts's example, the value of this measure is 41,022 for Koselsk, 26,663 for Moscow, 3574 for Vitebsk, and 9521 for Smolensk. The number for Koselsk represents the total number of one-, two-, three, . . . , eight-step paths from Koselsk to itself and to all other places on the 13th-century Russian river network. By this measure, Moscow ranked fifth and was not the most connected place. However, when Pitts computed the accessibility index, the topological distance from a vertex to all others in the network, and ranked the 39 places, from the most connected to the least connected, he found that Moscow was the second most accessible node after Kolomna.

It will be noted that there were 418 eight-step paths between Smolensk and Chernikov in the 12th- and 13th-century Russian river network. Obviously, many of these represent redundant paths, and it would be desirable to develop a way of identifying their number. Luce and Perry (1949) provide an illustration of this problem in a study concerned with matrix analysis of group structure.

Although our main focus here is on networks consisting of links between places, it is of interest to note that a network consisting of acquaintanceships between individuals, i.e., a personal communication network, shares many of the properties of transportation networks. Connections are reciprocal; some individuals are better connected than others; there are cliques and intermediaries (relay nodes). Anthropologists have used the techniques of matrix algebra to study the relationships among individual members of groups such as clans, neighborhoods, civic associations, and other such social networks. The importance of word-of-mouth information transfer as a precondition to the diffusion of innovations is highlighted in Chapter 11.

Just as not all places are connected with one another directly, not all individuals are directly connected either. Therefore, in establishing a connection between a pair of remote places or persons, it is necessary to go through a number of intermediaries, i.e., to establish *n*-step paths. The powering of binary connectivity matrices is useful in this context also and sheds light on questions such as the channels along which information moves.

Evaluating the Connectivity of a Network

Graph-theoretic measures are useful in evaluating not only the accessibility of nodes, but also the connectivity of networks. Kansky (1963) introduced a large number of graph-theoretic measures in the geography literature. Many of these are index numbers whose utility appears to be marginal. We have selected those measures that seem to have a greater degree of utility in the analysis of transportation networks.

Beta index. The *beta index* is the number of linkages per place or node, i.e., linkage intensity. It is computed as

$$\beta = \frac{e}{v}$$

in which e is the number of edges and v is the number of vertices. A beta index of 0.8 indicates that, on the average, there is 0.8 link for each vertex, while one of 2.5 indicates that, on the average, 2.5 routes lead into or out of each vertex in the network. Obviously, index values of more than 1 suggest the existence of alternative routings between some pairs of nodes. The value of beta is 1.49 for the Martinique road network in Figure 5-1.

The size of the index value is generally high in developed countries and low in underdeveloped ones. Moreover, in any one country the index value increases through time as alternative links are constructed.

An empirical value of the beta index, as well as of some of the other network measures, stems from the fact that it has an upper and lower bound, which enables the analyst to treat the index as a scale with two fixed endpoints. Any particular network can be evaluated with reference to the relative distance from the specified limits. The range of the beta index (β), for a planar graph, is $0.5 \leqslant \beta \leqslant (v - 1)/2$, that is, from 0.5 to approximately 3.0. For a nonplanar graph, the upper bound is infinity.

Gamma index. The gamma index is the ratio between the actual and the maximum possible number of edges in a graph. It is defined as

$$\gamma = \frac{e}{3(v - 2)}$$

For the Martinique road network, the value of gamma is 0.52.

Consider Figure 5-4*a* and *b*. In both *a* and *b* there are five nodes at the same coordinate locations, but while in Figure 5-4*a* the nodes are simply connected by means of a tree, in Figure 5-4*b* the maximum number of possible

Figure 5-4 Simple networks showing (*a*) a tree; (*b*) a fully connected planar graph; (*c*) a fully connected nonplanar graph.

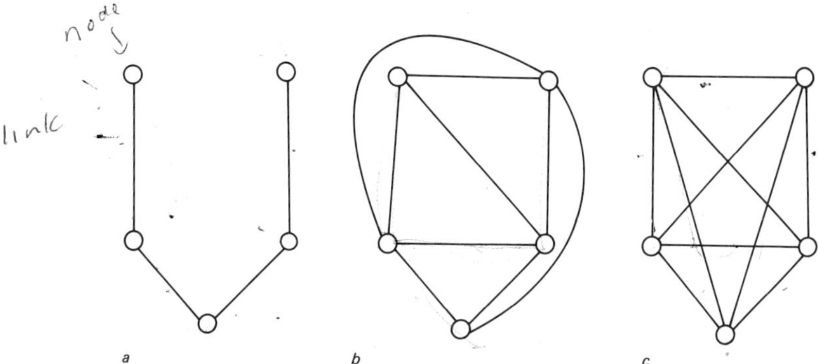

connections among the five nodes is shown as a planar graph. The minimum number of links, $v-1$, is 4 in this case, and the maximum, $3(v-2)$, is 9. Consequently, the gamma index of the graph in Figure 5-4*a* is 4/9 or 0.44, while for Figure 5-4*b* it is 9/9 or 1.00.

Like the beta index, the gamma index also has a direct correlation with levels of economic development: in the richer countries of the world, there are alternative and possibly redundant links which improve the level of accessibility between nodes.

The limits of the gamma index are 0 and 1.0, for both planar and nonplanar graphs. This index can also be expressed as a percentage so that its value of 0.44 for Figure 5-4*a* can be interpreted as representing a 44 percent level of connectivity.

For a nonplanar graph, the appropriate formula of the gamma index is

$$\gamma = \frac{2e}{v(v-1)}$$

For the five-node locational system in Figure 5-4*c,* the gamma index is 1.0, indicating a fully connected network with 100 percent connectivity.

The major difference between a well-connected network and one that is not so well connected stems from the presence or absence of loops. Poorly connected networks such as that of the Sri Lanka (Ceylon) railroad network tend to be trees, in contrast to the Martinique road network which is characterized by the presence of loops. It is evident that while in Figure 5-5*a* there is a direct connection between vertices 1 and 5, in Figure 5-5*b* the path from 1 to 5 is via 2, 3, and 4. Figure 5-5*a* constitutes one loop while Figure 5-5*c* is said to have three *fundamental loops* connecting vertices: 1–2–5, 2–3–5, and 3–4–5.

Cyclomatic number. Since well-connected networks are, by definition, those that contain a number of loops, one way of evaluating network connectivity is simply by counting loops. This number may be computed with the use of the *cyclomatic number*, defined as

$$\mu = e - v + g$$

Figure 5-5 Graphs of networks with varying number of fundamental circuits

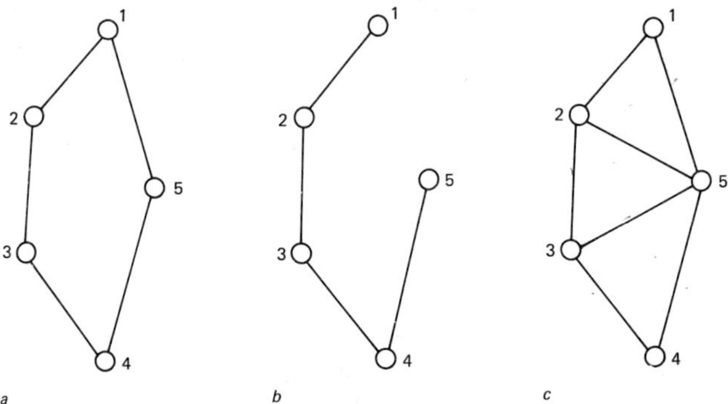

where g is the number of subgraphs. In poor countries of the world, in spatially fragmented ones, e.g., Indonesia, and at earlier stages of economic development of presently rich countries, the national transportation network is made up of disjointed entities, each of which is known as a *subgraph*.

Figure 5-6 is a hypothetical region with two separate subgraphs. The rail-

Figure 5-6 Hypothetical region containing two subgraphs

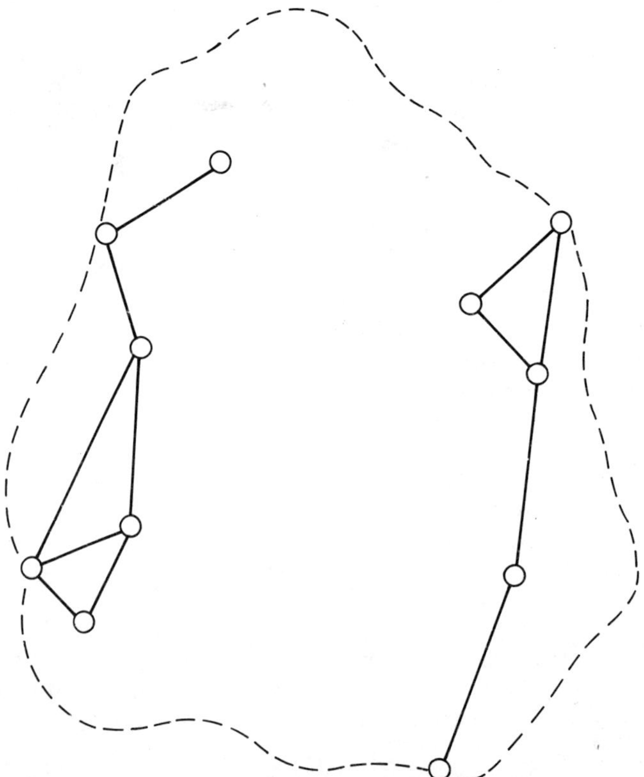

road network of the United States was constructed independently by literally hundreds of private entrepreneurs. Consequently, maps of the American railroad network in its infancy show the existence of numerous subgraphs.

The cyclomatic number fòr the graph in Figure 5-5 is 3, while that for Martinique is 19. The limits of the cyclomatic number are from 0 to $(2v - 5)$ for a planar graph and for a nonplanar one from 0 to $(v - 1)(v - 2)/2$.

Alpha index. The alpha index is a further refinement of the cyclomatic number. It is defined as

$$\alpha = \frac{e - v + g}{2v - 5} \qquad \text{or} \qquad \alpha = \frac{\mu}{2v - 5}$$

and it measures the ratio between the actual number of loops in a graph and the maximum possible number. Thus, for the Martinique road network, the existing number of loops is 19 while the maximum possible is 69, resulting in an alpha index of 0.28. This measure can also be expressed as a percentage, so that we may say that the Martinique road network is 28 percent connected according to this index.

For a nonplanar graph, the index value is computed as

$$\alpha = \frac{e - v + g}{v(v - 1)/2 - (v - 1)}$$

The range of the alpha index is from 0 to 1.0 for both planar and nonplanar graphs.

Regional networks can be compared using the alpha index. In the United States, with over 3 million miles of road and with approximately 1 mile of road per square mile of area, the highway network is so intricate that it contains, quite literally, hundreds of thousands of loops. While the alpha index for the U.S. road network has not been computed, it is safe to assume that its order of magnitude is high.

Dispersion or Shimbel index. The degree of compactness of a network is a function of the spatial arrangement of vertices with reference to the network. Two relatively extreme cases of elongation on the one hand and compactness on the other are represented by Chile and France. The *Shimbel index*

$$D(G) = \sum_{i=1}^{v} \sum_{j=1}^{n} d_{ij}$$

which measures total distances between all vertices along the shortest paths, enables us to evaluate the compactness of a network. For the graphs of Figure 5-5*b* and *c*, the values of the Shimbel index are 40 and 26, respectively. The value of 26 is computed as follows:

	To 1	2	3	4	5	Σ
From 1	0	1	2	2	1	6
2	1	0	1	2	1	5
3	2	1	0	1	1	5
4	2	2	1	0	1	6
5	1	1	1	1	0	4
						ΣΣ = 26

1. The graph is converted to a distance matrix on page 91, where the cell values represent the shortest distance between a pair of nodes. Thus, d_{14} (first row, fourth column) is 2, going via V_5, but 3 via V_2 and V_3.
2. Compute the row sums.
3. Compute the sum of the row sums.

The value of the Shimbel index is inversely related to the degree of compactness of a network. In countries such as Chile and in the case of the Trans-Siberian railroad and the two Canadian railroad networks, the arrangement of nodes and the patterns of the networks are distinctly linear. There are only a few edges crisscrossing the basic orientation of these networks. By contrast, the national railroad networks of Germany and Switzerland have links which lead to such places as the foot of the Jungfrau glacier, despite the ruggedness of the terrain. The differences in the values of the Shimbel index, as between an elongated network and a compact one, stem from the number of peripheral nodes. In an elongated network there are only a few peripheral nodes, while in a compact one there are many. It must also be reemphasized that the meaning of "distance" in graphs varies from the ordinary usage of the term and refers to the number of intervening links between a pair of nodes, rather than to mileage.

Table 5-2 is a convenient summary of the several measures of accessibility and connectivity of nodes and networks that have been considered above. Werner (1968) tested the efficiency of three connectivity indices, alpha, beta, and gamma, in terms of their ability to discriminate between six alternative

Table 5-2
Summary Table of Selected Graph-theoretic Measures

Name of index	Computational formula	
König index or associated number		$K_i = \max d_{ij}$
Accessibility index		$A_i = \sum_{i=1}^{n} d_{ij}$
Beta index		$\beta = \frac{e}{v}$
Gamma index	$\gamma = \frac{e}{3(v-2)}$ (planar)	$\gamma = \frac{2e}{v(v-1)}$ (non-planar)
Cyclomatic number	$\mu = e - v + g$	
Alpha index	$\alpha = \frac{e-v+g}{2v-5}$ (planar)	$\alpha = \frac{e-v+g}{v(v-1)/2-(v-1)}$ (non-planar)
Dispersion or Shimbel index	$D(G) = \sum_{i=1}^{n} \sum_{j=1}^{n} d_{ij}$	

where
v = vertex
d_{ij} = distance between the ith vertex and the jth vertex
e = edge
g = subgraph

networks of approximately the same size. He found that all three measures ranked each of the networks in the same sequence, although none of the indices was able to discriminate between alternative configurations such as square and circular networks. Moreover, his contention is that since all three indices use the values of e and v as the basic inputs, they are all mathematically equivalent and that, in addition, beta and gamma are theoretically redundant. Consequently, Werner recommends the use of the alpha index in preference to beta and gamma in order to evaluate network connectivity. James et al. (1970) found that the indices considered in this chapter do not discriminate adequately between networks of different sizes. For example, the three graphs in Figure 5-7 have three, four, and seven vertices, respectively. Both the beta index and the cyclomatic number of these three graphs equal 1.0 despite the varying number of edges and vertices.

It should also be noted that when different measures are computed for a particular network, different values result. Thus, we found that according to the alpha index the road network of Martinique was 28 percent connected, while according to the gamma index the same network was 52 percent connected. This difference raises a legitimate question about the real connectivity of the Martinique network. The answer seems to be that each of the various indices measures a separate aspect of connectivity, which, indeed, is a complex concept that cannot be captured adequately by any one "fail-safe" index. The utility of these various indices stems from their ability to provide a yardstick of comparability for interregional or international transportation networks.

Thus far in this discussion of graph-theoretic concepts and associated measures, consideration has been limited to topological distance in which distance between a pair of vertices is measured by counting the number of intervening edges, regardless of the physical distance of each edge. This method does present the advantages of abstraction and simplification. If one's interest is in studying the geometric or structural properties of a network, physical distances between vertices is not of much consequence and therefore may be ignored. However, there are many operational situations where the actual distance between nodes is crucial because of its direct bearing on construction costs and elapsed time needed to travel between nodes. Certainly, this is the case in transportation planning, business logistics, and individual route selection. Not all the indices discussed here can be modified to accommodate physical or economic distance. Those that can be modified include the König index, the accessibility index, and the Shimbel index.

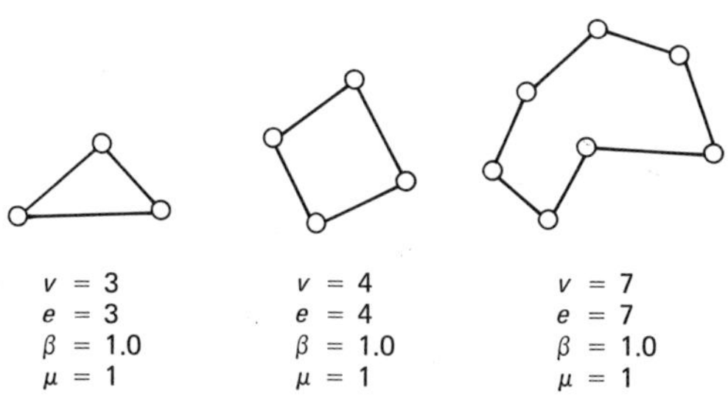

Figure 5-7 Relationship between selected graph-theoretic measures and increasing size of networks

International Variations in Network Structure

Just as much as a maple leaf and a leaf of a banana plant are very different in shape, size, and the pattern of their veins, transport networks also differ as between regions or nations. Moreover, like leaves, transport networks are functional. They were created for a purpose which may be related to the physical and socioeconomic context of a nation.

Garrison and Marble (1962) selected 25 countries, computed a number of network measures for each, and correlated these measures with certain indices of socioeconomic development and physical characteristics. Table 5-3 is an extract from the Garrison-Marble study showing the alpha and gamma indices for the railroad networks of 10 of the countries. The index values are expressed as percentages, and it may be noted that the rank-ordering of the values of both indices is similar.

In general, relatively advanced countries, such as Sweden and Hungary, exhibit higher index values than less developed ones, such as Ghana, Turkey, and Iran. Ghana and Nigeria, although neighbors in West Africa and both former British colonies, had significantly different alpha indices: 1.30 for Ghana and 10.70 for Nigeria. Such contrasts suggest certain underlying variations in the socioeconomic as well as physical makeup of the several nations included in the sample.

Berry's (1960) study of 95 countries identified several of these basic dimensions of variation. Factor analysis of 43 developmental variables, such as energy consumption per capita, educational attainment, international trade turnover, birthrates, and the like, yielded four underlying, nonredundant dimensions or factors of economic development.

Two of these factors were identified as "technological level" and "demographic status." The former represents a scale made up of the level of urbanization, degree of industrialization, income, intensity of transportation, and so on. Countries that rank low on this scale are those which are highly urbanized and industrialized and in which per capita incomes are high. The demographic status is a synthetic index made up of birthrate and death rate, population density, population per unit of cultivated land, and so on. Again, each of the 95 countries can be ranked on this scale as to relative position.

In addition, three physical characteristics were selected by Garrison and Marble: size, shape, and relief. Size of nations was simply measured as the area in square miles. The measure of shape was the ratio of the width of the

Table 5-3
Alpha and Gamma Indices of Railroad Networks of Selected Countries, 1960

Source: Adapted from W. Garrison and D. Marble, *The Structure of Transportation Networks*, 1962, p. 47, Northwestern University, The Transportation Center.

Country	Alpha	Gamma
Sweden	19.30	46.20
Hungary	15.68	44.00
Nigeria	10.70	41.00
Cuba	10.20	40.40
Mexico	7.54	38.50
Tunisia	5.00	37.30
Finland	3.00	35.60
Ghana	1.30	35.00
Turkey	0.45	33.60
Iran	0.00	32.45

Table 5-4
Partial Regression Coefficients, Network Measures, and Independent Variables

Network measure	Technological level	Demographic status	Size	Shape	Relief
Alpha index	−.049	.068	1.208	−3.306	−.090
Gamma index	−.031	.043	.412	−2.419	−.071
Cyclomatic number	−.012	.027	.354	− .799	.001
Diameter	−.092	.012	10.101	7.447	.347

Source: Garrison and Marble (1962, 38).

longest axis to the shortest one, the shortest being drawn as a perpendicular to the midpoint of the longest axis. Relief was measured as the ratio of the airline distance between two points and the distance on the ground between these same points. For each country, three random traverses were averaged in order to compute a measure of relief.

Regression and correlation analyses were then used to evaluate the relationships between selected network measures and the five explanatory variables discussed previously. Table 5-4 provides the partial regression coefficients whose values depend upon the absolute value of the particular independent variable. Thus, it is inappropriate to compare, for example, the coefficient associated with the level of technology with that pertaining to shape in explaining the place-to-place observed variations in any of the network measures. However, the coefficients may be compared columnwise, and thus we can conclude that the size of a nation contributes 10 times as much to the variation in the diameter of the networks as it does to the alpha index.

Further, the sign preceding the coefficient suggests the direction of the relationships. The coefficient of 1.208, with respect to the size of a nation and the alpha index, indicates that the larger the country, the higher is the value of the alpha index; i.e., there are a larger number of loops in the railroad network of large nations. On the other hand, elongated nations have a high shape index which is associated with low values of the alpha index.

Reading across the row, we can observe that higher levels of technology, higher demographic status, larger size, compact shape, and relatively insignificant relief variations tend to be associated with both high alpha and high gamma indices. Further, the number of loops, or cyclomatic number, is strongly influenced by the technological level, demographic status, size, and shape, but relief plays a minor role in contributing to country-to-country variations in the cyclomatic number. The diameter or span of a railroad network is also high in the case of technologically advanced nations with high demographic status, nations of large size, elongated shape, and relatively rugged relief. Czechoslovakia is an example of a nation illustrating four of these conditions, size being the only exception.

More significant than the partial regression coefficients are the multiple coefficients of determination (R^2), whose values are shown in Table 5-5. These represent levels of statistical "explanation." The 42 percent R^2 associated with the level of technology and the alpha index can be interpreted thus: 42 percent of the place-to-place variation in the value of the alpha index is influenced by

Table 5-5
Marginal Incremental Coefficients of Determination* between Network Measures and Independent Variables

Network measure	Techno-logical level	Demo-graphic status	Size	Shape	Relief	Total
Alpha index	42	2	2	8	3	57
Gamma index	37	3	1	11	4	56
Cyclomatic number	54	2	3	3	0	62
Diameter	62	0	5	8	5	80

* Figures have been multiplied by 100 to eliminate the decimal.
Source: Garrison and Marble (1962, 40, adapted from Table 10).

the variation in the level of technology. Demographic status makes an additional contribution of 2 percentage points, shape 8, relief 3; the five together explain 57 percent of the variation in the alpha index. The residual or unexplained variation due to factors that have not been incorporated in the model is 43 percent.

For all the network indices, the technological level is the single most important independent variable contributing, in general, more than two-thirds of the total explanation provided by the five variables. Shape seems to be the second most important explanatory variable, followed by size and relief. The demographic status, although the second most important factor identified by Berry in his study of world economic development, is the least significant in terms of its ability to explain international contrasts in railroad network connectivity.

The highest R^2 in Table 5-4 is 62 percent, which is the relationship between the level of technology and the diameter of the network. Of what value is this finding? Not much, it may be argued, because in comparing two countries of equal size, the one with the greater number of nodes and therefore ipso facto the greater number of edges would also have the larger diameter. As long as one is considering only railroad networks, every vertex is on the network, and vertices not on it are automatically excluded from consideration. Moreover, one would expect that in most cases a nation with a large number of nodes on its railroad network would also have a high level of urbanization and therefore a concomitant level of technology. Under these circumstances, to use technology as an explanatory variable is tantamount to circular reasoning, if not begging the question somewhat. After all, one would expect rich nations to be at least a bit dependent for their wealth upon the ability of their transport networks to facilitate the movement of people, goods, and information from place to place. Equally, the demand for a highly connected transport network would be higher in affluent nations, and only they would be in a position to finance the high level of investment necessary to build such a transport network.

There is something of a symbiotic relationship between transportation facilities and economic development. Therefore, the conclusion that "the technological development was the more important factor conditioning the character of transport systems" (Garrison and Marble, 1962, 53) seems peculiar, to say the least.

In a review of the role of transportation in economic development, Gauthier (1970, 619) concludes that our knowledge of spatial economic growth does not clearly suggest the temporal sequence and relative importance among the transportation network, the differentiation of the subregional economic systems, the spatial structure of the urban hierarchy, and overall regional economic development. The honest answer to the question, Which comes first, the economic-development chicken or the transportation-network egg? is: We don't know, but probably both come first.

Network Regionalization

In a complex network, certain pairs of nodes are better connected than others. It may be expected that nodes that are relatively close together tend to be highly connected, in contrast to those that are far apart. Therefore, it may be possible to partition a national network into a series of regional subsystems. In the United States, the feeder airlines in the Midwest and other regions provide a high degree of connection to some nodes, such as Kansas City and Denver, which are, in turn, the articulation points "hooking" their regions with the rest of the country via other articulation points, such as Chicago and Atlanta.

All networks, apparently, have a hierarchical structure. A useful analogy is that of communications networks consisting of many types of organizations, such as television broadcasting, newspapers, trade journals, professional and fraternal associations, and church socials, all of which aid in the dissemination of information. In the United States, at the national level we have the national television companies for whom the operating space is at least coextensive with that of the nation. Lower down the hierarchy, there are fraternal organizations such as the Lions Club, Rotary, American Legion, and others, each of which has lodges or chapters whose "market" area is localized. Information is exchanged at the local level, but to the extent that many of these orders have a national organizational structure, information is also transmitted between regions. In this way, information is diffused by means of a communications network which is characterized by many overlapping hierarchical levels.

The question is now raised, How can we best identify the regional structure of a network in terms of its partitioned subnetworks? A widely used procedure is factor or principal component analysis of binary connectivity matrices.

The binary connectivity matrix is a square one with identical numbers of rows and columns. A correlation coefficient, r_{ij}, can be computed, telling the degree to which each node is connected with every other node. The total variance in the matrix can be "factored out" by successively extracting components so that the first one accounts for the maximum amount of variation. Then, a residual correlation matrix is recomputed and factored again to extract the second component, and so on. In this way, by iteratively extracting diminishing amounts of the initial variation, a final residual correlation matrix is left, with zeros in the off-diagonal elements. At this stage, the component analysis is complete in the sense that all the original variance has been accounted for.

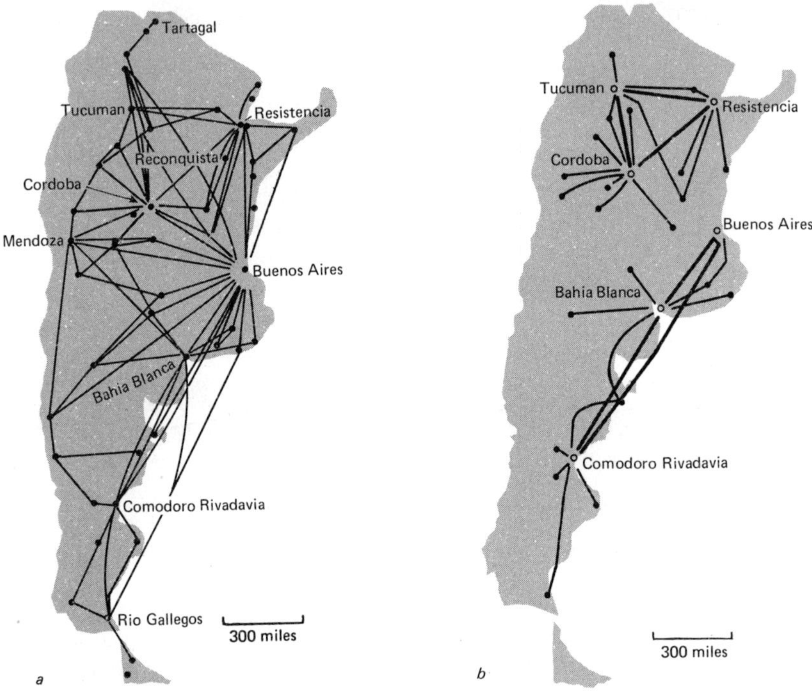

Figure 5-8 Regionalization of the Argentinean airline network showing (*a*) the network; (*b*) major regionalization effect; (*c*) the field effect of Buenos Aires; (*d*) minor regionalization.

Each *component* is a package of nodes such that within any one component there is maximum homogeneity, and between any one component and any other there is maximum heterogeneity. Components are said to be *orthogonalized*, meaning that there is zero correlation between them. By mapping what are termed *component loadings*, which in this case are the correlation of each node to each component, it is possible to identify the nature of each of the components. This was done by Garrison and Marble (1962) for the airline network of Argentina, and the results are presented in Figure 5-8.

Table 5-6 reports the proportion of the total variation explained by the component analysis. The total variance was 192.00, of which 100.55, or 52.36 percent, was explained by the component analysis in terms of the first

Table 5-6
Results of the Components Analysis of the Argentinean Local Service Airline Network

Source: Garrison and Marble (1962, 62, Table 22).

Component	Percent variation
1. Size scale	21.94%
2. Major regional systems	10.76%
3. Buenos Aires field	9.47%
4. Minor region (*a*)	5.71%
5. Minor region (*b*)	4.48%
Total (five components)	52.36%

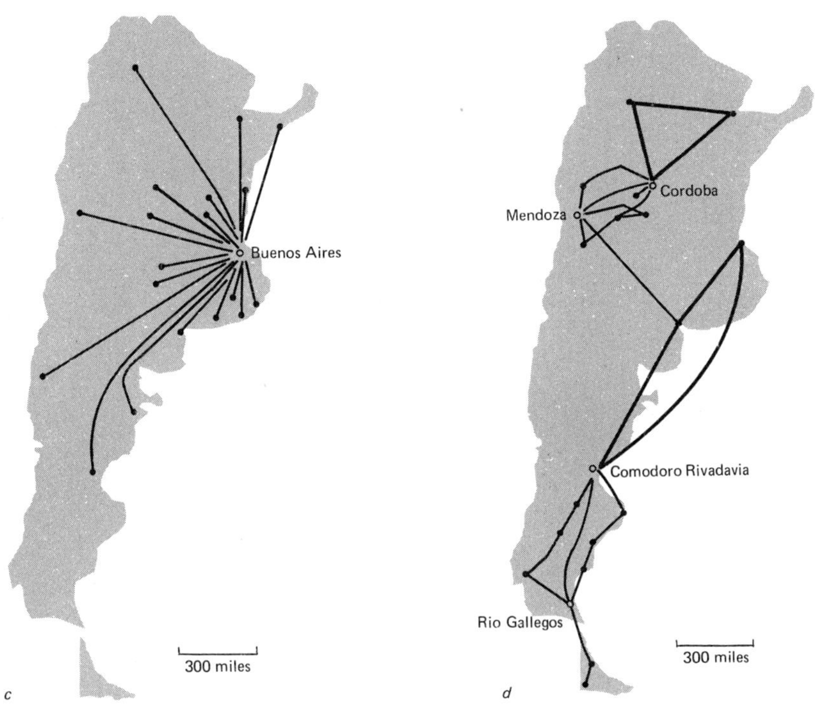

five components extracted and interpreted. The unexplained variation, due to other components, amounted to 47.6 percent. Garrison and Marble interpret this unexplained variation as largely being due to the "neighborhood effect" since the analysis concentrated mainly on the off-diagonal clusters. The data matrix was organized on the basis of a north-south listing with contiguity of places maintained insofar as possible. On such a matrix, a series of 1s close to the principal diagonal indicates connections to the first, second, third, and other close neighboring places. Generally, most of the places are connected with their nearest neighbors, rather than with more distant ones, and since this mode of principal component analysis identifies and collapses node clusters columnwise, these neighborhood effects escape the analysis. Therefore, the 52.4 percent explanation is over and above that of the pattern of neighborhood connectivity and can be broken down as follows.

Population size (component 1, 21.9 percent) simply represents a linear scaling of the nodes in the Argentina airline network by means of their relative population size. This interpretation is confirmed by an examination of the component loadings on which Buenos Aires had a value of 3.148 and Cordoba 2.334, while a small town such as Tartagil had a value of 0.007.

Major regionalization (component 2, 10.8 percent) is, actually, the first component to focus specifically upon the characteristics of the network as a network. This component breaks down the graph into a triangular system of cities, Cordoba–Resistencia–Tucuman, each of which is directly connected with Buenos Aires and to each of which there are feeder routes from smaller nodes in their sphere of influence. The second region corresponds to two linear axes, Buenos Aires–Bahia Blanca–Commodoro–Rivadavia. Thus, Reconquista is connected with Buenos Aires via Commodoro–Rivadavia.

Figure 5-8*b* shows the basic major regionalization effect which, as Garrison and Marble note, is "merely suggestive" of the results of the component analysis, rather than being mathematically precise. Nevertheless, it does tend to show that, within each of these two regions, there is a certain level of connectivity in that Tucuman, Cordoba, Resistencia, Bahia Blanca, and Commodoro Rivadavia are the articulation points hooking up their regions to places in other regions, as well as to Buenos Aires at the top of the national urban hierarchy.

Field effect (component 3, 9.5 percent) symbolizes the attraction of Buenos Aires as a sort of magnet or focal point for the entire Argentinean urban system, in whose orbit are all the locations except those in the southern extremity of the country. Evidently, southern Argentina is not well connected with the rest of the national system (see Figure 5-8*c*).

Minor regionalization (components 4 and 5, 5.7 and 4.5 percent) also indexes regionalization effects focused (1) on Cordoba and Mendoza and (2) on Rio Gallegos, all three of which, in turn, are connected with Buenos Aires (see Figure 5-8*d*).

In a parallel analysis of the local-service airline network of Venezuela, Garrison and Marble arrived at essentially similar conclusions. There were, however, two differences: first, the total percentage variance explained was significantly lower, a factor which they interpreted to mean that the Venezuelan network was somewhat less structured. Second, the field effect centered upon Caracas emerged as a more important component than in the analogous case in Argentina.

Garrison and Marble developed connectivity matrices for the surface transportation networks of each of the 25 nations in their sample. The dominant characteristic was shown to be that edges tended to link urban centers to their nearby neighboring ones. Surface transportation modes represent heavy capital expenditures and, once built, cannot readily be eliminated. Airline routes, on the other hand, have a great deal of flexibility, their only physical limitation being the availability of air fields. Service can be provided or eliminated between pairs of nodes almost at will. Thus, surface transportation networks exhibit a marked "neighborhood effect," while airline networks tend to have much more elaborate structures that are amenable to partitioning into regional substructures. As nations develop and become more affluent, even the surface transportation modes acquire the basic characteristics of an airline network, and Garrison (1960) has described the interstate highway system of the United States as being more akin to an airline network than to a conventional road system.

Alternative Network Configurations

A given number of nodes can be linked in a number of alternative ways, yielding different network configurations (Figure 5-9). In each configuration there are five nodes at identical coordinate locations. The first graph (Figure

Figure 5-9 Alternative network configurations: (*a*) Paul Revere's ride; (*b*) hierarchical; (*c*) traveling salesman; (*d*) fully connected nonplanar.

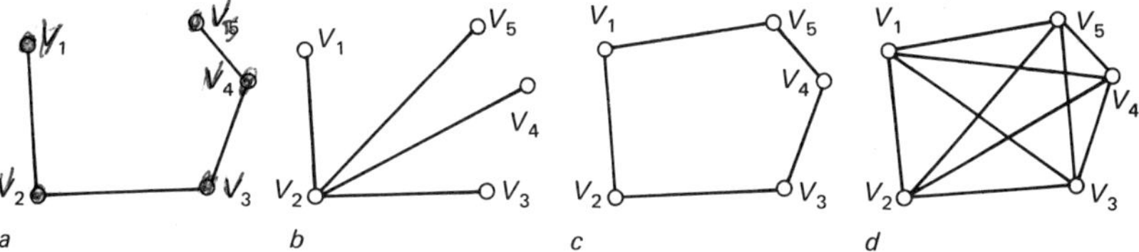

5-9*a*) belongs to the general class of trees and is more specifically identified by Bunge (1966) as *Paul Revere's ride*. It will be recalled that Paul Revere had to contact the largest number of nodes in the shortest possible time, the while shouting, "The British are coming, the British are coming." For his purposes, it was not material that the last node did not have a direct connection with the first node since, after accomplishing the mission, he could backtrack from V_5 to V_1 via V_4, V_3, and V_2. In this graph, direct connections are only to the immediately adjacent neighbors on either side, except for the V_1–V_5 pair of nodes. Consequently, regardless of the origin of a particular journey, in order to reach all nodes and to return to the origin, it is necessary to traverse eight links. If, on the other hand, only one-way trips are involved, unlike Paul Revere's ride, V_3 is more central than any other node as measured by the Köning index of 2, and therefore it is an optimal location for, say, a warehouse.

Figure 5-9*b* is a *hierarchical network* in which, as in Figure 5-9*a*, there are four links. However, there is a major difference: only V_2 is connected directly to the other four vertices. Since there are no loops, this is also a tree. Travel from V_4 to V_5, although they are close to each other in terms of physical distance, involves a circuitous journey through V_2. Indeed, travel from any node to any node other than V_2 must pass through V_2, giving it a strategic role in the network.

Garrison and Marble (1962, 5) provide a real world example of a hierarchical network, using the case of the airline network of Guatemala (see Figure 5-10). Note that from Dos Lagunas to Carmelita, which are less than 50 miles apart, the airline trip has to be via Guatemala City because of the network configuration, and this route covers a total distance of approximately 600 miles. Contacts between units in a political-territorial system follow this hierarchical principle. The communications network, designed to maintain administrative control, is such that while each constituent unit must have a direct link to the capital, it is not essential that each unit be connected even to its nearest neighbor. Thus, in the halcyon days of the British Empire, India,

Figure 5-10 Hierarchical network configuration: the Guatemala airline system

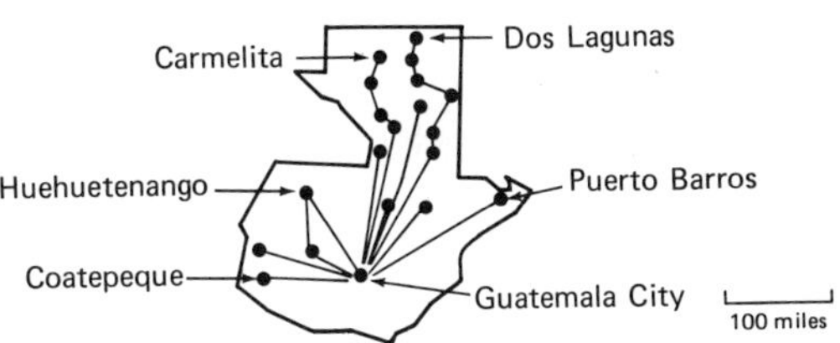

Burma, Ceylon, and the Federated Malay States all had ties with London, rather than with each other, despite being in the same region of the world. Communication systems necessary to maintain the command and control functions in the military also tend to be tightly hierarchical.

Figure 5-9*c* is a loop, sometimes known as a Hamiltonian circuit, labeled by Bunge as the *traveling salesman* definition of distance. The major difference between this type of network and Paul Revere's ride is that if we start from any vertex, the other four vertices can be reached by overcoming a total topological distance of 5 units in contrast to 8.

Moreover, while in the case of Paul Revere's ride V_3 stood out as being relatively better located vis-à-vis the other nodes and in the hierarchical network V_2 is the only node directly connected with the other four, in a loop such as that in Figure 5-9*c* the notion of relative location evaporates. The König index for each node is the same.

Figure 5-9*d* is a *fully connected nonplanar network* in which there are ten links between five nodes, and thus the value of the beta index is 2. If the points are settlements and the links are highways or railroads, then this network yields the shortest possible topological distance between any pair of nodes. In turn, this network minimizes user costs, in contrast to Paul Revere's ride in which all five nodes are connected by means of the shortest total distance of four edges. The latter configuration minimizes builder costs, a factor which, of necessity, increases user costs. This distinction is basic to the discussion of optimization problems in which key questions are, Optimal for whom? What is being optimized — time, costs, flow, or distance? Explicit consideration of optimization problems is reserved until Chapter 12.

Table 5-7 is an attempt to show that the computation and application of graph-theoretic measures should not be made uncritically. Thus, although the index values for the Paul Revere's ride and the hierarchical network are both the same across the row, the configurations as depicted in Figure 5-9*a* and *b* are very different, as are the distances between nodes and the relative accessibility of the nodes. Thus, it is apparent that different networks can give rise to the same index values. James et al. (1970) recognized this point and developed an alternative index, $S - I$, which enabled them to discriminate among alternative network configurations such as Hamiltonian circuits, star graphs, cobweb graphs, completely connected graphs, and others.

NODAL AND ROUTE HIERARCHIES

One advantage of considering a transport network as a graph is that, as we have seen, we can reduce the real-world network to its fundamental properties

Table 5-7
Beta and Alpha Indices for Alternative Network Configurations

Network configuration	Number of vertices	Number of edges	Beta	Alpha
Paul Revere's ride	5	4	0.8	0.0
Hierarchical	5	4	0.8	0.0
Traveling salesman	5	5	1.0	0.2
Fully connected	5	10	2.0	1.00

of nodes and links. This advantage, however, is not obtained without paying a price. By assuming all nodes to be of unit size and all links to be of unit length, a certain amount of information is sacrificed. While such trade-offs are characteristic in any model-based approach, the consequences of information loss can be minimized by the reintroduction of real world complexities. The most important complications that must be introduced in this context are size variations among nodes, capacity variations among links, and real world distances versus topological ones.

Nodal Hierarchies

It appears that the hierarchical principle runs as a recurrent theme among apparently widely disparate sets of phenomena. Social systems have their rank ordering, corporations and administrative bureaucracies have line and staff organizations, and drainage networks constitute a well-ordered hierarchical system. The essential properties common to all hierarchies are the existence of two or more levels and a pyramidal structure (so that the number of objects at any one level decreases as we go up the hierarchy).

It is easy to demonstrate that in many regions and nations, as indeed in the world, there are a small number of large cities, a larger number of medium-sized cities, and a very large number of small towns. Table 5-8 shows that in the United States, as well as in Texas and Oregon specifically, there is a regular and consistent increase in the number of cities through the nine decreasing-size classes.

With respect to a settlement hierarchy, it is possible to state as testable propositions (although tests conducted have met with varying degrees of success) the following:

1. There are a certain number of discrete-size classes of settlements.
2. The number of settlements in each size class increases down the hierarchy.
3. There is some characteristic spacing between nearest neighbors at any particular level.

A theoretical construct which relates the size, number, and spatial arrangement is central place theory, and the following set of diagrams serves to illustrate the spatial-hierarchical structuring of an idealized Löschian landscape.

Table 5-8
Size Distribution of Urban Places

Source: U.S. Census of Population (1970, Table 5).

Population size classes	Number of cities: United States	Texas	Oregon
1,000,000 or more	6	1	—
500,000–1,000,000	20	2	—
250,000–500,000	30	3	1
100,000–250,000	100	4	—
50,000–100,000	240	17	2
25,000–50,000	520	19	3
10,000–25,000	1385	80	17
5000–10,000	1839	95	20
2500–5000	2295	152	29

Figure 5-11 Theoretical evolution of a settlement system (after Lösch)

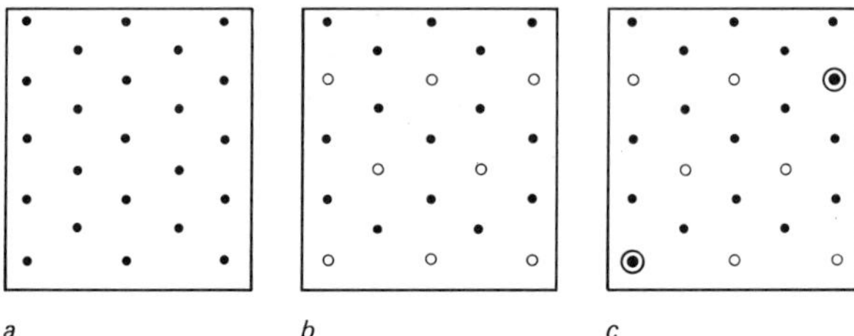

Figure 5-11, Haggett's modification of the ideas initially presented by Lösch, shows the sequence of development with the following stages:

1. Initially, there is an undifferentiated nodal pattern with a uniform or regular spacing. The 23 settlements in Figure 5-11*a* are arranged in the form of a triangular lattice network.
2. At the second stage, shown in Figure 5-11*b*, eight of the smaller nodes have become intermediate-size settlements, and the average distance between these is larger as compared with that between the smaller settlements. There is, however, uniform spacing between pairs of nearest neighbors which belong to the second level in the hierarchy.
3. In the third stage, shown in Figure 5-11*c*, two of the eight intermediate-level settlements have become major agglomerations, and they are located still farther apart in comparison to the second-level places.

There are 15 small places, 6 intermediate-level places, and 2 large ones in the hypothetical landscape shown in Figure 5-11*c*. If the size of the region were to be enlarged, a similar progression of size classes could be expected. In his study of trade centers in a part of the Canadian great plains, Hodge (1965) has provided empirical corroboration of the theoretical expectations concerning the number of settlements in the different size classes and their characteristic spacing. From Table 5-9, it is evident that smaller towns are lesser distances apart and that there is a regular progression so that as the median size of settlement increases, the average spacing between settlements of the same size increases also.

The size of nodes, whether considered as origins or destinations, and the distance separating an origin from a destination are, in general, the two prime determinants of the volume of spatial interaction.

Table 5-9
Relationship between Size and Spacing of Settlements in the Canadian Great Plains

Source: Compiled from G. Hodge, "The Prediction of Trade Center Viability in the Great Plains," *Papers*, Regional Science Association, **15:** 92, Table 1; 99, Table 6 (1965). Used with permission.

Median size	Number of centers	Mean spacing (miles)
103,800	2	144.0
10,000	9	67.5
1,800	29	39.5
610	85	22.5
360	100	19.8
210	150	13.5
50	404	9.6

Route Hierarchies

The transport network, regardless of the mode, is made up of many links, some small and others large. Just as there are discrete-size classes of nodes, there is also a frequency distribution of segments of the transportation network classified by capacity and length.

The unit of measurement required to designate a route hierarchy is different from that used to denote a nodal hierarchy, the appropriate measure being the number of miles of different classes of routes. In the United States, there are over 3 million miles of highway, but of these, the preponderant share consists of rural roads and city streets, both of which are low-order segments. At the top of the hierarchy is the Interstate Highway System, amounting to 42,600 miles (1970), or approximately 1.1 percent of the total highway mileage.

Another difference between the nodal hierarchy and the route hierarchy is that, while city size is measured usually in terms of population, route sizes are evaluated according to their capacity to accommodate traffic. Thus, while a country road may be two lanes wide with narrow bridges, a freeway may have six or more lanes with limited access.

A hierarchical route network exists not only at the national level but also within regions and particularly within metropolitan areas. Creighton (1970, 96–98) has analyzed data pertaining to the frequency distribution of route mileages and traffic volumes classified by type of road in the Chicago metropolitan area. Of the 10,262 miles of roadways, 72.2 percent are local streets, 27.2 percent are arterials, and only 0.6 percent are expressways. However, of the 36.2 million daily vehicle-miles of travel, local streets carry only about 16 percent, while expressways and arterials carry the balance.

The same hierarchical progression may be observed in a variety of other modes: there are feeder airline routes traversing short distances, intercity routes over longer distances, and international lines around the planet. Pipeline networks with small average diameter diverge from the oil-field area of the Gulf coast, merging subsequently to constitute larger pipes as they converge toward megalopolis.

Ullman (1949) noted that there is as much difference between the poorest and the best railroads as there is between a minor country road and a superhighway. Similar to the flows on the Chicago highway network in which the expressways carry the largest amount of traffic, the most heavily used 10 percent of the U.S. railroad mileage carried 50 percent of the total ton-miles. At the bottom of the hierarchy, the least used 10 percent of the national mileage carried less than 0.5 percent of the national freight traffic. The highest-order links are four-track lines on the Pennsylvania Railroad from Pittsburgh to New York and the New York Central from Cleveland to Albany. Three-track sections at the next level in the hierarchy extend westward to Aurora, Illinois, and southward to Washington, D.C. Two-track lines intensify the pattern of connections in the northeastern portion of the United States. In addition, the two major transcontinental lines, Union Pacific and Santa Fe, as well as the Atlantic Coastline, provide interregional, high-order linkages. The preponderant proportion of the total mileage consists of low-order, single-track links of relatively short lengths.

The variations in capacity and length among route segments and the

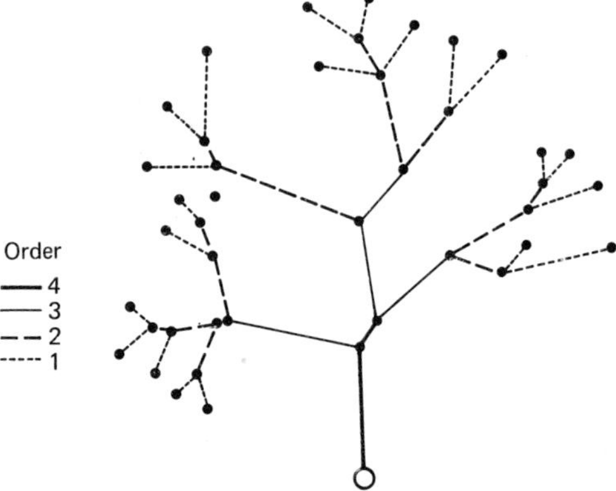

Figure 5-12
Stream ordering in a drainage network (after Strahler)

spatial distributions of the different sizes of routes all have distinctive relationships. These relationships are not haphazard or random but occur in a patterned way which suggests functional order and spatial organization.

Haggett (1967) recognized the isomorphism between transport networks and drainage systems. Borrowing from the work of the hydrologist Horton and the geomorphologist Strahler, he studied the major structural regularities of dendritic, or treelike, transport systems. All segments of a stream system located at the outer edges are considered to be in the first or lowest order of the hierarchy. Two first-order streams merge to form a second-order stream, two second-order streams combine to yield a third-order stream, and so on. The result is a branching hierarchy (Figure 5-12).

Haggett applied these notions to a portion of the English road system as well as the road network centering on Oporto, Portugal. He was able to recognize strong similarities between drainage networks and road networks in their hierarchical ordering. A path belonging to a higher order is formed by the merger of two or more lower-order paths.

Haggett subsequently summarized the observed relationships in terms of certain laws:

1. Path order is inversely related to path number so that the smaller the path order, the larger the number of path occurrences; i.e., there are more driveways than expressways (Figure 5-13*a*).

Figure 5-13 Generalized relationship between path order and (*a*) number, (*b*) length, (*c*) flow, and (*d*) tributary area.

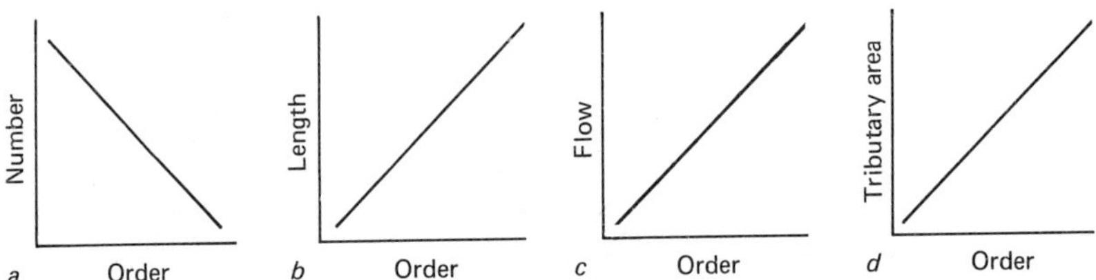

2. Path order is directly related to path length. The higher the order, the greater is the mean length of the path; i.e., the mean lengths of driveways and local streets are small in comparison with that of transcontinental expressways (Figure 5-13*b*).

3. Path order is directly related to flow or capacity, so that driveways can accommodate one or two automobiles, while, as was shown in the case of Chicago, the capacity of urban freeways runs into the tens of thousands (Figure 5-13*c*).

4. Path order is directly related to the size of the tributary area. Every path has a service area that contains the nodes from which its traffic is generated or consigned. These generating units are analogous to springs in a drainage system. The service area of a driveway consists of a single-family home, while a major arterial may serve an entire quadrant of a city with many small roads feeding traffic into it (Figure 5-13*d*).

In each of the four laws specified above, path order may be viewed as the independent variable, contributing to variations in number, length, flow, and tributary area. The term "order" here refers to a hierarchical ordering in which the frequency of occurrences is very high at lower orders and low at higher orders.

The hierarchical organization of routes just described is quite general. Although the discussion has been couched in terms of driveways, arterials, and freeways, which are parts of the highway system, the same principles are also evident in the case of other transportation and communications networks. The telephone system constitutes one of the best examples of a highly elaborate and finely articulated hierarchical network.

Correspondence of Nodal and Route Hierarchies

Movement originates at nodes, and flows occur on route networks. Both the nodes and segments of the network exhibit hierarchical structures that are meshed in an organized way.

Regardless of the distance separating them, larger nodes that generate larger volumes of movement are linked by means of high-order routes which also, incidentally, link smaller nodes that lie athwart the path. Dumfries, Virginia, with a population of 1890, is linked by Interstate 95 to both Washington and Richmond, purely by virtue of its fortuitous location. Smaller routes connect a larger node with smaller nodes in its vicinity.

The meshing of the nodal and route hierarchies has been modeled by Haggett (1966) for the Löschian landscape described earlier. Figure 5-14 shows the relationships between hierarchical position of nodes and hierarchical order of paths. There are about 150 distance units of the lowest-order paths in the network in Figure 5-14*a*. Note that each of the 23 low-order nodes is at the intersection of six links and that each node is connected with its six nearest neighbors. At this stage, there is neither a nodal nor a route hierarchy. Small villages and country roads are all that exist.

In the next stage of development (Figure 5-14*b*), the eight medium-sized nodes are linked to each other by means of second-order paths. The total length of the link segments belonging to this order is about 90 distance units.

Figure 5-14 The correspondence between nodal and route hierarchies in a theoretical settlement pattern

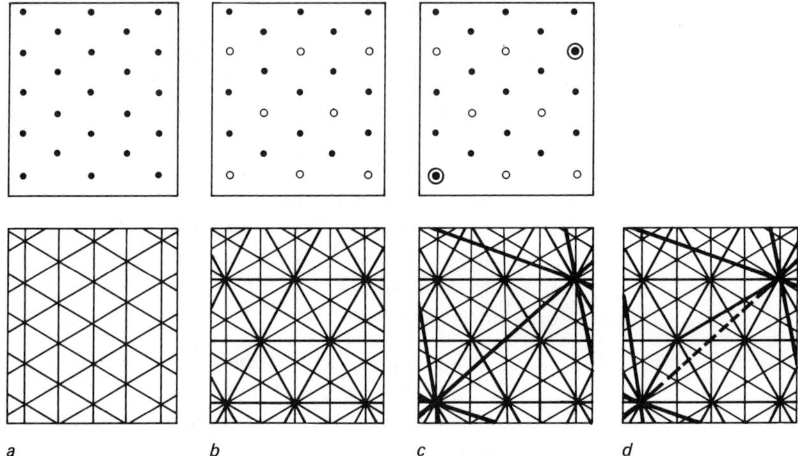

Each second-order node has six links converging on it from each of its nearest neighbors of the same order. The second-order network is superimposed on the first-order network, and none of the second-order routes serves any of the first-order nodes. There appears to be a rigid stratification of hierarchical orders, a sort of route caste system, as it were.

In Figure 5-14*c*, the two third-order places are connected by means of a third-order route. Again, each of these two is connected to its other five nearest neighbors belonging to the third order (not shown on the map), as well as to each other, by means of high-order links. This network, totaling 40 units of distance in length, is again superimposed on both the second- and the first-order networks. As before, no second-order node is served by a third-order link.

The net result is that, by now, we have a nodal-hierarchical spatial pattern consisting of villages, towns, and cities and a network consisting of country roads, state roads, and superhighways. It is obvious that this model can be extended sequentially to the *K*th level, but the general principles remain unaltered.

Two consequences arise from the pattern in Figure 5-14*c*. The route density is inordinately high, with the total distance units amounting to 240 although the size of the area has remained unchanged since the initial stage. Directly arising from this fact is a strong redundancy which has crept in because of the theoretical necessity to keep separate the functions of route segments at specific hierarchical levels. In particular, there are too many unnecessary low-order routes.

In the real world, since network development is a sequential process and since nodal development is also a function of time, the high-order link between the two high-order nodes is likely to be realigned, as shown in Figure 5-14*d*. The low-order route has now been upgraded, and consequently the intervening low-order places, the Dumfries of this world, are also served by the high-order link, although the rigid hierarchical route stratification has been undermined. Moreover, functions tend to get a bit mixed up: it is not unusual to see both tractors and interstate buses on some U.S. highways. Thus it is that, through time, the route caste system is destroyed.

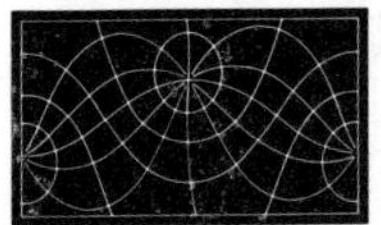

6 The Temporal Development and Prediction of Transportation Networks

POSING THE PROBLEM OF CHANGE

Signs such as "Your highway taxes at work," "Road under construction for the next ten miles," "Squeeze left," and "Detour ahead" are roadside sights familiar to every American motorist and indicate that the transportation network is undergoing change. What is happening today is, of course, just a continuation of long-term trends in the historical geography of transportation networks. Figure 6-1 shows the sequence of development of Western railroads from 1870 to 1930, derived from Paullin's *Atlas of Historical Geography.*

The evolution of transportation networks occurs not only at the macroscale of nations and large regions, but also at the microscale or urban scale. In cities that developed over the course of many centuries, e.g., in Europe and Asia, the road pattern has sometimes evolved from an initial series of trails, through a system of ancient paved roads, to a complex network of modern freeways. In many of the old sections of ancient cities, narrow, winding roads paved with cobblestones are still in use along with more modern macadamized links, and traces of the past are still visible on the urban cultural landscape. With developments in transportation technology, the circulation system is made up of separate modal networks that intersect at some points.

While, in general, change has involved the intensification (space-filling), augmentation (spatial diffusion), and articulation (well-defined spatial structuring) of the transportation network, the process has by no means been unidirectional. Thus, for example, Figure 6-2 shows the long-run trends in mileage of surfaced roads and railroads operated over nearly a century from 1860 to 1958 in the United States. It can be seen that the mileage operated by railroads began to decrease somewhat after 1930. The closing of link segments of the overall transportation network can be observed at a variety of scales.

In urban areas, a "No thru traffic" sign effectively removes a particular link from the total inventory of transportation facilities.

A new political boundary superimposed on an already settled area with an existing transportation network partitions the network into subgraphs, especially if the newly created nations are hostile toward each other. Thus, in recent years, there has been no through highway or railroad service between India and Pakistan, North and South Vietnam, and North and South Korea, despite the existence of through roads and railroads. The Suez Canal, which served for several decades as a major link in the British Commonwealth's lifeline from London to Sidney, from 1967 to 1974 was similarly withdrawn from the world's stock of transportation routes, compelling costly long-distance travel around the Cape of Good Hope.

In some cases, transportation networks seem to undergo a complex form of reincarnation, including both birth and death cycles. After the Normandy invasion in World War II, the brilliant American tank commander General George S. Patton found himself confronted with a situation in which the Germans were fully in control of both the all-weather, motorable road network in western France and the nodes linked by this network. Patton unearthed maps of the Roman road system in the British Museum and found that the Roman roads, were, in many instances, orthogonal to the modern road system and, further, that they crossed rivers at their narrowest and shallowest fordable stretches. From then on, his tactics were designed so as to move his tanks on the traces of the old Roman network. These tactics were successful, at least in part, because the Germans were geared to operate on a completely different network that intersected little with the one that Patton was using.

Studies of the history of transportation networks, such as those by Taylor (1951), Jackman (1916), and Dyos and Aldcroft (1969), demonstrate that network change does not proceed in a constant manner but rather is spasmodic in character. There have been transportation revolutions, much like the agricultural and industrial revolutions, in which very rapid change occurred in short periods of time. In the United States, Taylor (1951) has characterized the period from 1815 to 1860 as being the revolutionary period in the development of the American transportation network during which not only the building of canals in particular but also the spread of the fundamental railroad network in the eastern United States transformed the space-economy. "Canal booms" and "railroad manias" in both the United States and Great Britain were distinguished by frenzied activity and speculation that resulted in high levels of connectivity between nodes and numerous Hamiltonian circuits that, in retrospect, were redundant more often than not. In the United States, the total mileage of railroads in operation increased from 35,085 in 1865 to 166,700 in 1890 (Gottmann, 1961). The railroad network continued to expand, although at a much slower pace, until 1920, when it reached its maximum extent. The highway network, on the other hand, expanded very slowly from 1860 to 1920 and from then on started an exponential climb. The period of "highway mania" is perhaps ending in the United States, not only because of the near completion of the Interstate Highway System, but also because of widespread public concern regarding environmental quality and certain aspects of the energy crisis.

Figure 6-1 Evolution of the railroad network in the western United States: (*a*) to 1870; (*b*) to 1880; (*c*) to 1930.

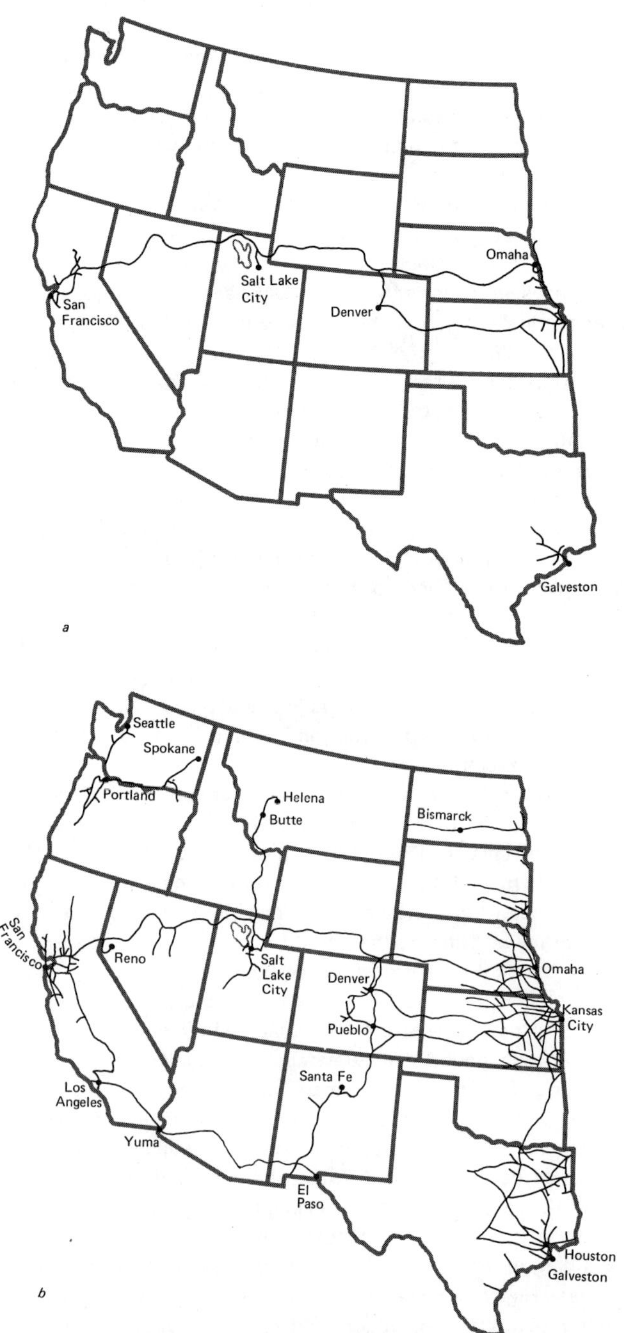

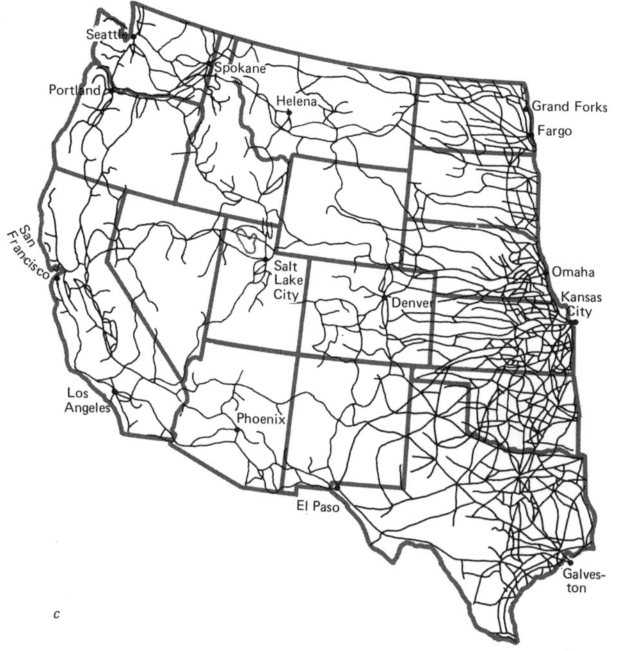

c

Figure 6-2 Long-term trends in highway and railroad mileage in the United States

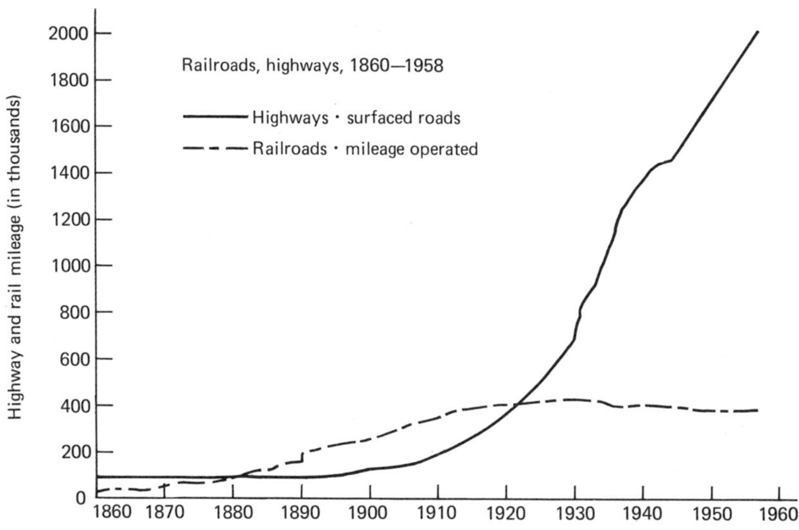

In 1972, the Governor of Massachusetts supported a complete ban on freeway construction in the city of Boston, and in many other cities citizens' action groups are trying to prevent the proliferation of urban freeways.

A transport network is built not *in vacuo,* but in the context of the location of nodes. Through time, the network adjusts itself to the changing characteristics of nodes, and the nodes themselves, in turn, undergo change as a function of the developing network. The relationships between the transport network on the one hand and urban and regional development on the other and the attendant topic of spatial reorganization are considered in Chapter 13.

The evolutionary process of transportation network development appears to be, to use a Churchillian phrase out of context, "a puzzle wrapped in an enigma, rolled in a mystery." It seems futile to attempt to disentangle piece by piece the different strands in a tightly knotted network that evolved at varying rates in time. On occasion, literally everything seemed to happen at once! This being the case, how is one to approach the study of temporal processes in networks?

Sorre (1954, 411) has suggested that the organization of a network can result from two different processes. On the one hand, it can develop from a diffused movement in response to local, perceived needs, the subsequent meshing of previously unconnected links, and competition among routes leading to the emergence of some routes that are more important than others. Ultimately, the route pattern is reorganized to give the major routes their optimal alignment. But one can also imagine the establishment of the major routes according to a predesigned plan. At first, loops are constructed connecting major nodes, and then there is a space-filling sequence during which secondary routes interconnect nodes within the loop, one with another and with the loop. Sorre notes that both these processes must be kept in mind in order to highlight certain general aspects applicable to all modes of transportation. Nevertheless, thus far there is no general theory or comprehensive framework within which to understand, much less explain, the processes of network change. What we have at our disposal is a series of partial models which, despite their lack of much theoretical content, still represent valiant attempts to shed light on the temporal development of transportation networks. We can categorize the available modeling approaches into stages-of-growth and simulation models, even though they are not mutually exclusive.

STAGES-OF-GROWTH MODELS

Many continuous growth processes can be viewed *as if* they occurred in a series of discrete stages. Some familiar examples are the stages of physical and psychological development of human beings, the Rostovian stages of economic growth, and the Davisian cycle of erosion. In the same way, the continuous process of network change can be disaggregated into sequential stages each of which contains a characteristic network pattern.

This class of models can be subdivided further into those models that pertain to coastal penetration and those that refer to midcontinental in-filling, each of which represents a variation on the basic theme of stages-of-growth.

Model of Coastal Penetration

Taaffe, Morrill, and Gould (1963) were the first to construct a model which represents a generalized description of transportation network development in underdeveloped countries. Their model is an inductive one based largely on data concerning Ghana and Nigeria, although they also examined the network expansion process in Brazil, Kenya, Tanganyika, and Malaya. Rimmer (1967) has subsequently applied portions of this model to New Zealand. These comparative studies show that in all these nations there are broad similarities in the way in which network development proceeded.

Figure 6-3 shows the six stages of network development conceptualized by Taaffe, Morrill, and Gould. In the first stage, there is a series of scattered ports along a segment of coastline. There is no size variation among ports: they are all equally small. Small trails extend toward the interior from each of the ports to their limited hinterlands. There is really no transport network in this phase: instead there are a number of independent networks.

In the second stage, some of the ports have disappeared since their functions have been captured by two ports, P_1 and P_2. Port competition has been a characteristic feature of many nations. In Ghana, Sekondi (which merged subsequently with Takoradi) and Accra had become the two dominant ports by 1920. In the United States, New York and Philadelphia were able to outcompete Boston and Baltimore. Favorable location at the mouth of navigable rivers or with respect to access routes to the interior (e.g., the Susquehanna River and the Hudson-Mohawk valleys) and aggressive entrepreneurship, present in some ports and not in others, are factors involved in the differential growth of ports. In any event, a few ports become larger, and from these there are penetration lines reaching to interior mineral or agricultural resource areas. These initial penetration lines may be roads, railroads, or canals, depending upon the available technology and environmental context. I_1 and I_2 are interior nodes that acquire their importance partly by virtue of their direct connection with the two major ports. There are at least two trees at this stage, with a small number of links per tree.

This stage may be identified as the most crucial one since it establishes the fundamental alignments of the future network pattern. The current alignment of U.S. 40 and the New York State Thruway were basically laid out in the 18th century or perhaps even earlier by the Indians.

In underdeveloped countries, there appear to have been three major reasons for the penetration of the interior. Many of these nations were subjected to imperialistic exploitation, and rail lines were built to the interior in order to establish and maintain military control. Gandhi once characterized the network of British-built railroads in India as iron chains that bind the nation. Indeed, the 200-mile-long railroad from Madras to Bangalore runs relatively straight without linking even some of the major nodes that would have required only a small deviation from the straight-line short path.

The second motive for interior penetration stems from the notion of complementarity. Since many underdeveloped nations contained mineral resources that were in demand in the mother country but unavailable there, access was

Figure 6-3 Network development in the context of coastal penetration

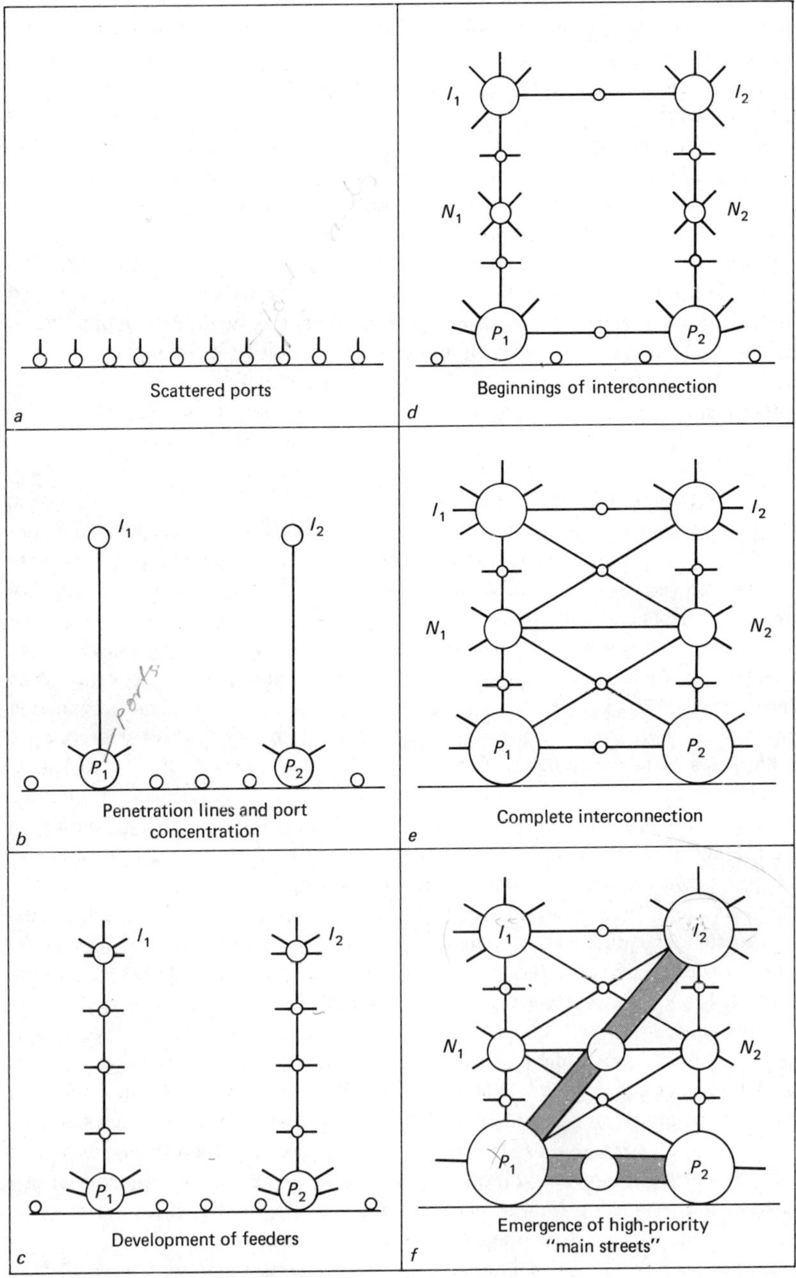

created to the resource areas, linking them with the ports and thereby with the outside world. In this way, railroad links were built to the tin mines in Malaya and the iron-ore ranges in east central India.

The third motive, also involving complementarity and like the second one somewhat exploitative, led to the linking of ports with areas that had a potential for cash crops for which there was an export market. Thus, linking rice-growing areas was given low priority in contrast to linking areas where coffee, cacao, and other plantation crops could be grown. In Sri Lanka, the road network is much denser in the hilly tea-growing areas, in which some of the roads required engineering feats, than the network in the flatter rice-growing north-central province.

In the third stage, diagramed in Figure 6-3*c, d,* and *e,* the major theme is one of the development of feeder routes and lateral interconnections. Some agglomerations emerge on the initial penetration lines, and, from these, small feeder routes reach out. The interior centers I_1 and I_2 become larger, and a lateral connection is developed between them as well as between P_1 and P_2. Thus, the disjointed trees become a more fully connected network or Hamiltonian circuit. The development of feeder routes can also be visualized as a diffusion process, in which the density of the road network decreases with distance from the major agglomerations and the high-density area spreads outward through time. Just as much as there was port competition in the initial phase, there is also competition between the interior nodes in the third phase, and it will be noted that N_1 and N_2 have emerged as the two larger places between the coast and the interior. These two nodes are halfway between P_1 and I_1, and P_2 and I_2, respectively. They may represent places at which an overnight stopover on a journey to the interior is convenient. Such an initial advantage is subsequently enhanced by the development of lateral and diagonal links, as is shown in Figure 6-3*e*. Although this phase may be drawn out, there is almost complete interconnection by the end of the third stage. In Figure 6-3*e*, it can be seen that there are diagonal links between N_1–I_2–P_2 as well as N_2–I_1–P_1.

The last stage, depicted in Figure 6-3*f,* is labeled by Taaffe, Morrill, and Gould as the development of "high-priority linkages." Since there is differential growth of both ports and interior nodes, inevitably some centers will tend to acquire a dominance over a substantial hinterland at the expense of other centers. The demand for transportation will be higher at these centers, as will the volume of movement between the larger centers. The consequence of these changes is that certain routes emerge as "high-priority main streets." In the model, these are the routes linking P_1 with I_2 and P_2. These routes now become corridors between two locations, with a high level of interaction between them. Consequently, nodes on the route also benefit and grow. In the United States, the high-priority link is between Chicago and New York, distinguished by the heaviest airline and railroad schedules, the largest number of roads, and the highest volume of telephone traffic.

Model of Network Development on a Bounded Isotropic Surface

Rather than collecting data pertaining to portions of the real world and then arriving at a generalized model of network development, it is possible to establish a hypothetical landscape such as an isotropic plane and then hypothesize the stages in the growth of a transportation network. This is the approach taken by Lachene (1965). Although his major purpose was to study the relationship between the geographic distribution of economic activities and transportation networks, his model of network development is presented here. This approach is based upon plausibility and common sense, rather than inevitable logic leading to particular events and relationships. Therefore, questions such as, Why did this node or route develop here and not there? cannot be answered. Nevertheless, it is possible to argue that irrational human behavior may result in haphazard spatial patterns such as those developed by Lachene. Figure 6-4 is a sequence from Lachene as adapted by Haggett and Chorley (1969, 262).

In the first stage, the region is sparsely populated, and there is a low level of economic activity distributed more or less uniformly throughout the region. A network of trails or footpaths, requiring minimal levels of capital investment, constitutes the transport system. Assuming a rectilinear land-subdivision system, such as that in the midwestern part of the United States, the settlement pattern and the transport network both have a rectilinear configuration, as shown in Figure 6-4*a*. The total mileage of the network is the highest in this initial stage, but the capacity of individual link segments is quite low.

The second stage can be partitioned into two substages (Figure 6-4*b* and *c*). In the first of these, towns form at some of the intersections, owing perhaps to comparative advantage, resource endowment, or irrational decisions. One of the towns has a peripheral location, and Lachene suggests that it owes its preeminence to its bridgehead location with reference to the outside world. The interfaces between two different physical environments are often favorable locations for such bridgehead towns, for example, the forest-grassland or desert-savanna boundaries.

In the second phase of stage 2, a road network links the settlements, again following a rectilinear alignment, and in fact is superimposed directly upon the original trails. Some of the trails have become paved roads. Since the supply of capital acts as a constraint, the total distance of this paved-road network is smaller than that of the original dirt-road grid.

Lachene emphasizes that frequently route capacity exceeds the potential traffic or demand at the time when routes are built. Therefore, there is a low marginal cost to the provision of additional transportation services. Moreover,

Figure 6-4 Network development on an isotropic plane

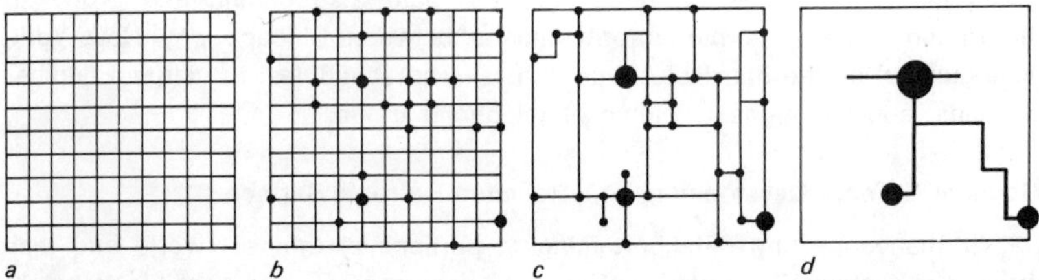

the expected life of routes, given proper maintenance, is almost unlimited. These factors create what he calls an "accumulator effect," and in the long run they influence the relative growth of nodes.

By the end of the second stage, owing to rural-urban migration, economic activity becomes strongly concentrated in the urban centers, and the gradual depopulation of the countryside results in the abandonment of some of the older trails.

In stage 3, the process of differential growth of nodes culminates in the emergence of three dominant urban centers. These are connected by a superior, more expensive route network, perhaps a railroad or a freeway. The total length of this network is the shortest of the entire sequence.

Ekström and Williamson (1971) also make use of a hypothetical approach to study the development of transport systems in time. In the *initial phase,* a new mode of transportation is established in space. In the *spread phase,* there is spatial diffusion of the network. This is followed by a *coordinating phase,* in which there is an integration of different transport networks and a reorganization of the production and distribution systems.

Two additional phases may emerge subsequently, after either the spread phase or the coordinating phase. These are (1) a *concentration phase,* in which there is a channeling of flows between certain terminals and relay nodes located at certain places, serving to give a well-defined but complex structure to flows, and (2) a *liquidation phase,* in which a particular mode of transportation disappears or is less used because it cannot satisfy the changing requirements of the space-economy.

In any given nation, different regions may be undergoing different phases simultaneously. Thus, from the national viewpoint, the passenger railroads in the United States may be undergoing a concentration phase, but this change may require that in certain areas the railroad service be liquidated.

The models described above are subject to criticism on a number of grounds. Any stages-of-growth approach, whether it be to the study of transportation networks, economic development, or whatever, risks the inherent danger of artificially partitioning what, in fact, is a continuous and evolutionary growth process. To the extent that all models represent simplifications, this danger may be unavoidable. However, in that the general conclusions are impressionistic, it is not easy to manipulate or test these models. Moreover, the stages are not equal in length to each other; nor are they readily identifiable. The exceptions may be the initial and the spread, or diffusion, phases. The fact that the first railroad was built between two nodes in a certain area at a specific date is readily verifiable. The subsequent rapid diffusion in the form of railway manias and canal booms has also been extensively documented in the historical record. Beyond that, the latter stages are very difficult to recognize, because the situational context is drastically transformed from simple to complex, and the stages, if they exist, seem to overlap.

Additionally, the Taaffe, Morrill, and Gould model is areally specific and applies to nations with a particular political history — those that were subjected to colonial exploitation. The nations in which the development of transport networks was studied, using this model, are tropical or subtropical coastal nations. The Lachene model, aside from being strictly a hypothetical one, applies to a restricted midcontinent region in a nation in which massive rural-to-urban migration has occurred.

These models, of course, do not accord with the real world facts, but it is not damning with faint praise to suggest that they offer considerable insight into the process of network development, albeit in a very simplistic manner. They also constitute an adequate framework within which to pigeonhole the movement-related facts of regional development.

SIMULATION MODELS

Television viewers of space shots and moon landings are familiar with videotaped clips in which there is a simulated picture of activities that are occurring simultaneously in outer space. If the caption "simulated" did not appear on the picture tube, few persons would recognize the fake for what it is. Simulations can be remarkably lifelike or, in some cases, clearer than life. Simulation models represent an attempt to replicate the dynamics of some selected facets of reality by employing substitute elements instead of real components.

In any simulation there is a systematic selection by which only a certain number of features are chosen for manipulation. While this selection is a characteristic of all models, in simulation, the dynamics of any situation can be explicitly built in. In addition, time can be collapsed or expanded, and the past, present, and future can all be considered. In an operational situation, a segment of time or generation is one computer run, and by means of successive iterations long durations can be compressed, much as in a drama. Thus, by their very nature, simulation models lend themselves to the study of the temporal development of transport networks.

After the elements that one wishes to study are identified, explicit rules must be established concerning the operational procedures and the relationships among the elements in the system being simulated. Computer models require the specification of formal rules as part of the program.

One class of simulation models, known as the Monte Carlo type, allows chance to play a role. Monte Carlo models have been widely used in as disparate fields as physics, epidemiology, and geography. In approaching the past, where many things are unknown, or in approaching the future, which contains many uncertainties, an appropriate modeling strategy is to conceive of both the past and the future as if random processes were and will be at work. This approach can be taken even though there may be grounds to believe that there are deterministic relationships among the elements of reality.

Simulation models enable repeated runs of a basic theme with minor variations on it. This flexibility and versatility allow us to test the impact of alternative combinations of circumstances. After calibrating a model by studying the past and acquiring confidence in the model, we can project and compare many futures, and the most desirable one, according to some standard, can then be selected. Simulation models have been used to study the location of links and the development of networks.

Simulation of Alternative Links

Before the Northern Pacific Railroad was constructed in the Pacific Northwest interior, several possible routes were surveyed. Each of these was technically feasible and was designed to satisfy some specific strategic objective of the builder. Figure 6-5 shows the array of proposed routes and those that were ultimately chosen. Meinig (1962, 413) suggests that intimate knowledge of the area concerned and detailed archival research would be needed to discover the basis of decisionmaking for each particular link segment of a railroad network.

An alternative approach to the problem of why certain nodes were connected and others were not can be formally stated: "Given a spatial distribution of *vertices,* and their incident *edges,* isolate criteria which will result in the replication of the graph being examined" (Black, 1971a, 283). Black conceived of the railroad network in Maine as a tree branching out from Portland, growing outward through time to connect outlying peripheral nodes. He first stipulated the variables that are relevant to the temporal development of a railroad network and the relationships among these variables. The result was the construction of a general link-location model, as follows:

$$\Gamma_{ij}{}^{(t+1)} = f\left[\left(\sum_{k=1}^{n} r_{ij}{}^{k}\, x_{ij}{}^{k}\right)^{(t)} - b(c_{ij}\, l_{ij})^{(t)}\right] + da_{hij}$$

where

$r_{ij}{}^{k}$ = net revenue obtained from shipping a unit of the *k*th commodity from *i* to *j*; this value, of course, varies from commodity to commodity

$x_{ij}{}^{k}$ = total amount of the *k*th commodity flowing from *i* to *j*

Figure 6-5 Network of constructed and proposed rail lines in the Pacific Northwest

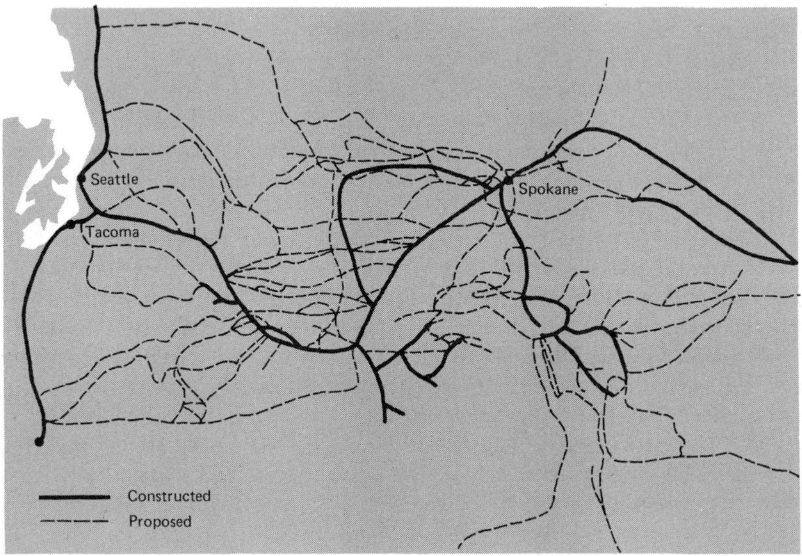

c_{ij} = construction cost of a single mile of track between i and j

l_{ij} = total track mileage between nodes i and j

b = a constant indicating the proportion of the initial construction expenditures which are to be repaid during the tth time period; this constant is determined by the amortization period and indicates by what time period a particular line segment will begin to pay off

a_{hij} = the cosine of the angle formed by adding the link ij to the existing link hi

d = a constant

$\Gamma_{ij}^{(t+1)}$ = 1 if its value is $\geqslant \lambda$, and 0 if its value is $< \lambda$. (λ is a discriminant score. If the value of $\Gamma_{ij}^{(t+1)}$ is 1, then a link has been constructed from i to j by time $t + 1$; otherwise, there is no link.)

This formidable-looking equation simply says that the presence or absence of a link between a pair of vertices at a particular time is a function of (1) the revenue obtainable from the potential ton-miles of traffic between a pair of nodes for a number of commodities, and (2) the construction cost of the trackage between that pair of nodes. These two are offsetting factors in the sense that the probability of a link's being built between a pair of nodes is directly related to revenue and inversely to construction cost. Accordingly, if a pair of nodes is close together, construction costs are low; and if expected flow volumes and revenues are high, then the probability of a link's being constructed is very high. A pair of remote nodes that are separated by rugged terrain and that have limited traffic-generation potential has a low probability of being linked. This probability will be somewhat enhanced if the expected flow volumes are high and/or the terrain conditions lend themselves to low construction costs.

Additionally, a constraint, in the form of the cosine of the angle, is built into the model to preclude backtracking, i.e., low-angle route branching. In developing a treelike network, ideally one would want to enlarge the reach of the branches outward in many directions. Backtracking involves building a link whose orientation is toward the original starting point (much like a downward hanging branch pointing toward the roots). If there are many instances of backtracking in a network, the overall link length will be so large that the initial budget would be exhausted before the tree had an opportunity to develop fully. Therefore, in this model links that branch out at a low angle have a low probability of being built.

Although the model incorporates the most important factors that enter into link-location decisionmaking, it is not operational. For most regions, systematic historical data are not available so that we cannot identify the k commodities, the amounts shipped, the respective origins and destinations, or the expected or obtained revenues. Therefore, Black operationalized the model by employing nine surrogate measures, such as distance from Portsmouth, New Hampshire, a potential-flow function, intervening opportunities, and the like. Using least-squares regression procedures, he correlated Γ_{ij} with each of the variables and combined the three best-fitting ones into an operational model. This model incorporated potential traffic (the population of j divided by d_{ij}), distance to the *j*th end node from Portsmouth, and the angular measure. The resulting three-variable equation for the first time period was

$$\Gamma_{ij}^{(t+1)} = 0.0001\frac{P_j^{(t)}}{d_{ij}} - 0.013d_{ij} + 0.150a_{hij} + 0.310$$

This equation was recomputed for each 10-year interval from 1840 to 1910, yielding values of Γ_{ij} as discriminant scores.

In attempting to classify phenomena such as towns versus cities or, in the present context, built links versus those that could have been but were not built, it is useful to have a means of discriminating among the classes so that the probability of misclassifying any given object is minimized. We want both to avoid "building" links that were not in fact built and, conversely, to promote the construction of links in the model that were in fact built in the real world. Using a form of the multiple regression technique, it is possible to compute what are termed "discriminant functions" and obtain a score for each of several observations, in this case, links. Such scores can be ranked and the median or midpoint used as a cutoff to discriminate between links that were constructed and those that could have been constructed but were not. In Black's case, a discriminant score of 0.235 segregated the 200 constructed links from the 1185 unconstructed links, with 80.6 percent efficiency — that is, any potential link that obtained a score of 0.235 or over was regarded as a constructed link in the model.

He then simulated the growth of the network as a tree. All links were added to the existing network, and no subgraphs were allowed to emerge so that excessive mileage of links would not be simulated. The 216 miles of railroads actually constructed between 1840 and 1851 were stipulated as a budget constraint, and this had to be allocated as link segments connecting particular nodes.

The simulation process was an iterative one in which at each stage (1) all possible links in a planar graph were examined, (2) the link for which the value of the discriminant score, $\Gamma_{ij}^{(t+1)}$, was the largest was built, and (3) its length was subtracted from the budget. Each iteration added one link, and the procedure was terminated when the budget was exhausted or, alternatively, when all discriminant scores were less than 0.235.

The simulated network is shown in Figure 6-6*a* and may be compared with the actual network shown in Figure 6-6*b*. Of the 50 nodes connected by the simulated tree, only 5 were not connected in the network actually built in Maine between 1840 and 1851.

Simulation of Circuits

In an earlier study, Kansky (1963) took a slightly different approach to the Sicilian railroad in that he did not build it up link by link, but rather constructed a model that would replicate the developed pattern as it existed in 1908.

He first established an axiomatic, or more precisely, semiaxiomatic, system of statements. These are not entirely verifiable because they are only partly based upon empirical observation. Further, some of these axioms contradict others. Nevertheless, Kansky's construct represents an interesting approach to the problem of network development. Axioms 3 through 9 (Kansky, 1963, 125–126) are restated below:

Axiom 3: All networks undergo an evolutionary process of structural change and become more complex through time so that "the network N_i which is prior to the network N_j in time is of a simpler structure."

Axiom 4: However, the nature of evolutionary process in some regions is such that, through time, some modes of transportation, e.g., canals, are abandoned, so that the later network is simpler.

Axiom 5: Simultaneous with the increasing complexity of networks is the enlargement of nodes, i.e., more people and more economic activity resulting in more movement, etc.

Axiom 6: In any given region, a subsequent network consists of a larger number of nodes and routes in comparison with the earlier network. Alternatively, if the number of vertices remains constant through time, at least one vertex becomes larger in size.

Axiom 7: The length of individual link segments in the network becomes progressively shorter through time as a result of the development of a large number of intervening nodes between two that are relatively far apart. As we saw in the Taaffe, Morrill, and Gould (1963) model, the creation of intervening nodes fosters the development of feeder routes (third stage).

Axiom 8: Through time, in any given region, the remote places, in contrast to those in the focus of economic activity, are the last to be connected. Therefore, later networks have a larger number of terminals (dead ends) than earlier ones.

Axiom 9: Through time, the number of circuits in a network increases so that there are a large number of redundant connections (four major highways between Washington and Baltimore) providing several alternative ways of traveling between a pair of nodes.

Kansky used the logical structure outlined above in conjunction with the graph-theoretic indices presented in Chapter 5 to develop a quantitative predictive model of network structure. Since there is a functional relationship between network structures and regional characteristics, we can write $(c_1, c_2, c_3, c_4) = (\beta, V, N) = T_S$, where the c_i are the regional characteristics, β is the beta index, V is the number of vertices, N is the mean edge length, and T_S is the transportation network structure. Thus, a definite group of transportation nodes has a definite probability of being connected by certain transportation routes. The regional characteristics treated were technological scale, size, relief, and shape. By fitting the observed value of measures of regional characteristics into a regression equation, Kansky computed the expected values of the Sicilian network as follows: number of railroad vertices = 16.48, beta index = 1.13, and average edge length = 17.62 miles.

Having empirically determined these network measures, he then selected the 16 settlements in Sicily which by 1908 would have been on the railroad network. The selection was effected by (1) the computation of population and income scores for each of the 30 major settlements, (2) the computation of

Figure 6-6 The railroad network of Maine in 1851: (*a*) simulated; (*b*) actual.

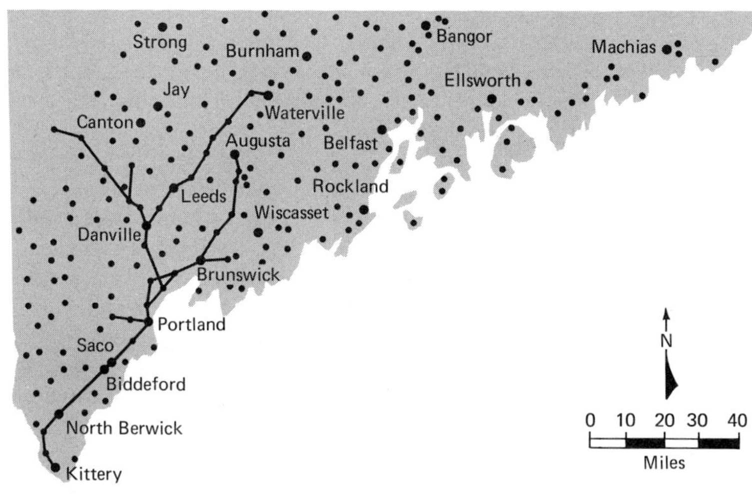

a

b

proportionate income shares, and (3) the assignment of simulation scores. For example, the town of Augusta's share was 0.57 percent of the total urban income, and it was assigned numbers from 00084 to 00140. Then, if in consulting a table of random digits the first number picked happened to be 00101, Augusta was assigned a railroad location. In this way, all required vertices were randomly selected. Since the range of simulation scores assigned to towns with larger incomes was higher, this insured that towns such as Palermo (05163 to 08878) had a near certainty of being picked.

Using the calculated beta value, Kansky then connected the two largest centers, as measured by population from those selected above. Then, he gradually added edges such that the next largest center joined the largest and closest center already located on the network.

The result of this simulation yielded an average edge length of 42.60 miles in contrast to the computed 17.62. The evident circuity was reduced by employing a *delta-wye* transformation, originally proposed by Akers (1960). Basically, this transformation assumes that three points, located in a triangular pattern, will be connected by means of a Y-shaped route rather than a delta-shaped loop. Akers suggests methods for this transformation.

Using maps showing topography, drainage patterns, and passes, Kansky made a further subjective change in the simulated railroad network, and the result shown in Figure 6-7*b* may be compared with the actual 1908 network shown in Figure 6-7*a*.

Garrison and Marble (1962, 86), after concluding that a pair of stochastic models designed to simulate the railroad network in Ireland did not yield adequately realistic results, constructed a deterministic model. They established a set of three rules to allocate links to a network according to the "field," "regional," and "neighborhood" effects that were described in Chapter 5. Each place was connected with its nearest neighbor in order to account for the neighborhood effect. This step resulted in a series of subgraphs. The second rule, to account for the regional effect, was to connect each subgraph to its nearest subgraph. Finally, the field effect in this experiment was restricted to Belfast, and it was required that each subgraph be linked to other subgraphs along a Belfast axis, with a 20-degree deviation allowed. Using these three rules, Garrison and Marble simulated the Northern Ireland railroad network.

A comparison of the actual with the simulated network showed some discrepancies, owing to a lack of consideration of field effects other than those centering upon Belfast. As Garrison and Marble note, the rules established were arbitrary, but nevertheless, they apparently enabled a fairly close replication of the network pattern.

In contrast to the approaches described above in which nodes are connected to each other because of their characteristics, Kolars and Malin (1970) used a broader framework which incorporated both point and area. Invoking Warntz (1966), they noted that transportation arteries occur on major ridge lines as defined by a population-accessibility surface. Accordingly, they constructed an isoplethic population map of Turkey, where each isoline represents 100,000 people within 25 miles. The peaks are connected by ridge lines which are the loci of points having the largest rural population within a day's journey by traditional transport modes, and consequently they represent optimal routes.

The first step in the simulation was the computation of an interaction potential between all pairs of peaks using the conventional gravity model, $I_{ij} = P_i P_j / d_{ij}^2$ (elaborated upon in Chapter 9). The lowest-order peak was connected to the higher-order peak with which it shared the greatest interaction value. This was repeated for all peaks in ascending order, and the results are shown

Figure 6-7 The railroad network of Sicily in 1908: (*a*) actual; (*b*) simulated.

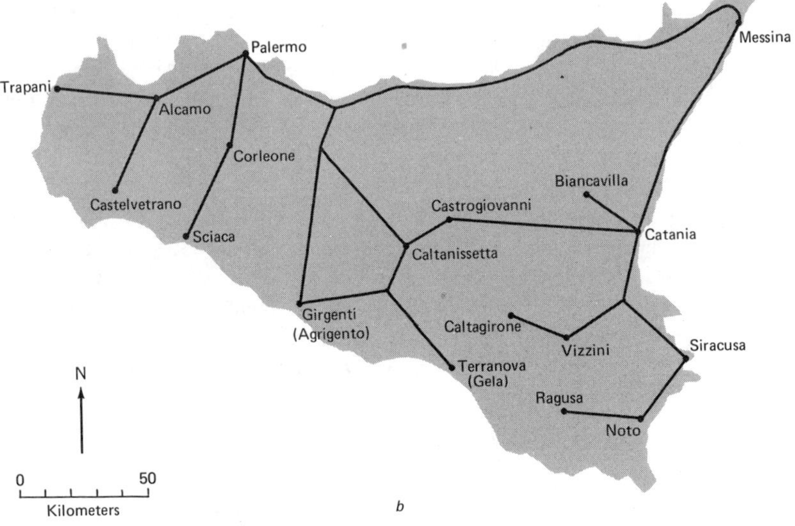

in Figure 6-8*a*. The correspondence between this network and the hierarchical network shown in Figure 5-9*b* is noteworthy.

Obviously, this network contains a number of redundant links, maximizing total network length. Therefore, in the second step, nearly parallel routes were eliminated by combining them into a single route, whenever a certain high-order peak was linked to several low-order peaks in roughly the same direction. The resulting rectified network is shown in Figure 6-8*b*. This network is still a tree and contains a number of dead-end nodes that the authors considered to be inefficient.

Therefore, in the third step, all the endpoints were connected to their nearest neighboring peaks, regardless of the values of I_{ij}. The result (Figure 6-8*c*) is a network consisting of nine loops which minimizes the point-to-point distances, even though closing the loops involves a greater total route mileage.

Finally, in the fourth step, the graph was converted to a more realistic railroad network by rerouting certain segments to follow intervening ridge crests between population peaks, natural passes, and the coastal lowlands (see Figure 6-8*d*).

Figure 6-8*e* enables us to assess the degree of spatial correspondence between the real and the simulated railroad networks. Numerically, the degree of correspondence was 67.1 percent. Kolars and Malin observe that their results substantiate the motivations for network development as proposed by Taaffe, Morrill, and Gould. Link by link, they categorize the motivations into four groups: administrative, agricultural exploitation, nonagricultural resource exploitation, and exogenous political origin. The vast majority of the routes had multiple motivations. Using knowledge of the region, they finally attempt to explain the discrepancies between the simulated and the actual in terms of rail lines both predicted but not present and present but not predicted. Exogenous political and military factors are believed to be the most important ones that account for the observed deviations.

It should be noted that Kolars and Malin, in their attempt to predict the spatial arrangement of links as it changed from 1860 to 1964, use the 1960 distribution of population as an independent or explanatory variable. This procedure is somewhat peculiar because, as we pointed out in Chapter 5, the development of transportation and the spatial aspects of economic development, including population distribution, bear a symbiotic relationship.

CHANCE AND NETWORK DEVELOPMENT

Vidal de la Blache once observed that men establish new relationships between scattered features. Just as no two individuals are carbon copies of each other, so also no two places are exactly alike in a literal sense. Each place has what we may refer to as "local conditionality" which, in the absence of human intervention, is a concatenation of circumstances. The result is somewhat like a conductorless orchestra in which all players insist on playing their own tunes. The role of individuals or society in this context is to institute a coherent system of interlocking forces that ultimately leads to a semblance of order. In this way, there is a human organization of space and there is no need to invoke any teleological or cosmic-order forces at work. Large-scale order at the macroscale can be the result of much indeterminacy at the smaller scale.

On the other hand, Curry (1964, 138) notes that while every locational decision may be optimal from a particular point of view, the resulting actions, as a whole, may appear to be random. Moreover, the vast amounts of physical capital in place (transportation and communication networks) have a locational stability which is greater than the individual components making up these networks. Their economic viability may be regarded as a function of the lag effect of individual decisions.

Early in this chapter, we referred to the notion of alternative futures. It is equally possible to speculate on alternative pasts. How many things that did not happen could have happened? From a given event *A,* the possible outcomes may be defined as a set $\{B_1, B_2, B_3, \ldots, B_k\}$. Why was the particular outcome chosen in preference to any of the alternative $k - 1$ outcomes? It is apparent that these are rhetorical questions that cannot be answered in a deterministic manner.

In view of the foregoing discussion, a probabilistic approach, using probability theory as a language, appears to be appropriate model conceptualization. We proceed *as if* events were random, even though we may have grounds to believe that the actors were motivated by such considerations as profit maximization. In the absence of good historical data, a great virtue of the probabilistic approach is that it amounts to an explicit admission of considerable ignorance (Curry, 1966, 611). We say, We don't know what happened, so let us consult a table of random digits and use it as a device to replicate the role of chance in real world decisionmaking. Of course, the various models presented above are not purely random. Although they may start with independent random variates, there are constraints in the form of angles, budgets, distance, population size, construction costs, and the like that can be built in to make the results fairly realistic. It is easier to build in constraints than to write the complex structural equations that would be required in order to describe the many ramifications involved in a human geographic process, such as that of the temporal development of transport networks. Thus, the notion of randomness is useful in cases where a range of possibilities exists.

One difficulty with this approach is that while a given set of premises contains logical consequences which are in agreement with reality, that fact by itself is no guarantee that a model is realistic (Curry, 1964, 146). Thus, it is quite possible that several different models may give the same result. Harvey (1967), in a different context, used such probability functions as the Poisson, negative binomial, and Neyman type A to test Hägerstrand's simulated diffusion patterns, and Harvey found that many of them did yield similar results. The discrimination among the different probability functions is not merely difficult but impossible in the absence of theory. Since each probability function has a mathematical process underlying it, unless we are in a position to match a physical process with a particular mathematical process, we lack the criteria to discriminate among alternative formulations.

In addition, the simulation of transport networks, as well as the simulation of other phenomena in human geography, has been confined to small areas such as Sicily, middle Sweden, and Maine. Therefore, it seems to us that this

Figure 6-8 Development of the Turkish railroad network: (*a*) lower-order nodes connected to higher-order ones; (*b*) parsimony of route length; (*c*) population centers connected to centers of highest interaction values; (*d*) railroad routes predicted on the basis of population-distance isopleths; (*e*) simulated railroad network compared with the actual network.

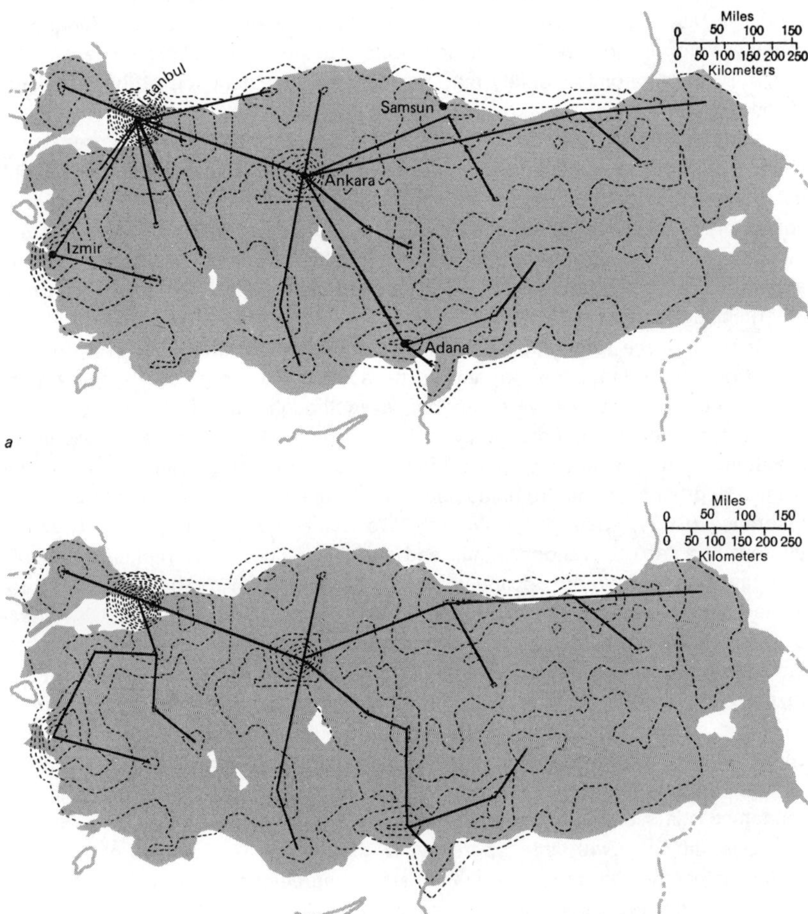

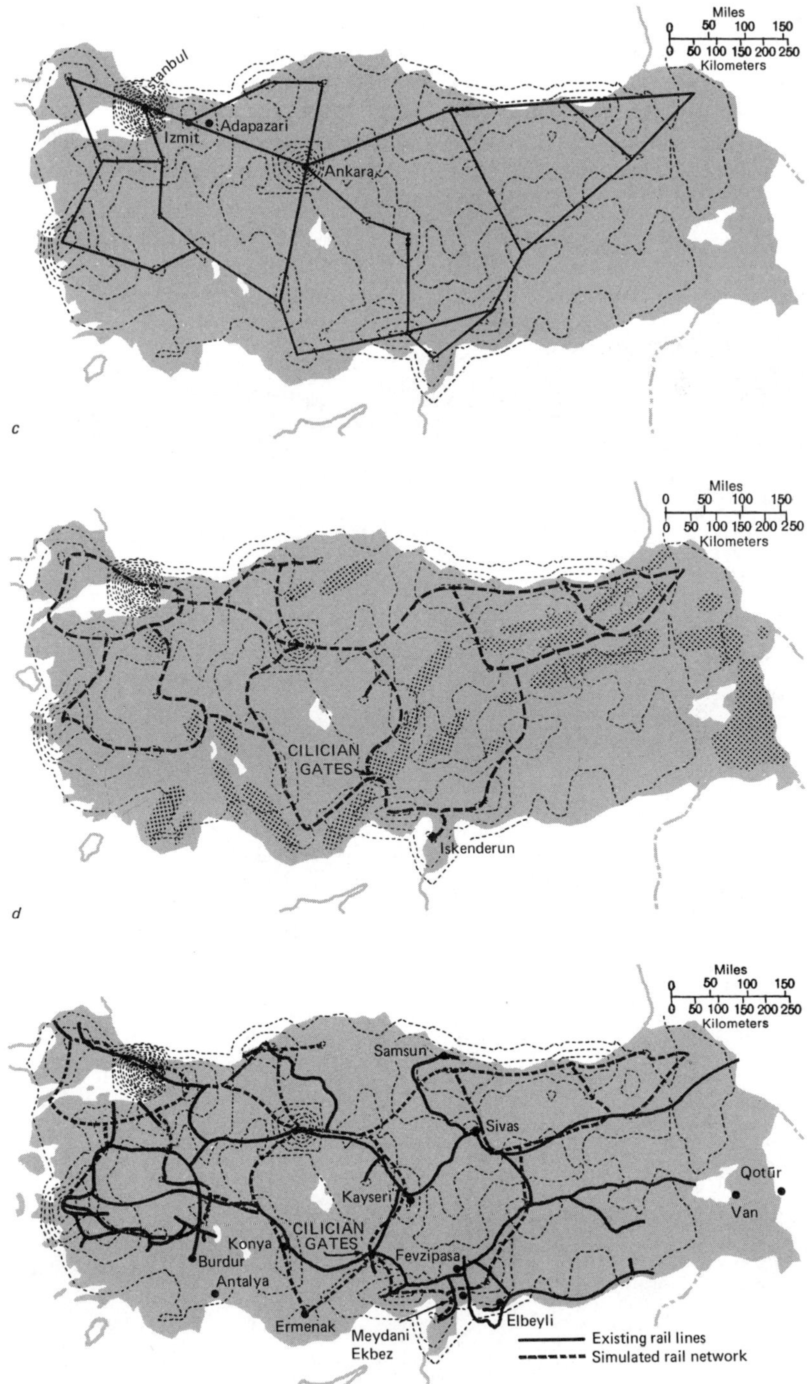
Miles
0 50 100 150
0 50 100 150 200 250
Kilometers
Istanbul
Izmit
Adapazari
Ankara
c
Miles
0 50 100 150
0 50 100 150 200 250
Kilometers
CILICIAN
GATES
Iskenderun
d
Miles
0 50 100 150
0 50 100 150 200 250
Kilometers
Samsun
Sivas
Qotūr
Van
Kayseri
CILICIAN
GATES
Konya
Burdur
Antalya
Fevzipasa
Ermenak
Meydani
Ekbez
Elbeyli
Existing rail lines
Simulated rail network
e

type of work can be properly evaluated only when the available models are expanded and elaborated to the point where a whole theoretical structure exists. In the meantime, as Curry (1964, 146) notes, exploration is all that is possible, and the models described in this chapter should be regarded only as pioneering attempts at understanding and opening up certain avenues of approach. As Thiele once said, models are to be used and not to be believed.

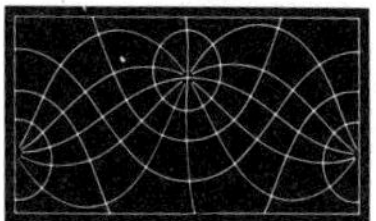

7 Propensity for Interaction

The major sequence in the last three chapters has been nodes, routes, and networks. Such a rigid spatial approach, concentrating on the elements of what may be called the "geometry of movement," has unfortunately but inevitably resulted in the exclusion of people. While undoubtedly the spatial behavior of individuals is affected by spatial elements, it is equally apparent that psychological, cultural, and socioeconomic variations among individuals play a role in the way that they interact in space. The propensity to interact manifests itself physically in point-to-point and area-to-area flows.

Before considering flows, however, it must first be understood that propensity for interaction can be illustrated in two important ways: (1) distance of contacts from an origin and (2) frequency of contacts at particular distances from an origin. The volume of contacts may be measured either in terms of repeated trips within a given temporal interval to the same location (5 trips a week from home to place of work, 4 trips a month to the grocery store) or in terms of a single flow of large volume (a person ordering 10 books from a publisher, a supermarket ordering 100 heads of lettuce from a warehouse). Flow maps showing volume of movement of persons, of products, or of information are cartographic portrayals of the consequences of interaction propensities.

TERRA COGNITA AND MENTAL MAPS

Since movement is purposive to a degree, we have to assume that an individual has either knowledge or the willingness and ability to search space. Obviously, he will have to know or find out the distribution of available opportunities for various purposes, e.g., the geographic distribution of bars and gas stations. As we shall see below, the search process is not entirely unconstrained, but rather there are certain prejudgments made on the basis of preferences and prejudices. Filtered, possibly distorted, images of reality result in patterns of both place avoidance and place preference. Word associations such as "darkest Africa," "the mysterious Orient," and "the Windy City" reinforce such prejudices and may influence modes of spatial behavior.

Space-searching is most conveniently accomplished with a map showing the relative location of objects of interest. The Washington Center for Metropolitan Studies has recently compiled data and published detailed maps showing apartment locations and rents, as well as the locations of single-family housing developments and their prices in the Washington suburbs. Such maps facilitate the selection of residential location, but they are somewhat rare, and individuals normally have to undertake a search procedure and code the results in a sort of maplike format. This mapping is quite different from that of geodetic cartographers, whose "objective" maps result from the compilation of data collected at particular locations measured according to cartesian coordinates. Assuming no human or machine errors, two topographic maps of the same portion of the world, at the same scale, made by two different cartographers would look exactly alike.

In contrast, individual space-searching and evaluation are usually undertaken with a private map on which information is not standardized, there are no conventional signs or symbols, and scale relationships are highly distorted. Such maps are based not on detailed surveys but rather on unsystematic and biased samples. The result has been called a *mental map,* which is a subjective image that is an integral part of our consciousness. Since we require not one map but several, on which different areas are recorded, we may speak of *mental atlases.* These serve the same purposes as conventional atlases — information storage and retrieval. Just as cartographic atlases vary in size from the *Penguin Pocket Atlas* to the five-volume *Times Atlas of the World,* the mental atlases of certain people are larger and more detailed than those of others. One by-product of geographic training may be the refinement and the expansion of one's mental atlas. When the need arises to look up a place, we use our mental atlas in the same manner as we would a dictionary or a conventional atlas and "flip" to the appropriate "page," depending upon whether our question of interest is worldwide (Where is the Plaines de Jarres?), regional (Should I move to California or Minnesota?), or intracity (Which are the crime-free areas in this city?).

The World

It is interesting to broach briefly the topic of "the known world" or terra cognita of the Europeans. "Cognized" territory, of course, implies that there is "uncognized" territory. While Babylonian tablets have been unearthed that show the location of some cities, the first map of the world was Ptolemy's map (A.D. 90–168). His "known world" extended through 180 degrees of longitude from a prime meridian to present-day China. Mountain chains are shown in imagined locations, and there is a gross exaggeration of the size of some islands such as Sri Lanka (Ceylon). Nevertheless, apparently there was a distance-decay effect to the accuracy of knowledge, and areas nearer Greece are shown more accurately than those farther away. Bagrow (1964) has argued that the mistaken conceptions of the configuration and the relationships between areas contributed to the long delay in attempting to reach Asia by circumnavigating Africa. The point is that routes cannot be charted unless both relative location and distances are known with some degree of accuracy.

During the Roman era, the status of cartography degenerated as mathematical geography, latitudes and longitudes, astronomical measurements, and projections were forgotten. However, the Romans were not entirely oblivious to the importance of relative location. They probably were the first to conceive of the "triptik" idea as is shown by the Peutinger table, a cartogram depicting the imperial highways on an elongated world map with military posts as major nodes.

In the Middle Ages, theological considerations influenced space perception. The Holy Land occupied an enormous area, and paradise was relatively far away at the top of the map. Given the great difficulties of long-distance travel in ancient times, the mere availability of maps, distorted though they were, did not automatically stimulate movement. Some hardy souls, however, did embark on long journeys on which they were aided or hindered by the varying accuracy of the maps they used. Finally, the known world was rather restricted in that it did not include the New World, thereby eliminating the possibility of travel to it.

Nations and Regions

Ancient and medieval cartographic ideas of the world were subjective. Today, at a national or regional level, subjective images are not often portrayed cartographically, although there are some well-known examples, such as the New Yorker's and the Bostonian's view of the United States.

Gould (1966) was the first systematically to study individuals' perceptions of geographic space. His major premise was that many of the locational decisions made by individuals are related to the differential evaluations they place upon various portions of their potential action space. Thus, migration, industrial location, and other aspects of spatial behavior must be understood in the context of the various mental images of an area. In his studies, Gould asked students in beginning geography courses at the state universities of California (Berkeley), Minnesota, Pennsylvania, and Alabama to rank the 48 conterminous states of the Union in order of residential desirability. The resulting data were subjected to principal components analysis in order to partition the total variation in space preferences into (1) that portion representing a general or common viewpoint applicable to all the respondents in the given sample, and (2) a residual or unique portion applicable to a specific individual in the sample. In this way, individual preferences were filtered out, and the focus of attention was on group preferences. The resulting surface of general preferences varies primarily according to the location of the group of viewers, and thus there are maps of the United States as seen from California, Minnesota, etc.

The configuration of preferential contours on many of Gould's maps does occasion a measure of surprise. From Figure 7-1*a*, we can see that Californians sharply discriminate between Kentucky and West Virginia even though, in terms of objective socioeconomic conditions, there is little difference between them. The preferred area is the home region itself. Eastward, there is a steady decline

Figure 7-1 The view of the United States from (*a*) California; (*b*) Alabama.

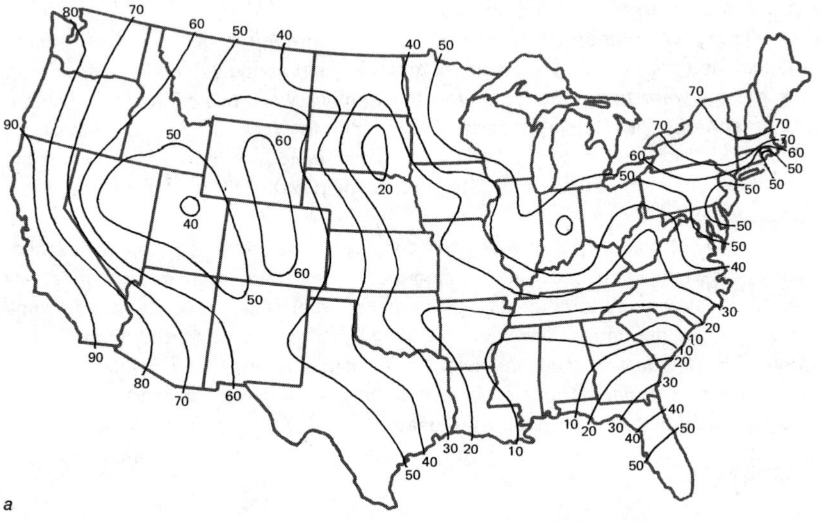

a

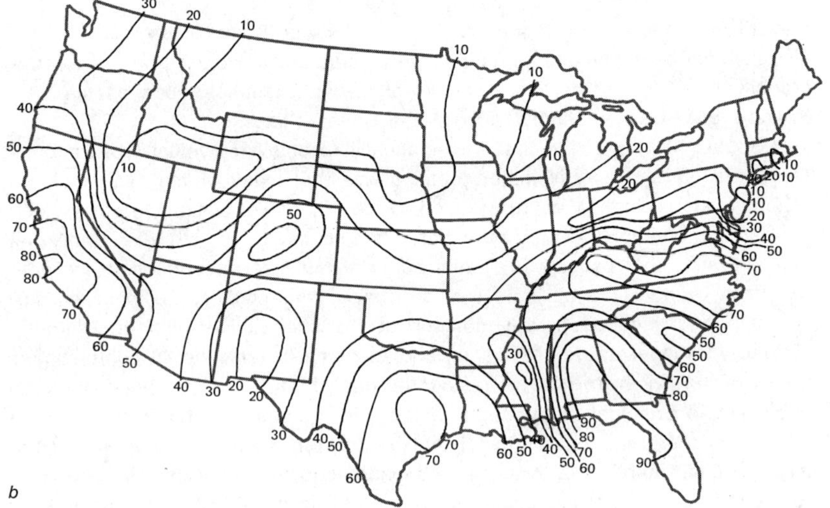

b

in perceived desirability, South Dakota forming a "sink," and thereafter the preferential surface rises toward New England, slopes down toward the Southeast, and rises again in Florida. Gould speculates that the image of blue-grass pastures causes Kentucky to be rated higher than its next-door neighbor and that the perceptual trough in the Deep South is due to Californians' image of civil and social unrest.

While there is only one objective United States, it is evident from Figure 7-1*b* that Alabamans' view of it is completely different from that of Californians. Alabamans rate their own state at the top, but whereas Californians tended to lump Alabama and Mississippi into the same category, Alabamans are keenly sensitive to differences at small distances from home. The level of information available concerning neighboring states is likely to be higher than that for more distant ones. North of the Mason-Dixon line, the perceptual surface falls off steeply, so that New York, Connecticut, and Massachusetts are rated low and discrimination is not significant among the various Yankee states. California, however, is highly preferred, despite the intervening distance, while New Mexico gets an unusually low rating in contrast to the neighboring states of Texas and Arizona. Such anomalies cannot be readily explained although Gould suggests that possibly the name "Mexico" conjures up an image to the white Southerner that produces its undesirability. Subsequently, Gould studied the mental images of individuals in Nigeria, Ghana, and England.

Certain general implications directly related to the propensity for movement appear to emerge from these parallel studies. For example, it is difficult to motivate bright administrative personnel to move to those back-country areas of underdeveloped nations which they view as undesirable. On the contrary, areas perceived as highly desirable, such as California, may continue to be destinations for interstate migrants despite the realities of smog, traffic congestion, and other negative environmental aspects. Also, mental maps are in part the result of the information flows to which we are subjected. To the extent that these flows are spatially biased, both our spatial perceptions and our propensities for travel are similarly biased.

The City

At the city level also, individuals evaluate the attributes of space and rearrange them in the form of mental maps. The outstanding work in this area is that of Lynch (1960), who by means of interviews, questionnaires, and sketches derived a synthetic "image of the city." Figure 7-2 shows the visual form of Boston drawn by a trained observer who used the concepts of city imageability as developed by Lynch on the basis of how people visualize their city. The major elements used by people to distinguish the contents of city images are as follows:

1. *Paths* are well-traveled routes such as streets, commuter lines, and railroads. Most of the observation of the city is done while moving along paths, so that these are the basic reference lines in relation to which the other elements are arranged.
2. *Edges,* although linear, are not considered to be paths by the observer;

Figure 7-2 A trained observer's generalized impression of the form of Boston

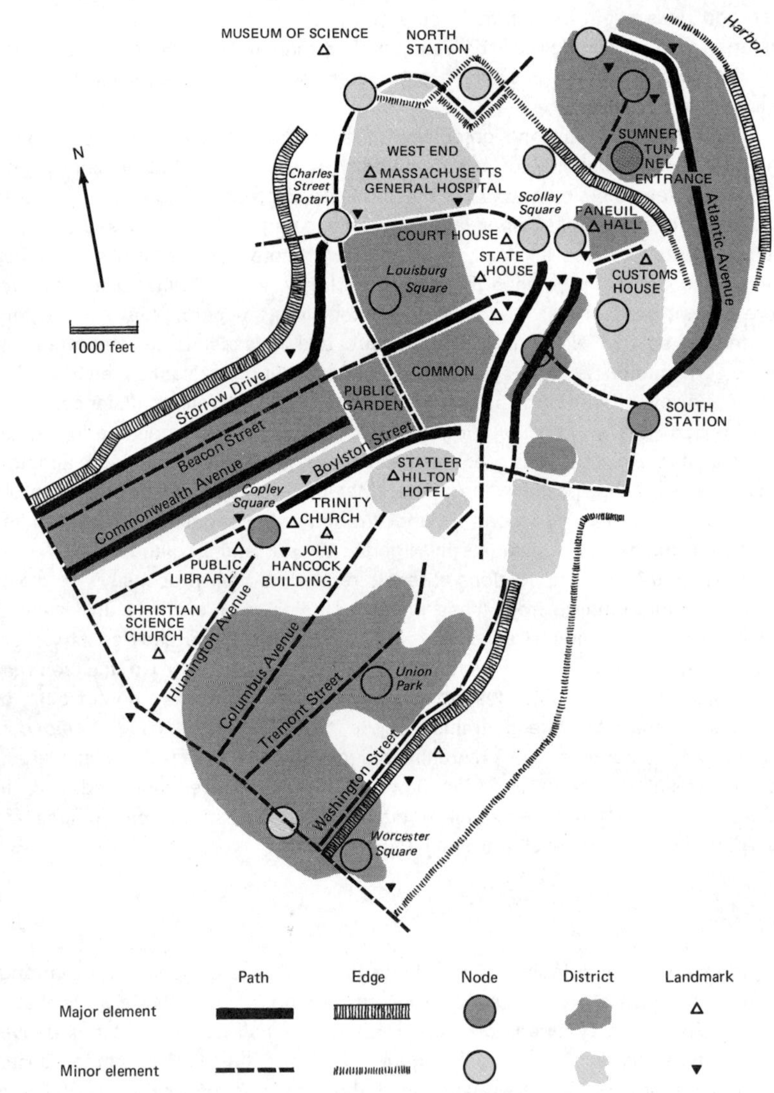

rather they are barriers such as railroad tracks or interfaces where two different regions are juxtaposed.

3. *Districts* are segments of the city which the observer enters "inside of."

4. *Nodes* are often the foci of transportation networks. Some nodes are also familiar meeting places where individuals congregate to exchange information.

5. *Landmarks* are reference points. Monuments, church spires, peaks of hills, and so on are some familiar examples of landmarks.

In particular, paths are the principal "resource" in the organization of imagery at the city scale. Nodes, as well as many landmarks, are at the major intersections and terminuses on the path network. Paths often bound districts so that in fact our images of the city are mainly molded by the view from the road. Klein (1967) confirmed Lynch's findings with reference to Karlsruhe and further suggested that well-traveled paths, especially those from home to work, contribute much to the formation of city images.

In Boston, interestingly, certain portions of the total urban space were gaps in the images of the respondents, and so we see that mental images not only deemphasize certain areas but also ignore some of them, giving rise to a Swiss-cheese-like spatial pattern. The ignored areas become virtually nonplace locations, and, consequently, a commercial business (e.g., clothing store) located in such an area may not be a popular destination in contrast to a similar establishment located within a well-recognized district. Further, not all city streets are perceived as paths even though, in reality, they are usable for city travel. In turn, this implies that traffic congestion is partly related to people's subjective notions concerning the preferred street segments or paths.

ACTION SPACE AND THE ROLE OF DISTANCE

The preceding considerations may lead to the hypothesis that human decisions concerning any activity are based upon a choice of alternatives or, more strictly, perceived alternatives. We have seen that these perceived alternatives are, on the whole, quite limited in range and spatial extent for any one individual. A direct consequence is that the spatial extent of that individual's location-related activities would be similarly spacebound.

In the short run, mental maps provide the outer limits of potential *action space,* which may be defined as that area which contains the majority of destinations of a particular individual. It is a subspace within the mental map and frequently tends to be discontinuous in the sense that between certain preferred areas there are some stretches of unknown, possibly undesirable, territory. The configuration of action spaces is frequently linear, especially in automobile-oriented societies. Moreover, from an individual's home base, the movement patterns that define the action space may have well-marked directional biases so that the elongation in one direction is offset by an attenuation in other directions.

The dimension of an individual's action space is a function of a number of variables. One determinant is the locational pattern of potential destinations. If each residential neighborhood in a city has one or more "Mom and Pop" stores as well as other types of businesses, then the neighborhood may be the dominant action space of an individual. Most wants can be satisfied within a relatively small area. On the other hand, if there are major regional shopping centers dispersed throughout a metropolitan area and if there are expressways connecting them with residential neighborhoods, an individual's action space would be much larger. These alternative spatial schemas have direct implications for mean distances traveled, and while the former is still characteristic of Third World nations, the latter is the familiar situation in the United States.

Time and cost budgetary constraints are other determinants of the physical dimensions of action spaces. Time is a finite resource which must be allocated among different uses. Thus, since movement, even by the most rapid mode of transportation, requires the expenditure of time for which there are other competing uses, individuals presumably try to maximize their return on the expenditure of time by adjusting their movement patterns and action spaces appropriately. Cost budgets influence the mode by which interaction occurs and, therefore, partly also the distances traveled. Personal action spaces are relatively small in size because most of the movement involves personal trips and because of the need to return daily to home base. However, by using the mail system, with its uniform national postage rates regardless of distance, a national contact field can be rather easily established. In the same way, relatively inexpensive long-distance telephone service enlarges the field beyond that of the daily commuting shed.

Regardless of the dimensions of the action space, in most instances the intensity of contacts decreases with distance from the home base. If a given area is densely populated, the mean distance of contact would very likely be low, but there still may be a decline in the volume of contacts with increasing distance from the origin.

Individual and Household Action Spaces

There are few empirical studies of individual movement patterns and their attendant action spaces. An exceptional worker along these lines has been the sociologist Chombart de Lauwe who was one of the first to introduce notions of social space in the literature. Figure 7-3 shows the movement patterns, over a period of 1 year, of a young woman living in the 16th arrondissement of Paris. The width of the lines is proportional to the frequency of travel from home to each of the many destinations. The pattern of movement in this real world example is largely conditioned by the location of particular destinations of this anonymous young woman. The intense triangular pattern, oriented eastward,

Figure 7-3
An example of individual action space in the real world

(Adapted from P. H. Chombart de Lauwe, *Paris et L'Agglomération Parisienne,* 1952, Paris: Presses Universitaires de France, p. 106, Figure 1.)

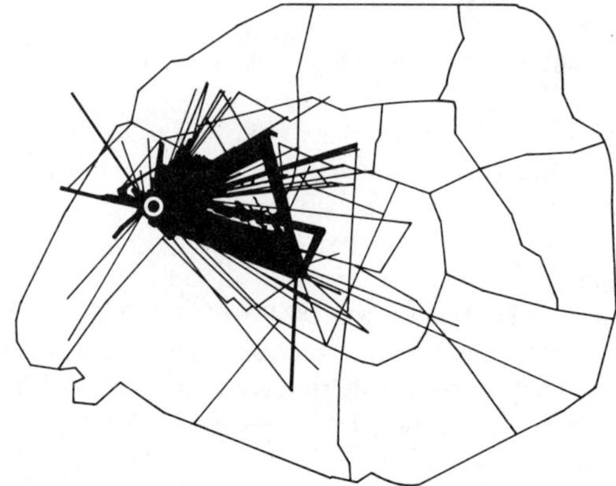

is the outstanding feature of the map. The vertices are home, the location of the piano teacher, and the college at which the young woman took courses in political science. Further, although there were occasional trips to other unspecified locations, few of these were to destinations outside the 16th arrondissement.

Figure 7-3 represents an individual's movement during 1 year for all purposes. In contrast, Figure 7-4*a* and *b* pertains to the movement pattern of all

Figure 7-4
Variations in contacts of members of households in Cedar Rapids, Iowa: (*a*) a household with a low level of contacts; (*b*) a household with a high level of contacts.

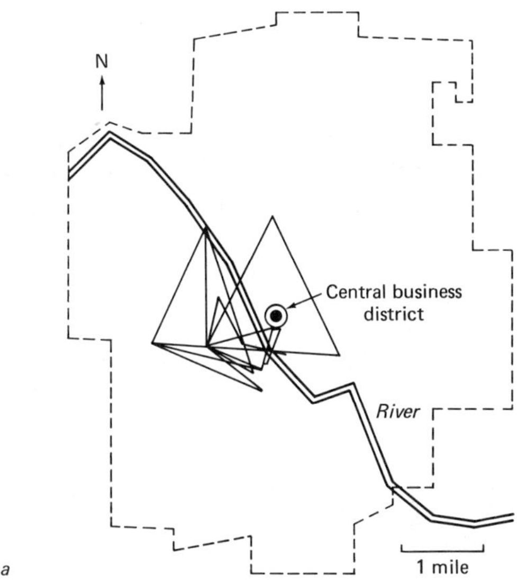

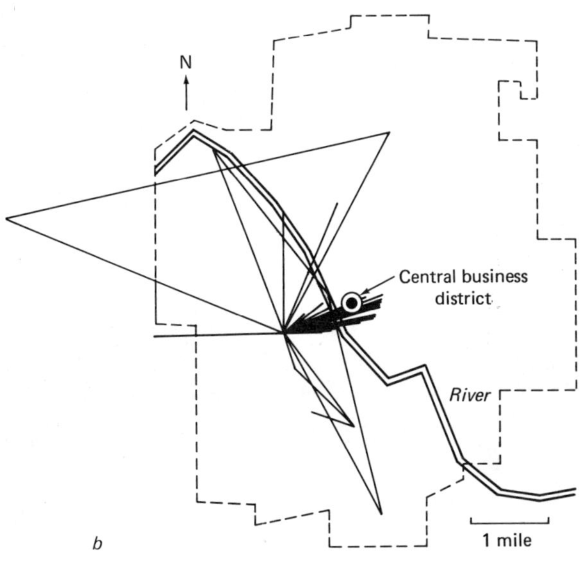

members of two sample households (except those related to work and education) during a 30-day surveillance period in Cedar Rapids, Iowa. Although these two households resided in the same part of the city, it is evident that the patterns of movement were quite dissimilar. The members of the household in Figure 7-4*a* made many fewer trips to the central business district than did the members of the household in Figure 7-4*b*. Marble and Bowlby (1968) suggest that the observed differences in those patterns reflect the influence of such nonspatial factors as the stage in the family life cycle and socioeconomic differences.

Socioeconomic Differences in Action Spaces

It is possible that the mapping of individual or household movement patterns may reveal differences that stem from more or less unique behavioral motivations. However, differences in destinations of a sample of individuals from two different and contrasting areas of a city can also be ascribed to the socioeconomic variations between the neighborhoods. Chombart de Lauwe used

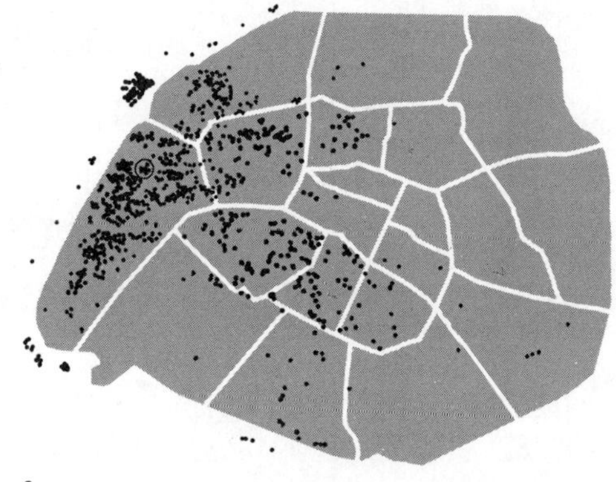

a

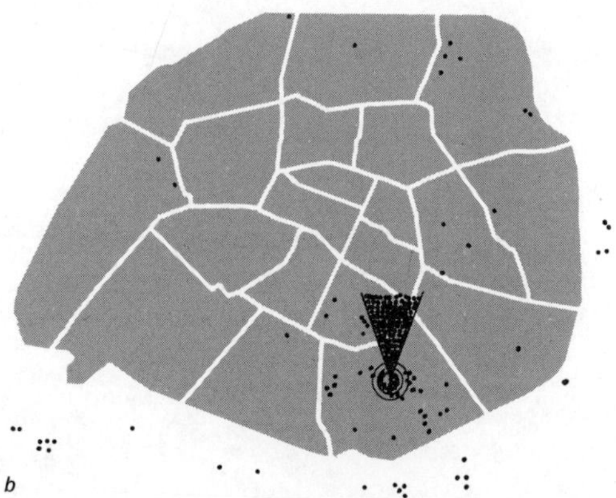

b

Figure 7-5
The social contact field of five families in (*a*) the 16th arrondissement in Paris, (*b*) the 13th arrondissement in Paris.

(Adapted from P. H. Chombart de Lauwe, *Paris et L'Agglomération Parisienne,* 1952, Paris: Presses Universitaires de France, p. 107, Figures 2 and 3.)

this process, and Figure 7-5*a* shows the locational distribution of contacts of the five families residing in the 16th arrondissement of Paris, a high-income, upper-class neighborhood. The contact fields of these upper-class families are widespread and not directly related to distance even though the largest number occurs within the arrondissement itself.

In contrast, Figure 7-5*b* shows the location of personal contacts of five families living in the 13th arrondissement, a low-income, working-class neighborhood populated by many newcomers from the provinces. Consequently, apart from their income constraints, they had not yet had time to develop a network of acquaintances, and the aggregate field of contacts is small in size and intensity. Further, most of the contacts are within the neighborhood in which the home is located.

Cultural Variations in Action Spaces

Chombart de Lauwe's maps exhibit the role of social and economic factors, especially that of income variations, on the extent of contact fields. Human variations are multidimensional, and, apart from social and economic factors, there are also cultural and other factors. Two individuals belonging to the same socioeconomic rank but to two contrasting culture groups may be expected to have different interaction propensities; consequently, their action spaces and location of contacts may also be expected to differ widely.

In order to understand how cultural variations affect store patronage, Ray (1967) studied a sample of farmers in southern Ontario that was made up of two distinct culture groups: French-Canadians and English-Canadians. He then collected data concerning their travel patterns to purchase certain specific goods and services. He found that for low-order convenience activities, especially food stores and banks, all individuals traveled to the nearest available opportunity. In contrast, for high-order services, especially those that required a measure of confidence and face-to-face interchange, both English-Canadians and French-Canadians were highly selective in their choice of destinations. They engaged in comparison shopping for medical and legal services, so that English farmers, for example, bypassed a nearby French doctor to go to a relatively distant English doctor. It would appear, therefore, that interaction propensities are not always motivated by the desire to minimize distance or the cost of overcoming it.

In a similar study, Murdie (1965) analyzed the differences between a sample of "modern" Canadians and old-order Mennonite farmers with respect to their shopping habits. Distances traveled were considered for eight functions ranging from food stores to dentists. For "traditional goods," e.g., clothing, shoes, harness repair, and yard goods, the Mennonites traveled to the nearest settlement where these goods and services could be obtained, while "modern" Canadians traveled to Kitchener, Ontario, the regional capital, bypassing nearer, smaller places (Figure 7-6*a* and *b*). For modern services, e.g., dentistry, there was no difference in observed travel behavior. In spite of the variations of action spaces among individuals and socioeconomic and cultural groups, it is possible to make certain generalizations concerning the propensity for interaction in a spatial context.

Figure 7-6 Travel patterns for traditional goods (clothing and yard goods) of (*a*) "modern" Canadians; (*b*) old-order Mennonites.

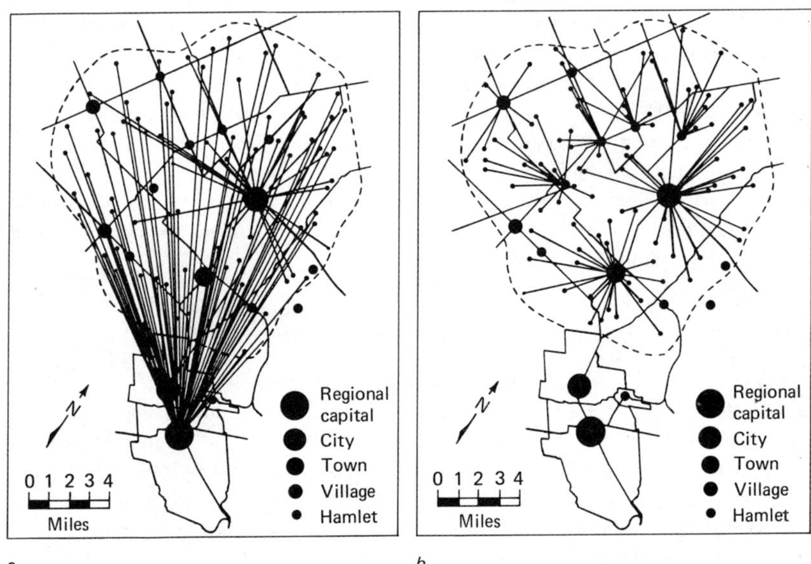

EMPIRICAL REGULARITIES IN THE PROPENSITY FOR INTERACTION

Hägerstrand has remarked, "Population is fluid and each individual has a moving pattern of his own, with turning points at his home, his place of work, shopping center" (Hägerstrand, 1957, 27). Each individual has his own field, variously called action space, "awareness space," "choice space," and so on, within which there is an intense pattern of movement. However, the study of the movement patterns of each individual in a metropolitan area, a nation, or the world is a physical impossibility. It is particularly the task of historians to study the biographies and the exhaustively chronicled movement patterns of individuals such as Ibn Batutta, Fa Hsien, Marco Polo, and other long-distance travelers. A hallmark of both physical and social sciences is the study of samples and, on that basis, arriving at inferences about some characteristics of the "statistical population." Since adequate generalizations cannot result from the study of the travel behavior of specific individuals, the preferred approach is to search for regularities in human behavior.

Distance-decay Functions

The most common approach, used to discover empirical regularities in the relationship between the volume and distances of interaction, begins with sets of data as shown in Table 7-1. In this table, space has been aggregated into distance bands to which the number of actual moves is recorded. Neither specific origins nor specific destinations are directly relevant in this aggregative context although, as Figure 7-7 shows, the pattern of contacts between

Table 7-1
Seattle, Marriage Distances

Source: Morrill and Pitts (1967, 408, Table 3). Reproduced by permission from the *Annals* of the Association of American Geographers, Volume 57, 1967.

Distance band in miles	Number of marriages
0–1	47
1–2	41
2–3	30
3–4	28
4–5	20
5–6	22
6–7	22
7–8	17
8–9	14
9–10	10

bride and groom produces numerous crisscrossing lines. Each line connects the home address of a particular bride with that of her groom. The hypothesis is that people select partners within a somewhat circumscribed area. Distances separating 251 groom-bride pairs are aggregated and tabulated by distance bands in Table 7-1. It will be observed that there is a consistent decrease in the number of marriages with increasing distance, the only exception being in the 4- to 5-mile distance band.

Spatial interaction data pertaining to different trip purposes have been organized in this manner for a number of areas. Figure 7-8 is a plot of the raw data concerning migration in the Cleveland area, number of contacts in

Figure 7-7
Lines of contact between pairs of brides and grooms in Seattle, Washington, 1962

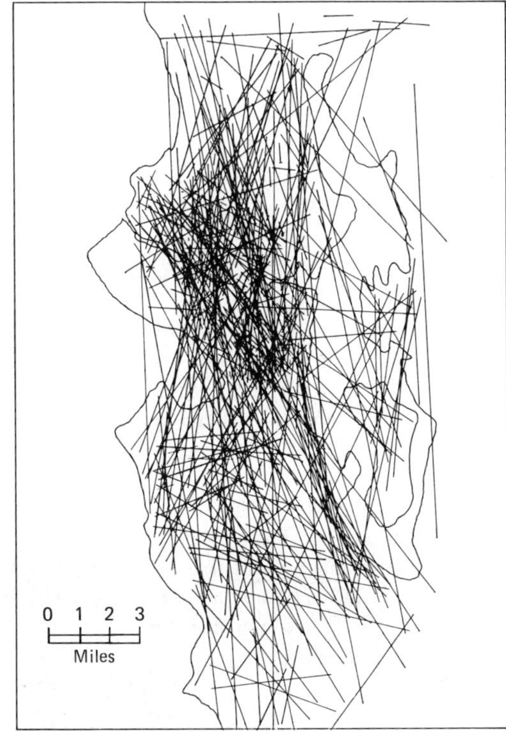

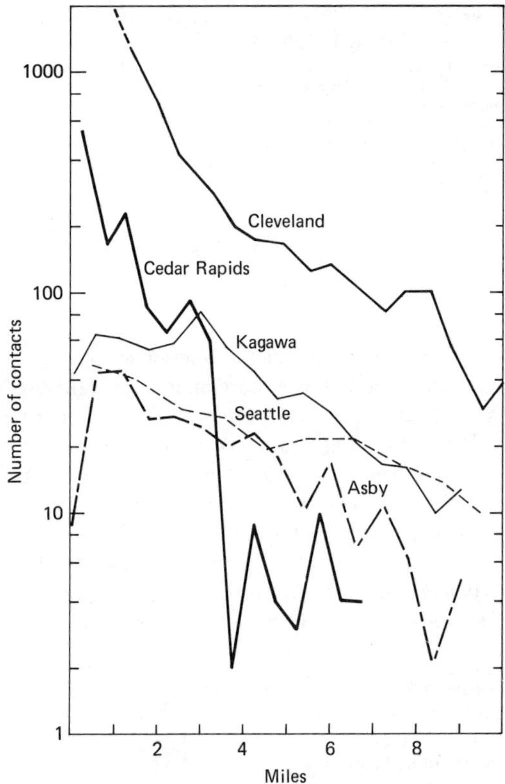

Figure 7-8
Volume of contacts, by distance, for selected areas and different purposes

Cedar Rapids, marriage distances in Seattle and in Kagawa, Japan, and both marriage and migration in Asby, Sweden. The five curves in Figure 7-8 have a general downward orientation in that the number of moving units, marriages, or contacts is greater at shorter distances than at longer ones. However, the lines joining the midpoints of the several distance bands are not smooth ones. The peaks and troughs are rather sharp, especially in the Cedar Rapids case, making it difficult to interpret the curves in a general manner other than by recourse to the possibly self-evident statement that interaction generally declines with distance. These general tendencies can be approximated by certain mathematical functions, so that a smooth *distance-decay* trend results.

Kulldorf (1955), Morrill (1963a), and Morrill and Pitts (1967) have considered in some detail the problem of fitting curves to observed movement-oriented data. While the fitted mathematical functions can be viewed as sophisticated descriptions of observed frequencies of contacts at varying distances, it must be emphasized that each function may have a different underlying generating process and set of assumptions.

Figure 7-9 shows the jagged actual frequencies of migration and marriage in Asby, Sweden, as well as the smoothed exponential, pareto, and pareto-exponential functions. Before plotting them, the data pertaining to

Figure 7-9 Actual and predicted moves per unit area in Asby, Sweden

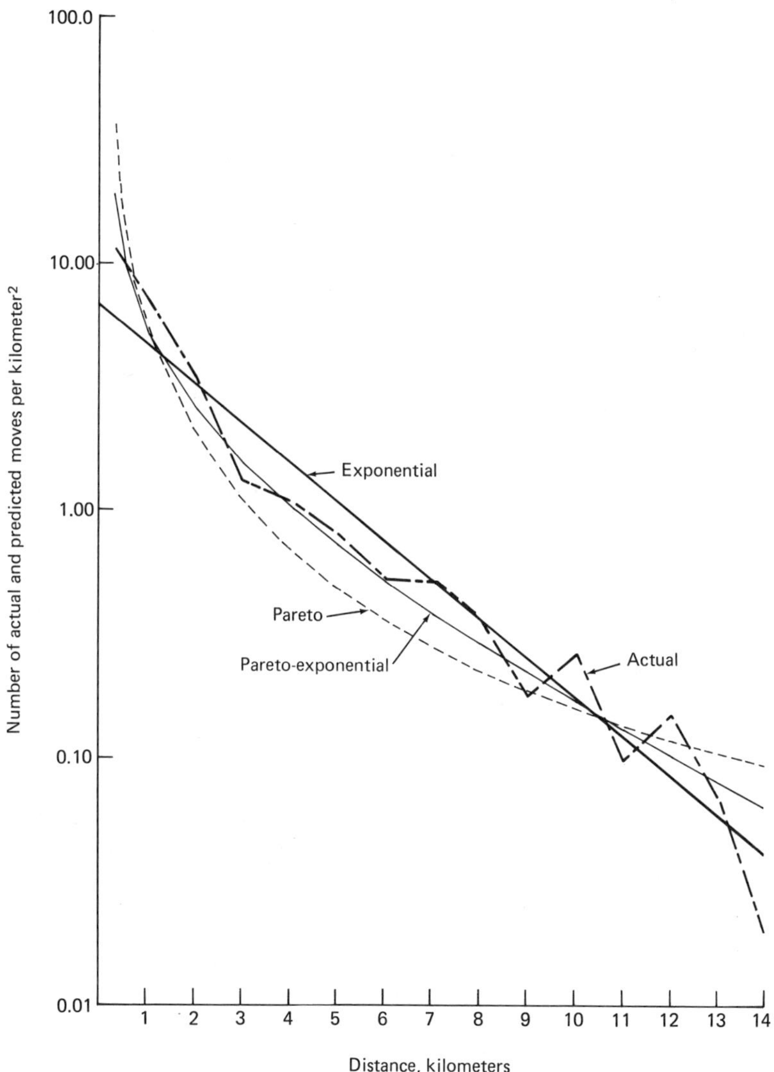

movement distances, such as those shown on Table 7-1, must be standardized by area. The area of any particular distance band, of course, increases with distance from a common origin. Since we are interested in analyzing the relationship between volume of contact and distance, it would defeat our purpose if we were to work with the raw data on the number of moving units by distance band. For example, in the Asby case, the number of moving units (marriage partners and migrants) in the 0.0- to 0.5-kilometer band was only 9, but when standardized, the moving units per square kilometer were 11.39. In the immediately adjacent distance band (0.5 to 1.5 kilometers) the number of moving units was 45, which turned out to be 7.17 per square kilometer. We see, therefore, that despite the increase in the actual number of moving units, as between these two distance bands, the movers per unit area declined with distance from a common origin. It is with reference to these standardized values that a variety of curves can be fitted. The most commonly fitted curves are described below.

The pareto function is of the form $y = ad^{-b}$, where y is the computed volume of interaction at a distance, d is distance, and a and b are empirically derived parameters. This function is generally useful in cases where there is a large volume of contact at very close distances, although it tends to grossly exaggerate contacts at these distances. Thus, while there were only 11.39 contacts per square kilometer in the 0- to 0.5-kilometer distance band in the case of Asby, the pareto function predicted 28.5 contacts, an exaggeration of about 300 percent.

The exponential function is of the form $y = ae^{-bd}$, where e is the base of the natural logarithm, 2.7183. Its use is appropriate in cases where successive moves on the part of either one individual or several individuals within a small unit area are strongly correlated with the length of such moves. However, in contrast to the pareto function, the exponential function grossly underestimates short-distance contacts. On semilog graph paper, the exponential function is a straight line, and it can be seen from Figure 7-9 that the origin of this line is considerably lower on the vertical axis than the actual number of marriages and moves. In terms of predicted frequencies, the exponential function yielded a value of 4.87 per unit area in the closest distance band, or about half of the actual number of moves.

In view of the errors of estimation produced so far, the pareto and the exponential functions may be combined into a pareto-exponential function of the form $y = ad^{-b}e^{-cd}$, where a, b, and c are parameters that must be empirically estimated. This function seems to yield relatively good fits in cases where movement is partly purposeful and accidental. Although there are other more complex functions such as the chi-square and the more general gamma function, these are difficult to work with compared to the ones just described for which the relationship between distance and frequency of moves may be obtained by standard least-squares regression procedures.

For the Asby data, the linear forms of the function and their derived parameters for unit areas are as follows:

Pareto:
$$\log y = \log a - b(\log d)$$
$$y = 6.26d^{-1.585}$$

Exponential:
$$\log y = \log a - b(d \log e)$$
$$y = 6.8e^{-0.365d}$$

Pareto-exponential:
$$\log y = \log a - b(\log d) - c(d \log e)$$
$$y = 6.55d^{-0.8}e^{0.18d}$$

Distance-decay functions using any of the above formulations can be computed on the basis of both moving units per distance band and moving units per unit area in each of the distance bands. However, different numerical estimates of y may result in the two cases.

For any distance, the number of moves, marriage contacts, or whatever can be computed, and appropriate curves can be fitted. The volume of movement predicted by the equation and the derived curves may then be compared with the known actual frequencies for goodness of fit. An appropriate test for this purpose is the Kolmogorov-Smirnov test (Siegel, 1956), which shows whether two frequency distributions are "significantly divergent" from each other, a condition which is, in turn, indicative of whether the pair belongs to the same population.

Instead of fitting a variety of curves to a given set of data in a hit-or-miss fashion, it is more logical to think through the underlying processes involved in movement and then to select the most appropriate function. In this way, real world physical meaning and interpretation may be obtained. Most data in this area of interest — for example, the location of those who have moved from a certain origin — will tend to be highly leptokurtic, i.e., the actual frequencies are greater than expected at small distances as well as at large ones. The constraints of time and distance as well as the nature of daily routines restrict many of our movements to short distances within a small area around the home base. However, the concentration of population, e.g., the spatial pattern of metropolitan areas and the locational distribution of economic activities, produces an opposite bias as well, in that some moves may be over greater distances than one might anticipate. For example, if we observed the migratory behavior of a sample of households from Peoria, Illinois, and plotted a frequency distribution, we might well find that the majority of the moves were to nearby locations, especially Chicago, and faraway locations, such as Los Angeles, rather than to intermediate locations, such as Denver and Minneapolis. This distribution could be explained, in part, by relative size and attraction of these possible destinations.

The Mean Information Field

It must be emphasized that the distance-decay concept is one of the most general concepts in human geography. Further, it does not matter whether we are considering individuals or groups. The frequency of moves considered in the previous section represents an aggregation of movers in terms of both a common origin and distance zones, although the specific origins of each individual mover may have been different. Thus, for example, one individual might have moved from Washington to New York, and another from Madras to Bangalore. The intervening distance in both cases is about 200 miles, although both origins and destinations are very different. On a worldwide basis, a sample of movers who migrated over distances of 10, 100, 1000 miles, etc. can be studied and a curve can be fitted, irrespective of origins and destinations. The resulting function would still be a negative one, and propensity to move would decline as intervening distance increased.

For an individual, the frequency of contacts at various distances from a specific home location also follows the same pattern. Generally, the action spaces and distance-decay functions of various individuals are quite different.

The action space of individuals for whom distance is a tight constraint can be described by steep curves. In contrast, the action space of individuals whose behavior is only loosely constrained by distance can be described by flatter curves. Therefore, it is possible to think of a whole family of curves, describing the generic behavior of numerous individuals, as well as that of an average individual.

Any distance-decay function can be rotated 360° to yield a cone of interaction resting over a circular area. Figure 7-10*a*, *b*, and *c* shows the steps in the derivation of a *mean information field* from a distance-decay curve. This field indicates the probability of the number of contacts at various distances on the part of an average individual located at the center of an isotropic plane. This probability refers to accumulated frequencies of contacts.

The mean information field treated here is a private or personal one in the sense that only face-to-face contacts are diagramed, not those by mail, telephone, and other means of communication. It represents the most important portion of an individual's action space. Since circular areas cannot be partitioned into regular subareas, squares are frequently used to record the number of contacts to particular unit areas at different distances from the locational origin of an individual.

THE CONCEPTS OF MASS AND MASS PROPENSITY FOR INTERACTION

If the phenomenon located at the center of the mean information field represented not an individual but rather a household, the resulting spatial pattern of the frequency of contacts would still be the same. The numerical size of the interactions would, however, be different. Assuming equal propensities for interaction among individuals, we may multiply by the number of individuals in a household (or the number in a high-rise apartment building or in a city) to yield the number of contacts at specific distances from the origin.

The action space around an individual household, apartment, city, or perhaps even a nation may be compared to a field around a magnet. Just as the reach of a magnetic field is a direct function of the power of the magnet, individual and urban contact fields are also direct functions of their force or gravitational pull.

Figure 7-10 Derivation of the mean information field

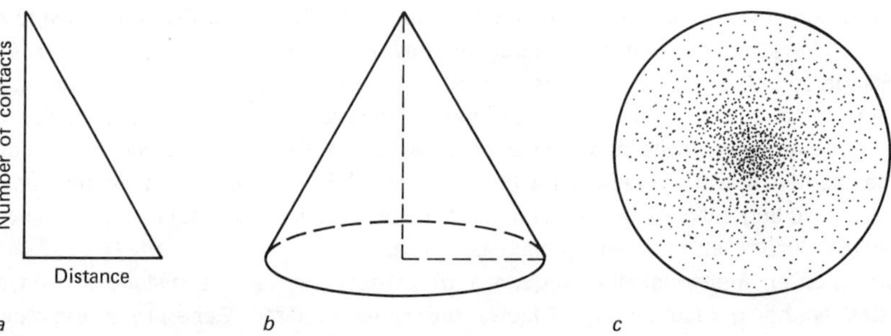

Carey, as long ago as 1858, suggested an analogy between man and molecule. In a well-known statement he said, "Man, the molecule of society, is the subject of Social Science. . . . The great law of *Molecular Gravitation* [is] the indispensable condition of the existence of the being known as man . . . . The greater number collected in a given space, the greater is the attractive force that is there exerted" (Carrothers, 1956, 94). Since Carey first drew attention to the possibility of this isomorphism, Ravenstein, Zipf, Stewart, and Warntz have made leading contributions to what is sometimes known as "social physics," in which social and physical phenomena are conceptualized as being subjected to similar sets of forces.

A key concept in social physics and its operational derivatives, including gravity and potential models, is that of *mass.* Single individuals are like molecules, and groups are aggregates of molecules. The focus of attention of social physics is on the aggregate rather than on its elemental components. The range of behavior of any particular individual particle may be not only unknown, but also unknowable. Consequently, the behavior of any atomized portion of a mass is unpredictable and subject to possibly aberrant behavior.

Brownian motion in physics suggests that the physical behavior of elemental components of matter is subject to random disturbances. Thus, the occurrence of an event can be predicted only in probabilistic terms. The limits of confidence, however, are relatively narrow and finite, at least in physics. The possibility of making errors in the study of the behavior of matter is considerably diminished if larger aggregates are considered. In that case, certain stable relationships may exist and predictable regularities may emerge. The trend in physics, starting from Boyle's studies of the effect of pressure and temperature on the volume of gases, has been to focus upon "wholes," i.e., masses of molecules, rather than upon any particular molecule.

Progress in the physical sciences, especially the discovery of numerous laws concerning the behavior of matter, has been made possible partly by concentrating attention on aggregates. In the same way, it is assumed that if human beings are regarded as existing in groups (that is, as a sociological mass), their intergroup interactions may be described and predicted with relative accuracy. This assumption of macrogeography may be a heroic one because, unlike molecules, individual human beings are decisionmaking units who are not subject to primordial natural forces in the same way as physical matter is. Nevertheless, it is possible to argue that in a large mass there is a sort of averaging so that individual decisions cancel each other out. Thus, we may speak of a "modal individual" (i.e., the most frequently found type of person). Since there are many such modal individuals, it may be argued that the impact of mavericks is negligible and may be ignored.

Unlike physical masses that are three-dimensional, sociological masses are conceptualized as being abstract, dimensionless, and identified as a point located on a two-dimensional *x,y* coordinate system. Further, there is some numerical value (a measure of the mass) located at that point. This mass exerts its influence over a geographic area on other masses located at other points, and this mass is also subject to the influences of these other masses. Sociological masses exert a gravitational force, and the interaction between two sociological masses is like that described in newtonian physics: the product of the masses divided by the distance between them (P_iP_j/d_{ij}, in which P is a measure of mass and d_{ij} is the distance between points i and j). As such, this force declines with increasing distance between the masses.

In social physics, the mass is considered to be greater than the sum of its parts. New York is not just composed of 11.5 million New Yorkers, but rather, by virtue of its functional importance and agglomerative nature as a mass, it exerts a greater pull over other masses than would be expected simply on the basis of its population size. On the other hand, smaller areas may have a lesser pull or gravitational attraction than would be expected on the basis of their population size alone. Evidently, the molecular weight of different individuals varies. In the geographic context, it may be said that the molecular weight is an individual's capacity for spatial interaction, that is, the propensity to move or cause things and people to move to the individual.

BEHAVIORAL DEPARTURES

The general notions of distance-decay functions, constrained action spaces, and the mean information field, as outlined earlier, are probably typical of most of the world. Especially in Third World nations such as China and India, where the most important mode of movement is pedestrian, are these concepts accurate reflections of real world patterns. Cost factors play a significant role in poorer nations, virtually prohibiting long-distance trips, except possibly for those that occur once in a lifetime. The locational system in these societies adjusts itself to short-distance movement, so that clustering of activities results. Stores and places of work are close to the home, as are the temple and relatives, a situation which leads to aggregate distance minimization. In terms of both intraurban or village movement and intraregional movement, the role of distance is a powerful one; it is the prime determinant of flows, constrained, however, by the uneven geographic endowment of resources.

In a worldwide context, the United States and other affluent, technologically advanced nations represent deviant situations. The widespread affluence, mass ownership of automobiles, and relative unimportance of transport costs in relation to the general price and income levels all result in patterns of movement in which the role of distance is decreasing, especially in the intraurban realm. People do not necessarily choose residences close to work; on the contrary, they sometimes live on the "other side of town" in order to obtain certain residential amenities not to be found near the place of work. With ever-increasing suburbanization and the concomitant large volume of trips from suburb to central city and suburb to suburb, the frequency of trips within a single urban area may have only a tenuous relationship to distance. The same is true in shopping, migration, and other forms of spatial behavior.

The difficulty of matching observed flows with expected flows has inspired attempts to manipulate distance in the context of extremely complex functions, including the quadratic, the gaussian, the chi-square, and the Fourier. These are very difficult to interpret. For example, Burch (1961), in a study of intercity person-trips (M_{ij}) with respect to five cities in North Carolina, fitted a quadratic equation to the observed data as follows: $M_{ij} = 0.04(P_i P_j / d_{ij}^2)^2 + 4.9(P_i P_j / d_{ij}^2) + 160$. In this equation, the quantity d_{ij}^2 appears twice because the quadratic is a convex function. The real world meaning of this equation is not readily apparent, and increasing disenchantment with this kind of curve-fitting has led some geographers to revert to the study of individual behavior.

Wolpert (1965) has observed that the prediction of interstate migration flows using gravity and regression models is less and less successful with each succeeding decade, necessitating selection of unique weights for each area, for distance functions, and for subgroups of both in- and out-migrants. "Plots of migration distances defy the persistence of the most tenacious of curve-fitters" (Wolpert, 1965, 159). The best fits for interstate migrations were obtained for 1935 to 1940, the period of the Great Depression, a time when unemployment was in excess of 29 percent, job opportunities at potential destinations were scarce, and cash was in short supply. Therefore, in the Depression era, interstate migrations were adequately explained by the intervening distance between the states of origin and the states of destination. What was an economic catastrophe in the United States is very nearly the normal situation in many parts of the Third World.

Another reason why interstate migration flows do not correlate well with distance is that the prime motivation for moving is to search for better economic opportunities. As Bunge (1966) has suggested in the "law of nearness," nearer things are more alike than more distant ones. The objective of moving from West Virginia to Kentucky to seek better job opportunities is not a very rational one, since better jobs are available in Texas and California. Therefore, complex distance functions are required to describe even these relatively infrequent moves, despite the difficulty of attaching physical meaning to complex functions.

At a microscale, the relationships between movement and distance become even less clear, and the problem of predicting point-to-point volumes of flow becomes more intractable. For example, Marble (1959) studied the movement behavior of 100 households during a 2-week period in Cedar Rapids, Iowa. For the purpose of this study a "trip" was defined as a movement which has both its ultimate origin and destination at home. Movement from home to work to shop to home is counted as one trip in this study. In conventional origin-destination surveys, this journey would be counted as three trips. He computed trip frequencies (except for the purpose of pleasure driving and visiting friends) for each household and attempted to predict these in light of 14 independent variables, by incorporating all the variables in a regression equation. He concluded that trip frequencies are not related strictly to the location of retail activities in the city. He also analyzed the relationship between total miles traveled and residential location; again, very low levels of statistical explanation resulted. Only 14 percent of the total variation in total distance traveled could be accounted for by the same model. Even at this low explanatory level only three variables were significant: the distance to the nearest transit line and distance to the nearest high-order and the nearest low-order retail centers. In general, socioeconomic variables were of greater significance than distance variables in contributing to the observed variation in trip frequencies. Consequently, Isard's contention that space preferences are determined by social and economic factors exogenous to the spatial system would appear to be confirmed by the results of Marble's study.

The elements of consumer space preference were categorized by Huff (1960), who argued that each individual has a particular space preference, defined as a desired level of social contact, so that when he is placed in the same spatial context as another individual, he may behave differently (see also Isard, 1956). Among the elements included were *desideratum,* which is a consumer's readiness to secure an object that satisfies his needs aroused by some stimulus or physiological drive; *value system,* which is affected by such elements as ethical and moral code, income, occupation, and mental synthesizing abilities; and *movement imagery,* which is a hypothetical construct in the mind of the potential mover who envisages possible paths, modes, and attendant costs to reach a particular destination. Huff constructed a connectivity matrix of all these elements as well as others, powered it, and was able to rank the elements in terms of order of contribution to space preferences.

In the same vein, Rushton, Golledge, and Clark (1967) applied the economist Samuelson's "revealed preference theory" to study shopping behavior in Iowa. Their contention was that individuals apply a subjective preference function to real alternatives (in this case, the actual locations of grocery stores, movie theaters, banks, etc.). A comparison among alternatives leads to overt behavior that can be observed as a trip. In order to obtain an understanding of "revealed space preferences," they compared the ratio of possible to actual grocery purchases in towns of various sizes and at varying distances from the location of the residences of a sample of persons. Their major conclusion was that large centers attracted relatively more grocery purchases than smaller ones, as long as the towns were below 6000 in population, seemingly a critical size and functional threshold. People preferred to shop in a town with a population of 5000 rather than one with 4000, but they did not discriminate between a town with a population of 6000 and a town with a population of 10,000. Since it is not necessary to travel to a town of 6000 people just to buy groceries, even in Iowa, the inference is that individuals travel to higher-order centers in order to combine grocery purchases with other purposes that cannot be satisfied in low-order centers.

Since many existing planning models of trip behavior yield poor results, Marble and Bowlby (1968) observed that there is a need to develop an understanding of individual travel behavior. If two households located in the same part of Cedar Rapids (see Figure 7-4), or any other city for that matter, exhibit contrasts in spatial behavior, the inference is that nonspatial factors are playing a major role in their movement patterns. They examined these differences in light of two factors: (1) the "opportunity set," that is, the locational alternatives, and (2) the degree of repetition with which particular locations were visited. Repetitive behavior is to be expected, especially in connection with the purchases of standardized products and convenience goods. For a sample of 116 households, it was found that the mean number of stops (99.8) for the members of a household over a 4-week period included 85 locationally repetitious stops. Repetitious spatial behavior becomes stable after some time and may be interpreted as the culmination of a search process. Initially, a newcomer to an area has to learn about the opportunity set by trial and error, with a view to satisfying his subjective place-utility function.

Olsson (1967) has observed that Huff's ideas concerning individual consumer space preferences may easily be translated into Wolpert's (1965) conceptualizations of place utility, the field-theory approach to search behavior, and family cycles. Wolpert, borrowing from the work of organization theory, has generalized some of the behavioral considerations outlined thus far in this chapter. He identified three important concepts:

1. *Place utility.* Each individual has a threshold of net utility that he evaluates in a binary fashion — satisfactory and unsatisfactory. In the context of migration, satisfaction leads to a decision to stay while dissatisfaction is a stimulus to move. An individual tries to match the utility at the existing location with expected place utility at each of several possible destinations. The role of information concerning the opportunities at the destinations is crucial to the evaluation process.
2. *The field-theory approach to search behavior.* As we have seen earlier, neither the world nor the nation nor the region can constitute the field of an individual. Action space is restricted, and individuals undertake a nonformal sampling approach to the search procedure. It is easier to sample (obtain information) from nearer locations than from more distant ones, and so information is generally spatially biased (a nonrandom sample). The mass media enlarge the range of sampled information, but they also provide more bits of information concerning larger and crisis-ridden areas rather than smaller and more tranquil ones. Further, one's position in relation to a hierarchical social network conditions the amount of information available so that company presidents, for example, are locationally more acute than junior clerks in the same company.
3. *Life cycle.* As a person grows in age and status, there are critical thresholds at each of which the action space and distances of contact change drastically.

In view of the various behavioral and other ramifications outlined above and on the basis of the location of opportunities, Schneider, a leading transportation planner, has concluded that "distance does not matter" (Berry and Horton, 1970, 541). At first glance, this is a thunderbolt that attacks the very foundations of physical and human geography. The importance of distance is almost an article of faith for a geographer. A number of geographers, dissatisfied with low levels of explanation produced by various distance variables in their studies of movement, have been prompted to incorporate socioeconomic and behavioral variables in an attempt to obtain higher levels of statistical explanation. There has been a concerted effort along these lines, and the studies discussed above represent an infinitesimal selection from what is a plethora of behavioral studies in this area of geography.

These studies raise a major question. In the absence of a spatial focus, emphasizing relative location and distance, what is the geographic relevance of any of these studies? If it is found that distance explains only 20 percent of the length of shopping trips in a certain city, the balance is a residual which may be more appropriately treated by a sister discipline for which the role of distance, in turn, is a residual. Quite apart from these parochial considerations, it may be suggested that those who deny the importance of distance have the obligation to show that distance-decay functions have a nonnegative slope (i.e., the value of b is equal to or greater than 0). Moreover, studies which have apparently demonstrated the negligible importance of distance have focused upon microdistances in an intrametropolitan context where the locational arrangement of objects overwhelms distance considerations. This relation may not hold at a broader scale and in many other nations. Therefore, we do not have to take recourse to either theological or parochial considerations to assert that, indeed, distance does matter.

INDIVIDUAL OR MASS PROPENSITY?

In the consideration of the propensity for interaction outlined in this chapter, two basic themes stand out. (1) Individuals minimize distances that they have to overcome in order to satisfy their wants. This tendency is called *efficient* or *optimal behavior.* The tendency to make a larger number of contacts at nearer locations results in consistent distance-decay functions that may partly be explained by time and cost budgetary considerations. (2) Individuals make locational decisions (i.e., where to shop, to play, to pray, and so on) in the context of psychological, cultural, and other behavioral considerations, resulting in *suboptimization.* In a sense, suboptimization can be considered a luxury available to richer nations and richer peoples. A poor man has so little to squander on wasteful travel that it may be presumed that he will quickly finish his search process and identify his nearest opportunities.

In view of the foregoing, there are two ways to study the propensity for movement and the resulting flows:

1. Study large-scale spatial regularities, using existing macroscale constructs such as the gravity model. Conventionally, this has been a rigidly deterministic framework although, as we shall see later, there are recent probabilistic variants. Existing constructs are, by and large, quite satisfactory despite the qualifications that have been entered concerning the impact of affluence. The utility of these macroapproaches is especially great in the study of aggregated large-scale flows between major agglomerations and interregional movements. However, the manipulation of distance exponents is often required, the technical aspects of which are treated in Chapter 9.

2. Every change of scale brings about the statement of a new problem. Therefore, large-scale model constructs should not be applied uncritically to small-scale situations where the role of the individual decisionmaking apparently is crucial. At this level (for example, intraurban residential mobility) the propensity for interaction probably is best analyzed by studying individuals as individuals, using behavioral postulates derived from psychology and sociology. To date, work in geography along these lines has been largely based on data, some going back to 1949, from what is possibly the most researched city in the world in this context, Cedar Rapids, Iowa. However, any lesson learned and findings obtained by such studies cannot be applied to other larger or smaller cities, even in the American cultural context. This restriction exists

not only because Cedar Rapids may be a biased sample or a unique case, but also because, as we have suggested earlier, New York City or any other agglomeration is more than *just* the sum of its individual parts.

Finally, Gould (1972) notes that even at microscales, the combinatorial possibilities are quite literally astronomical. For example, 10 people shopping at 4 stores (locational opportunities in an awareness or action space) can generate 1 trillion (1,000,000,000,000) possible travel configurations. Each of these may represent single, combination, and multiple sequences of shopping trips by these 10 persons. In addition to the combinatorial possibilities, the human being will probably be the last mystery to be unveiled, and at this juncture it is impossible to specify which properties of individuals are related to their spatial behavior as individuals. These considerations prompt Gould (1972, 694) to write: "Indeed, it should give a number of behavioral geographers considerable pause as they continue their headlong stampede to the individual level." Therefore, it seems to us that the only reasonable way to understand the generation of spatial interaction is via the use of macroscale (aggregate) models.

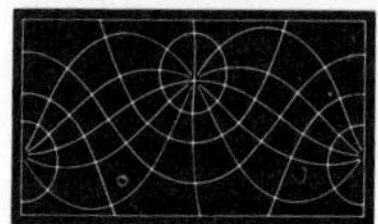

8 Nodal Characteristics as the Bases for Modeling Flows

Geographers focus their interest on movement of two basic types. One of these (for lack of better descriptive terminology) results in the areal spread of phenomena and is referred to as *spatial diffusion.* The other type of movement occurs among specified origins and destinations and is referred to as *flows.* Both diffusion and flows involve the locational transfer of people, things, and information.

While it is not easy to establish a distinction between diffusion and flows, some clues may clarify the differences. The former frequently involves the movement of intangibles, such as ideas, although once the intangibles have moved, the manifestations are clear enough. We cannot actually see communism moving and traversing space as we can see a coal train. However, when communism reached Cuba from the Soviet Union, we all knew that it had "arrived" at a particular destination from a specific origin.

Furthermore, in the case of diffusion, the question of time (rate) is more significant than that of volume. How fast an idea spreads is something that can be empirically determined, enabling us to mesh space with time. Unlike tons and liters, the flow of ideas cannot be measured in conventional units of weight or volume. The more relevant measurement of volume typically used is the number or proportion of a given population in a specific subareal unit that has adopted a given idea by a particular time.

In either case — diffusion or flows — the processes of spatial transfer are imbued with pattern, structure, and certain empirical regularities which may be described and analyzed by a variety of models. These models form the subject matter of this chapter and the ensuing Chapters 9 to 11.

All models require effort in data collection, and their use is contingent on our capability to manipulate them. The latter is partly a function of the available technology (both hardware and software) as well as the availability of a pool of expertise to make use of the technology. It is always useful to have at our disposal a kitbag of simple techniques or modeling strategies that enable a quick scan of the data to determine if some order can be recognized, if only in a preliminary manner. These quick-scan strategies are the major focus of this chapter.

In Chapter 9, we introduce more complex models that require a greater amount of information and a higher level of technical competence. The ensuing generalizations are also more sophisticated. Subsequently, in Chapter 10, flow structures are considered, and Chapter 11 is devoted entirely to the topic of diffusion.

FLOWS AND FLOW MAPS

Unlike the propensity for interaction, which is a somewhat inferred or derived concept, a spatial flow is an observable phenomenon which can be measured directly as the specific volume passing a point during a particular time interval. A familiar example is that of the flow of water, measured as cubic feet per second, which incorporates both volume and time. Traffic counters are analogous to stream gauges, and thus, in the case of human movement, a typical measure is that of vehicles per hour passing a particular intersection. Other examples of measures of human movements include number of arrivals or departures per day at an airport, number of long-distance calls between two points during a week, and tons of coal moving from one region to another per year.

The possibility of measuring the flow of phenomena does not imply the existence of such measures. Indeed, there is a woeful lack of flow data on a consistent, comprehensive, and useful basis, even in the United States. Economic censuses include a wealth of data on mineral and manufacturing industries and retail and wholesale trade, as well as selected services, in a spatially disaggregated framework. One can find out how many hogs there are in a specific county and how many car-wash establishments in a given city. However, despite the wide recognition that the circulation of people, goods, information, and money is what keeps a complex and integrated space-economy such as that of the United States functioning, there is no systematic monitoring of flows.

Those few flow data that are available in the United States include the following:

1. Airline, bus, and train schedules. As an example, airline schedules are conveniently released in a compendium available twice monthly, *The Official Airline Guide.* It is a quick-reference book, in which scheduled air carrier services are listed.

2. The Civil Aeronautics Board (CAB) publishes monthly volumes of air passenger movement between individual cities above a certain population size.

3. The volume and value of imports and exports by countries of origin and destination are published monthly and in annual summaries by the U.S. Bureau of the Census.

4. Many individual port authorities furnish data from bills of lading for

in and out commodity movement, enabling the study of cargo hinterlands such as those by Patton (1958) and Kenyon (1970).

5. The Interstate Commerce Commission (ICC) formerly published statistics on state-to-state commodity movement that were based on a 1 percent rail carload-lot waybill sample. Ullman's *American Commodity Flow* (1957) was based on this source. Unfortunately, the ICC has discontinued publication of the waybill statistics which pertained strictly to railroad movement. Even so, since increasingly larger volumes of freight are being carried by trucks, if one wished to obtain a complete picture of point-to-point commodity flows in the United States, one would have to piece together information from diverse and noncomparable sources.

6. For the periods 1955–1960 and 1965–1970, migration data from each State Economic Area (SEA) to each of the other SEAs have been published in special volumes by the U.S. Bureau of the Census. SEAs are made up of single or groups of counties so that each metropolitan area comprises one SEA. Consequently they may be regarded as economic functional areas.

7. Starting in 1963, a census of transportation has been carried out in the United States at 4-year intervals. While most of the data contained in this series are not amenable to spatial analysis, they do provide information on such matters as a state-by-state breakdown on the number of trucks by body type, size class, age, and mileage traveled, as well as their use. These data may be correlated with other information concerning each of the states. The Commodity Transportation Survey is based on a sample of bills of lading from the files of manufacturers rather than carriers. The resulting data are classified by commodity groups and geographic areas. These basic data, such as ton-miles by mode of transport, length of haul, and origin and destination areas, provide the raw materials for flow studies.

Apart from the kinds of data on movement enumerated above, there have been occasional surveys of which the most famous, by now possibly the most notorious, is that concerning Cedar Rapids, Iowa, referenced in Chapter 7. Nystuen and Dacey (1961) were able to obtain point-to-point volumes of telephone calls in the state of Washington. While their findings are reviewed subsequently, this type of study has seldom been replicated, owing to a lack of data, and therefore comparative generalizations are not readily possible. Metropolitan area transportation studies, such as the Chicago Area Transportation Study (CATS), are occasional and very expensive undertakings, and to the extent that metropolitan areas are constantly changing, the reported patterns of flows may quickly become obsolete. The lack of readily available movement data in the United States is aggravated by the fact that transportation services are performed by a multitude of private enterprises. Thus, in 1969 there were 1894 independent telephone companies, 1311 class 1 common and contract carrier trucking businesses subject to ICC regulations, numerous private carriers (for example, A&P supermarket chain), as well as 721 railroad companies. Consequently, the collection of unpublished data can be tedious and borders on the impossible.

The spatial structure of flows is the result of the spatial manifestation of factors introduced in the preceding chapters, including individual and mass propensity for interaction, the characteristics of nodes, the frictional factor of distance, as well as the nature of supplies and demands. One way to start the analysis of flows is to consider their graphic presentation.

Anything that is observable and measurable and has a distribution is also mappable. Figures 8-1 to 8-4 represent a sample from the wealth of maps in the geography literature, chosen explicitly with a view to portraying spatial flows of diverse phenomena at a variety of areal scales. Figure 8-1, showing tobacco shipments from the production regions of the United States, Brazil, Rhodesia, and India to the consumption regions of western Europe, illustrates the roles of complementarity leading to the orientation of flows. There is also a flow from Turkey to the United States, even though the latter is by far the largest tobacco producer and exporter, as is shown by the width of the flow lines. This carrying of coal to Newcastle, as it were, makes it possible to blend American tobacco with Turkish varieties in the manufacture of cigarettes.

Massive international labor migrations are also a function of both surplus at the source and deficits, or demand, at the destination. The differential in the prevailing wage rates between origin and destination acts as a further incentive to labor mobility. A distance-decay effect is more clearly evident in Figure 8-2, which depicts labor movement in Europe, than in Figure 8-1. This difference is due largely to the fact that in the transportation of commodities, the transport charge is borne by the producer. In contrast, in the case of labor movement or other forms of person-movement, movers usually pay their own expense; therefore, distance and associated costs are likely to have more of an inhibiting effect. Moreover, the constraints on the international mobility of labor are far more rigid than those imposed on commodities. It may be noted that the largest flows originate from Italy, long noted for its high and chronic unemployment, as well as from Spain, North Africa, Greece, and Turkey, all of which rank low on Berry's technological scale (Chapter 5). In contrast, the destinations, mainly France, Germany, and Britain, rank high on the same scale.

Figure 8-3 shows the movement of patients to physicians in western

Figure 8-1 International tobacco movement

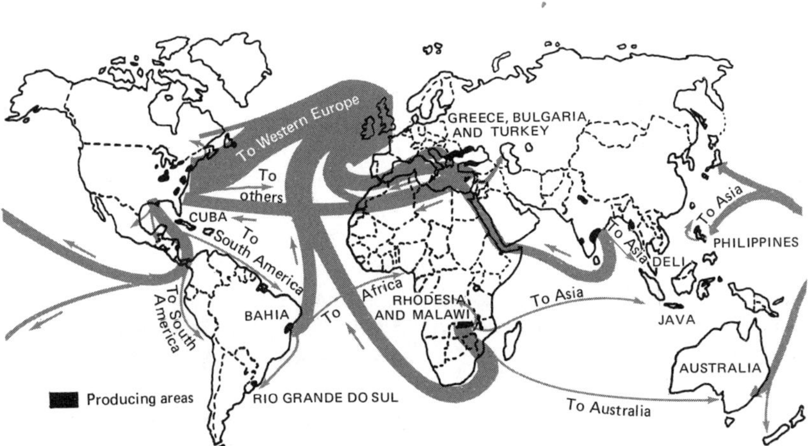

Figure 8-2 Spatial pattern of international labor mobility in Europe

From *A Geography of Mankind* by J. Broek and J. Webb, p. 503. Copyright 1968, 1973, McGraw-Hill Book Company. Used with permission of McGraw-Hill Book Company.

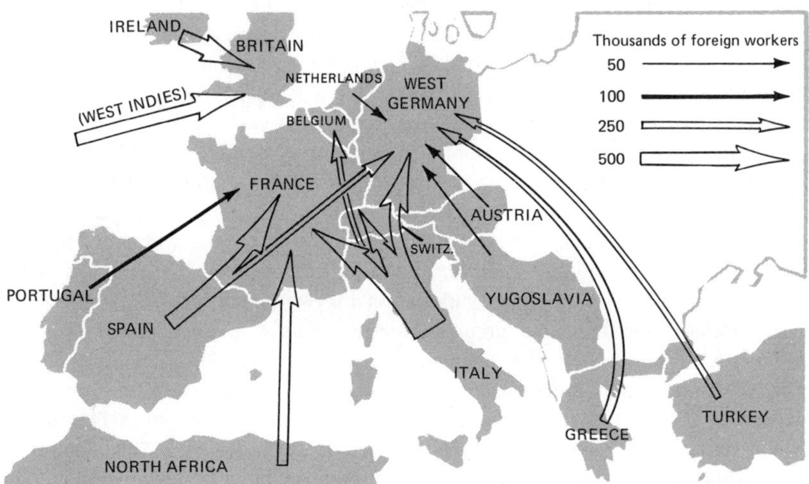

Pennsylvania. The dominant characteristic of movement is that it is from rural to urban counties, again illustrating the role of complementarity. While the counties that contain Pittsburgh, Cumberland, Elmira, Altoona, and Johnstown have a surplus of physicians, rural counties are characterized by a deficit. There is also a good deal of reverse travel across county lines which is due to the particular spatial distribution of both population (consumers) and physicians (suppliers). In certain areas, there is an imbalance between the geography of physicians and the geography of population, necessitating a cross-county movement of people to doctors. In addition, there is a certain amount of comparison shopping for personal services which was alluded to in Chapter 7 with reference to the spatial behavior of the Canadian farm population. Moreover, the configuration of the transport network, the highway system in this case, structures the accessibility of certain physicians in terms of certain patients.

Cultural and ethnic differences are also important factors that contribute to variations in both the volume and distance of movement. Figure 8-4*a* and *b* shows the flows of black and white employees to the Argonne National Laboratory. The locational origins of black employees are largely in the city of Chicago itself, as well as in lower Cook County, while whites come from a broader region, with only a few originating in the city of Chicago. The peculiar commuting shown on these two maps may be explained in part by existing patterns of residential segregation which may frequently prevent distance minimization. Also, the choice of residential sites sometimes leads to long-distance commuting in which desired amenities are traded for a greater transport cost.

Despite the differences in the areal scales among these four maps, there are three common elements present in each one: origins, destinations, and volumes of flow between them. Further, the notion of complementarity can be

Figure 8-3 Intercounty movements of patients to physicians in western Pennsylvania. Figures represent proportion of patients leaving one county for another.

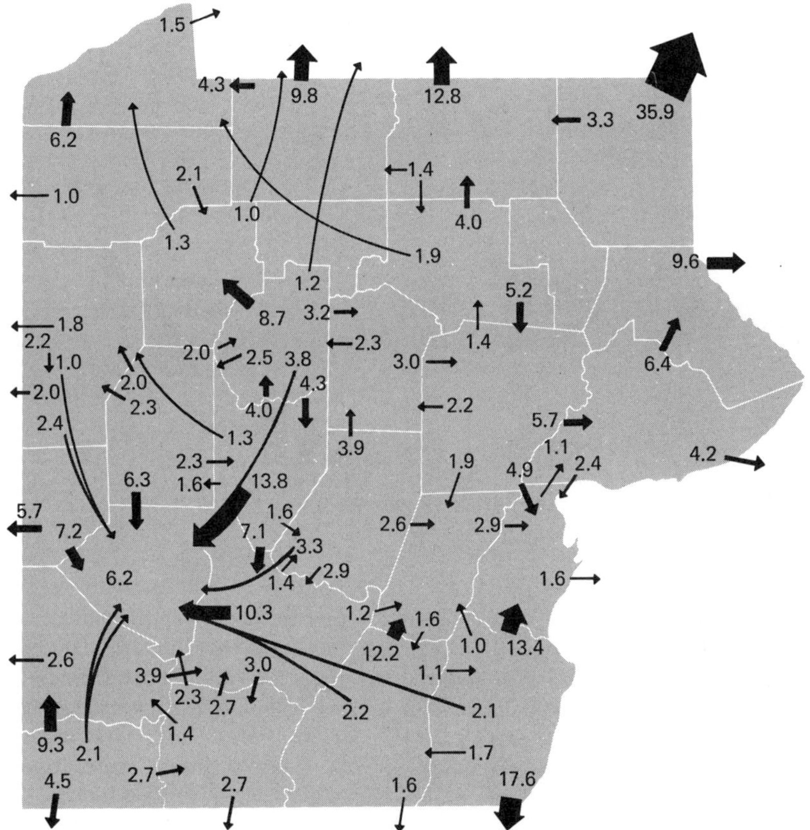

inferred from each map since the observed flows link supply and demand areas. The concept of complementarity, introduced in Chapter 1, can be specified to a certain degree, and Smith (1964) has attempted to do so with an analysis of flows of agricultural commodities to New England. By computing ratios of actual to expected flows, he obtained an index of complementarity. Specifically, he correlated predicted volumes of shipments of agricultural products to New England, using the gravity model, with the actual shipments. The predictions were based on the assumption that the volume of agricultural commodity flow between any one of the 34 non-New England states and New England as a whole would be (1) directly proportional to the product of the agricultural surplus of that state (supply function) and the population of New England (demand function), and (2) inversely proportional to the distance from that state to New England. For each state, the dependent variable represented the volume shipped to New England, weighted by that shipment's share of imports to New England. The division of the regression-predicted volume of flows by the weighted actual shipments yielded a measure

Figure 8-4 Flows of employees to the Argonne National Laboratory: (*a*) black employees; (*b*) white employees.

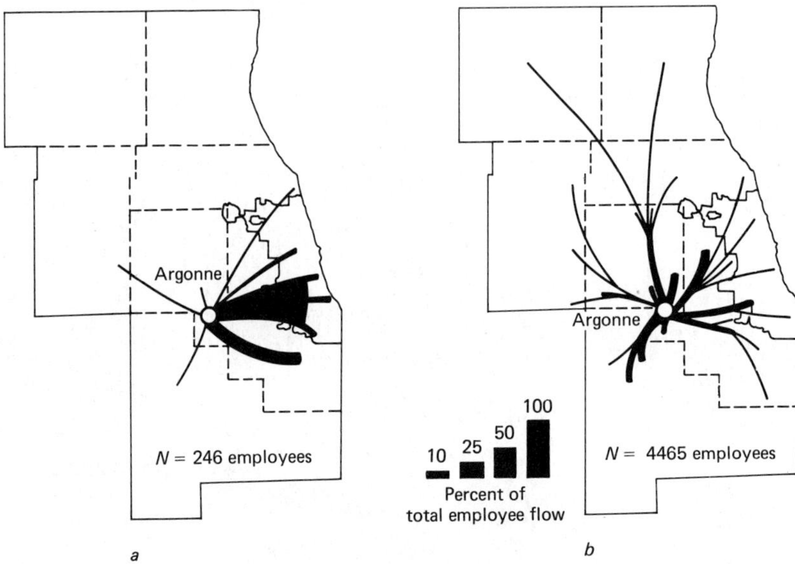

of complementarity. For Illinois, this measure was 10.1, which suggests that the 3108 tons of agricultural products sent from Illinois to New England were 10 times greater than was expected on the basis of distance and surplus, as well as the share of imports by New England accounted for by Illinois. In general, states nearest to New England had indices of less than 1; for example, the index for Maryland was 0.3, indicating that rail shipments were three-tenths of the volume expected.

FLOW TYPOLOGIES

It is possible to establish typologies in order to recognize some order in flow patterns. This grouping can be done in three different ways: (1) on the basis of distance, (2) on the basis of time, and (3) on the basis of both time and distance. The first two typologies are treated below, while the third belongs more properly in Chapter 11 under general considerations of diffusion processes.

The United States may be conveniently divided into three accessibility regions: high, intermediate, and low. Figure 8-5 shows accessibility contours of the entire U.S. national market by combined land and sea transport, specified as a percentage below that of New York City. For example, the accessibility of Chicago to the national market is 20 percent less than that of New York City, while Birmingham and Minneapolis have approximately the same degree of accessibility (35 to 40 below New York City). Miami and Oklahoma City have an accessibility value of 40 to 45 percent below New York City. The 25 and 40 percent contours may be regarded as the outer limits of areas of high and intermediate accessibility, respectively. All places to the west of the 40 percent

Figure 8-5 Accessibility to the United States national market, shown as a percent below New York City

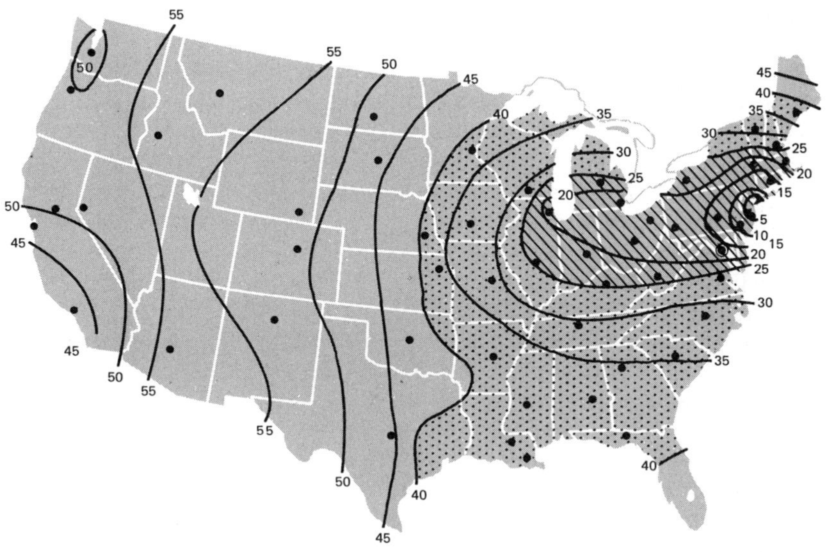

equipotential contour have low accessibility to the national markets (Pred, 1964).

With these considerations in mind, one may ask two questions:

1. What will be the locational orientation of a specific manufacturing activity? Weber (1929), one of the early contributors to classical location theory, classified manufacturing industries into three locational categories: transport orientation (either market site or material site), labor orientation, and "agglomeration-deglomeration." For our purposes, this categorization can be modified to (1) raw material and fuel, (2) market, and (3) labor and agglomeration.

2. Given these orientations, is there a difference in the characteristic types of flows generated by either material-, market-, or labor-oriented manufacturing industries, in each of the three recognized accessibility regions?

The combination of three accessibility regions and three types of manufacturing industry orientations yields nine potential manufacturing flow categories, which have been analyzed by Pred. While a detailed summary of this typology is out of place here, an illustrative example is useful.

The aluminum industry is well known for its material and power orientation, since the costs of bauxite, or alumina, and electrical power account for the major proportion of its total material input costs. By analyzing the cumulative percentage of total aluminum flows, classified by distance, for each of three states, Pred found that (1) 60 percent of the flows from Ohio (a high-accessibility region) were short-distance ones (less than 800 miles); (2) those from Louisiana (intermediate accessibility) had a high percentage of medium-distance flows (800 to 1599 miles); and (3) a high proportion of shipments by producers in the low-accessibility region of Washington state were over long distances (in excess of 1600 miles). The conclusion is that distant producers, while reaping the benefits of cheaper raw materials and power, have to ship their output over longer distances. One can extrapolate from this example and conceive of a wide-ranging typology of shipment of different products cross-classified by length of haul.

By their very nature, the movements of commodities and ideas do not usually experience periodicities. Obvious exceptions are strawberries, which are shipped in the summer, and the mailing of Christmas cards in mid-December. In contrast, many types of person-movement exhibit well-defined periodicities (Morrill, 1970, 135–140). We can classify the movement of persons as being temporary, transient, or permanent.

Temporary movements include (1) interestablishment interactions (home delivery of milk, a visit by the Fuller-brush salesman), (2) consumers shopping for goods and services, and (3) the journey to work. The last, owing to the spatial separation between place of residence and place of work, amounts to very large volumes of flows that exhibit a regular periodicity with peaks around 8:30 A.M. and 5:30 P.M. Lynch (1972) notes that to a large extent the smooth operation of a complex society depends upon the synchronized functioning of its individuals and its activities.

Transient movements include the following: (1) Military reassignment and rotation of diplomatic personnel. (2) Movement of migratory labor. In the United States, agricultural labor moves seasonally from the Mexican border northward along the West and East Coasts as well as the Great Plains, following planting and harvesting demands. (3) Movement to obtain a college education may last 4 years, more or less.

The permanent relocation of people is usually called *migration.* Some examples include (1) migration in search of improved economic opportunity (e.g., from Ireland to the United States or from West Virginia to Michigan); (2) migration for social and psychological reasons (e.g., movement of blacks from the rural South to urban areas in the North to escape overt racial discrimination); (3) migration associated with political and military turmoil (e.g., from India to Pakistan, and the flow of Jews from prewar Germany); (4) migration for retirement (e.g., to Florida or Arizona).

Although migration is usually considered to be permanent, in a highly mobile society it may actually be only temporary. On the average a U.S. resident moves 5 times during his lifetime. Three of these moves may be of relatively short distance, while two are much longer ones. In some underdeveloped countries, the migration from rural to urban areas is a chain process up the urban hierarchy, including some moves in the reverse direction.

The different types of movements considered above, whether classified by distance or by time, can be mapped. In transportation planning studies, there are maps of the journey to work and of the journey to shop, and many texts in demography contain maps of interstate and international migrations. Such cartographic descriptions of flows, however, have a limited analytical value, and as Smith (1964) has pointed out, the relationships between nodal or regional characteristics and flows have to be exhumed from these maps. However, if the information contained in maps is translated into matrix form, certain kinds of sophisticated analyses become possible, and one can attempt the identification of the spatial structure of flows.

DETERMINISTIC AND STOCHASTIC APPROACHES

In a review of methods and concepts in commodity flows studies, prepared for a symposium of the International Geographical Union's Commission on Quantitative Methods, Smith (1970) notes that the available studies deal with (1) volume of shipments, (2) efficiency of flows, and (3) structure of flows. While the topic of flow efficiency will be dealt with in Chapter 12 and flow structure in Chapter 10, flow volumes are treated in this and the next chapter. A first consideration is that the study of flows as a function of nodal characteristics can be approached from either a deterministic or a stochastic point of view.

Deterministic Approaches

One way to analyze shipments is to make diagnostic statements about volumes in the form of "more than" or "less than" some established yardsticks. Three useful yardsticks are described below.

Location Quotients

A *location quotient* is a measure of the relative importance of one phenomenon when compared to a larger entity. Operationally, it is a ratio of ratios. For example, employment in the coal mining industry is 2 percent of total U.S. employment, and in West Virginia mining accounts for 12 percent of total state employment. West Virginia is said to have a location quotient of 6 (12/2) with reference to this industry. In turn, this quotient indicates that the coal mining industry is 6 times more important in West Virginia than it is in the nation as a whole. This statistic may be regarded as an index of the characteristics of employment or industrial structure of destinations and origins. Therefore, it may be used as a basis for the assessments of flows. Obviously, one may expect that places having a location quotient greater than 1 are exporters of a particular industry's products, while those having a quotient of less than 1 are importers. Consequently, it may be possible to relate specific shipments between pairs of states on the basis of their respective location quotients.

Shift Techniques

Changing volumes of inbound and outbound shipments through particular nodes can also be described by means of the *shift technique,* which compares the actual change to the expected change in a region between two points in time. The latter is based upon changes that occurred at the regional or national level between the same points in time. With the use of this technique, the dimensions of port competition have been studied. For example, if between two time periods the total volume of seaborne trade in a nation has changed by +20 percent, while that of port *A* has changed by +10 percent, port *B* by +30 percent, and port *C* by −5 percent, it is evident that in terms of freight reallocation, port *A* is an absolute gainer but a relative loser, port *B* is both an absolute and a relative gainer, and port *C* is both an absolute and a relative loser. The resulting ratios can then be used as yardsticks to make diagnostic assessments of observed flows. Rimmer (1967) has used shift analysis to examine the changes in the volumes of coastal shipments of New Zealand seaports.

Regression Analysis

Regression and correlation techniques can also be used to study the volume of commodity, migration, or information flows from many origins to one destination or from one origin to many destinations. Typically, the volume of flow to the *j*th destination or from the *i*th origin is used as the dependent variable, while per capita income and other surrogates of demand, such as population or employment in selected activities in each of the origin or destination nodes, are being used as the independent or explanatory variables. The specific selection of independent variables has depended upon the nature of the study. The expected or predicted flows to a specific origin or from a specific destination can be computed using the resulting regression equation. These flows can then be compared with observed flows, and the differences, called *residuals,* can be mapped and used as a point of departure for further analysis.

A recent study of freight flows in Britain (Chisholm and O'Sullivan, 1973) provides an example of the use of regression analysis for a quick scan of the data prior to more elaborate analyses. Chisholm and O'Sullivan had data on freight shipments (disaggregated by commodity group) by road and rail between 78 origin and destination zones. The study focused initially on determining the bases on which to estimate the volume of commodities that will be generated in each zone and attracted to it. As independent variables, Chisholm and O'Sullivan (1973, 41–42) selected population, employment, and retail turnover, in order to "explain" the tonnage of freight moving in or out of each of the 78 zones. They also computed simple coefficients of determination (R^2) which may be interpreted as the percent of the variation in the volume of flow that is determined statistically by the variations in population size, etc. For road traffic destinations, the values of R^2 with respect to population, employment, and retail turnover were .79, .78, and .74, respectively. The performance of the model with respect to rail tonnage destinations, however, left something to be desired. The comparable values of R^2 were as low as .13, .08, and .05. The authors suggest that the poor results for rail traffic in Britain are due to the domination of rail freight by mineral commodities and other bulk goods which originate from a limited number of zones (e.g., the South Wales region) and are consigned to a small number of destination zones in which there is much manufacturing activity.

Frequently, the effect of distance will be the prime residual if it has not been explicitly incorporated into the original list of explanatory variables. Generally, regression models tend to exaggerate the volume of shipments between two large places that are far apart and to underpredict the volume between small places close together. The deficiencies of regression models can be corrected somewhat by incorporating distance explicitly into the regression formulation of the gravity model that is presented in Chapter 9.

Stochastic Approaches

In a deterministic model of the form $y = f(x)$, the change in the magnitude of the dependent variable y — in the present case, the volume of flows — is determined by the magnitude of variation of the independent variables x — for example, population size. This relation means that given information on variations of the independent or "explanatory" variable, it is possible to "predict" or "explain" the volume of flows with some degree of confidence.

In contrast, the stance is completely different in stochastic modeling approaches. A *stochastic process* is one in which there is uncertainty about the outcome of events, and consequently statements can be made only in the context of odds. A familiar example is that of weather prediction in which, due to the large number of uncertainties and interacting variables, the forecast is couched in terms of a specified "chance" of precipitation.

Many geographic phenomena can be conceptualized as if they were chance or stochastic processes, making it possible to use the powerful mathematics of probability, such as Markov chain analysis. Studies in this context include those by Brown (1970), Brown and Horton (1970), Brown and Longbrake (1970), Harvey (1967), and Musham (1963).

Markov Chain Analysis

In order to use the Markov chain as a tool of research, we must be reasonably certain at the outset that the phenomenon being modeled is a *"Markov process,"* i.e., that there is a dependence between an event and the immediately preceding one. For example, in the context of intraurban migration, events or "states" can be defined as residence in a low-, medium-, or high-income neighborhood. Studies of social and economic mobility suggest that most moves are from one state to the immediately following or preceding one, e.g., a low- to a medium-income neighborhood or from a high- back to a medium-income neighborhood. There may be some lucky individuals who suddenly strike it rich, enabling them to move from a hovel on the wrong side of the tracks to a mansion in the ritzy part of town. The probability of such an occurrence, of course, is very low.

If we know the initial state S_i (e.g., the number of people living in particular neighborhood types who have moved to other neighborhood types), it is possible to compute *transition probabilities* (the probability of making a transition from one state to another). Given two states S_1 and S_2, we can write the transition probability matrix P as follows:

		To S_1	S_2
From	S_1	P_{11}	P_{12}
	S_2	P_{21}	P_{22}

P_{11} is the probability that state S_1 will occur, given that state S_1 occurred on the previous trial, i.e., the probability of staying in the same type of neighborhood. This probability is likely to be very high in contrast to moving from S_1, a ghetto, to S_2, an expensive address such as Chevy Chase, Maryland, or Westchester County, New York.

In migration studies, it is reasonable to assume that the process is a reversible one. There are two kinds of processes that can be identified from an examination of a transition probability matrix: (1) *transient,* in which every state can be reached from every other one and, once reached, can be left; (2) *absorbing,* in which there exist one or more states which, by themselves, are *ergodic,* i.e., once reached from any other state, cannot be left. According to this classification, most geographic phenomena are probably transient so that, for example, economic troubles may lead to a reverse movement from high-income neighborhoods to low-income ones, as well as to movement from suburbs back to the central city.

Borrowing from an idea originally suggested by Horton and Shuldiner (1967), Yeates (1974) provides a clear illustration of the application of Markov chain analysis to commuting. The phenomenon of commuting may be viewed as constituting a closed system in that an individual within a labor market area is likely to remain within it. On a regular basis, this individual travels from home to a particular work location and returns to home base. While the location of home base is fixed, at least in the context of this problem, that of the work location poses a number of alternatives. Consider Figure 8-6, which illustrates three land-use parcels. A commuter may be located at any one of these, and during each time period he must either leave the parcel on which he is located and travel to either of the other two parcels or remain on that specific parcel. It also seems reasonable to assume that there is some distance-decay function operating in this context, so that the probable destination for each trip is some function of the distance between a pair of land parcels. On this basis, we can specify the transition probabilities, which are indicated in Figure 8-6. The appropriate matrix representation* is:

	To *A*	*B*	*C*	Σ
From *A*	.5	.3	.2	1.0
B	.3	.4	.3	1.0
C	.2	.2	.6	1.0

In the above tabulation, the cell values P_{ij} specify the probabilities of moving from one parcel to any other during a particular time period, and the row sums equal 1.0 (because each cell in a row represents a particular proportion of the total probability — 1.0 or 100 percent). Thus P_{CC} (0.6) is the probability of one individual staying on parcel *C* after 1 time period. These values can be used to compute the probability that an individual will remain on parcel *A* or move to parcel *B* or parcel *C,* for example, after 2 or more time periods.

For an individual originating on any parcel, the possible commuting paths and the probability of each path are termed a "Markov chain." Figure 8-7 shows the Markov chain applicable to an individual originating at *B,* and the transition probabilities in that chain are those shown in the previous tabulation. Thus, the values of 0.3, 0.4, and 0.3 (column 1) refer to the probabilities of moving from *B* to *A,* remaining at *B,* or moving to *C* during the first trial. From any location, the individual path probabilities can be assigned.

* From *An Introduction to Quantitative Analysis in Human Geography,* by Maurice Yeates, p. 177. Copyright 1974, McGraw-Hill, Inc. Used with permission of McGraw-Hill Book Company.

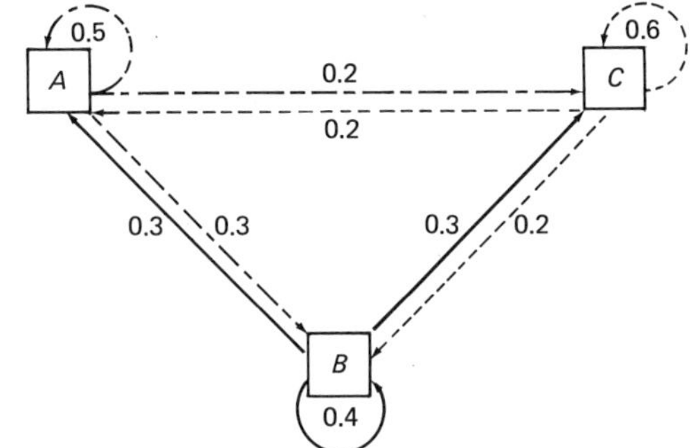

Figure 8-6
System of hypothetical origins and destinations in an urban area. (Values represent probabilities of movement from any location.)

From *An Introduction to Quantitative Analysis in Human Geography* by Maurice Yeates, Figure 7-8, p. 176. Copyright 1974 by McGraw-Hill, Inc. Used with permission of McGraw-Hill Book Company.

In order to obtain the probability of remaining at *B* after 2 time periods, it is necessary to make use of the multiplication rule for conditional probabilities, that is, $(0.3 \times 0.3) + (0.4 \times 0.4) + (0.3 \times 0.2) = 0.31$. From where did these values originate? From Figure 8-7 we can see that the path probabilities of remaining at *B* after two steps are (1) moving to *A* and then back to *B* (0.3×0.3); (2) remaining at *B* (0.4×0.4); and (3) moving to *C* and then back to *B*

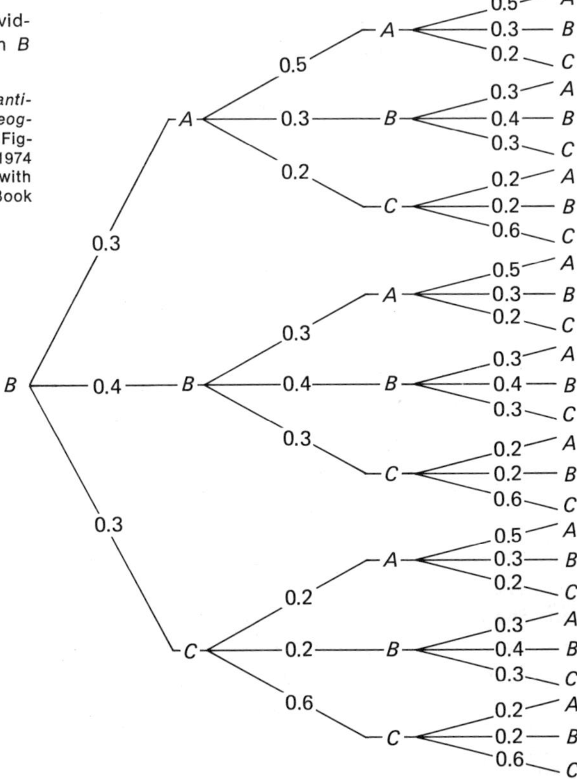

Figure 8-7
Markov chain for an individual originating at location *B* in Figure 8-6.

From *An Introduction to Quantitative Analysis in Human Geography* by Maúrice Yeates, Figure 7-9, p. 180. Copyright 1974 by McGraw-Hill, Inc. Used with permission of McGraw-Hill Book Company.

(0.3 × 0.2). Summing the products of these paths yields the probability of remaining at B after two steps.

The multiplication procedure just suggested yields just the probability of moving from B to any other location after two steps. This procedure needs to be repeated if we wish to determine the probability of moving from A or C after two steps. The repetitive operations can be substantially eliminated by recourse to matrix multiplication by successively powering the transition probability matrix, which will yield the probability of moving to any location after n number of steps.

For an individual starting at any particular location, squaring the initial transition probability matrix yields the probability of reaching any location after 2 time periods, just as cubing the matrix yields these probabilities after three steps. For the example considered here, the applicable powered matrices (P^1 to P^9)* are

$$P^1 = \begin{bmatrix} .5 & .3 & .2 \\ .3 & .4 & .3 \\ .2 & .2 & .6 \end{bmatrix}$$

$$P^2 = \begin{bmatrix} .38 & .31 & .31 \\ .33 & .31 & .36 \\ .28 & .26 & .46 \end{bmatrix}$$

$$P^3 = \begin{bmatrix} .345 & .300 & .355 \\ .330 & .295 & .375 \\ .310 & .280 & .410 \end{bmatrix}$$

$$P^4 = \begin{bmatrix} .3335 & .2945 & .3720 \\ .3285 & .2920 & .3795 \\ .3210 & .2870 & .3920 \end{bmatrix}$$

$$P^5 = \begin{bmatrix} .32950 & .29225 & .37825 \\ .32775 & .29125 & .38100 \\ .32500 & .28950 & .38550 \end{bmatrix}$$

$$P^6 = \begin{bmatrix} .328075 & .291400 & .380525 \\ .327450 & .291025 & .381525 \\ .326450 & .290400 & .383150 \end{bmatrix}$$

$$P^7 = \begin{bmatrix} .3275625 & .2910875 & .3813500 \\ .3273375 & .2909500 & .3817125 \\ .3269750 & .2907250 & .3823000 \end{bmatrix}$$

$$P^8 = \begin{bmatrix} .32737750 & .29097375 & .38164875 \\ .32729625 & .29092375 & .38178000 \\ .32716500 & .29084250 & .38199250 \end{bmatrix}$$

$$P^9 = \begin{bmatrix} .327310625 & .290932500 & .381756875 \\ .327281250 & .290914375 & .381804375 \\ .327233750 & .290885000 & .381881250 \end{bmatrix}$$

From these matrices, we know that an individual starting at A has a 31 percent probability of being at B after 2 time periods, a value that decreases to 29.14 percent after six steps.

The results of Markov chain analysis depend a great deal upon the initial operational definition of "states." These states can be either locations or locational categories. For example, Brown, Odland, and Golledge (1970) have used each of 100 standard metropolitan statistical areas (SMSAs) in the United

* From *An Introduction to Quantitative Analysis in Human Geography,* by Maurice Yeates, Table 7.6, p. 182. Copyright 1974, McGraw-Hill, Inc. Used with permission of McGraw-Hill Book Company.

States as the S_i to study intermetropolitan migration patterns. Accordingly, they developed a 100 × 100 transition probability matrix. Alternatively, a classification of neighborhood types derived from a factor analysis was used by Brown and Longbrake (1970) to study intraurban residential mobility in Cedar Rapids. The typology of origin and destination zones included middle-life-cycle, middle-class family households; late-life-cycle, upper-middle-class households; lower-economic-status households; sound, rented two-family dwelling units; and so on.

If it is possible to assume that transition probabilities are stable and that population remains constant, then one can estimate the state of the system at some future time period. After some number of steps (usually five or six) there is rapid convergence toward some average or "equilibrium" state. The vector of convergence is termed the "unique fixed-point probability vector" and may be regarded as a state of equilibrium in which movement between these states would serve to maintain the system at the same level.

Two deficiencies of the application of the Markov chain approach in geography must be briefly noted. (1) Depending upon the level of disaggregation, mobility within any particular state, of course, is not captured by the analysis. For example, a move from a high-income neighborhood to another that may be 50 miles away is not counted as a move, since the definition of the state prevents the identification of geographic mobility as such. If a state is identified as "suburb," no distinction can be made between a suburb of, say, London and that of Birmingham. A household which has moved between these suburbs cannot be differentiated from another household which has moved from one London suburb to another. (2) In the absence of the specification of relative location and distances, geographic Markov chain models are essentially aspatial.

Simulation

Although the emphasis in this chapter is mainly on quick-scan strategies that enable the modeling of point-to-point flows, we nevertheless wish to introduce here a simulation approach to modeling migration that explicitly incorporates distance as a convenient transition to the next chapter. Morrill (1963b) studied the growth and development of towns in Sweden over a 200-year period from 1750 to 1960. The major components in his model were central-place activities, non-central-place activities (primarily manufacturing and transportation), and migration. We shall limit our consideration here solely to migration.

In this model, migration is viewed as a function of (1) distance between an origin and all possible destinations; (2) the relative attractiveness (most importantly, economic opportunity) as between an origin and potential destinations; and (3) availability of information concerning destinations which, in turn, is largely a function of destinations of prior migrants from a certain origin.

These considerations may be incorporated simultaneously in a simulation model which recognizes that locational decisions are subject to both errors and uncertainties that we can neither specify nor ignore. Generally, at any particular point in time there are more potential destinations for migrants than potential migrants, leading to a certain inherent randomness in the real world. Moreover, the combined effect of many small forces that operate in variegated ways may also be random. Therefore, a simulation approach to the modeling of migration may be one of the most appropriate ways to understand the process of place-to-place migration. Simulation as a topic has already been considered in Chapter 6, and therefore we shall proceed directly to the workings of Morrill's model. The allocation of migrants is made as follows:

1. Each area is assigned an index of attraction for migrants, A_k for the kth subarea, reflecting the existing population, the level of urbanization, and location with respect to the transport network. For example, a rural parish may have an index of 0.7, while one with a major urban center at a railroad junction may have a value of 4.4. The mean for the whole region is 1.0.

2. The probability of migration from the jth origin to the kth destination is defined as

$$P_{jk} = \frac{A_k}{d_{jk}{}^b}$$

where d is distance and b is an empirically derived exponent. The migration relationship stated above is a probabilistic one which varies directly with the relative attractiveness of the possible destination, and inversely with distance. The sum of probabilities for migrating from one area to all possible destinations equals 1.0. With respect to any one origin this total probability can be distributed to each of the several destinations. For example, if the value of P_{jk} with respect to subarea 1 is 2.0, then digits 1 and 2 are assigned to it; if P_{jk} of subarea 10 is 19.0, then digits 16 through 34 may be assigned to it. In general, areas close to an origin would have a larger number of numbers assigned to them. In this way, 100 numbers from 1 to 100 are assigned. Note that a different set of P_{jk} must be recomputed for each origin since both relative attractiveness and pairwise distances vary.

3. Following the assignment of probabilities which results in a "migration probability field," random numbers are used to select the specific destinations. Assume that we have to allocate specific destinations for each of 20 migrants from a certain origin. We draw random numbers in sequence. Let the first number be 76. This may correspond with area 20 because it has been allocated numbers 73 to 96. The destination has now been chosen by means of matching a random number with a specific destination. Perhaps the second number is 23, corresponding with area 10 (numbers 16 through 34). We proceed in this way until all the 20 migrants are allocated to their respective destinations from one subarea during one generation, which is a computer iteration (see Figure 14*a* to *d*, Morrill, 1963b, 13).

The process is repeated with respect to each of the different origins, aggregated into the total number of migrants between all pairs of areas; in this way, the net gain or loss due to internal migration can be computed. In turn, this calculation is used as a basis for modifying the index of relative attractiveness for the next generation, such that areas with excessive outmigration would have a lower index value.

Morrill's study was concerned with Småland in middle Sweden, and with 155 subareas it was necessary to compute $155 \times 155 = 24{,}025$ probabilities for each time period. If simulations are run at 10-year intervals for two centuries, the total number of probabilities that must be computed approximates 0.5 million! Hence, the use of electronic computers is a sine qua non for such large-scale simulations.

The major criticism that must be made of this approach concerns the index of attraction. Essentially, this is a weight that must be empirically determined and statistically tested. The simplicity and elegance of a simulation model are somewhat distorted in the result. Nevertheless, as a stochastic approach used in the study of internodal flows, simulation models are extremely valuable for the insights they can provide about spatial processes.

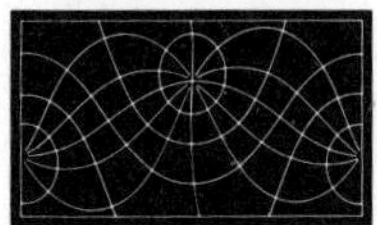

9 Distance as the Basis for Modeling Flows

This chapter is concerned entirely with the family of gravity models. We begin with a narrative account of the historical development of the model, and since the utilization of this model has been so widespread, we present its derivation in some detail. Then, from countless studies we have selected three for the explication of its practical application. Subsequently, the operational problems that have been encountered in the use of the traditional gravity model are discussed, and an evaluation is provided. Finally, a new approach to modeling flows which incorporates notions from general systems theory, in particular "entropy maximization," is introduced.

FLOWS AS A FUNCTION OF NODAL MASS AND DISTANCE: THE GRAVITY MODEL

In many studies of point-to-point movement, it has been found that distance between two points and the size of their populations (mass) provide a surprisingly high level of statistical explanation for the volumes of flows. Evidently, population stands as a surrogate measure for demand and subsumes the impact of many other factors. An adequate point of departure in modeling spatial flows is an adaptation to human phenomena of the gravity model in physics of the form

$$I_{ij} = \frac{M_i \cdot M_j}{d_{ij}} \tag{9.1}$$

where I_{ij} is the volume of interaction between points i and j, M_i and M_j are the masses of points i and j, respectively, and d_{ij} is the distance between them.

Development and Derivation of the Gravity Model

Historical Development

The logical underpinnings of the gravity model in social science were first articulated by Carey (1858, 42–43) in his *Principles of Social Science:*

> Man tends, of necessity, to gravitate towards his fellow man. Of all animals he is the most gregarious, and the greater in number collected in a given space the greater is the attractive force there exerted . . . .
>
> Such being the case, why is it that all the members of the human family do not tend to come together on a single spot of earth? Because of the existence of the same simple and universal law by means of which is maintained the beautiful order of the system of which our planet forms a part. We are surrounded by bodies of various sizes, and some of these are themselves provided with satellites, each having its local center of attraction, by means of which its parts are held together . . . .
>
> . . . London and Paris may be regarded as the rival suns of our system, each exercising a strong attractive force, and were it not for the existence of the counter attraction of local centers like Vienna and Berlin, . . . Europe would present to view one great centralized system, the population of which was always tending towards these two cities.

Evidently, since the days of Carey, new suns such as New York and Tokyo have evolved, the process of spatial evolution being faster than that of stellar masses.

Carrothers (1956), in an excellent review of the historical antecedents of the gravity model, points out that the first attempt to use Carey's concept in an operational context was in a study of migration flows between English cities (Ravenstein, 1885). Destinations were treated as centers of absorption, and volumes of migratory movement were shown to decrease with increasing distance between a given origin and destination. The formulation used by Ravenstein

$$M_{ij} = \frac{(f)P_j}{d_{ij}} \tag{9.2}$$

where M_{ij} is the volume of migration between the *i*th origin and the *j*th destination is not, *sensu stricto,* a gravity model inasmuch as the mutual attraction $(P_i \cdot P_j)$ between *i* and *j* is neglected.

Subsequently, a proportionality factor and a distance exponent were incorporated into a study of farm population migrations in the United States (Young, 1924). His model took the form

$$M_{ij} = K\frac{Z_j}{d_{ij}^2} \tag{9.3}$$

where *K* is a proportionality constant and Z_j equals the force of attraction of destination *j*. As with Ravenstein's formulation, there is no multiplication of the masses. However, the squaring of the distance is tantamount to weighting its impact, and indeed, much of the technical discussion in the literature on the gravity model is concerned with the question of the most appropriate distance exponent.

Still later, a variation of the gravity model was used to delineate the trade areas of two competing masses by estimating the volume of trade generated by the inhabitants of the intervening space (Reilly, 1929, 1931). The point of equilibrium between these two adjacent trade centers identified a location at which an individual is indifferent about which center he or she will patronize. The location of this equilibrium point is described by

$$\frac{P_i}{d_{xi}^2} = \frac{P_j}{d_{xj}^2} \tag{9.4}$$

where x is the point of equilibrium on the line between i and j and d_x is the distance from i or j to point x. Equation (9.4) does not lend itself readily to computation, and therefore the equilibrium point can be determined by

$$d_{xi} = \frac{d_{ij}}{1 + \sqrt{P_j/P_i}} \tag{9.5}$$

Stewart (1941) and Zipf (1949) were the first to revert to the early gravity formulation of Carey with a direct analogy between physical and social interaction of the form

$$I_{ij} = K\frac{P_i \cdot P_j}{d_{ij}^2} \tag{9.6}$$

In order to calibrate the model, a constant of proportionality must be introduced in Equation (9.6) by explicitly incorporating the total magnitude of the phenomenon, e.g., total telephone calls, bus passenger traffic, and the like. Stewart regarded this constant as being equivalent to the total energy of interaction of a given region i, that is, the sum of the energy of interaction of i with each of the other regions or cities into which the larger region has been partitioned. Thus, the proportionality constant K may be regarded as a scalar which is necessary to adjust the model to the magnitude of the phenomenon. Alternatively, K can be interpreted as an interaction propensity function. For example, in studying intercity air passenger traffic, since not all individuals are air travelers, the proportionality constant (K) serves to deflate the total population, thereby calibrating the model.

A Derivation of the Gravity Model and Its Operational Version

Isard et al. (1960, 493–568), in an extensive review of the gravity and potential models, synthesized a large amount of material available up to that time. Drawing on the work of Carroll and Bevis (1957), Dodd (1950), and Iklé (1954), they derived the gravity model without having to depend upon an analogy.

Assume the existence of a metropolitan region with a homogeneous population P. The total number of trips (or telephone calls, commodity flows, or whatever) between each subarea of the region and every other one is T. If movement were costless (i.e., there were no friction of distance), the percentage of trips of a typical individual in subarea i to subarea j would be given as

P_j/P. Since the population is assumed to be homogeneous, there is no variation among individuals with respect to their movement propensities. Therefore, the number of trips that any individual in any subarea i undertakes in a given time period is equal to the number of trips per capita for the entire metropolitan region, that is T/P, which can be designated as k. Thus, the number of trips per individual in subarea i to subarea j is $k(P_j/P)$.

Since we know that there are P_i individuals in subarea i, the total number of person-trips from i to j is

$$T_{ij} = k\frac{P_i \cdot P_j}{P} \tag{9.7}$$

In this way, by serially substituting pairs of areas in the equation, it is possible to estimate the total number of hypothetical trips for every possible combination of subareas.

Of course, movement is not costless, and therefore the next consideration is to estimate the quantitative impact of distance on the volume of movement between the subareas. Suppose that we have at our disposal data provided by an area transportation origin and destination study which record the volumes of interaction (I_{ij}), as well as distances between them. On double-log graph paper, the ratio of actual to expected trip volumes (I_{ij}/P_{ij}) can be plotted on the vertical axis and d_{ij} on the horizontal axis, as is done in Figure 9-1. Each of the points on this graph represents a pair of subareas. Thus, point L, for example, refers to a pair of subareas located 3.6 miles apart, for which the ratio I_{ij}/P_{ij} is 0.4. As depicted here, the relationship between distance and the ratio of actual to expected interaction is log-linear. While area transportation studies have shown that the relationship between interaction and distance is quite complex, a regression line can always be fitted by means of standard least-squares procedures, in which the object is to minimize the sum of the

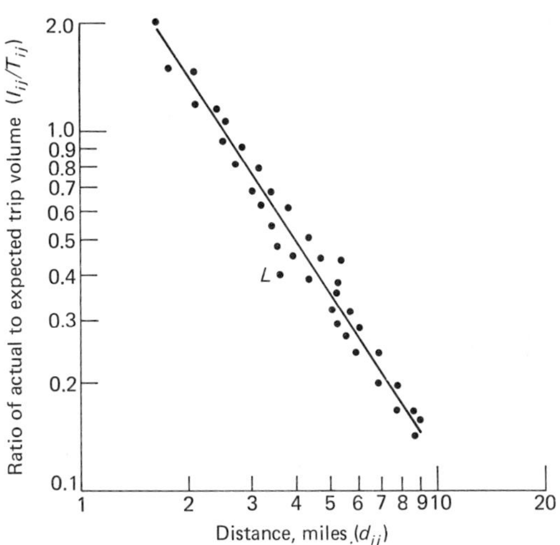

Figure 9-1
Scatter diagram and regression line showing the relationship between interaction and distance

squared deviations from the line. The equation of the regression line in Figure 9-1 is

$$\log \frac{I_{ij}}{T_{ij}} = a - b \log d_{ij} \tag{9.8}$$

for which the computed values are $a = 3.9$ and $b = 1.5$.

If the logs are removed from Equation (9.8) and c is made to stand for the antilog of a, the resulting form of the equation is

$$I_{ij} = \frac{c \cdot T_{ij}}{d_{ij}^{\,b}} \tag{9.9}$$

The slope of the line in Figure 9-1, described by the b value (which is 1.5), can then be directly entered as the distance exponent. In this way, a measure of the friction of distance is obtained.

Since T_{ij} has already been defined in Equation (9.7) as

$$T_{ij} = \frac{k \cdot P_i \cdot P_j}{P}$$

and k has been defined as T/P, Equation (9.9) may be fully written out as

$$I_{ij} = \frac{(c \cdot T/P)\,(P_i P_j/P)}{d_{ij}^{\,b}} \tag{9.10}$$

In order to simplify this equation, the expression $c \cdot T/(P \cdot P)$ in the numerator may be replaced arbitrarily by a constant K. Inasmuch as the gravitational constant is a complex one in newtonian physics, it is perhaps appropriate that the K derived here is also quite obscure in meaning. Therefore, Equation (9.10) may be rewritten as

$$I_{ij} = K \frac{P_i \cdot P_j}{d_{ij}^{\,b}} \tag{9.11}$$

a familiar structure which has been constructed rather than simply borrowed.

The assumptions concerning homogeneity of population and costless movement have been relaxed, and Isard et al. (1960, 498) write, "We might conclude that the relationship [expressed in Equation (9.11)] reflects a basic principle underlying the structure of metropolitan areas and systems of metropolitan areas."

It should be clear by now that the major operational problem in the formulation and testing of the gravity model lies in the empirical estimation of the two parameters K and b. In practice, the estimation is made with the use of multiple regression procedures, so that Equation (9.11) can be rewritten as

$$I_{ij} = K \cdot P_i \cdot P_j \cdot d_{ij}^{\,-b} \tag{9.12}$$

In this linear form, the exponent of distance becomes a negative one. The specific impact of distance, termed its "weight," is neither universal (in a spatial sense) nor invariant (in a temporal sense) in human interaction as it is in newtonian physics; rather, it varies from problem to problem. It has to be estimated each time, and the value of *b* as computed for Cedar Rapids cannot be used for contacts in Vasteras, Sweden. In addition to weighting distance, there is also the more fundamental question of how to measure it, i.e., time, cost, number of traffic lights, and so on.

Like distance, mass can also be measured in a number of ways, e.g., number of inhabitants, number of telephones, number of hospital beds, personal income, and the like. In order to obtain a good fit between the gravity model and a set of observed data, the masses are also weighted with empirically derived regression coefficients. Thus, the operational version of the gravity model becomes

$$I_{ij} = K \cdot P_i^{b_1} \cdot P_j^{b_2} \cdot d_{ij}^{-b_3} \tag{9.13}$$

where b_1, b_2, and b_3 are the exponents to be estimated and K is a constant term.

Equations with powered terms, such as (9.13) are difficult to compute and have to be modified further, if possible. Moreover, as we have shown in Chapter 8, distance-decay functions of human interaction are generally highly skewed, with a very large number of contacts at short distances and a small number at larger distances. Further, since interaction is the function of the product of two masses, a plot of values of interaction intensity with values of the product of the masses is also likely to be skewed. For example, the product of the population of London and that of New York is many times greater than that of Alice Springs and Timbuktu. Similarly, the volume of interaction between the two large cities is overwhelmingly greater than for the other two. On a worldwide scale, there would thus be numerous small combined population values and a few large ones, given the nature of the world's settlement hierarchy. The resulting curves drawn on arithmetic graph paper would resemble those shown in Figure 9-2*a* and *b*. These sharply skewed curves can be straightened out by converting the values to their logs, thus establishing a linear relationship. In this way, data can be manipulated with linear algebra, more specifically by the technique of multiple regression analysis.

The logarithmic version of Equation (9.13) can be written as

$$\log I_{ij} = \log a + b_1(\log P_i) + b_2(\log P_j) - b_3(\log d_{ij}) \tag{9.14}$$

in which $\log a$ is a replacement for K in Equation (9.13) and b_1, b_2, and b_3 represent the former exponents.

In order to compute the parameters a, b_1, b_2, and b_3, two data matrices and a column vector are required. These are as follows:

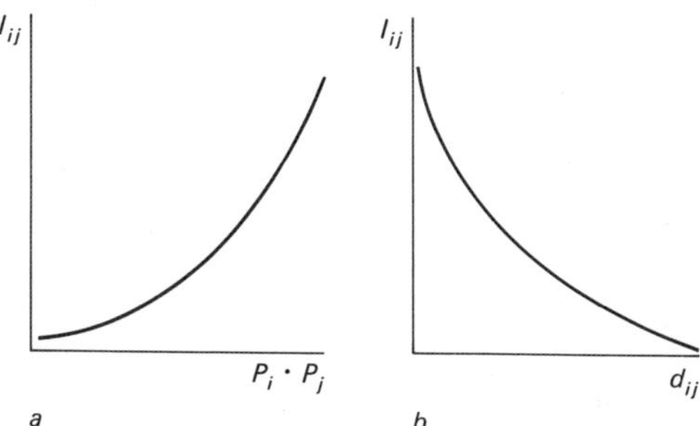

Figure 9-2
Pair of skewed functions showing (*a*) relationship between interaction (I_{ij}) and the product of the masses ($P_i \cdot P_j$); (*b*) relationship between interaction (I_{ij}) and intervening distance (D_{ij}).

1. A flow matrix. For the 50 states of the United States for example, this would be a 50×50 matrix, recording the pairwise interactions between each state and every one of the other 49 states.

2. A distance matrix, also of dimension 50×50, recording, perhaps, the airline distance from the largest city in each state to the largest one in each of the other states.

3. A 50×1 column vector, recording the population or other measures of mass of each of the states. In this example, each state is treated as a single mass, and it is assumed that the entire weight is aggregated at a point, be it the central business district of the largest city or the population center of the state.

Examples of the Application of Gravity Models

There are, quite literally, hundreds of studies which have made use of a form of the gravity model to analyze human interaction. Indeed, it is possible to speak of an extended family of gravity models with many tribal cousins. Most of these studies, however, are in the field of transportation planning, and, surprisingly, there is a paucity of gravity model-based analyses in the geography literature. Moreover, most geographic studies have employed a relatively primitive P_iP_j/d_{ij} or P_iP_j/d_{ij}^2 version. Three studies are reviewed here in some detail in order to illustrate the procedures necessary to fit a gravity model to a set of flow data.

Modeling Multimodal Passenger Flows

A study of air, rail, bus, and auto traffic volumes between selected pairs of California cities is one of the clearest examples of the application of the logarithmic version of the gravity model in the literature (Alcaly, 1967). For air-passenger movement only, from Los Angeles to each of the other cities, the data requirements and the organization of the basic matrix are shown in Table 9-1. The volumes of flow and the values of d_{ij} would, of course, be different

Table 9-1
General Schema for the Arrangement of Data with Respect to a Gravity Model

City pair	Passenger volume	Population origin	Population destination	Distance
Los Angeles (1)–Sacramento (2)	I_{12}	P_1	P_2	d_{12}
Los Angeles–San Diego (3)	I_{13}	P_1	P_3	d_{13}
Los Angeles–San Francisco (4)	I_{14}	P_1	P_4	d_{14}
Los Angeles–San Jose (5)	I_{15}	P_1	P_5	d_{15}
Los Angeles–Santa Barbara (6)	I_{16}	P_1	P_6	d_{16}
Los Angeles–Stockton (7)	I_{17}	P_1	P_7	d_{17}
.	.	.	.	.
.	.	.	.	.
.	.	.	.	.
Los Angeles– . . . (*j*)	I_{1j}	P_1	P_j	d_{1j}

for other modes of movement while both the values of the P_i and P_j would remain the same. These various data are then converted to logarithms.*

The data are then subjected to multiple regression analysis. The analysis would yield log a, b_1, b_2, and b_3 as well as the computed log I_{ij}, which may then be compared with the observed log I_{ij}.

In the study of California traffic some of the fitted equations were as follows (Alcaly, 1967):

$$\log I_{ij}\,(\text{air}) = -46.769 + 2.0899 \log P_i + 2.0175 \log P_i - 0.3566 \log d_{ij}\,(\text{air})$$
$$R^2 = 0.90827 \qquad (9.15)$$

$$\log I_{ij}\,(\text{auto}) = -0.3033 + 0.9818 \log P_i + 1.0308 \log P_j - 2.5623 \log d_{ij}\,(\text{highway})$$
$$R^2 = 0.91612 \qquad (9.16)$$

$$\log I_{ij}\,(\text{total}) = -3.3909 + 1.0759 \log P_i + 1.0831 \log P_j - 2.4599 \log d_{ij}\,(\text{air})$$
$$R^2 = 0.94321 \qquad (9.17)$$

The I_{ij} for all modes of travel were also computed using mileages by rail, highway, air, as well as an average mileage incorporating all three. The major purpose was to test the effect of aggregation on the results yielded by the gravity model. It was found that indeed the model performed more robustly, as measured by the coefficient of determination (R^2), when the flows by all modes were aggregated. This result does suggest that the gravity model is a macroscopic and inclusive one and, therefore, is powerful in describing and predicting mass behavior in spatial interaction. Similar conclusions were reached by Mera (1971) who found that the gravity model yielded better fits when applied to aggregate commodity flows than when applied to disaggregated flows (cement, confectionery, metal cans, etc.).

How may we interpret the numerically estimated parameters in Equations (9.15) and (9.16)? The constant terms −46.769 and −0.3033 in the air and auto travel regressions, respectively, represent the quantities required to make the equations balance. In practice, however, they may be regarded as measures of the average propensity for interaction by the two different modes. Since the cost of air travel is much greater than that of auto travel on a per-mile basis, the value of the constant is higher for air travel. In comparing these two constants, both of which take on a negative value, the one with the lower absolute value (auto) indicates a higher propensity for interaction.

In the case of air travel, if log P_i rises by 1, then log I_{ij} increases by 2.0899. If log P_j increases by 1, then log I_{ij} increases by 2.0175. The differences in the b values, applied to P_i and P_j for air and auto travel, suggest that approximately twice as many people are needed to generate a given volume of air travel in contrast to auto travel. An alternative interpretation may be that individuals drive between small towns and fly between larger ones if the intervening distance is not too great.

*Assuming that the data are to be subjected to computer analysis, cards are punched, with each card representing the whole or portion of a row in Table 9-1. There are a number of canned computer programs available in all university computer centers, the most widely used being the UCLA Biomedical Library Package (Dixon, 1971), in which BMD 02R is the multiple regression program.

As expected, the coefficients of log d_{ij} are negative in all the equations. This means that, for air travel, if log d_{ij} increases by 1, then log I_{ij} decreases by 0.3566 and for auto travel by 2.5623. These values, the distance exponents in Equations (9.12) and (9.13), indicate that the friction of distance is considerably greater for auto travel than for air travel.

The computed values of I_{ij} reflect average relationships over all the city pairs in the data set. Therefore, the actual interaction between a specific city pair does not necessarily equal that generated by the model. In order to compute the expected value of auto travel, for example, between Los Angeles and San Francisco, the following procedure is used. The logarithm of Los Angeles's population is inserted in Equation (9.16) and multiplied by 0.9818; the log of San Francisco's population is multiplied by 1.0308; the log of the highway distance between these two cities is multiplied by —2.5623; and finally the constant value of 0.3033 is subtracted. The resulting value is the logarithm of the volume of flow predicted by the model. Then the actual flow volume can be compared to the predicted one after converting the computed log I_{ij} to its raw form. If it is found, for example, that the gravity model underestimates flows for a number of pairs of cities, the location of the respective origins and destinations might be examined on a map only to reveal that they are separated by mountainous terrain. In this case, a more appropriate measure of distance may be travel time. In fact, Alcaly experimented with different measures of distance and found that for auto travel a better fit was provided by using travel time (as a result, R^2 increased slightly to 0.92602).

The utility of the regression version of the gravity model stems from the fact that it enables us to obtain statistical estimates or projections. Suppose, for example, that an airline wanted to initiate service between San Francisco and Eureka. One way to assess the economic feasibility of this venture would be to compute the expected magnitude of flows between the two cities with Equation (9.15), by inserting the logarithms of the populations of San Francisco and Eureka and the logarithm of the distance between them. The result may then be used as one decisionmaking criterion to initiate or not initiate the service. A cautionary word is necessary, however. Gravity-model parameters are areally and temporally specific and vary according to purpose. Consequently, it would be inappropriate to use the parameters derived by Alcaly in his intra-California study to attempt to forecast air traffic volumes between Los Angeles and Peking.

Modeling Communications Flows

A variant of the gravity model is the "potential" formulation of the model, the major difference being that it is written as

$$I_{ij} = K \frac{P_j}{d_{ij}^{\,b}} \tag{9.18}$$

rather than

$$I_{ij} = K \frac{P_i \cdot P_j}{d_{ij}^{\,b}} \tag{9.19}$$

The major difference in the "potential" formulation is that the impact of P_i is ignored, and thus there is no multiplication term in the numerator. This model conceptualization is appropriate when we are concerned with flows between one origin and many destinations or one destination and many origins.

The potential model can also be written as a linear equation

$$\log I_{ij} = \log a + b_1 \log P_j - b_2 \log d_{ij} \tag{9.20}$$

This formulation was used to study the inhibiting influences of political boundaries upon spatial interaction (Mackay, 1958). In the gravity model, regardless of its formulation, distance is assumed to be a smoothly continuous function. While there is an exponential decline of interaction with distance, the relationship can nevertheless be expressed as a straight line. Mackay's thesis was that boundaries introduce a sharp discontinuity both at the subnational and at the international levels.

Consider Figure 9-3, in which city *A*, located at distance $O - A$ from city *O*, may be expected to have a volume of interaction with *O*, amounting to $O - R$, according to the intersect along line 1. Line 1 in this figure represents a regression of hypothetical interactions over varying distances. If, however, between cities *A* and *O* there were a subnational boundary at *B*, then the volume of interaction would be only $O - Q$. In this context, $R - Q$ is a measure of the inhibiting impact of the boundary. If the boundary at *B* were an international one instead of a subnational one, the decrease in the expected level of interaction between *O* and *A* would be even greater. The volume would be as low as $O - P$ instead of $O - R$, and the difference between *P* and *R* may be assumed to represent the quantitative impact of the international boundary upon the level of interaction.

These suppositions were tested by fitting a potential version of the gravity model to telephone-call volumes between French Canadian and English Canadian cities on the one hand, and French Canadian and U.S. cities on the

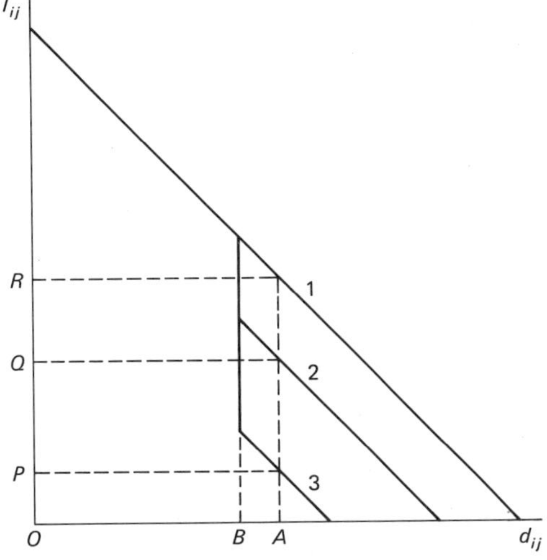

Figure 9-3
The role of political boundaries on distance-decay functions of interaction, showing (1) function without a boundary; (2) function with a provincial boundary at *B*; (3) function with an international boundary at *B*.

other. Figure 9-4 is a scatter diagram of telephone-call volumes from Montreal to Quebec cities; to English-speaking cities in the provinces of Ontario, Manitoba, Saskatchewan, Alberta, and British Columbia; and to U.S. cities. The fact that the U.S. cities are located toward the lower right-hand corner of the scatter diagram indicates that the volume of interaction is less than it might have been in the absence of the Canada-United States boundary.

Telephone traffic from Montreal to each of 22 of the largest cities in Quebec, 29 in the rest of Canada, and 18 in the U.S. was plotted against a theoretical P_j/d_{ij} (Montreal being the *i*th city) (Figure 9-4). Three dominant patterns of interaction emerge: (1) intra-Quebec flows, with the highest volumes relative to distance; (2) Quebec–English Canada, and (3) Quebec–United States. The frictional role of the boundary between French and English Canada is equivalent to an increased distance factor of 5 to 10. This means that the number of telephone calls between a pair of cities located 100 miles apart across the border is equivalent to the volume between two other cities in Quebec 500 to 1000 miles apart. Further, the effect of the international boundary is equal to a 50-fold increase in distance within the same province.

Mackay's study suggests that, despite linguistic and other cultural differences, English and French Canadians have a greater demonstrated affinity than do Canadians and Americans.

Mackay also fitted the following equation to the data pertaining to telephone-call volumes between Montreal and other cities in Quebec:

$$\log I_{ij} = 1.8 + 1.1 \log P_j - 0.9 \log d_{ij} \tag{9.21}$$

Since the coefficients 1.1 and 0.9 are both very close to 1, in this case the relationship P_j/d_{ij} is an adequate representation which requires neither weight-

Figure 9-4 Scatter diagram of telephone-call volumes between Montreal and other selected cities during a 10-day period

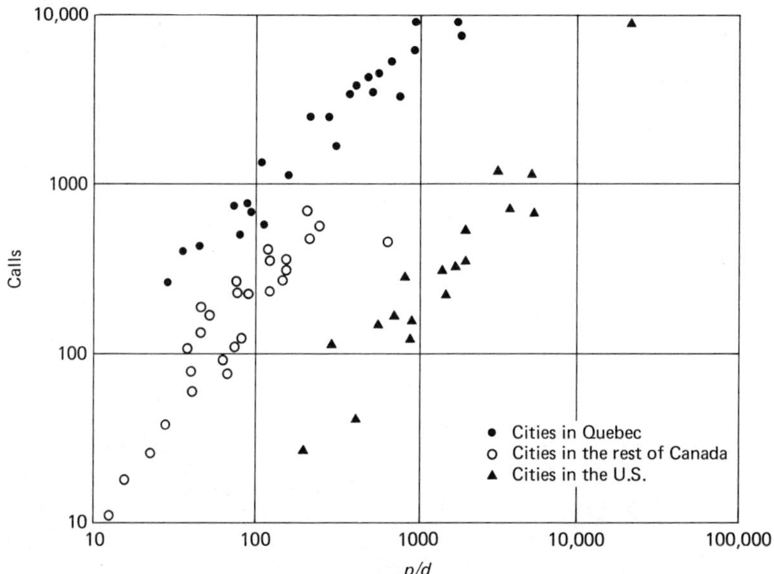

ing the mass or the distance, nor adding an exponent. The elimination of U.S. and English-Canadian cities had the impact of simplifying the relationships among population, distance, and human interaction.

Modeling Intrametropolitan Consumer Shopping Trips

One way to model flows between areas is to consider the pairwise mutual attraction between a set of cities, as has been done in the preceding section. However, it is known that in a system of cities the people and activities of each city exert some attractive force on those of *every* other city and are, reciprocally, attracted by each of the others. Consequently, it may be expected that the flows between several cities or several subareas within a metropolitan region are directly proportional to the relative attraction of each city or subarea (in comparison with the alternative attraction of all other areas) and inversely proportional to distance.

The simultaneous attraction among a number of areas is of major interest in transportation planning studies, where the goal is to allocate flows in an accounting framework. Specifically, all outgoing movement from all areas must equal total incoming movements to all areas. For any one area, the volume of outgoing movement is partitioned among each of all the other subareas.

The following modification of the gravity model explicitly incorporates the concept of relative attractiveness, enabling the spatial allocation of both inbound and outbound movement:

$$T_{ij} = T_i \frac{A_j/d_{ij}^b}{A_1/d_{i1}^b + A_2/d_{i2}^b + \ldots + A_n/d_{in}^b} \tag{9.22}$$

or

$$T_{ij} = T_i \frac{A_j/d_{ij}^b}{\sum_{j=1}^{n} A_j/d_{ij}^b} \tag{9.23}$$

This model states that destination zone j attracts trips T_{ij} (1) in direct proportion to the total outbound number of trips T_i from zone i, (2) in direct proportion to its own attractive force A_j, (3) in inverse proportion to the distance between the two zones d_{ij}, and (4) in inverse proportion to the relative attractive function of competing opportunities defined as

$$\sum_{j=1}^{n} (A_j/d_{ij}^b)$$

The specific index used to measure the force of attraction A_j varies according to the purpose of the trip generation study. For journey-to-work studies, the obviously appropriate index is the number of employment opportunities (jobs) available at each of the destinations. Floor area of retail trade establishments is commonly used as a measure of attraction in modeling consumer movement. For intercity tourist movements, the number of hotel rooms could be used as the measure of attraction. Thus the concept of attractiveness lends itself to a great deal of flexibility in operational situations.

The output of the model [Equation (9.23)] is initially a percentage or fractional allocation of trips from one origin to each of several specific destinations.

When multiplied by the total number of trips from that origin T_i, the product is a complete allocation of all trips between that origin and all destinations. By extending this procedure to all possible origins, a regional allocation is produced.

The allocation of consumer trips and expenditures in the Baltimore metropolitan area was studied by Lakshmanan and Hansen (1965a, 1965b). The total sales generated at all shopping centers were assumed to be equal to the total available personal consumption expenditures for all retail goods in the region. By introducing a realistic situation of overlapping competition among all shopping centers, the study was a significant departure from the traditional assumption of closed trade-area boundaries where consumers shop at the nearest available opportunity.

The goal of the Baltimore study was to predict consumer spending S_{ij} for retail goods by people living in zone i and shopping in zone j. Money flows can also be modeled using the same gravity formulation, and whether money is sent via the mail in the form of a check or is carried by individuals and spent in zone j is only an operational question. Conceptually there is not much difference. However, since the cost of movement for personal consumption expenditures varies with distance in contrast to mail flows (10 cents from any place to any other in the U.S.), it may be expected that consumer travel would exhibit steep distance-decay functions, *ceteris paribus.* Additionally, the location of competing facilities, differentiated by price, quality, variety, and other attributes, has been demonstrated to have a crucial role in consumer travel behavior. With these considerations in mind, Lakshmanan and Hansen tested a slight modification of the model given in Equation (9.23) and compared the results with actual shopping trips. The model yielded an R^2 value of 0.91. When the shopping trips from each of the 78 origin zones to the central business district were aggregated, the model predicted 16,425 shopping trips, which was 5 percent below the daily 17,466 actual trips recorded by the origin-and-destination survey of the Baltimore Metropolitan Area Transportation Study.

The preceding paragraphs have described how gravity models are tested and calibrated. If the deviations between the predicted and the actual flows are beyond some specified tolerance limits, then the parameters of the model need to be reestimated.

Some Operational Problems

Since the gravity model is fundamentally an analytical device used to predict or model interarea flows, in most situations the aim is to replicate observed flows as closely as possible. Consequently, maximizing the goodness of fit, as evaluated by R^2 and other measures, is an important consideration which has led to the manipulation of the components of the model in a number of ways. Many of these manipulations have little or no conceptual justification, but if the aim is prediction in a planning context, it may be argued that empirical validation is all that matters and that theoretical ramifications should take a back seat. Attempts at such empirical validation have frequently encountered a number of operational problems, a categorization of which includes the following topics.

Measuring the Mass

In the nomenclature used throughout this chapter, P_iP_j has referred to the masses of two areas. To the extent that individuals are the fundamental elements of social masses as well as decisionmaking units, and since population totals can be regarded as surrogates for demand, numbers of people have been a standard measure of mass. However, depending on the exact nature of the problem under investigation, other measurements are perhaps more appropriate. In migration studies, for example, labor surplus in the ith area and number of unfilled job opportunities in the jth area would probably yield a better fit than population when they are used to measure the mass. In retail market potential studies, dollar volumes of sales and retail floor area are useful measures. Harris (1954) used the number of tractors as the measure of mass in analyzing the location of producers of farm equipment. The number of families, automobile registrations, hospital beds, commodity output, value added by manufacturing, and so on are alternative measures of mass.

Measuring Distance

For intermetropolitan and intercity studies of movement, a simple airline measure of distance has proved to be quite adequate. However, as the size of the area under consideration becomes smaller, airline distances tend to yield poor fits. The correlation between road distance and airline distance is a function of scale, as was shown in Chapter 2.

Travel time is one of the most widely used measures of distance in metropolitan transportation studies. In industrial location studies, transport costs, or, more broadly, transfer costs, are certainly more relevant measures than physical distance. In both types of studies, the measure of distance must include terminal costs (costs of parking, loading, and unloading) in addition to the over-the-road cost.

Alternative measures include mileage along specific routes rather than straight-line distances, fuel consumed in transport, number of gear shifts, stop signs, traffic lights, etc.

Weighting the Mass

If aggregates of people are regarded as the mass, it is evident that the different individuals who compose the mass make varying contributions to the interaction potential. These variations are especially important in interaction studies in which the two masses are located in different cultural or economic regions. There are at least three ways of differentiating masses:

1. One way involves the recognition that the propensity for interaction varies between groups which are regionally identified. Stewart (1947) argued that, contrary to the assumption in his early formulations in which a value of 1.0 was assigned as the weight of the masses, it was necessary to stipulate different weights that are more reflective of average regional interaction propensities. Accordingly, he assigned regional values of 1.0, 0.8, and 2.0 as weights of the masses in the American North, Deep South, and Far West, respectively. The potential for movement of individuals in a city in the Far

West was twice that in a city located in the North, while interaction propensity in the Deep South was assumed to be 80 percent of that in the North.

The interaction propensities in peasant societies, such as those in India and China, when compared to those in the United States, may justify the assignment of a weight of say 0.1. Such weights also change through time. In order to incorporate weights in the gravity model, it is rewritten as

$$I_{ij} = K \frac{w_i P_i \cdot w_j P_j}{d_{ij}^{\,b}} \tag{9.24}$$

in which w_i and w_j are weights modifying the populations of the origin and the destination, respectively.

If *i* refers to Los Angeles and *j* to Calcutta and their masses as measured by population amount to 4 and 5 million, respectively, while weights of 2.0 and 0.1 are used, we are saying that the population of Los Angeles should be regarded as 8 million while that of Calcutta is only 0.5 million, insofar as potential interaction between them is concerned. Within the United States, Stewart found that the weights he used were appropriate and adequately predicted the movement of bank checks.

By experimenting with weights of masses for the flow of telephone calls, it has been found that city weights were 0.34 for Flint, Michigan, and 2.94 for Los Angeles. For airline traffic, the range of weights was from 0.14 for Baltimore to 7.61 for Miami. This means that the volume of inbound and outbound movement from and to Miami's airport is over 7 times that which could be expected solely from the unweighted, raw population of the city (Hammer and Iklé, 1957).

2. The second approach to weighing the mass is by incorporating a qualitative factor to adjust the quantity. In contrast to Stewart's procedure, this method gives an empirically derived weight which can be directly computed. Thus, in studying airline passenger movement, the population weighted by per capita income may be a more appropriate measure of potential air traffic, since the propensity to travel by air depends largely on income. It is possible to keep on adding weights, such as educational level, family size, occupational characteristics, and so on, and Equation (9.24) may then be rewritten as

$$I_{ij} = K \frac{w_{1i} w_{2i} w_{3i} P_i \cdot w_{1j} w_{2j} w_{3j} P_j}{d_{ij}^{\,b}} \tag{9.25}$$

3. Another way of approaching the problem of differentiating masses is to raise each one to some power as a way of incorporating either agglomeration or deglomeration economies of different cities. In a study of intercity travel, Mylroie (1956) fitted a number of exponents and found that the best fit was given by

$$I_{ij} = K \frac{P_i^{0.5} \cdot P_j^{0.5}}{d_{ij}^{2}} \tag{9.26}$$

or, alternatively,

$$I_{ij} = K \sqrt{\frac{P_i \cdot P_j}{d_{ij}^{2}}} \tag{9.27}$$

Weighting the Distance

Strictly from a geographic point of view, the modification of distance is the most important operational problem in the use of gravity models to study spatial interaction. Since we are concerned with the specific frictional impact of distance, we need to compute the most appropriate distance exponent. If one remained rigidly within the framework of newtonian physics, of course there would be no difficulty. Thus while Stewart was amenable to manipulating the masses, he resolutely refused to weight distance. Instead, he argued either that d_{ij} should be left without an exponent (i.e., an exponent of 1) or that it should be squared. Many transportation studies, however, have shown clearly that distance functions in social physics are much more complex than in the newtonian formulation. The coefficient (b value) or distance exponent in Equation (9.14) is empirically determined as are all the other exponents.

By now, an extensive number of gravity model-based studies have been accumulated, especially in the field of transportation planning. In comparing the frictional impact of distance in these studies, as measured by the b coefficient relevant to distance, one is struck by the widely divergent values. In the absence of a theory it is impossible to provide credible explanations of these differing values. Nevertheless, it is possible to suggest a number of interpretations, each of which may be applicable to a particular situation. Among such interpretations, we wish to emphasize the impact of distance itself, the size of the mass, the size of the study area, aggregation by commodity and type of movement, and modal split.

The impact of distance itself. Carrothers (1956, 97) claims that "the exponent may be a variable function related inversely to distance itself rather than to population." If so, the impedance role per unit distance is greater for short distances than for longer ones. The distance-decay functions plotted in Chapter 8 showed this to be the case. Thus, for example, if store A is 2 miles from someone's home and store B is 10 miles away, and both are offering the same goods at the same prices, an individual will patronize store A. On the other hand, whether Vladivostok is 9000 or 10,000 miles away from an origin is a matter of little consequence; i.e., there is a sort of "marginal friction of distance" which decreases with distance.

In calibrating the gravity model, it has been found that if distances (as measured by travel time) are small, then the exponent is large. Thus, in small towns where distances are short and activities are located close together, the travel time factor b is high. In contrast, it is well known that in Los Angeles, where activities are widely spread out, people travel long distances both as a matter of habit and out of necessity. One of the difficulties encountered in gravity-model studies is that with increasing distance from a given origin the area under search increases as does the number of alternative opportunities. Therefore, the allocation of flows from a specific origin to a specific destination can frequently become erroneous even though total inbound and outbound movement balance out.

The impact of the size of the mass. It has been suggested that the distance exponent is a variable one which is inversely related to the size of the mass. One way to interpret this notion is that a large mass may be expected to generate a large volume of interaction of which many of the component flows will be over relatively long distances (i.e., many New Yorkers fly to

Sydney). Furthermore, the functional complexity of a large agglomeration and its role in the national or international urban hierarchy mean that many kinds of interaction in great volumes would tend to occur over long distances. In contrast, in a traditional peasant society, not only are the masses small in size, but the functional simplicity would lead to short-distance interactions.

The size of area. One unsolved and probably unsolvable problem in many aspects of geographic research is that of areal aggregation. Geographic space can be conceived of as a continuum of points. Information about geographic space, on the other hand, is usually highly discrete, being bundled and recorded on the basis of arbitrarily defined areas such as census tracts, enumeration districts, counties, trip-generation zones, states, and so on. While the gravity model incorporates mass and distance explicitly, it perforce ignores shape and size of the area. If, as may frequently happen, the individual sizes of the areas under consideration are widely varied, then it may also be true that much of the regional movement is confined within the larger areas, i.e., intrazonal, and consequently escapes the analysis completely. When the basic study unit area is especially large, as in the case of Black's (1973) study of commodity flows between economic regions such as New England and the Pacific Northwest, it is impossible to identify intraregional movements. It may actually be that more movement occurs *within* these large regions than between the regions.

Aggregation by commodity and type of movement. In this context, Alcaly (1967) found that in California aggregated intercity passenger volume, including air, rail, bus, and auto movements, yielded a better fit, as compared to disaggregated passenger trips.

In much the same vein, Black (1971b) compared the exponents as they varied between the 1967 flows of 80 different commodity groups among the nine census regions of the United States. Using an iterative procedure where *b* begins with a value of 0 and is allowed to increase in increments of 0.05, Black was able to compute exponents whose contribution to the marginal change in the correlation between predicted and actual flows was equal to 0. In comparing the more aggregated with the less aggregated shipment groups, he found that the model performed slightly better for the aggregated data. For the disaggregated data, it was found that the distance exponent varied widely, from 11.25 for hydraulic cement to —0.05 for general industrial machinery and household appliances. Other values included 1.05 (miscellaneous fabrics and textiles), 2.00 (miscellaneous nonmetallic minerals), 5.25 (dairy products), and 0.25 (drugs). Thus, while the exponent for hydraulic cement suggests a very steep distance decay (distance has to be raised to its eleventh power!), the shipment of drugs and photographic equipment is relatively unimpeded by the friction of distance. In terms of the bases of spatial interaction (Ullman, 1956), it may be said that the former is less transferable than the latter.

In a study of commodity flows in the Bengal-Bihar industrial complex in India, a potential formulation of the gravity model was used to analyze the volumes of flows. The distance exponent for coal was 1.04 while that for "other machinery" was 0.39 (Reed, 1967). Further, for the shipment of iron and steel within the Calcutta region, the exponent was 0.95 in contrast to

2.12 for movement from the region to the rest of India, indicating that iron and steel shipments are mostly within the industrial complex itself.

When distance exponents by trip purposes were computed for the Detroit metropolitan area, it was found that while school trips had a high exponent (great frictional impact of distance), the exponent for social contacts was relatively low (Carroll and Bevis, 1957).

Modal split. In evaluating the current performance of the transportation facilities in a metropolitan area, and in attempting to project the number, kinds, and locations of transportation links required at some future time, it is necessary to disaggregate a gravity model by mode. That is, we wish to know the volume of I_{ijk} (the volume of movement between origin i and destination j via the kth mode of travel: auto, pedestrian, subway, etc.). Based on cost and convenience factors, the distance exponent applicable to each of these modes will probably differ. Modal split, although of peripheral interest in geography, is a crucial operational consideration for transportation planners.

Temporal and Locational Aspects of Parameters of Gravity Models

Without question, the wealth of migration and other movement data available in Sweden, disaggregated areally and comparable for a long period of time, is somewhat unique. Thus, it is no wonder that some of the most detailed geographic studies on movement, including the diffusion of innovations, have emerged from Sweden. Indeed, it may be said that the studies of spatial diffusion have diffused outward from Lund, Sweden. Thus, Hägerstrand (1957) had access to large amounts of data on who moved when and where for his study of Asby Parish.

Figure 9-5 shows the relationship between migration and distance for two decennial intervals, 1860 to 1869 and 1930 to 1939. The distance exponent for the earlier time period was 3.0 and for the latter 2.4. The difference between these is apparent in Figure 9-5 as the slope of the line for 1930 to 1939 is distinctly less steep than that for 1860 to 1869. This difference suggests that, through time, migration fields become larger as more people move over longer distances.

Some of the factors that are probably associated with the temporal decrease of distance exponents are the location of prior migrants from a certain origin area who may have moved long distances and who transmitted encouraging information back home, greater information availability generally about opportunities at distant locations which leads to an increase in the awareness space, and better and cheaper transport facilities. Indeed, in terms of the last factor, in Aarhus, Denmark, it was calculated that the distance exponent for migration from rural parishes with railroad stations was 1.4, and for parishes without railroad stations it was 1.8 (Hägerstrand, 1957, 116).

Long-run trends in gravity-model parameters may mask short-run fluctuations. Indeed, in the short run, the trend may actually be counter to that observed over very long periods of time. In the United States, we know that with growing affluence, better transportation facilities, a higher level of connectivity between nodes, better information about job opportunities at distant places, dispersal of manufacturing and other activities through the space-

Figure 9-5 Temporal variations in distance exponents for Swedish migration data: (*a*) 1860–1869; (*b*) 1930–1939.

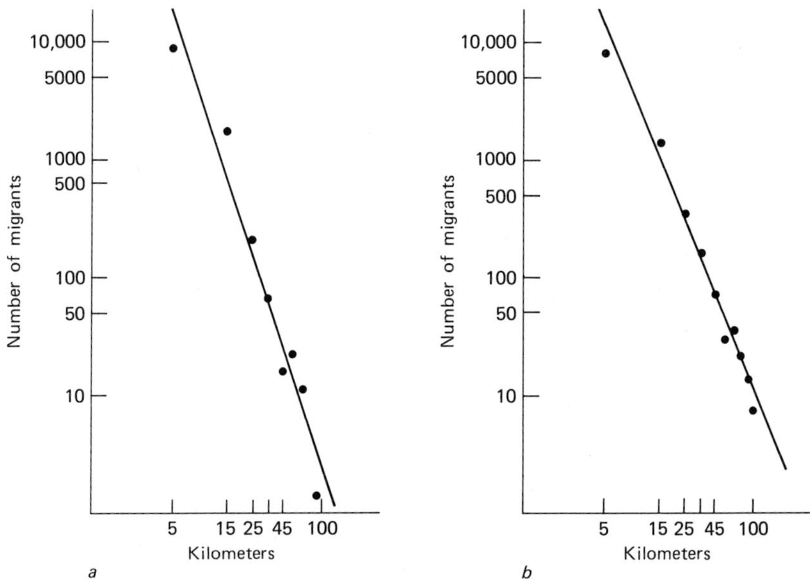

economy, and the decline of employment in farming, etc., in the course of the last century or so families have become more mobile. The frictional role of distance has been decreasing.

We nevertheless find that a comparison of migration between five origins (the State Economic Areas of Boston; Jackson, Mississippi; Des Moines; Pueblo, Colorado; and Fresno) and twenty common destinations shows a modestly increasing role of distance between 1955 to 1960 and 1965 to 1970. The origins were chosen with a view to obtaining broad geographical coverage. The 20 destinations, also State Economic Areas, were chosen by means of a stratified random-sampling procedure. Using the population of the origins and destinations and the airline distance between them, Conmy (1973) fitted the logarithmic form of the gravity model as in Equation (9.14). The resulting *b* values applicable to distance were —1.28141 for the 1955–1960 period and —1.32739 for the 1965–1970 period. The difference between the two *b* values is modest. The slight increase, indicative of the greater frictional role of distance in the later time period, is perhaps suggestive of a higher level of place utility.

There are not only temporal differences, but also place-to-place ones in the size of the distance exponent at any given time. These differences are associated with urban-rural contrasts in awareness space, opportunities, the differential characteristics of individuals, and, of course, the availability of transportation facilities. Hägerstrand has shown that there are geographic clusters of high exponents indicative of isolation, as well as clusters of low exponents that index a lesser degree of distance-boundedness. Again, in Aarhus, the distance exponent for small towns was 1.3, in contrast to 1.6 for rural parishes.

Critique and Evaluation of the Gravity Model

Gravity-model studies and the concept associated with the gravity model have been extensively reviewed by Olsson (1965) and Isard et al. (1960). An overall evaluation of the gravity model should be undertaken from two entirely different perspectives: from the viewpoint of a model builder and from the viewpoint of a philosopher of science.

The first vantage point from which to evaluate and criticize the gravity model is that of the model builder or user. For example, from a transportation planner's viewpoint, the "proof of the pudding is in the eating." In numerous applications, the gravity model has shown a remarkable ability to mirror the observed patterns of spatial interaction. Some of these applications have made use of complex "black-box" formulations, and while we may not know why they work, the fact that they do more than justifies their repeated and continued use. The model is generally a robust one.

Additionally, the gravity model is simple to compute, at least in its elementary version, easy to understand intuitively, and lends itself to delicate calibrations as a result of which it can be made sensitive to small differences in the volumes of interarea flows. Consequently, it has become one of the standard operational techniques in metropolitan area transportation studies.

As was shown earlier, the fit of gravity models is especially good in the context of aggregated mass movement and particularly at the intrametropolitan scale. When the mass is disaggregated, the performance is less satisfactory. Studies of interregional movements must come to grips with the problem of resource localization, and since there is no simple or consistent relationship between movement and resource availability, alternative modeling strategies such as multiple regression or flow factor analysis may be more appropriate. At the international scale, the gravity model is least satisfactory because of the sharply attenuating effects of political boundaries on distance-decay functions, as was shown by Mackay's study of telephone traffic between cities in Quebec and the U.S. Certainly, if the masses of the U.S. and the U.S.S.R. were multiplied and the product divided by the distance between them, the resulting predicted interaction volume would be far off the mark, owing to the relative impermeability of the so-called Iron Curtain, no matter how much one manipulated the model and adjusted its parameters.

We must also scrutinize the gravity model from the viewpoint of the philosopher of science. Noting that "under the general umbrella, spatial interaction and distance decay, it has been possible to accommodate most model work in transportation, migration, commuting, diffusion and location theory." Olsson (1970, 223) has attempted to examine spatial interaction models in terms of epistemological principles. A frequently used schema of scientific explanation is that initially proposed by Hempel and Oppenheim (1948), which is of the form

$C_1, C_2, \ldots, C_k$	(which is a statement of initial conditions)
$L_1, L_2, \ldots, L_k$	(which are general laws that lead via logical deduction to E)
E	(which is a description of the empirical phenomenon to be explained)

In this schema, there is a perfect symmetry between explanation and prediction, which means that doing one necessarily involves doing the other. Olsson objects to this symmetrical relationship on the ground that while explanation is a necessary prerequisite for prediction, the reverse is not necessarily true. Thus, on the basis of an examination of data, it is possible to arrive at inductive generalizations which are useful for predictive purposes but which are not necessarily the same thing as an explanation. One important criterion that any explanation must satisfy, in order to be properly called an explanation, is that it must have the ability to predict deviant behavior.

Moreover, a model provided with a theory is completely interpreted while one without a theory is subject to several different interpretations, each of which may be valid under different circumstances. Therefore, in the absence of theory we lack any basis to discriminate among the alternative interpretations. For example, if T_{ij} is significantly higher in the real world than was predicted by the model, the difference may be caused by an incorrect specification of the values of K and P. To argue that these deviations may be due to income, ethnic, or other variations is really circular reasoning and amounts to going back to the real world. This return to the real world is self-defeating, since an important purpose of model-building is to eliminate some of the confusion inherent in the real world.

The only underlying theory that can be associated with the gravity model is that of "least effort," a vague notion at best. The gravity model is really just an analogy drawn from physics, and Chorley (1964) has noted some of the dangers in drawing analogies. A high level of comparability must be present in order to make a satisfactory analogy; therefore, broad analogical leaps into different domains should not be made indiscriminately. Social physics in general and the gravity model in particular raise such questions as, Are people like molecules? Are places masses? Is the relationship between interaction and distance continuous and smooth? Is the migration field a continuous one like the gravitational field? Is the propensity for interaction an invariant constant? Is the relationship between mass and distance invariant through time as in the physical domain?

Isard et al. (1960) have noted that in empirical studies using the gravity model different exponents have been used, just as many different weights have been applied to the masses. Nevertheless, there is no theoretical rationale for using one particular exponent rather than another in any situation. This being the case, we often do not know why we are doing what we are doing, and further, in the absence of theory a substantial component of arbitrariness creeps in. A telling example of such arbitrariness is the multiplication of c by k, the division of the product by P^2, and calling the whole thing K in the derivation of the model, which bears only a spurious relationship to the newtonian gravitational constant G. Indeed, as the gravity model becomes increasingly more complex, with numerous weights as in Equation (9.25) and with different exponents for different commodities as in Black's study, it eventually becomes something of a "black box." Input data are manipulated by the model, and eventually an output emerges. From the geographer's point of view, the numerous weights blur the effects of distance, and as a result we are not able to filter out the unique contribution of distance to human interaction.

A final criticism, from an epistemological point of view, is that gravity models are deterministic. Olsson (1967) has argued the need for rooting the gravity model in a firm probabilistic framework. This has recently been done by Wilson (1970).

ENTROPY-MAXIMIZING MODEL: A NEW DEPARTURE

In the last half decade, the most significant and innovative work in modeling and analyzing flows has been that of Wilson (1970). In his work, the major departure from the traditional gravity-type interaction models has been the introduction of formal systems theory (concepts such as "equilibrium" and "steady state") and information theory (concepts such as "entropy"), as well as probability theory.

The Idea of a General System

We have pointed out earlier that a model without a theory is ambiguous and open to several interpretations, while one supplied with a theory can be interpreted in only one way. Wilson's model is founded upon general systems theory. It must be stated at this point that any system (but especially a social one) is infinitely complex, and therefore, "it is advisable to think of systems not as real things at all, but as convenient abstractions which possess a form which facilitates a certain style of analysis" (Harvey, 1969, 448). In this sense, a system is really a model of the real world.

A *system S* may be defined as a set of objects or elements (possessed of a set of attributes or characteristics). The set of elements, $A = \{a_1, a_2, \ldots, a_n\}$ is one in which the elements interact with each other. If r_{ij} represents the interaction between two elements a_i and a_j, then we can denote the set of all r_{ij} by R. Such a specification leads to the definition of a system as $S = \{A, R\}$. In a spatial system, the elements are nodes and routes, the attributes are their functions such as population size, capacities, etc., and the relationships are manifested in flows. The essential characteristic of any system is that everything is related to everything else. In the spatial system, it is movement that ties the elements of the system together and keeps it functioning. In comparing a metropolitan region to a system, we are not making any analogical leaps, as in the case of the classic gravity model which assumes that metropolitan regions obey the laws of the solar system.

States of a System and Alternative Configurations

In order to function, every system requires some level of energy input. It is possible to define the *state of the system* as being the composite structure resulting from the amount of energy supplied to it, as well as the distribution of that energy among the individual components. The analogy to the familiar economic system may serve to make the point clear. If we can conceptualize the total personal income of a nation or area as being the total energy, then the distribution of that income among individuals is a description of the state of that economic system.

A most important question attacked by Wilson is the conceptualization and operational modeling of "the most likely state" of a regional system. Since the meaning of "likelihood" is not intuitively obvious, consider first the income distribution among a population as being a representation of the state of an economic system. We can visualize two contrasting situations, as in Figure 9-6*a* and *b*. The first of these is said to be a *descending* series in which a few people make very high incomes and most people make relatively low incomes. In the *ascending* series (Figure 9-6*b*), a lot of people earn very high incomes and a small number of people earn low incomes. Thus, every distribution has a configuration, in this case, how many people earn how much income. In addition, every configuration can occur in some number of alternative ways, and so it is possible to shift the allocation of the total annual income (energy) among the individuals and in that way arrive at the same configuration.

Between an ascending and a descending income series, which one is the most likely to occur? We all know that in every nation in the world there are a few very rich people and that the majority of the population are poor or have moderate incomes. Therefore, we may conclude that in any system, a descending series is the most likely or probable state of that system. This is a characteristic which belongs to many classes of phenomena: a few large cities and many small towns, a few giant corporations and numerous small companies, and a few very long routes and many very short links.

The state of a system can change through time in two different ways: (1) the total amount of energy available can become greater or lesser, and (2) simultaneously, the distribution of energy among the components can also change. For example, the overall income level in a nation changes through time (generally it increases), and the income distribution can become more or less equitable through time.

In this model, we conceptualize a metropolitan area (or any other place, for that matter) as being a system. The elements are (1) people at places, (2) activities at places, and (3) routes connecting them. The relationships are flows between specific origins and specific destinations. Of course, these flows can occur only with the infusion of money (energy). As a finite resource, money must be allocated among a number of human wants, keeping in mind that if more money is spent on travel, less will be spent on food, and so on. Just as income distributions vary, people's spending patterns on travel vary also. Again, we can think of a descending series where in any metropolitan area most people will spend a little money on travel, while some will spend a lot. From our perspective so far, we know that a descending series is more likely to occur than an ascending one. However, we have embarked upon a search for *the* most likely state of a system. It can be defined as that par-

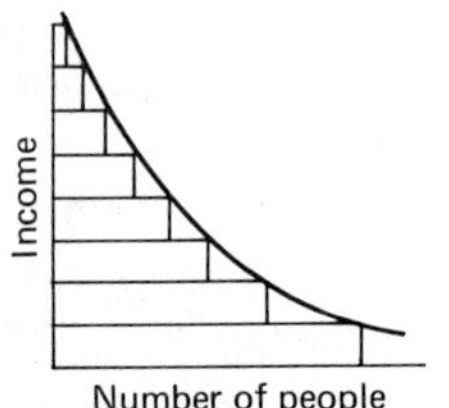

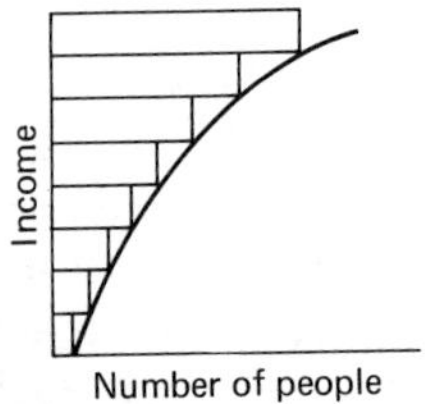

Figure 9-6
Two income distributions: (*a*) descending; (*b*) ascending.

ticular state for which the number of combinatorial possibilities is the greatest. As an example, we may write the combinatorial expression

$$W = \frac{n!}{\prod_{i=1}^{6} n_i!} \tag{9.28}$$

where $\Pi_1^6 n_i!$ means that starting from the first factorial number $i = 1$, we serially multiply six numbers such that $n! = n \times (n-1) \times (n-2) \times (n-3)$. . . . Thus, $6! = 6 \times 5 \times 4 \times 3 \times 2 \times 1 = 720$.

The notion of the maximum number of ways in which a particular configuration can occur can be better understood by considering a hypothetical descending series such as that shown below. An area has 10 people, and the total commuting budget is set at $80/week. This money is distributed among the population so that four individuals are at the "ground state" or zero-energy level, in that they live close to work and spend very little money or time on commuting. They may be considered to be optimizers. In contrast, there is a maverick who spends as much as $30/week on commuting. The commuting budget is allocated as follows:

Number of individuals	Dollars/week
1	30
1	20
2	10
2	5
4	0
10	80

The number of ways in which this particular configuration can occur can be computed by using the combinatorial formula [Equation (9.28)]:

$$W = \frac{10!}{1!\,1!\,2!\,2!\,4!} = 37{,}800$$

Consider next an ascending series with reference to the same system of 10 individuals and a commuting budget of $80:

Number of individuals	Dollars/week
4	10
3	8
2	6
1	4
10	80

This particular configuration can also occur in a number of ways

$$W = \frac{10!}{4!\,3!\,2!\,1!} = 12{,}600$$

Although the above two examples represent, in each case, only one of many possible descending-ascending configurations with respect to a system of 10 individuals and a total energy supply of $80, we can see that the descending series can occur in many more ways than the ascending one (3 times more numerous). Therefore, a descending series is the "most likely state" of the system; i.e., in any metropolitan area, there will be aggregate movement minimization, where most people operate near "ground state," living relatively close to work.

Moreover, through time, in any nation or region the amount of money spent on travel probably increases. At any given time, people in peasant societies are more space-bound than those in affluent societies. Thus, in terms of ascending and descending series, the interpersonal distribution of the limited travel budget will be a very steep descending series. In affluent societies, in contrast, the total budget is high, and its distribution among individuals will tend to be more uniform. For example, most Americans travel about 10,000 to 15,000 miles/year, representing expenditures of approximately $1200 to $1800, not including parking. The contrasting travel-expenditure pattern between poor and affluent societies, as well as through time in any one society, is shown in Figure 9-7.

Intrametropolitan Journey to Work in the Context of Entropy

Now that we have described the concept of the "most likely" state of the system and its combinatorial possibilities, it is possible to consider the flow model specifically. Although Wilson has constructed a large number of models, the discussion here is limited to the most elementary one, specifically, journey to work in a metropolitan area. The relevant elements are number of employees at particular residential origins i and the number of employment

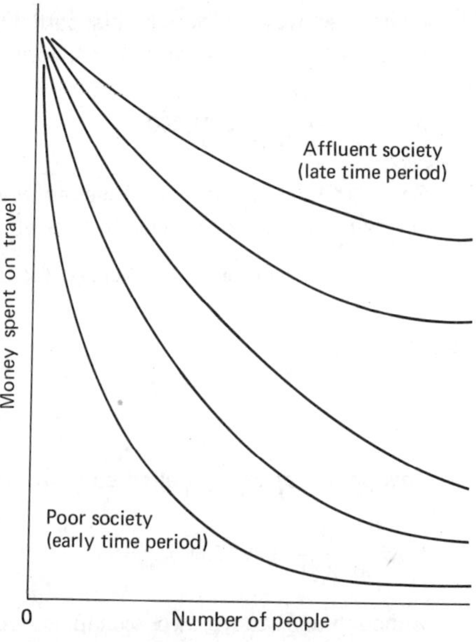

Figure 9-7
Travel budget allocations and states of the system, cross-culturally and through time

opportunities at particular destinations j. The number of employees traveling from i to j can be written as t_{ij}. The total travel cost or budget is C, and c_{ij} represents the amount of money spent by one individual in commuting from i to j. The flow matrix T_{ij} represents the actual, overall state (or megastate) of the system, which in turn comprises microstates (the individual t_{ij}).

What is the most likely state of T_{ij}? In physics, *entropy* is defined as the measure of unusable or unavailable energy in a closed thermodynamic system during an irreversible reaction. In a spatial context, entropy signifies "unnecessarily" long-distance travel or "unnecessarily" high expenditures on travel. The simplest way to obtain an intuitive understanding of the rather difficult concept of entropy is to treat it as a synonym for "waste" or "inefficiency." If there is motion without movement, as happens when we are stuck in a traffic jam and the engine of the automobile is turning, that is an example of entropy, for we are using energy but getting nowhere. In the same way, passengerless drivers who commute long distances are contributing to system-wide entropy. In light of Figure 9-7, we can see that a system in which a large proportion of the population is using large amounts of energy (cost, time, gasoline) is likely to be a wasteful, high-entropy system. Nevertheless, most systems have a tendency toward maximum entropy, and therefore entropy has the largest number of combinatorial possibilities or ways of occurring.

With respect to commuting flows, the maximum entropy of the system can be identified by finding the particular T_{ij} matrix, among all possible ones, for which the combinatorial possibilities are the largest. Viewed narrowly in this context, the notion that movement in an urban system tends toward maximum entropy is not inherently credible since maximum entropy would involve very high levels of travel expenditure on the part of a majority of the population in the area. Furthermore, maximum entropy implies something of an ascending series. We know from our everyday experience that even in affluent, wasteful societies such as ours in the United States the configuration of trip lengths in a metropolitan area conforms somewhat to a descending series.

Although not everyone engages in optimizing behavior, people do not go out of their way to travel long distances, especially on a daily basis. Thus, the goal in this model is to maximize entropy, but under severe constraints. Therefore, as between an ascending and a descending series, entropy maximization under constraints implies some form of a descending series, though not necessarily a very steep one in affluent Western nations (see Figure 9-7). We can identify the T_{ij} matrix in which there will be the largest number of possible combinations of pairwise interactions by means of

$$W(T_{ij}) = \frac{T!}{\prod\limits_{ij} T_{ij}!} \tag{9.29}$$

Let us ignore the matter of constraints for now and consider a metropolitan system in which there is one origin, five destinations, and ten workers. Some possible configurations of trips are as follows:

		Destination				
		A	*B*	*C*	*D*	*E*
Origin	10	10	0	0	0	0
	10	0	10	0	0	0
	10	·	·	·	·	·
	10	0	0	0	0	10
	10	5	5	0	0	0
	10	5	0	5	0	0
	10	5	0	0	5	0
	10	5	0	0	0	5
	10	0	5	5	0	0
	10	0	5	0	5	0
	10	·	·	·	·	·

Real world metropolitan systems, of course, are much more complex than that system depicted above. Recall that in the Baltimore metropolitan area, there were about 78 trip-generation zones, so that the microstates referred to a 78×78 matrix, i.e., 6084 cells. $T!$ in Equation (9.29) refers to the total number of work trips/day. In the Washington metropolitan area, there are more than 750,000 work trips/day. When a small number such as 15! equals 1,307,674,368,000, it is possible to perceive the formidable dimensions engendered by 0.75 million factorial. Consequently, in the operation of the model, the logarithms of $T!$ and $t_{ij}!$ are used rather than the raw numbers, but max $W(T_{ij})$ in logarithmic form is the same as that in the nonlogarithmic form. It is, therefore, convenient to keep the size of the numbers down: the logarithm of 15!, for example, is only 12.116.

Introducing Constraints on Maximum Entropy

In a pure entropy-maximizing model, many of the microstates (the cell entries) involve waste, that is, irrationally long travel distances as many individuals bypass intervening work opportunities. Because work opportunities and residential ones are not evenly distributed in a metropolitan area, their geographic patterns severely constrain the configuration of the aggregate journey to work. Therefore, let us introduce constraints concerning the number of employees in each origin zone as well as the number of job opportunities in each destination zone. With 4 origins, 5 destinations, and 28 daily trips, two possible allocations (from among many) are as follows:

		Destination				
		A (8)	*B* (5)	*C* (1)	*D* (10)	*E* (4)
Origin	1 (10)	4	3	0	2	1
	2 (5)	3	2	0	0	0
	3 (7)	1	0	1	5	0
	4 (6)	0	0	0	3	3

		Destination				
		A (8)	*B* (5)	*C* (1)	*D* (10)	*E* (4)
Origin	1 (10)	8	0	0	0	2
	2 (5)	0	5	0	0	0
	3 (7)	0	0	1	4	2
	4 (6)	0	0	0	6	0

In both of these matrices, the total number of employees in each of the origin zones and the total number of job opportunities in each of the destination zones have been reconciled. There are, of course, many ways of reconciling these figures to yield alternative configurations, each of which would represent a T_{ij}. The number of possible matrices would be very large if we did not know that the 28 workers are partitioned in a specific way among origins and, further, that 28 jobs are partitioned in a specific way among each of the destinations. These allocations are shown along the row and column headings, respectively, of the preceding two tabulations. The allocations can be treated as constraints, and in order not to end up with a situation in which "anything goes," the problem then is to maximize

$$W(T_{ij}) = \frac{T!}{\prod_{ij} T_{ij}!}$$

subject to the three constraints given in Equations (9.30), (9.31), and (9.32)

$$\sum_j T_{ij} = O_i \tag{9.30}$$

that is, the total number of trips from each residential area to one or more destinations cannot exceed the known number of employees in that origin zone.

$$\sum_i T_{ij} = D_j \tag{9.31}$$

that is, the total number of incoming workers into any destination zone from one or more origin zones cannot exceed the known number of job opportunities in that zone.

The specific allocation of t_{ij} does not have to be known, although if it is, it can serve as a check on the accuracy of the model. The minimum data input consists of a column vector indicating the number of workers in each origin zone and a row vector indicating the number of jobs in each destination zone.

The amount of money spent on commuting is a finite quantity, and while it can and does change through time, in the short run it is likely to be fixed and therefore is the third constraint on entropy maximization. In the allocation of trips in the two preceding matrices, distance or cost of travel between individual pairs of zones was not incorporated. Indeed, there are no spatial constraints to the flow of commuters. Thus, the third piece of information required to make the model operational is a cost matrix C, in which the individual c_{ij} represent the commuting cost from origin i to destination j. It is generally easy to compile mileages between each origin and all possible destinations and to multiply them by a per-mile cost of travel to yield the c_{ij}. Finally, we need to know the value of the total commuting budget in the metropolitan area under study, a statistic that is not readily available but may be obtained by sample surveys.

Travel cost is stipulated as the final constraint on maximum entropy

$$\sum_i \sum_j t_{ij} \cdot c_{ij} = C \tag{9.32}$$

which states that each of the trips t_{ij}, multiplied by the cost of making it c_{ij} and summed, cannot exceed some known total travel budget C. This final constraint prevents the utilization of unavailable energy.

What do these three constraints do? One way to single out their contribution is to recall the traditional gravity model in its simplest version P_iP_j/d_{ij}. Suppose that an origin zone, such as Arlington, Virginia, had one worker and a destination zone, such as the Federal Triangle in the District of Columbia, had one job opportunity at a particular period in time. Under these conditions, P_iP_j is equal to $1 \times 1 = 1$; that is, there is one work trip between this pair of zones. If, through time, the number of workers and the number of employment opportunities are doubled, then P_iP_j is equal to $2 \times 2 = 4$. The gravity model suggests that there are four work trips between this pair of zones, although there are only two people to make them and two jobs at the end of the road. In practice, as we have seen earlier, an arbitrary scalar K is used to adjust the size of interaction. The entropy-maximizing model, however, eliminates this kind of nonsensical result with the explicit inclusion of constraints. For this reason, Gould (1972, 696) writes, "One of the most important and exciting things about Wilson's work is that it raises the gravity model Phoenix-like from the ashes of such absurdity, and places it upon a secure theoretical foundation for the first time."

In addition, the three basic constraints are interrelated and allowed to operate simultaneously; that is, the model operationalizes what is probably the key concept in general systems theory, namely, that everything is related to everything else. Thus, for example, if one considers a specific origin and a number of destinations, the allocation of workers to each destination in the model depends simultaneously upon the overall number of jobs available at each destination, the distance or cost of reaching that destination, and the relative location of any destination with respect to other origins which may be closer to that destination. We can conceptualize a metropolitan system as one in which the employees of every origin are in some sort of competition with those of every other origin for job opportunities located at all destinations, and simultaneously, destinations are also in competition with each other for employees from all possible origin zones. Indiviuals evaluate alternative destinations, take costs into consideration, and the end result is a certain overall configuration of work trips.

Commuting flows, as well as other flows, serve to maintain the regional system in some kind of equilibrium, at least in the short run. How will the equilibrium change if (1) new elements are introduced into the system? (2) existing elements take on a new value? (3) new employment opportunities are located in some suburban zone? (4) new residences are built in some central city zone? (5) travel cost is increased or decreased between a pair of zones or in the entire metropolitan area? (6) a new highway is built or an existing one widened? The alteration of any part of the system is a source of temporary disequilibrium, and a new equilibrium must eventually result. Technically we say that the system needs to "relax." Relaxation times in social systems such as urban areas are likely to be much longer than those in physical systems. Once again it is the constraints that enable us to trace the quantitative impact of changes in the system. Thus, for each origin and each destination zone, there is a specific numerical value to the individual constraint (termed a "lagrangian multiplier") which tells us how the maximum $W(T_{ij})$ will change if the constraint is slightly loosened or tightened with reference to any particular origin or destination zone.

Evaluation of the Entropy-maximization Model

The incorporation of constraints makes the entropy-maximizing version of the gravity model flexible. If it is possible to specify mathematically any constraint, such as parking expenses or the difficulty of on-street parking, then the constraints can be explicitly incorporated into the model. Further, the mass, routes, and modes can be disaggregated by adding suitable subscripts, making the model very realistic and complex. It has been applied recently in area transportation studies in Britain and has been found to yield extremely good results, although very large computer capabilities are required to accommodate the immense combinatorial aspects of the model, even in logarithmic form. As it is extremely sensitive to sampling biases, its prerequisite is a relatively elaborate data-gathering operation.

Since surrogates of two masses (supply and demand) and an inverse function of distance (see Entropy-maximizing Model: Technical Comments, page 206) are incorporated in Wilson's work, it is evident that his work represents a reformulation of the classic gravity model. However, its foundation is more secure for the following reasons:

1. In the classic gravity model, K or G is said to represent either a travel-propensity function or a gravitational constant. However, this "constant," as we saw, is actually a variable which changes through time according to trip purpose, nature of commodity, size of place, and so on, in contrast to the gravitational constant in physics which is invariant. In practice, K in spatial interaction models is used as a scalar to adjust the value of estimated flows in accordance with their known size. Clearly, sound theory should not have any element of arbitrariness in it.

2. The notion of an undifferentiated mass, even if disaggregated or weighted by income, etc., is still a deterministic formulation. In contrast, the alternative viewpoint of a frequency distribution, in which with increasing size one dominant configuration overwhelms all the others in terms of combinatorial possibilities, meets Olsson's plea for rooting the gravity model in a firm probabilistic foundation.

3. By seeking to maximize $W(T_{ij})$ and trying to find that flow matrix which has the greatest number of microstates associated with it, we are also explicitly recognizing individual behavior. Note, however, that this is done without recourse to studying individual behavior as such by means of a travel-diary approach. Deviant behavior (from some optimal norm) can be explained or predicted in this model by recourse to systems concepts rather than by going back to the real world.

4. Finally, by applying the concepts of general systems theory to a metropolitan area, we are in a position to understand that the system may assume any one of a number of states. The most likely state, however, is

characterized by constrained entropy; i.e., it contains the greatest number of feasible (not possible) microstates.

ENTROPY-MAXIMIZING MODEL: TECHNICAL COMMENTS

The discussion concerning Wilson's model in this chapter was deliberately kept simple and straightforward, emphasizing the conceptual underpinnings of the model, rather than a formal statement of it. Nevertheless, students who have acquired some level of mathematical competence may find the following technical notes useful:

1. The distance-decay function used in this model is an exponential one. The most likely state of any reasonably large system will be a descending series. In Figure 9-7, the curves can be described by means of

$$c_k = c_0 e^{-\beta e_k} \tag{9.33}$$

where c_k = number of individuals who spend k dollars for commuting
c_0 = number of individuals who spend no money for commuting (ground-state level)
β = a parameter to be estimated (a regression coefficient)
e_k = commuting budget k
e = 2.7183

Equation (9.33) is strictly analogous to Boltzmann's law concerning excitation levels of gas particles given a certain supply of energy.

The configuration of the most likely state depends upon the value of β, which in turn is a function of the mean energy (or commuting budget) level available to or used up by individuals in the metropolitan system. As individuals in the area become more affluent, the total energy supply increases, the numerical value of β becomes smaller, and many individuals can afford to travel long distances. This situation is shown in the topmost curve in Figure 9-7. On the other hand, if the total travel budget is low, the numerical value of β is large. In a peasant society, many individuals are at the ground-state level, as shown by the steepest and lowest curve in Figure 9-7; most people "stay put."

2. The modus operandi of obtaining the maximum value of some expression such as max $W(T_{ij})$, subject to some number of specified constraints, involves the use of what are termed "lagrangian multipliers."

The problem is to write an expression in such a way that a constraint is truly "binding"; that is, in an attempt to find the maximum value, the constraint should give us a particular lesser value and in this way stop us before we reach the unconstrained maximum value. Even for very simple expressions that can be graphed and visually examined, incorrect maximization solutions may be reached because the constraint is not binding. To avoid this situation, lagrangian multipliers are widely used by applied mathematicians, econometricians, and now, evidently, by geographers.

Specifically, each of the three constraint equations is rewritten, bringing everything to one side and setting each equation equal to 0. This method, of course, involves the introduction of a minus sign in the lefthand side of the equation. Thus, for example, the first constraint, concerning the trips from each residential area,

$$\sum_j T_{ij} = O_i$$

is now rewritten as

$$O_i - \sum_j T_{ij} = 0$$

In this way, each of the constraining equations is reformulated and incorporated in the function that we wish to maximize, together with some multiplier (the lagrangian) of each constraining equation. Once this process is completed, both the possibility of exceeding a constraint that should be binding and reaching an incorrect maximum as well as the possibility of not meeting a constraint are eliminated. Thus, a correct solution can always be obtained in the face of constraints. Additionally, a numerical value for λ, the lagrangian multiplier, is also obtained along the way. This calculation is very useful because λ tells us how the maximum would change if a particular constraint were slightly loosened or tightened up. For example, the second constraint refers to the number of employment opportunities in zone j. Once λ_j has been computed with respect to this constraint, it is easy to determine the impact on max $W(T_{ij})$ of additional or diminished job opportunities in any destination zone. The same use of constraints holds good for situations where more or fewer residential opportunities occur at any one of the origin zones, and for changes in the cost of transportation between specific pairs of origins and destinations.

By incorporating each of the rewritten constraint equations in the expression to be maximized, we have

$$\max W = \frac{T!}{\prod_{ij} T_{ij}!} + \sum \lambda_i(O_i - \sum_j T_{ij}) + \sum \lambda_j(D_j - \sum_i T_{ij}) + \beta(C - \sum_i \sum_j T_{ij} \cdot c_{ij}) \quad (9.35)$$

3. Equation (9.35) is extremely difficult to compute, and therefore in practice the combinatorial expression is first converted to natural logarithms. Furthermore, the evaluation of the expression depends upon a method known as "Stirling's approximation." What this involves, basically, is an iterative procedure, setting β to different values and obtaining different sets of lagrangian multipliers repeatedly, until such time as they converge on certain stable values. The technical details of this approximation are rather complex, but in any event, the expression to be maximized in the face of binding constraints becomes

$$T_{ij} = A_i \cdot B_j \cdot O_i \cdot D_j \exp(-\beta c_{ij}) \quad (9.36)$$

where, since O_i and D_j have already been defined, as constraining equations,

$$A_i = \exp \frac{-\lambda_i^{(1)}}{O_i} \quad (9.37)$$

which is equal to

$$A_i = [\sum_j B_j D_j \exp(-\beta c_{ij})]^{-1} \quad (9.38)$$

and

$$B_j = \exp \frac{-\lambda_j^{(2)}}{D_j} \tag{9.39}$$

which equals

$$B_j = [\sum_j A_i O_i \exp(-\beta c_{ij})]^{-1} \tag{9.40}$$

Despite the forbiddingly awesome-looking formulations above [Equations (9.36) to (9.40)], it is not difficult to obtain an intuitive understanding of what is happening. This new gravity model, inspired by statistical mechanics, requires neither analogical leaps to different domains nor an unbreakable contract with the concept of gravitation, and as a result, "thinking on spatial interaction [had] reached an impasse" (Pred, 1967, 18). It says that the most likely state of the system, in terms of probabilities or frequency distributions, is described by that flow matrix for which the combinatorial possibilities are the largest.

The interactions between home and work place, as in the traditional gravity model, are directly related to the number of workers (O_i) and the number of jobs (D_j). The lagrangian multipliers ensure that the system is in balance, by seeing to it that the constraints are met. Note from Equations (9.37) through (9.40) that λ_i and λ_j as well as $-\beta c_{ij}$ are all simultaneously estimated so that the constraints interact with each other. Further, a separate value of the lagrangian multiplier λ_i and λ_j is calculated for each origin and for each destination zone. With respect to the cost constraint, however, there is no such spatial disaggregation since the notion of energy is a systemwide one. The negative exponential function c_{ij} is controlled by the lagrangian multiplier β.

The distance-decay function in Wilson's model is exp $(-\beta c_{ij})$ which may be interpreted as the distance-deterrence function. The value of β, of course, is determined by the cost constraint equation and is related to average distance traveled or average transportation cost paid. The greater the value of β, the lesser the average distance traveled or, alternatively, the greater the frictional impact of distance. If C increases, then more is spent on traveling, and the average distances traveled will increase as the value of β decreases.

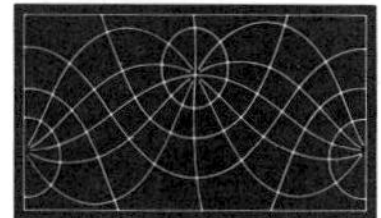

10 The Structure of Flows

In the preceding chapters, we have seen that a transportation network consists of a hierarchy of nodes and routes. Two basic elements of nodal and route hierarchies were chosen for particular emphasis: their numbers (or frequency) and their sizes (or capacities). Figure 5-14*c* showed an idealized landscape containing a large number of small places connected to one another by a few routes of short length and capacity.

At the upper end of the hierarchy, the few large places were connected to one another by long route segments of high capacity and to small and intermediate places by means of a large number of smaller route segments. We have also considered the probable volume of interaction that may be expected to occur between any two ultimate nodes as a function of their respective sizes and the intervening distance between them. An important "missing link" in the schema, so far, is the precise structuring of flows between any pair of nodes or in a system of nodes. We know that not all places are connected directly to one another, and therefore flows have to be routed in a complex and circuitous trajectory through a series of intervening (or relay) nodes.

The term "structure" appears to be one of those "primitives" in geography that is rather difficult to define. Although the notion of structure is developed throughout this chapter, it is nevertheless necessary to convey a preliminary understanding now, if only in an analogical fashion. Structure implies some recognizable order and organization. For example, in a house if the bedrooms, bathroom, and living room were randomly arranged in relation to one another, the resulting layout could be dysfunctional and further would lead to unnecessarily high volumes of movement.

Physical systems, be they hydrological or meteorological, tend to function in an efficient manner with regard to their utilization of energy. We have already referred to the relationships among the number, length, area of watershed, and stream order (Figure 5-16). Let us now consider the relationship between flow volume and stream order and, in particular, the channeling of flows, as a way of approaching the topic of flow structure. Low-order streams carry a small volume of water, and as we proceed up the hierarchy, each successively higher-order stream carries an increasingly higher volume. Further, any given-order stream joins a higher-order stream.

A drop of run-off somewhere in Minnesota (origin) ultimately ends up in the Gulf of Mexico (destination). By itself, this statement is not profound, but in the case of human interaction, all that flow models tell us is how much originated where and was consigned to which destination. A more complete understanding of the nature of flows requires an understanding of what happens in between.

The drop of run-off will find its way to a brook, to larger and increasingly larger streams in a hierarchical fashion until it eventually enters the Mississippi and flows to the Gulf. If we were able to consider the manner in which every drop of run-off anywhere within a region or a nation ultimately reaches the sea, we would get an idea of the nature of hierarchical flows in a drainage system.

In a national or regional system, flows are structured through a nodal organization which is probably hierarchical in character also. This hypothesis has not been fully verified up to now. Nevertheless, some empirical examples show that flows do indeed occur in a structured manner and that there are some regularities. The evidence, fragmentary though it may be, is presented here.

RATIONALE FOR FLOW STRUCTURE

Recapitulating the contents of previous chapters, we may note that a space-economy is composed of functional entities. In light of the categorization of nodes presented in Chapter 4, it is possible to see that such functional entities occur at a variety of scales, and so there are specialized individuals, establishments, settlements, regions, and also nations. A large region may specialize in the production of boots and shoes; particular cities within the region may specialize in the making of basketball sneakers, women's dress shoes, or children's shoes; certain establishments within these cities may specialize in the manufacture of soles, uppers, or laces; individuals in these establishments specialize in some narrow occupation such as cutting, stitching, and so on.

The foregoing discussion represents the supply or production side of the equation. The demand or consumption side in turn is also a function of the degree of specialization. Therefore, it follows that as nodes become more specialized, they also become more dependent for goods and services produced in other specialized locations of production.

Another consideration relevant to the functioning of the space-economy has to do with the fact that in technologically advanced and affluent nations the population has acquired the means to indulge in high mass consumption. The median family income in the United States, for example, is currently over $12,000, which represents a substantial ability to consume, i.e., market muscle. Moreover, despite regional disparities in income levels, the propensity to consume is becoming relatively uniform, just as are the products themselves. Hamburger and fried chicken are made according to standardized formulas, and a large variety of ice cream is available everywhere in the United States. It is evident that it is high mass consumption that facilitates production at high volumes. The manufacture of about 10 million automobiles per year, year after year, for example, could not continue unless an equivalent number of automobiles were also bought year after year. The same consideration holds true for all goods and services produced in the economic system.

The satisfaction of large-scale demand in a spatial sense, i.e., the delivery of goods from production locations to consumption locations, of necessity requires massive flows over a complex system of links of varying lengths and capacities. Further, it is only with continuous movement that functional entities can maintain varying levels of specialization. Finally, the large volumes of flows encountered in a complex system made up of variously specialized nodes require a rather rigid structuring of these flows if the aggregate costs of movement are to be kept within manageable limits.

In Chapter 9, we alluded to systems notions in rather formal terms. In spite of the broad conceptual framework, we focused narrowly upon modeling point-to-point flows. Thus, we considered neither the specific structuring of the flows nor the notion of a hierarchy.

The elements of many systems are arranged in a hierarchical order so that what may be considered to be an element at one level may be a system by itself at a lower level. Thus, if a region is a system, nodes or cities are its elements. If each city is considered as a system, then its neighborhoods and establishments are its elements. It may be concluded that we have systems embedded within systems, standing in a hierarchical relationship to each other.

Turning our attention to urban settlements as the centers of activity and the hubs of transport networks, we recognize that a system of cities is arranged in a functional hierarchy in which the role of metropolitan regions is crucial. American metropolitan spaces (core areas) and their peripheral spaces (or fields) are conditioned by driving time. Friedman and Miller (1965) suggest that the typical radius from most metropolitan cores is 2 hours driving time over modern freeway systems, that is, 100 to 120 miles. It is within and between major metropolitan areas that the dominant national flows occur. In addition, metropolitan areas serve as critical articulation points of messages, goods, services, and funds. Products move from specialized production areas to relay nodes which act as collecting centers for regional specialities. These relay nodes are usually located in or near dominant metropolitan centers. From these nodes, products are shipped to other metropolitan areas in exchange for a different array of specialized products originating elsewhere. From any metropolitan center, there is a process of distribution to other smaller nodes in its hinterland.

The preceding statements suggest a theoretical rationale for the structuring of flows. To the extent that the urban system is hierarchical, flows that occur between the elements of the system may also be expected to be hierarchically structured. Although such a structure is perhaps common to all modes of movement, the clearest example is that of a telephone network. Therefore, we present an illustrative example (Figure 10-1) drawn from a special issue of the *Scientific American* devoted to communications; however, we do not wish to imply that all flows in a national system are so rigidly structured.

Figure 10-1 Schematic diagram for a telephone network

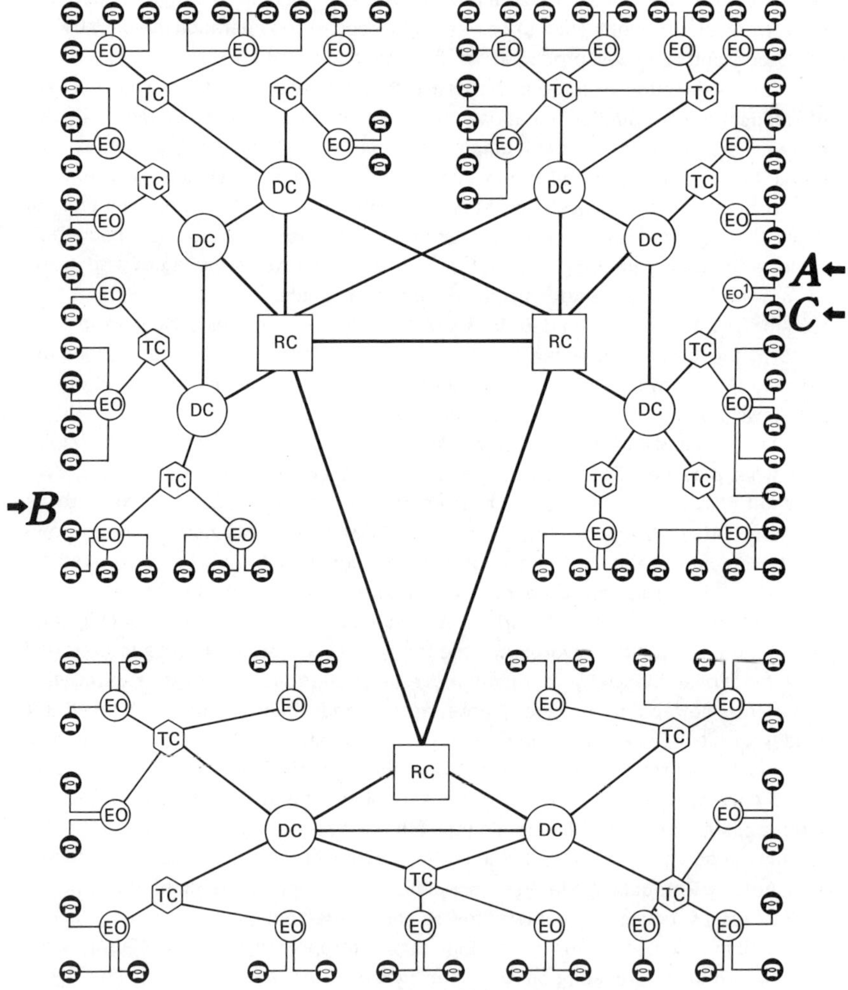

EO = end office, TC = toll center, DC = district center, RC = regional center

It has been demonstrated that in order for a telephone network to operate effectively, its design (spatial pattern) should minimize the number of branches (Inose, 1972). The more than 250 million telephone sets in the world are linked together into an integrated whole, or system. If direct connections were provided between each one of these sets and every other set, the required number of links would be astronomical. Clearly, the cost of constructing and maintaining such a network would be prohibitive. Therefore, switching centers, or relay nodes, are established to reduce the number of cross-points and thus minimize the overall length of the network.

Figure 10-1 is a diagram of a telephone network. Each of the telephone sets may be considered to be a node. In order to link telephones *A* and *B*, a path through EO, TC, DC, RC, RC, DC, TC, and EO is established. Since EO (end office) is the second lowest echelon in the hierarchy, TC (toll center) the third level, DC (district center) the fourth level, and RC (regional center) the highest, the routing of a call is very similar to the route one might take if one were to journey via the commercial airlines from a small town on the West Coast of the United States to another small town on the East Coast.

A call from *A* to *C*, however, does not have to go all the way up the hierarchy to RC and then down again, because these nodes may be considered to be two low-level nodes in the same subregion. For these two nodes, EO^1 may be considered to be the central node which articulates and relays messages between *A* and *C*.

The hypothetical network in Figure 10-1, a hierarchical one, channels and structures information flows in an optimal manner. The switching centers at the various levels in the hierarchy have larger and more complex functions as one moves up the hierarchy. The routes (twisted wire pairs or coaxial cables) are also hierarchical in capacity, so that those between a pair of RCs are considerably larger than the ones that link a telephone and an EO.

It should be noted, however, that in a communications network, the nodes at the different levels in the hierarchy are strictly relay nodes that do not perform any other function. Thus, at the very top of the hierarchy, a telephone regional center (RC) is not the same functionally as Atlanta, for example, which is the regional wholesaling and banking center of the Southeast. Telephone regional centers are not destinations as such, except in the internal workings of the telephone system. Furthermore, an example of the circuitry of the system is presented by the fact that from any RC to any EO, it is necessary to go through DC and TC, even though the origin and destination may be only a short distance apart. This type of circuitry is a special characteristic of flows in communications networks which are rigidly structured.

This illustrative example of a hierarchical network is a schematic one, although, in practice, telephone companies in the United States have endeavored to organize their networks accordingly. Of the many modes of movement, the telephone is only one, and although inferences from its flow structure can be made about other types and modes of movement, not much is really known about the structuring of migrations, commuting, mail, and other types of flows.

Although the hierarchical flow structure outlined in this section makes intuitive and obvious sense, as Berry (1964, 11) has emphasized, "it is mostly unsupported by substantive studies of the spatial organization of the economy of the United States."

FLOW STRUCTURES

The dearth of flow data series has hindered progress in transportation geography. Consequently, the analysis of hierarchical and other flow structures has been limited largely to the specific areas and particular time intervals for which data were available. There are two approaches to the identification of flow structures: (1) the simultaneous consideration of nodal hierarchies, specifically the "dominance order" of places, and the channeling of flows up and down through such a hierarchy, and (2) analysis of the extent to which sets of nodes (either as origins or as destinations) have similar movement characteristics, with a view to uncovering the significant regional connections.

Flows and "Dominance Order" of Nodes

The studies of air passenger traffic volumes by Taaffe (1956, 1958, 1962) and the telephone flow studies by Nystuen and Dacey (1961) and Soja (1968) have acquired wide currency in the literature on spatial interaction.

Working with volumes of long-distance telephone calls between city pairs in the state of Washington during one week in June 1958, Nystuen and Dacey (1961) were able to verify the existence of a flow structure which corresponded rather closely with the nodal organization of the state.

The procedures used in this study can be illustrated by first considering a hypothetical 12 × 12 matrix of direct flows between city pairs (see Figure 10-2*a*). The circled values represent the largest flow from an origin to a particular destination. For example, the largest flow (75) from *a* is to *b*, while the largest flow (38) from *h* is to *j*. The absence of a circled value along any particular row indicates that the largest flow is to a destination which is functionally smaller than the origin. Functional importance was measured by the total number of incoming calls (column totals). The largest volume of calls (69) from *b* is to *a*, but because the total volume for *b* is nearly 3 times as large as that for *a* (337 versus 113), *b* is regarded as a terminal node.

Figure 10-2*b* is a graph of the dominant connections between each origin and every destination, which indicates the nature of the hierarchical structure. It may be seen that the 12-node system has been partitioned into four subsystems; since it is the only one of its particular type in the system, node *e* stands by itself while node *j* is the ultimate terminal node of four other nodes *h*, *i*, *k*, and *l*. Moreover, *l* is connected to *j* via *k*, suggesting the following order of dominance: *j* → *k* → *l*.

Figure 10-2 Hypothetical telephone-call flows showing (*a*) associated matrix; (*b*) graph of dominant flows.

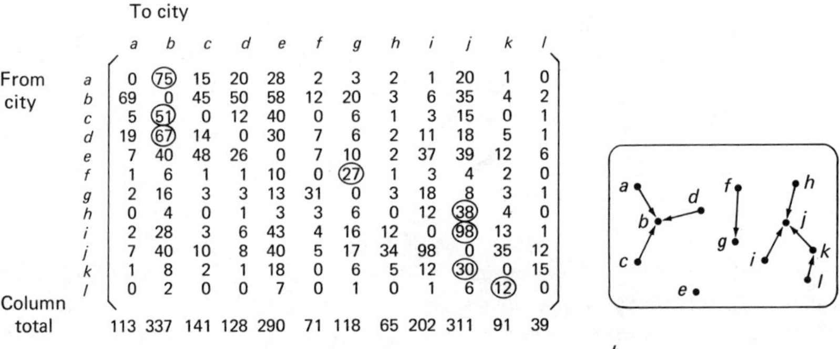

To city

From city	*a*	*b*	*c*	*d*	*e*	*f*	*g*	*h*	*i*	*j*	*k*	*l*
a	0	(75)	15	20	28	2	3	2	1	20	1	0
b	69	0	45	50	58	12	20	3	6	35	4	2
c	5	(51)	0	12	40	0	6	1	3	15	0	1
d	19	(67)	14	0	30	7	6	2	11	18	5	1
e	7	40	48	26	0	7	10	2	37	39	12	6
f	1	6	1	1	10	0	(27)	1	3	4	2	0
g	2	16	3	3	13	31	0	3	18	8	3	1
h	0	4	0	1	3	3	6	0	12	(38)	4	0
i	2	28	3	6	43	4	16	12	0	(98)	13	1
j	7	40	10	8	40	5	17	34	98	0	35	12
k	1	8	2	1	18	0	6	5	12	(30)	0	15
l	0	2	0	0	7	0	1	0	1	6	(12)	0
Column total	113	337	141	128	290	71	118	65	202	311	91	39

a

b

The initial flow matrix of long-distance calls between the 40 city pairs within Washington state was modified by Nystuen and Dacey so that the flow between each pair was proportionally related to the largest column sum in the matrix. This value was 154,192 for Seattle. The cell entries in the resulting matrix contain both direct and indirect long-distance calls between each city pair. This matrix was then further analyzed, using the procedures outlined above, and the resulting schema is shown in Figure 10-3. It can be seen that Seattle is the dominant node, as identified by the volume of flows, with two subcenters, Spokane and Yakima. There are also two small subsystems (Ephratta-Moses Lake and Pasco) located between Yakima and Spokane. The subsystems are relatively self-contained in that most of the flows are within the systems themselves.

This real world hierarchy is based on functional linkages, not population or some other index of size, and it is possible to see some strong similarities to the idealized Löschian landscape of Figure 5-14. The two high-level places, Seattle and Spokane, although located at almost opposite ends of the state, are linked directly. Small places are connected to the larger ones via an intermediate place (Goldendale is linked to Seattle via Yakima). Large places have a larger number of connections than do small ones, e.g., Spokane is connected to 10 other places while Yakima is connected to only 4. Note also

Figure 10-3 Washington state: nodal hierarchy as identified by analyzing flows of telephone calls

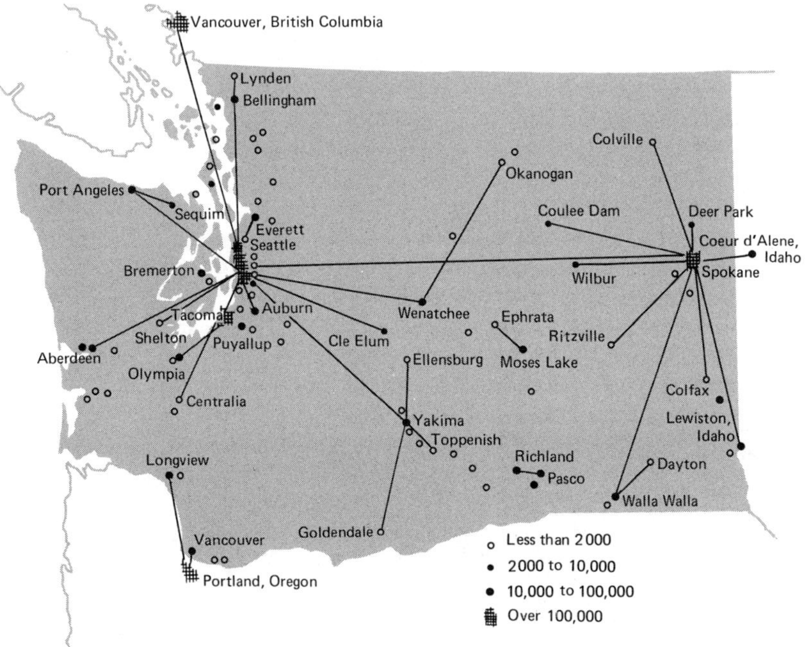

that there is one large place (Seattle), and, conversely, there is a large number of smaller places such as Ritzville and Centralia.

In studying intertown trading patterns for nine rail-shipped commodity groups among 25 towns in Nigeria, Hay and Smith (1970) also used the procedure described above. The results of their analysis are shown in Figure 10-4. Note that there are three "dominance orders" and that the number of nodes in a particular level decreases with increasing level in the hierarchy.

In particular, Ibadan and Kano are the foci of a large number of direct connections from other towns in the north and south, respectively. Although Zaria, at the lowest level in the hierarchy, is physically close to Ibadan at the highest level, it may be noted that the direct linkage is only to Iddo, which, however, is in turn connected to Ibadan. The flows are structured up the hierarchy. Likewise, Lagos Federal, Enugu, and Kaduna are like Iddo in that they collect flows from one or more low-order nodes and relay them to Kano, which is in the next higher order.

A study such as the one by Nystuen and Dacey based on flows of telephone calls is probably more meaningful in the interpretation of functional linkages in a nodal hierarchy in the context of an advanced technology-based nation such as the United States. The multiple roles and mass subscribership to the telephone within westernized nations allow for social, business, administrative, emergency, and other long-distance linkages. What happens in a Third World nation where a different economic, political, and cultural system may not require massive electronic voice communications for its orderly func-

Figure 10-4 Nigeria: nodal hierarchy as identified by intertown commodity flows by railroad

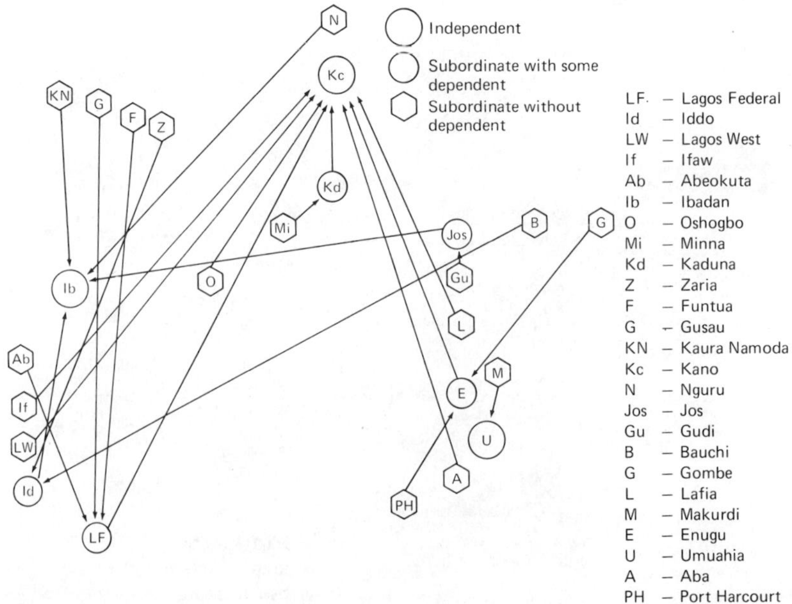

tioning? What is the flow structure of long-distance calls in such a society where only the elite, comprising the highly educated, the rich, and the politically powerful, have both ready access and a need for the telephone? The flow of telephone calls between large cities of East Africa was studied by Soja (1968) with a view to uncovering the degree of functional integration of cities across political boundaries.

Utilizing a transactions flow matrix of 24 telephone exchanges with flow magnitudes compiled during 9 hours over 2 days in 1961, Soja sought to determine the nature of major or "salient" flows, i.e., flows significantly greater in volume than might be expected otherwise. The concept of salience was defined as

$$RA_{ij} = \frac{A_{ij} - E_{ij}}{E_{ij}}$$

where RA_{ij} is the index of salience between exchanges *i* and *j*, A_{ij} is the actual volume of calls occurring between two nodes, and E_{ij} is the expected volume of flows. The computation of expectations was as follows: if Dar es Salaam received, say, 10 percent of all the calls generated in East Africa, then it was assumed that 10 percent of all the calls originating from each of the 23 other places were directed toward Dar es Salaam. Further, Soja selected arbitrarily an RA_{ij} value of 0.25 in both directions as a minimum measure of salience.

Having subjected the original transaction matrix to the preceding analysis, Soja mapped the results (Figure 10-5). This map suggests a hierarchical structuring of telephone-call flows within the region as a whole. As might be expected, both Nairobi and Dar es Salaam were identified as the most significant nodes, as can be seen from the number of salient flow lines converging on them in Figure 10-5. Two subsystems emerged also: one based on political autonomy, namely Uganda, which was centered upon Kampala, and the other, in southern Tanganyika (now called Tanzania), which was more of a regional subsystem. Further, the Tanganyikian system appeared to be more heavily focused upon Dar es Salaam, since most places were directly linked to it, suggesting a two-level hierarchy. In contrast, the Kenyan structure was arranged more loosely, with only the cities of Kisumu, Nakuru, and Mombasa linked directly to Nairobi.

In spite of the focus of this study upon Third World nations in Africa, a certain amount of evidence was presented in regard to the existence of a hierarchical flow structure. This evidence might support the conclusion that, irrespective of cultural, economic, social, and other variations, hierarchical flows exist in East Africa, in a West African nation such as Nigeria, and in the state of Washington in the United States. In all cases, a correspondence was shown to exist between flows on the one hand and the nodal hierarchy on the other. This correspondence is not just accidental, since continuous flows are necessary to sustain a nodal hierarchy in the first place.

Regionalization of Flows

It will be recalled that in Chapter 5 we regionalized the airline networks of Argentina and Venezuela in an attempt to understand the structure of networks. The starting point for these analyses was binary connectivity matrices simply

Figure 10-5 East Africa: "salient flows" of telephone calls

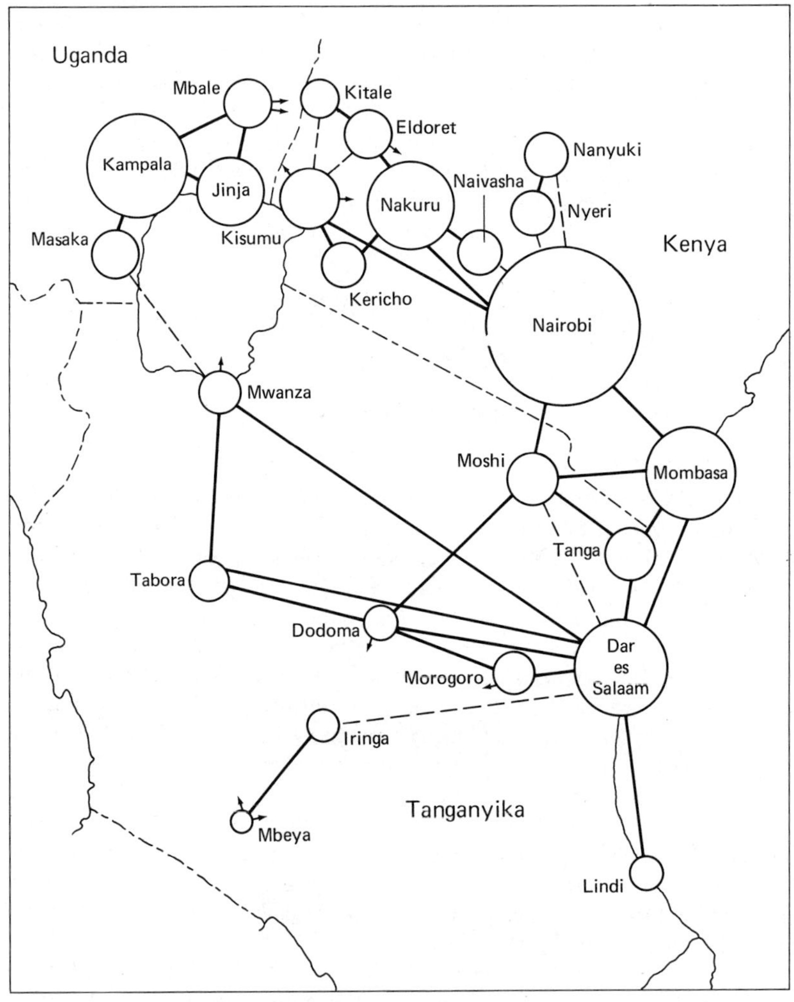

——— = RA < 0.25
– – – – = RA < 0 in both directions but > 0.25 at least one way
→ = RA < 0 in one direction only
Size of circles is in proportion to percentage of total trunk calls made between twenty-four exchange regions in East Africa.

showing the presence or absence of a direct link. The question of flow volume was completely ignored, and thus equal weight was placed on a once-a-week service as on say, 10 direct flights/day between pairs of nodes. Nevertheless, we were able to recognize a hierarchy of nodes and connections in the field and major regionalization effects. It may be assumed that the intensity of linkages between places, as measured by the number of flights or rail services, bears a close correspondence to the passenger or freight flows between such places.

Analysis of flow volumes, using the same procedures (factor analysis), enables us to regionalize nodes and flows as another way of identifying flow structures. More specifically, this type of analysis "involves the identification of generic locational characteristics of groups of origins, or groups of destinations, or of groups of origins and destinations (dyads)" (Smith, 1970, 411). Such an analysis enables us to delineate functional regions in a nation, based upon the similarities in flow patterns.

Every flow map has an analogous flow matrix in which the rows are origins and the columns are destinations. Accordingly, each cell records the transaction between the respective origin and destination. A flow matrix can be subjected to what is known as *dyadic factor analysis*.

The result is the identification of characteristic linkages between places on the basis of the kinds or intensities (volumes) of flows. Berry (1966) was the first to apply this type of analysis to flow data; since then, among others, Britton (1971) studied commodity movements in England, Wheeler (1972) studied trip purposes in Lansing, Michigan, and Goddard (1970) analyzed taxi flows in London. As examples of different kinds of movement at widely divergent scales, the results of Berry's and Goddard's work are summarized below.

Berry had various data available for each of 30 Indian states and 6 major port cities, concerning 63 different commodities for each of the 1260 dyads. The flows suggest a spatial economic system with (1) resource-based activities at certain locations interacting with one another and (2) a set of regional economies oriented around the major metropolitan centers. These metropolitan areas are intense economic cores that are surrounded by peripheries characterized by a relatively simple peasant economy. The metropolitan centers organize the spatial economy and are the articulation points (referred to as "relay nodes" in Chapter 4) which concentrate commodities and then distribute them to other metropolitan areas and rural regions within their "spheres of influence." Duncan et al. (1960) identified a similar metropolitan-dominated, regional structure of the United States; thus, despite the vastly different economic development and technological levels in India and the United States, certain repetitive themes are apparent.

Altogether, a 12-factor structure was shown to describe the spatial dimensions of the Indian commodity flows, in which each factor represents a specific group of commodities based upon characteristic origins and destinations. For example, factor 4 groups bones, dyes, rice in husks, manganese ore, center seed, til, and teak. Despite the differences in these commodities they form a coherent group in terms of their respective origins and destinations. The mapping of what are called "factor scores" with values greater than 3 for each of the factors enables a more precise identification of the nature of the factor structure. The dominant flows with respect to the first five factors are shown by means of directed arrows in Figure 10-6*a* to *e*.

The movement of eastern specialties to the south and of western specialties to the north is shown in Figure 10-6*a* (factor 1, 19.6 percent of the variance). The products consist of basic necessities, including cement, cotton yarns and fabric, glass, rice, wheat, four kinds of vegetable oils, kerosene, ghee (clarified butter), salt, and tobacco.

A second major flow pattern, eastward from the northern areas around Delhi to Calcutta and southward to Bombay (factor 2, accounting for 16.7 per-

Figure 10-6 Dominant linkages of Indian commodity flow as indicated by a dyadic factor analysis

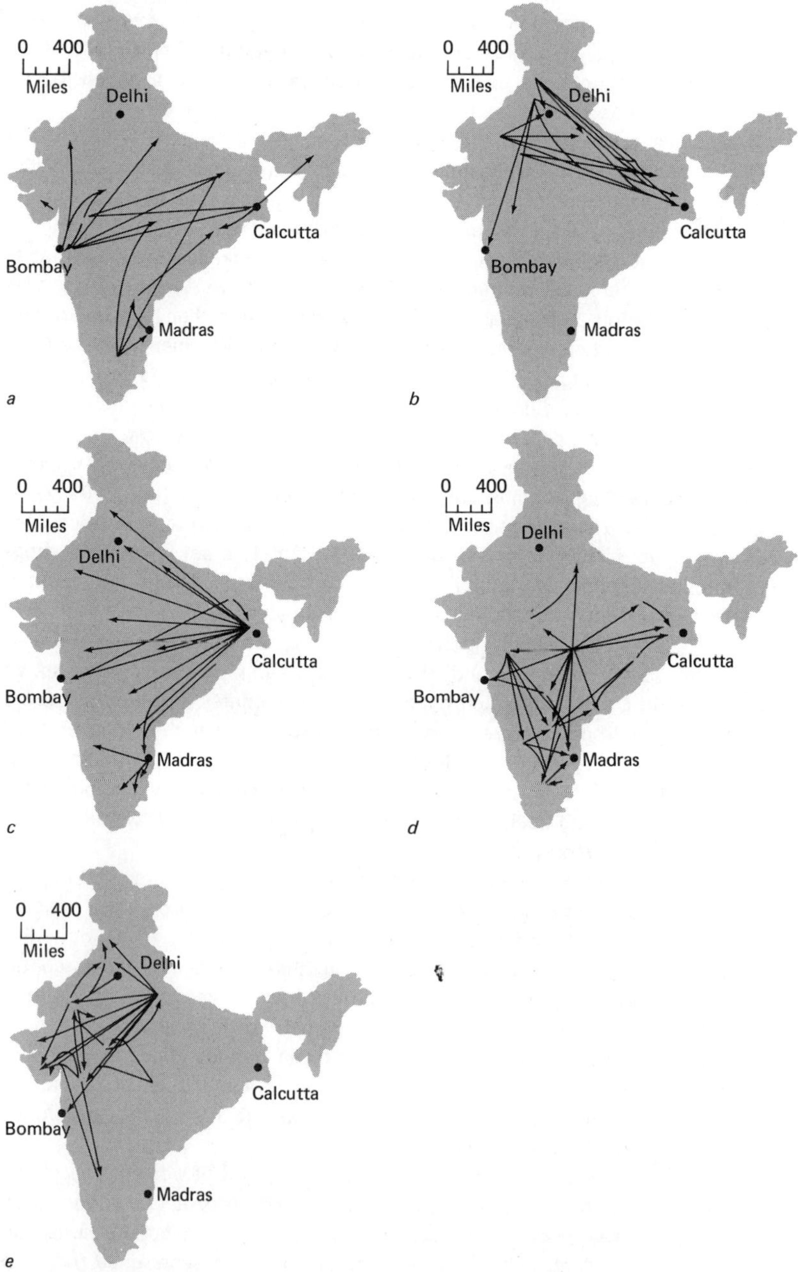

cent of the variance), includes cattle, certain maize varieties (jowar and bajra) widely consumed in Indian villages, gur (country sugar), and again oil seeds and vegetable oils (Figure 10-6*b*).

The dominant and distinctive role of Calcutta with reference to practically all the other 35 regions (factor 3, 12.9 percent of the variance) is shown by its shipments of coffee, raw jute, gunny bags, sugar, tea, and iron forms. In addition, the role of Madras as a redistribution center is highlighted (Figure 10-6*c*).

A complex spatial structure arising from the relationships between port hinterlands and manganese-producing areas (in north-central India) is shown by factor 4 (10.6 percent of the variance).

Finally, large-scale shipments of agricultural specialties produced in western and northern India are shown to take place within the Bombay-Delhi region (factor 5, 9.8 percent).

In summary, the commodity flow structure in India is a strongly regionalized one. Three major relationships emerged from the analysis: (1) Commodity flows between areas in western and southern India on the one hand and eastern India on the other are a function of the specialized manufacturing industries and metal-ore production. Thus, there is a transfer of industrial specialties from certain regions in return for agricultural specialties from others. (2) Commodity movements within the large regions, as well as within the hinterlands of the major ports of Calcutta and Bombay, take the form of intraregional redistribution of regional production specialties, e.g., the movement of rice within rice-growing areas. (3) There are also shipments of agricultural specialties between agricultural regions (e.g., rice moving to wheat-growing areas and vice versa), as well as transfers of manufacturing specialties (e.g., fabric from Bombay in return for boots and shoes from Kanpur) between industrial regions.

At the urban scale, Goddard (1970) analyzed intersectoral taxi flows within London, with a view to regionalizing the dominant flows. He utilized the journey logs kept by a 10 percent sample of all registered cabs in the London central area, which includes the central business district and the main-line rail terminals, which are major generators of taxi traffic. The 70 origin and destination zones were arrayed in a 70×70 flow matrix, in which the cells represent 24-hour average weekday traffic during the month of July 1962. Figure 10-7 is a cartographic representation of all the flows, and even though the flows of less than 10 vehicles/day were excluded, the map appears to be very "noisy," and no clear pattern or structure is readily apparent.

In order to extract a spatial structure, Goddard performed a principal components analysis which yielded six components that accounted for 60 percent of the initial variance. His results are presented in a series of maps (Figure 10-8*a* to *f*); Figure 10-8*a* is a reference or orientation map showing the locations of major nodes, districts, and paths, to use Lynch's terminology (see Chapter 7). Both component loadings and component scores were mapped to show common patterns of trip assembly. The maps show the links between each group of destinations (identified by loadings) and its respective set of common origins (identified by scores).

Figure 10-7 Average daily taxi flows in the central area of London

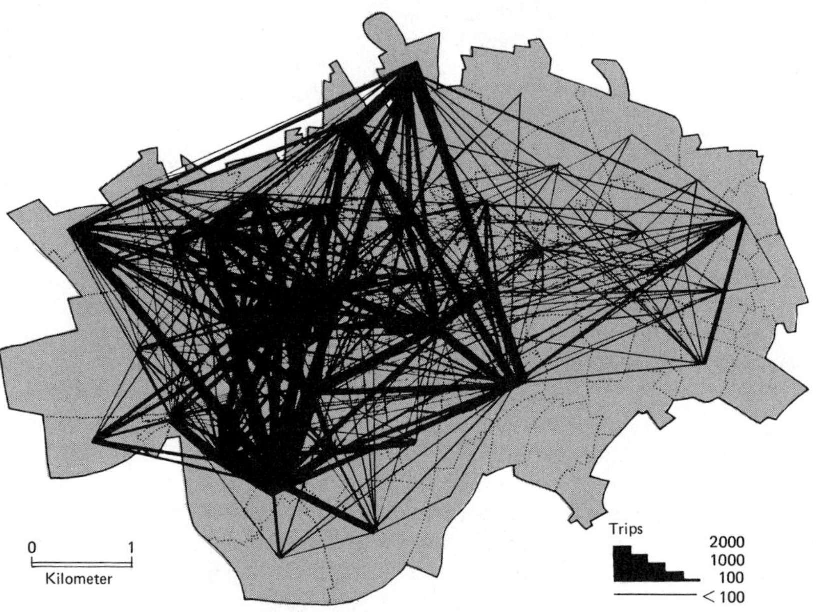

The dominant nodal subsystem of the West End, which includes the high-class residential area of Mayfair and Oxford Street as well as prestigious shopping facilities and offices, was identified first (component 1, 15.7 percent of the variance). Most of the movement is within the West End itself, and at the aggregated level (mass behavior) the pattern shown is analogous to the configuration of trips of the young woman in Paris's 16th arrondissement, identified in an earlier chapter.

A second nodal element was that centering on Westminster, which contains the houses of Parliament and government administrative functions (component 2, 12 percent of variance). The major destinations include the railroad terminals of Victoria, Paddington, King's Cross, and Waterloo, while Charing Cross stands out as a major origin, indicating transfers between railroad terminals.

The midtown portion of central London, including Soho, Fleet Street, and Covent Garden, which contains major entertainment facilities and the largest newspaper publishing area, emerged as a third "flow region" (component 3, 10 percent).

The eastern part of what Londoners term "the City" emerged as an independent region, as well as Bloomsbury, which contains major main-line terminals, the University, and many labor union offices (components 4 and 5, with 9 and 8 percent variances, respectively).

This analysis reveals pronounced spatial differentiation within the city of London with regard to the characteristics of the nodes and the corresponding structure of movement between them. The functional regions of London are

Figure 10-8 Taxi flows in the central area of London, showing (*a*) landmarks and districts; (*b*) West End component; (*c*) Westminster component. Continued on page 224.

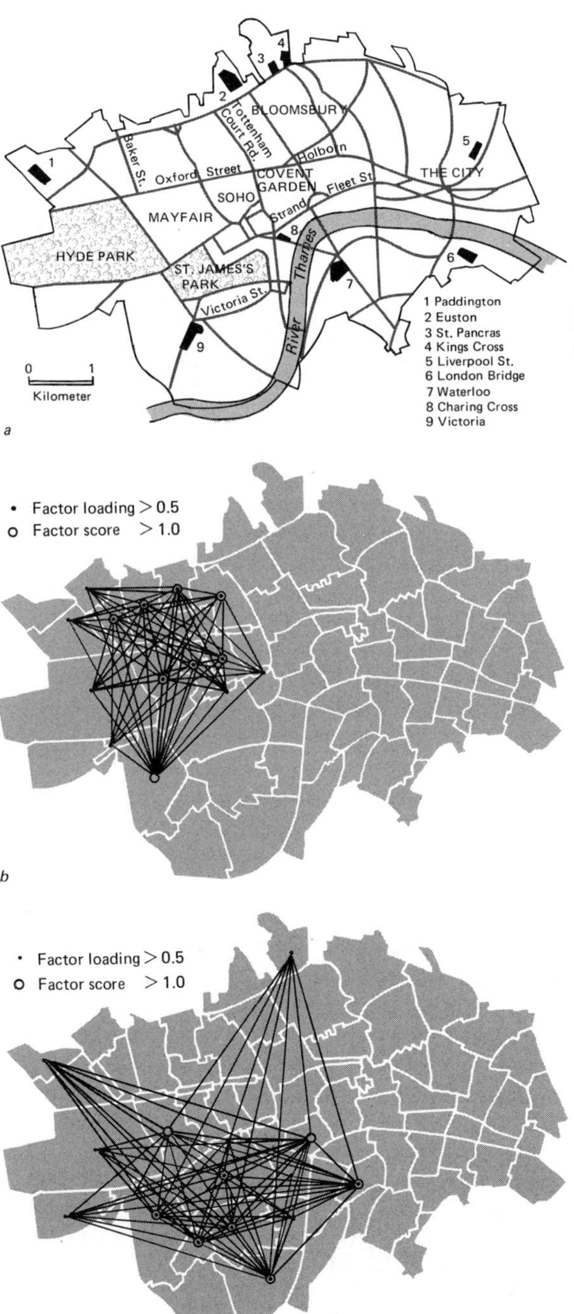

Figure 10-8 (*Continued*) (*d*) Covent Garden–Soho–Fleet Street component; (*e*) The City component; (*f*) Bloomsbury component.

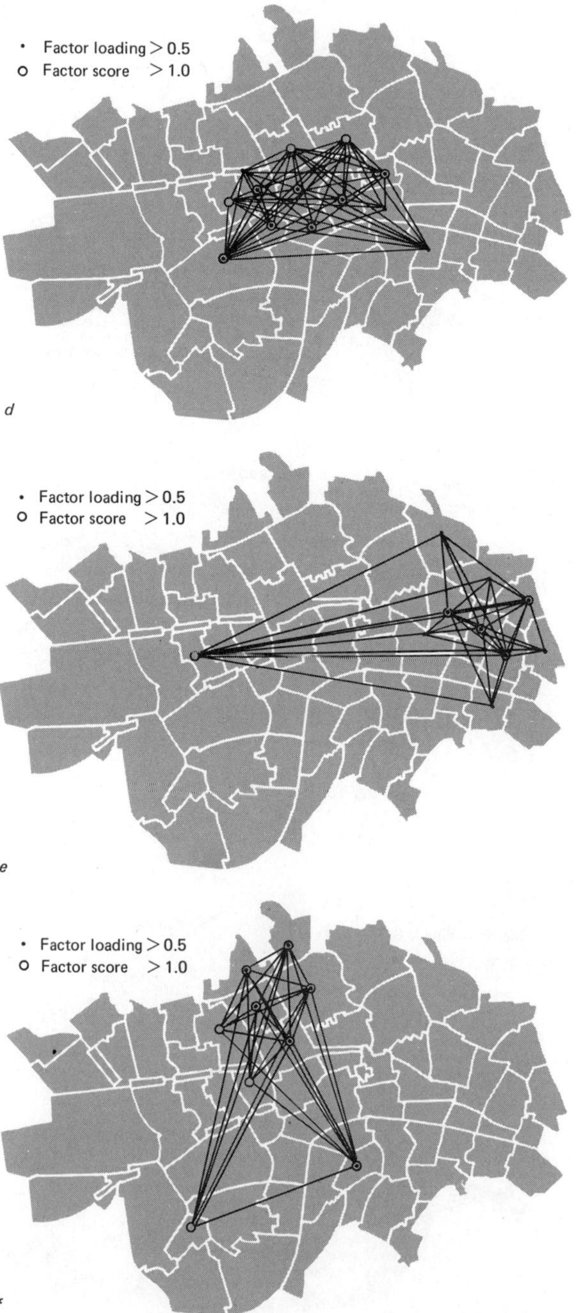

characterized by strong internal linkages which suggest that internal circulation is a prerequisite to maintaining functional entities.

Although a statement to the effect that all flows in a nation are structured in a hierarchical fashion may be unwarranted, the scanty evidential materials presented before all point in the same direction. Smaller volumes of flows originate at smaller nodes, are collected at intermediate-level places, and are then relayed to successively higher-order places. A well-defined hierarchical structuring of flows for which a theoretical rationale exists on the grounds of efficiency may also exist in the real world, although the structuring is not always easily recognizable as such.

While we are interested in flow structure for its own sake, we may also recognize that in any national system, many new ideas, products, technologies, and so on originate in the larger places and "diffuse" down the nodal hierarchy. The transmittal of information about a new thing is a prerequisite for its adoption. To the extent that information flows are hierarchically structured, we may expect that the diffusion of something new in geographic space is also hierarchically structured, at least in the initial stages.

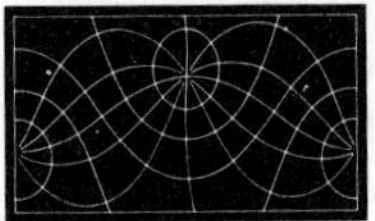

11 Spatial Diffusion Processes: Hierarchical and Contagious

Diffusion studies have a rich heritage in geography. In the postscript to his translation of Hägerstrand's (1967a) pioneering work, Pred states that Hägerstrand was influenced by the German anthropo-geographer Ratzel (1882), who introduced in the geography literature the fundamental idea of something starting somewhere and spreading out like ripples on a pond. Sauer's work on agricultural origins and dispersals (1952) is essentially a study of the spatial diffusion of crops and farming systems. It suggests how a particular agricultural practice originated in an area and was carried to one or more destinations. Kniffen (1949, 1951, 1965), a cultural geographer, has studied the areal spread of such items as covered bridges, agricultural fairs, and house types, all of which represent tangible objects on the American cultural landscape. Indeed, diffusion has often been regarded as a topic in cultural geography. However, after some geographers tried to model the process of spatial diffusion, it began to be considered as an element under the general spatial interaction umbrella, rather than as a component of traditional cultural geography.

Taking the broadest possible perspective, one can conceive of a host of phenomena whose locational shifts in time result in a spatial-diffusion process. Thus, we can speak of the diffusion of air in masses across continents, of the diffusion of oxygen through the body as blood circulates, or of the diffusion of epidemics. Inasmuch as this book is concerned with human spatial interactive processes, we are not dealing here, of course, with meteorology, human physiology, or epidemiology. However, it is conceivable that a synthesizer may someday, in fact, suggest a schema according to which a variety of forms of movement and phenomena can be viewed together.

MOVEMENT AS DIFFUSION

Diffusion can be defined simply as a process of spread in geographic space. As is the case in the flow of information, in the diffusion of innovations the destination node does not make a gain at the expense of the origin. Thus, when we speak of the diffusion of the Hong Kong flu, for example, the sender does not "get rid of it" by dumping it on somebody else. Therefore, it is not possible to establish an accounting framework for the diffusion of a phenomenon in the same way as one can account for the movement of 300 million tons of coal shipped out of West Virginia to each of several destinations. In addition, spatial diffusion cannot be identified or measured, and therefore at a particular point in space we can neither recognize cholera moving nor ask someone how much cholera he or she received. What *can* be measured is the number or rate of acceptors or adopters at a specific destination.

Despite these differences from more traditional flow notions, spatial diffusion is an important form of place-to-place movement or spatial interaction. Indeed, changes in a culture and many of the most important aspects of human progress have occurred as a result of the diffusion of innovations. Agriculture originated somewhere and diffused outward, just as all religions had particular origins and experienced a process of spread. In the same way, languages, artifacts, the industrial revolution, urbanization, democracy, technology, ideologies, disease control, and other powerful innovations have diffused in geographic space.

The dictionary defines "innovation" as "the introduction of anything new," a definition that lends itself to some confusion with the term "invention." In order to eliminate this possible ambiguity, we can make use of the following working definition: *innovation* is the implementation or adoption of something. Therefore, the spatial diffusion of innovations is the process by which a node (individual, establishment, settlement, or nation) receives and adopts something that was not there before. Thus, although communism was not new in the late fifties, when Cuba become a communist nation, communism as an ideology diffused across the oceans and occupied an area where it had not existed before. In much the same way, the use of the electronic computer in banking operations diffused from the United States to Western Europe and Japan but has yet to reach India, where bank tellers continue laboriously to write up accounts. The spread of many phenomena, such as disease, hot pants, women's suffrage, tuberculosis vaccine, farm loans, the intrauterine device, and a host or other "innovations" has been referred to as contagious diffusion processes.

A dichotomy can be established between hierarchical diffusion and contagious diffusion. A fundamental difference between the two types stems from the fact that hierarchical diffusion is a point phenomenon in which the process of spatial diffusion skips about geographic space even though a more or less definite flow structure is recognizable. As a result, it may happen that early adopters are located at relatively great distances from the center of diffusion, while nearer potential adopters are temporarily bypassed. In contrast, contagious diffusion is an areal process. As the term suggests, contagious diffusion proceeds by means of direct personal contacts with the result that nearer potential adopters receive an innovation before more distant ones. In the case of most innovations, it appears that there is a hierarchical process of diffusion initially, and subsequently the innovation begins to blanket a region or a nation in a contagious fashion. Therefore, it is appropriate to begin our discussion with hierarchical diffusion.

HIERARCHICAL DIFFUSION

Despite the fragmentary nature of the evidence presented in the preceding chapter, it seems reasonable to conclude that flows are structured in a hierarchical fashion. This conclusion is especially true of information flows. Moreover, it may also be assumed that significant impulses of social change are also transmitted downward through the hierarchy.

In the geography literature, Hägerstrand (1966) was the first to call attention to the hierarchical diffusion of innovations with his analysis of the spread of the Rotary International across Western Europe. In Figure 11-1, which shows a sequence of the diffusion of Rotary clubs, it can be noted that in 1922 there were only four clubs in the whole subcontinent: Paris, Amsterdam, Copenhagen, and Oslo. By 1925, the Rotary had spread from Paris to southern France and Italy and as far away as Austria and Portugal. Moreover, in Amsterdam, the number of clubs had increased to four. The process of diffusion continued into 1930, by which time a strong "neighborhood" or field effect was evident around Amsterdam, which now had 26 clubs in its immediate vicinity. The rate of spread slackened a bit during World War II (Figure 11-1*d*), but by 1950 had sharply accelerated again so that we see a relatively complete blanketing of Western Europe. The spread of Rotary Clubs was stopped cold by the France-Spain border and the Iron Curtain, and the failure to start even a single club in Spain and the Soviet Union underscores the role of political and/or ideological boundaries in inhibiting spatial interaction.

Today, Amsterdam, with 81 clubs in its vicinity, plays a leading role in the nodal hierarchy of Western Europe. Indeed, according to the *Official International Airline Guide,* Amsterdam has more direct flights in and out than any other place in Western Europe. It is the best connected node in Western Europe, and its accessibility or Shimbel index is the highest in Europe.

While the maps show the general process of spread, they do not indicate the structuring of movement. A closer analysis enabled Hägerstrand to reach these conclusions:

1. In any one nation, the primate (top-ranking) city generally adopts an innovation first, owing in part to the fact that in many nations the political and social elites, who are innovation-conscious, usually live in the primate city.

2. Other individuals in other cities engage in imitative behavior, and consequently many innovations diffuse from the primate city down the hierarchy. This diffusion is facilitated by the configuration of the transportation and communication networks which are focused somewhat on the primate city. Individuals there have intense and high-level contacts over longer distances, and members of the provincial elite (country squires) visit the primate city, frequently "taking back" new ideas for implementation in their own area.

3. At some point in time, hierarchical diffusion is overshadowed by a "neighborhood" effect so that nearer places, whatever their size or rank in the

Figure 11-1 The spatial diffusion of the Rotary International in Western Europe: (*a*) 1922; (*b*) 1925; (*c*) 1930; (*d*) 1950.

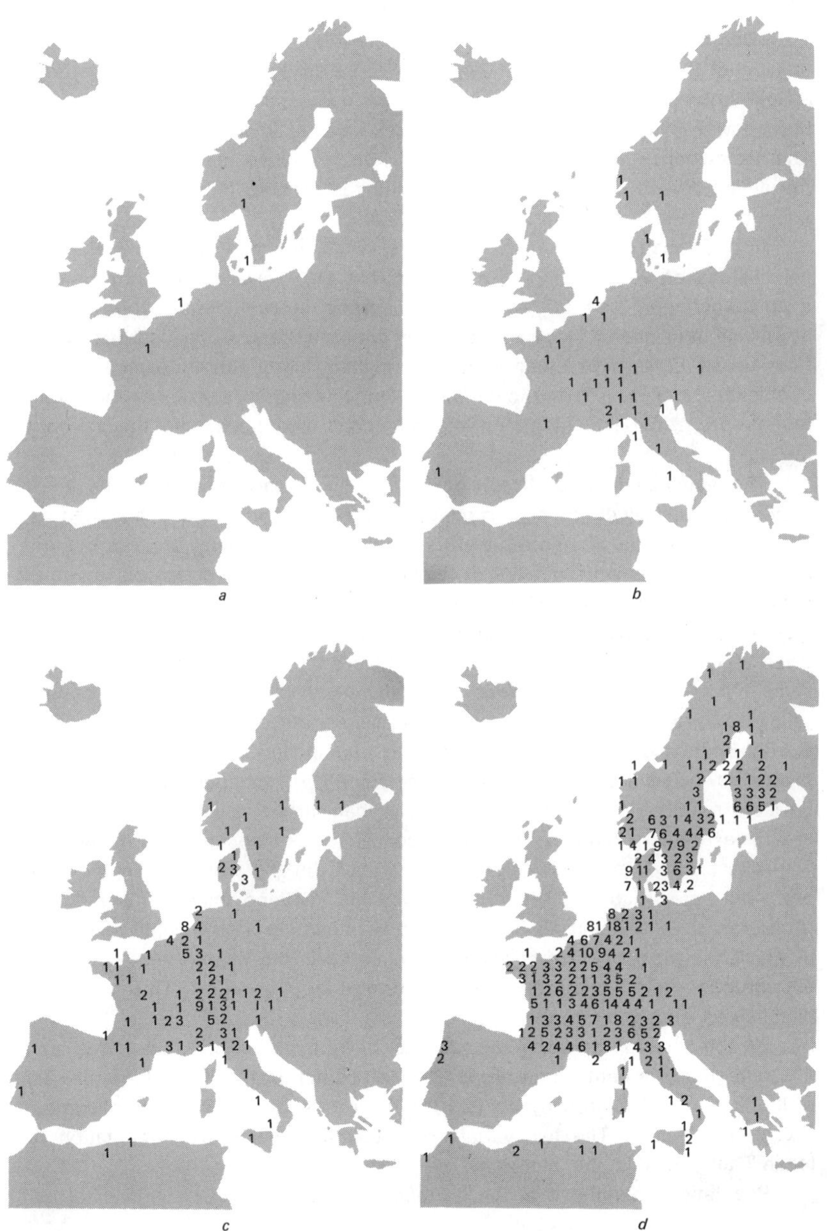

hierarchy, adopt the innovation in turn. At that juncture, physical distance or proximity becomes more important to the diffusion process than does either hierarchical position or functional distance.

Focusing on spatial diffusion processes within a country, Hägerstrand found that in Sweden by 1932 only nine of the largest places had established a Rotary club. By 1935, additional clubs had been started in other large places, but a lower-level place with a population of about 5000 had also started one. The somewhat regular downward progression continued until about 1946 when the neighborhood effect took over and the relationship between city size and adoption date became blurred.

In a detailed and formal study, Berry (1971) reached essentially the same conclusions as Hägerstrand. He argued that the overall diffusion process in a space-economy can be viewed as occurring in two steps: (1) a "filtering down" of innovations through the urban hierarchy, and (2) a "spreading out" from urban centers to other locations in their hinterland in something of a contagious process. This dichotomy in the diffusion process can be likened to entrepreneurial innovation on the one hand and household innovation on the other.

The establishment of television stations in urban centers in the United States can be viewed as a hierarchical process in which cities that had new stations were essentially entrepreneurs, while the "spreading" process occurred among purchasers and viewers of television sets. Berry suggested four basic reasons for filtering. (1) Entrepreneurs' search and evaluation of the market motivate them to penetrate larger places earlier and smaller ones last. Thus, given an urban hierarchy, with ranks of places 1 through n, the nth place or some nth-order place will adopt the innovations at the end of the diffusion process. Further, there is a chronological sequence of adoptions for 1 through n. (2) Economic activities are sometimes compelled to relocate in smaller places down the urban hierarchy as they search for cheaper labor, which may be more readily available in smaller towns than larger ones. (3) Entrepreneurs in smaller centers tend to mimic the behavior of those in larger places: the "big city slicker" generally appears "smarter." (In the world of Snuffy Smith, new ideas are frequently brought there by the "flatland inshorance peddler.") (4) Hierarchical diffusion may be modeled by means of a probability mechanism in which the probability of adoption depends upon the chance that a potential entrepreneur in a given town will learn of the innovation. This probability declines as a function of the size of towns.

On the basis of the foregoing reasons, Berry hypothesized that "the innovation potential of a center is a product of its position in the urban hierarchy and of the force exerted on it by centers that have already adopted the innovation" (Berry, 1971, 127). The two variables of this hypothesis are "population potential" and rank in the hierarchy.

Population potential V at the ith location is defined as

$$V_i = \sum_{j=1}^{n} \frac{P_j}{d_{ij}}$$

and has to be computed n times. Warntz (1964) computed this measure for each of the counties in the United States, using the 1960 population. Equipotential contours, joining places with the same value of *V*, are shown in Figure 11-2.

The rank-size rule suggests a statistical regularity between the rank of a city and its population. Essentially an empirical finding, it may be formally stated as $P_r = P_1/r^Q$, where P_r is the population of the city of rank *r*, P_1 is the population of the largest city in the system, and *Q* is an exponent. This equation means that if the population of the largest city is 1 million, that of the second largest should be about 500,000, that of the third largest should be approximately 333,333, and so on.

Figure 11-2 Hierarchical diffusion of television stations in the United States, 1940–1965

Reprinted with permission of Macmillan Publishing Co., Inc. from *Growth Centers in Regional Economic Development,* by Niles Hansen (ed.), p. 116. Copyright © 1972 by The Free Press, a division of Macmillan Publishing Co., Inc.

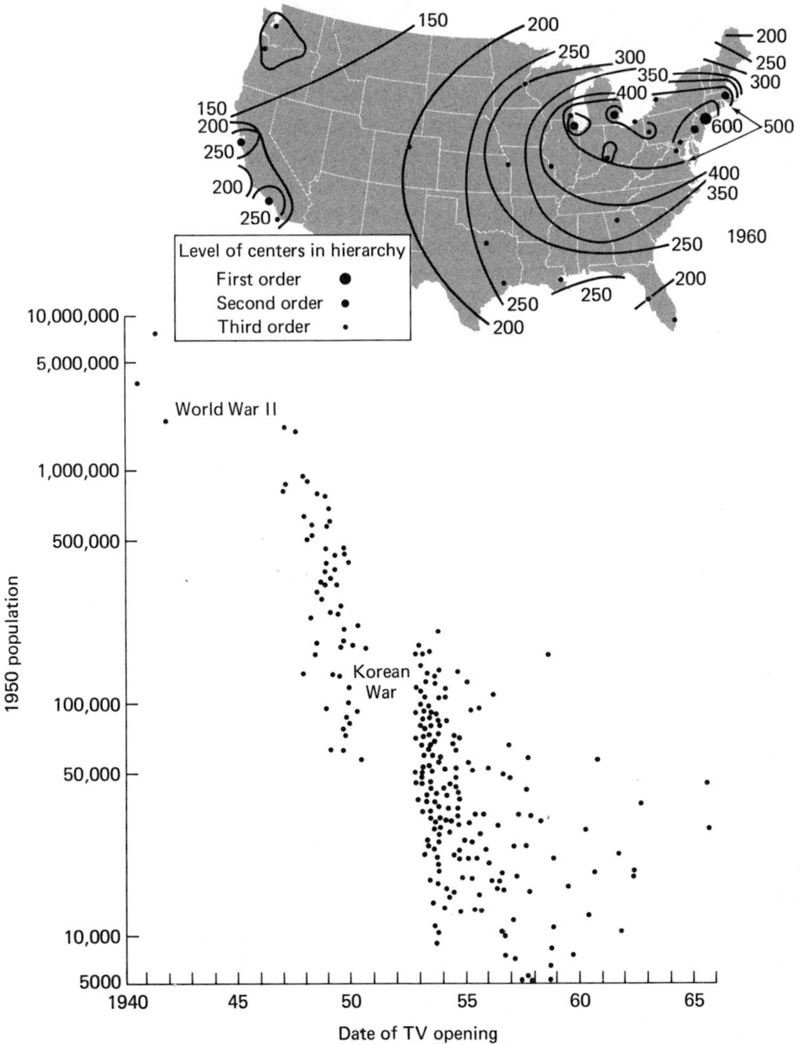

On the eve of World War II, the three top-ranking cities (New York, Chicago, and Philadelphia) established television stations. After a wartime hiatus, TV stations were established in 58 cities. Following another hiatus, related this time to the Korean War, 144 cities adopted TV transmitting facilities. By 1958, the diffusion of television stations was very nearly complete, and subsequently there were only 10 new adoptions.

Figure 11-2 shows the relationship between time of adoption and the 1950 population. A general rank-size pattern is readily evident in which the smaller cities tend to be among the last in the adoption process. The greater density of points after the Korean War demonstrates that the government-ordered freeze did indeed postpone the adoption by urban centers with populations of 100,000 to 250,000. In the absence of such an interruption in the diffusion process, the overall pattern would probably have been much more regular.

The role of population potential acts as a negative factor, and so in some areas with high population potential, competition from still larger metropolitan centers inhibited the adoption in medium-sized places, even though these were relatively high in the urban hierarchy. For example, to date, Fall River, Lawrence, Bridgeport, and New London have not opened TV stations because either Boston or New York offers readily accessible competition. The same is true of Ann Arbor, Michigan; Racine, Wisconsin; and Council Bluffs, Iowa, although Austin, Texas, which is too far from Dallas, has its own television station. High-order neighbors of nonadopting cities dominated the market earlier and consequently forestalled the diffusion of entrepreneurial innovations to nearby smaller centers.

The starting point in Berry's model of hierarchical diffusion was a rank-size distribution which, although still essentially an empirically observed regularity, has been the subject of some theoretical explanation (Berry and Garrison, 1958). Regardless of the attractiveness of one or another explanation, the conceptualization of an urban hierarchy as a rank-size distribution precludes the recognition of the "nesting" process in which each successively larger place contains the functions or the activities of the immediately preceding one. Nor is there any explicit consideration of the spacing between places at any particular hierarchical order. Central place theory, on the other hand, deals with these and other questions directly. Fundamentally, it suggests that in a central place system, there is a functional nesting of centers so that if the lowest-order center performs functions A, B, and C, then the next higher-order place performs A, B, C, and also D. This situation continues to the top of the hierarchy, so that the highest-order place performs n functions and the immediately lower-order one performs $n - m$ functions, where m is a specified number of functions. Moreover, there is a dominance relationship among the places in the system so that the highest-order place dominates some number (frequently called K) of the second-order places, each of which, in turn, dominates some number of third-order places, and so on. The resulting structure, diagramed in Figure 11-3, resembles the chain of command of a large corporation or a military bureaucracy.

Hudson (1969, 1972) has attempted to link spatial diffusion and central place theory explicitly and formally. In considering the filtering of innovations down the hierarchy, he developed the basic theorem

$$f(t) = \begin{cases} \dfrac{(m-1)!}{t!(m-1-t)!}\left(1-\dfrac{1}{q}\right)^{t}\left(\dfrac{1}{q}\right)^{m-1-t} & t = 0, 1, 2, \ldots, m-1 \\ 0 & \text{otherwise} \end{cases}$$

where $f(t) =$ the probability that a message will reach a town of a given hierarchical level at time t and $m =$ the order of the largest center in the hierarchy.

This equation represents the binomial frequency distribution, where t is a random variate. It states that innovations diffuse in such a way that the higher the order of a place, the greater is its probability of receiving information early. In this context, q is the number of orders in this hierarchy which have not received information at a particular time. (A familiar example is the probability of precipitation; if it is 70 percent, then there is a 30 percent chance of good weather, that is, $q = 30$.)

In this model, there is a one-to-one correspondence between time period and hierarchical order. Thus, in the first time period, the highest-order place adopts an innovation, and at the fifth time period, the fifth-order places adopt it.

Hudson's model is a very rigidly structured stochastic model which Pred (1971) has criticized on three counts. (1) There is no provision for lateral diffusion between any pair of places at any particular hierarchical order when both are not members of the same nest. Thus, if Boston and Philadelphia are dominated by New York and St. Louis and Denver are dominated by Chicago, the model does not allow for innovations to diffuse from Philadelphia to St. Louis. (2) There is no provision for lateral diffusion, even within the same nesting arrangement, as, for example, between Boston and Philadelphia. (3) The flow of innovation is strictly unidirectional, i.e., down the hierarchy. While this situation is obviously the most probable, there are occasions when some innovations do diffuse up the hierarchy. Not everything has to start in New York City, especially with modern means of communications. Many important innovations in the electronic computing field that are initially adopted in such places as Poughkeepsie and Minneapolis subsequently diffuse to Chicago, Los Angeles, and New York.

As an alternative schema, Pred suggests merging the Christaller central place hierarchy (which is largely concerned with tertiary activities) with a Löschian hierarchy (which incorporates nontertiary functions also) as well as a

Figure 11-3 Nodal dominance structure in a central-place system

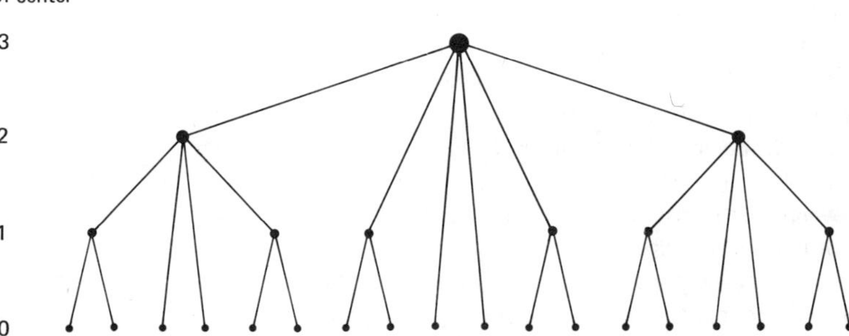

Figure 11-4 One among many possible flow schemas within a mixed nodal hierarchy

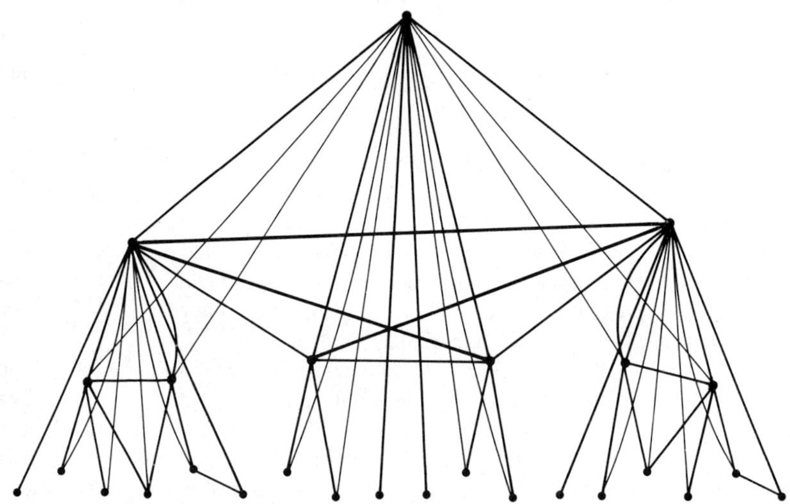

neighborhood effect. The results are shown in Figure 11-4. It must be noted, however, that this is only one permutation, and thus Pred's alternative yields an indeterminate model. By abandoning the Christallerian rigidity, we are left with a rather weak and anemic model which says, "there are many ways in which hierarchical diffusion can occur, and here is one of them." Nevertheless, Pred does present some evidence to substantiate his conceptual model.

Mathematically elegant models are often difficult to verify in light of real-world data because of their rigidly simplifying assumptions. In contrast, a loosely structured, nonformal conceptual or schematic model may be closer to the real world and may be verified by some form of circumstantial evidence. In comparing the two and assessing their validity, one is drawn to the judgment of most TV-viewers of courtroom drama who know that the same set of circumstantial evidence can have alternative meanings in terms of whodunit, the butler or the lord of the manor!

CONTAGIOUS DIFFUSION

The notion of contagious diffusion has its antecedents in epidemiology. A prerequisite for the occurrence of an epidemic, be it smallpox or a strain of influenza, is, of course, personal contact. Public health authorities endeavor to isolate or quarantine the carriers of a contagious disease and thus arrest its spread. From their perspective, the spread of a disease is viewed in terms of the number of people who are afflicted by it. However, there is also a spatial component in the process of contagion, which is of particular geographic interest. Because contagion depends upon interpersonal contacts which are characterized by distance-decay effects, contagious diffusion processes are spatially constrained.

There are basically two types of contagious diffusion processes: relocation and expansion. As a special exception to what we have stated before, in relocation diffusion the origin area loses the item being diffused. Thus, migration and even commuting (temporary though it is) can be viewed either as flows or as relocation diffusions. Indeed, a study of commuting in Chicago (Taaffe, Garner, and Yeates, 1963) attempted to treat the peripheral journey to work as a diffusion process. We shall, however, limit ourselves here to a consideration of expansion diffusion and, further, to the contagious diffusion of innovations.

Because it encompasses many apparently disparate items, spatial diffusion can be observed at a variety of scales. The following examples have been selected deliberately to illustrate the spread of agriculture, settlement, and women's suffrage as they occur at the world and national scales (Figures 11-5 to 11-7).

Figure 11-5 derives from a vignette entitled *Agricultural Origins and Dispersals* (Sauer, 1952), which has become a classic in cultural geography. In contrast to the other maps illustrating patterns of spatial diffusion contained in this chapter, this map does not have any dates or "generational intervals," since the topic it deals with is prehistoric. Nevertheless, the fundamental elements are clear. The hearths are the origin areas from which a particular innovation flowed along certain paths to one or more destinations. The original hearth of agriculture was southeastern Asia and the east coast of India. Subsidiary centers developed in the Middle East and West Africa. The grape, for example, originated in the upper Tigris-Euphrates basin, and from there grape culture moved across Turkey and southeastern Europe to northern Italy. This was just one route of penetration; others are shown on the map. Not only did plant culture diffuse, but also the domestication of the pig and fowl.

At a national scale, we can consider the diffusion of settlement in the United States from 1790 to 1890 (Figure 11-6). In this figure, the well-known westward expansion of American settlement can be seen as a general wavelike progression of the white man's occupancy of the land. In 1790, with the exception of Pennsylvania, the frontier of settlement essentially reached east of the Appalachians. In addition, there were a few clusters in Kentucky and Tennessee. At the same time, Spanish settlement began along the upper Rio Grande valley and along portions of the California coastline. By 1820, settlement had crossed the barrier of the Appalachians and had reached into the Ohio valley. Thirty years later, the eastern portion of the Great Plains was settled, and by 1890, the Rocky Mountains were being approached from the East.

The expansion of settlement from the Pacific Coast eastward was impeded by the obvious physical barriers as well as by the small scale of original settlement. The tongue-shaped contours define these routes of penetration. The American frontier effectively came to an end in 1890, by which time all the areas that were perceived as being habitable had, in fact, been settled. Although in general it is possible to describe the settlement process as being wavelike, the sequence here was rather choppy. Many intervening areas were leaped over, awaiting a subsequent spatial "in-filling" sequence. Thus, for example, the interior of West Virginia was not settled until 1820, even though the general settlement frontier had crossed into Ohio by 1800.

Many of us are used to thinking that in 18th- and 19th-century America,

Figure 11-5 The spread of agricultural practices and of the domestication of animals in the Old World

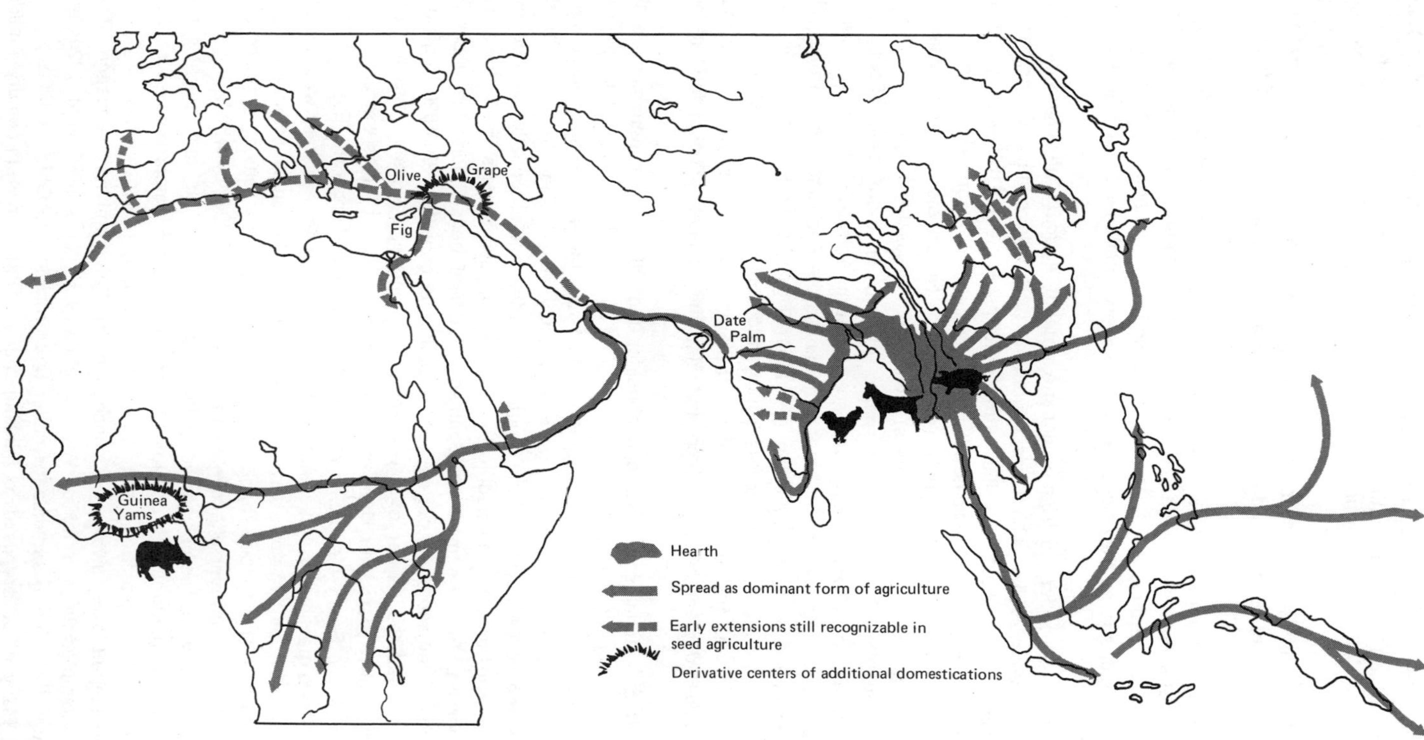

Figure 11-6
Expansion of United States settlement, 1790–1890. (Isochrones indicate, by decade, settlement with a population density greater than 2 persons per square mile.)

Figure 11-7 The spatial expansion of women's suffrage outward from Wyoming, 1870–1920

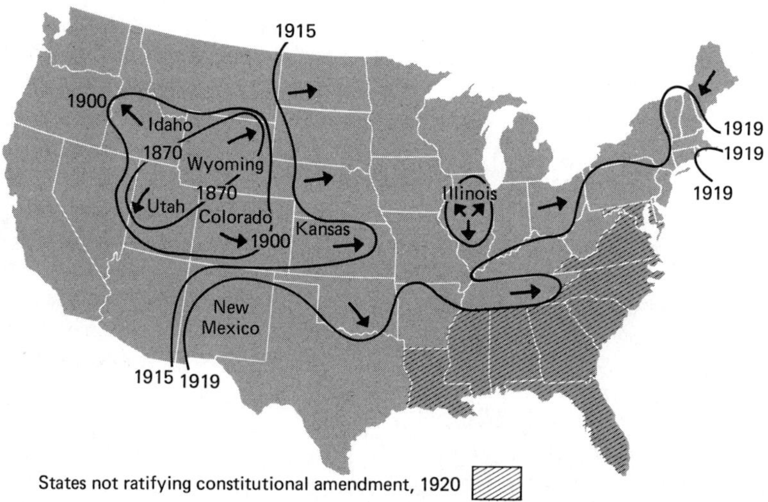

everything began on the East Coast. Figure 11-7 is an antidote to this bit of conventional wisdom in that it shows an innovation originating in the West and moving in the "wrong" direction, toward the East. Gould (1969b, 60) points out that many of the early western-type innovations involved individual rights, since frontiersmen and frontierswomen "chaffed under archaic and undemocratic laws carried earlier from the effete and decadent East." Wyoming was the first state in the Union to grant women the right to vote in state elections. It was a new idea that was adopted next by Utah. However, neighboring Colorado and Idaho resisted the innovation for 25 years. By 1915, the innovation had blanketed most of the Western states. From Kansas (1913), women's suffrage leaped over Missouri and Illinois. Although the year 1919 saw the rapid eastward advance of this wave of innovation, the conservative Southern states, nearly all belonging to the old Confederacy, did not ratify this amendment to the Constitution. Finally, in 1920, 50 years after the innovation originated in Wyoming, it had permeated the entire American national space. The diffusion of women's suffrage again presents certain characteristic aspects of the diffusion process: the existence of an origin and many destinations, a temporal interval in the diffusion, and a series of leapfrogs, each of which was a response to the existence of barriers. The unit of adoption in this case was the state, since once a state legislature had adopted the innovation, it had legal validity throughout the state. This kind of diffusion is in contrast to settlement expansion, which proceeded by small steps.

These examples of contagious diffusion contain certain repetitive themes and empirical regularities. The question arises as to what is the most appropriate perspective from which to study contagious diffusion *in general* (rather than studying just the diffusion of agricultural practices or settlement or women's suffrage). First, since the key to an understanding of contagious diffusion is the appreciation of interpersonal contacts, we shall continue with an analysis of the nature of contact systems. Second, since all movement is spatial and temporal simultaneously, we shall consider the time dimension within which diffusion processes operate, their overall rate of growth, and the spatial-temporal dimensions of their growth. With these two basic considerations in mind, we shall elaborate at length on the development of Monte Carlo simulation models used on the one hand to replicate spatial diffusion processes and on the other to uncover certain regularities in the process itself.

The Role of Contact Systems in Diffusion

To begin with, it is important to understand that the diffusion of an item in geographic space is seldom uniform, nor is it instantaneous. Moreover, information transmission is a prerequisite to the diffusion process, although, of course, the receipt of information does not necessarily mean the adoption of an innovation. Often, multiple tellings of some bit of information (propaganda) may be required before acceptance and adoption occur. A significant form of information transfer is still direct, personal, or face-to-face contact. In this context, Hägerstrand (1965, 263) writes, "Dissemination through private or group conversations easily outbalances other means of communications. Even today, we are very neolithic in that respect, I am sure." This statement was made about Sweden which enjoys mass ownership of radio and television and a high level of newspaper and magazine readership, as well as other sources of public information.

When one speaks of personal contacts, it is possible to conceive of them as a network in which the nodes are individual senders or receivers and the routes between them are communication channels. From this vantage point, we can refer to networks of personal contacts as trees, Hamiltonian circuits, fully connected networks, hierarchical networks, and so on, thus recognizing that social networks also have varying levels of connectivity. At one extreme, there is a cave-dwelling hermit who lives in both social and spatial isolation, while at the other extreme, gregarious persons are linked to a complex and widespread network of friends and acquaintances.

Figure 11-8*a* and *b* shows two illustrative schemas of networks of friends and acquaintances. The resemblance between the network configurations in this context and the network configurations in the context of nodes and routes is clear, and so graph-theoretic measures such as the beta and alpha indices

Figure 11-8 Networks of friends and acquaintances: (*a*) planar; (*b*) nonplanar.

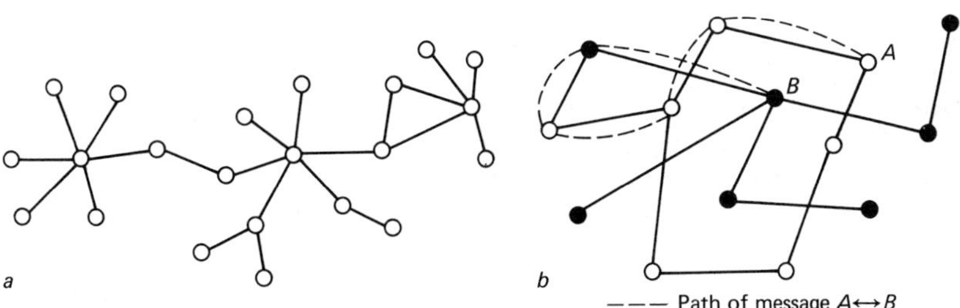

could also be computed for the social network (see Chapter 5). Some nodes are better connected than others and may be called the "kingpins" of their particular subsystems. In contrast, peripheral individuals or nodes at the "end of the line," as it were, are usually the last to hear a message. Messages can be routed through the network so that *A* tells *B* and *B* tells *C* and so on. "Neighborhood gossips" and traveling salesmen are often the best connected nodes (individuals) by virtue of their relative location in the network.

There may also be subgraphs within each of which there is a high degree of connectivity. However, connectivity between the subgraphs may be quite low. A racially polarized society may be viewed as one which consists of two entirely different networks. Social networks can be either planar or nonplanar. In a nonplanar network, the intersections are not necessarily nodes; rather, they overlap, making a network in which neighbors are not necessarily friends or acquaintances. This situation is well exemplified in many American neighborhoods of high-rise apartments. People live in apartment canyons as cave dwellers, and, despite spatial propinquity, there is no community within these "neighborhoods," a fact which makes a mockery of the concept. Home is just a place to park. Contacts are with people at places of work, in professional associations, in labor unions, and so on, rather than within the physical residential neighborhood. The notion of overlapping social systems does not mean that two subsystems of the network have nothing to do with each other. In fact, they may be in contact via one or more nodes. Thus, for example, in Figure 11-8*b*, *A* and *B* are neighbors in a euclidean sense, without any direct contact between them. A message from *A* to *B*, or vice versa, travels in a circultous path through three other members of *A*'s network and one member of *B*'s network. On a worldwide scale, a similar situation often exists in diplomatic contacts. Until the United States and China established quasi-diplomatic relations, contacts had to be routed through Poland and other third parties, who were in contact with both the communist and noncommunist networks.

The nature of circuitous paths and the role of intermediaries in a social network have been formally studied as the "small-world problem" (Travers and Milgram, 1969). The problem can be defined as follows: "Given two individuals selected randomly from the population, what is the probability that the minimum number of intermediaries required to link them is 0, 1, 2, . . . , *k*?" (Travers and Milgram, 1969, 426). The implication is that we live in a small world after all, which consists of tightly woven social networks in which unexpected connections exist between individuals who are apparently separated in both physical and social space.

In order to test this notion, Travers and Milgram selected an arbitrary "target person" (a Boston stockbroker living in Sharon, Massachusetts) who was to be the destination node. The 296 origin nodes (starting persons) were selected, and an effort was made to generate an acquaintance chain from each of these origins to the one chosen destination. Each starter was supplied with a document and requested to send it to the target individual if the starter knew the target individual on a first-name basis. In this case, the chain would have been zero. If, on the other hand, the target individual was not known on a first-name basis, the starter node was instructed to mail the document to a friend who was likely to know the target. The starting population was made up of 100 owners of stocks in Nebraska (1300 miles from Boston), another 96 randomly chosen Nebraskans, and 100 randomly chosen residents of the Boston metropolitan area. The detailed accounting which was kept revealed that, altogether, there were 453 intermediaries and that 64 of the 296 starters were able to get their documents to the target. The mean chain length (number of intermediaries) was found to be 5.2 and the maximum 11. Since social proximity is partly a function of spatial proximity, the chains originating in the Boston random group had a mean length of 4.4, versus 5.7 for the Nebraska random group. The Nebraska stock-owning starter group had a smaller social distance to the Boston stockbroker than did the other Nebraskans. Stockbroking channels were used, and consequently the mean chain length was 5.4.

It was found that there were a number of focal individuals in the networks; i.e., some intermediaries appeared in more than one chain. Figure 11-9 shows the common paths converging on the destination. Of the 64 letters which reached the target, 16 (25 percent) came through a single neighbor, 10 through one business associate, and 5 through another business associate. These are the penultimate links in the chains.

Even in a large population, such as that of the United States, the maximum number of intermediaries required to link widely separated individuals is only 11 in this case, indicating that there is some truth to the statement that

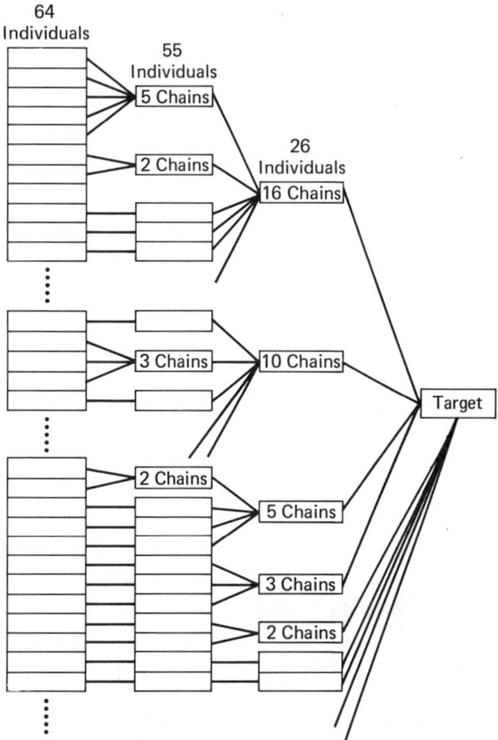

Figure 11-9 Common paths of communication as chains converging on the destination

this is a small world. In this context, society can be viewed as a binary matrix of interpersonal nonreciprocal contacts. By matrix-powering procedures, as was shown in Chapter 5, it is possible to analyze 1-, 2-, 3-, . . . , *n*-step connections between any two nodes. The same procedure is applicable to a social network, which can be partitioned and factor-analyzed, exactly like the Argentinean local airline service network. In this way, we can identify the structure of social networks and the pattern of connections.

The work of Travers and Milgram does suggest that it is possible to link any two individuals through some chain of individuals. In other words, under normal conditions a linkage can be made, however circuitous, and there is probably no such thing as an isolated node. The exact path (trajectory of the message) is a matter of chance, and therefore one can conceptualize interpersonal links in society as a random net. In considering spatial diffusion and information transfer between individuals, it is evident that numerous factors condition the precise configuration of the processes. The questions of why *this* individual originated a message and why *that* individual received a message and adopted an innovation or did not adopt it cannot usually be answered adequately. One way — possibly the only way — to incorporate all the behavioral aspects of particular individuals simultaneously, in an attempt to understand the diffusion process, is to conceive of a social network as being random.

As we have defined it before, a net consists of nodes connected by links. If these links are one-way, we may speak of a "directed" linear graph. Within such a graph, if the probabilities of connecting additional nodes (contacting individuals) which are not currently linked by the network are equal, then we refer to the net as *a pure random net*. On the other hand, if some bias is stipulated, i.e., if certain individuals or directions are favored over others, then the net is referred to as *a random and biased net*. Rapoport has suggested the incorporation of several different kinds of biases, and Brown and Moore (1969) have summarized his work, placing it in a geographical context. Random and biased nets make it possible to construct an idealized "island model," in which information exchanged between individuals in a village is a purely random process, while intervillage contacts are distance-biased. Alternatively, within a village or neighborhood, the members of an individual clique may be strongly linked by a system of contacts while there is little contact between members of two different cliques, as was represented in the overlapping networks in Figure 11-8*b*, a Hatfield-McCoy situation, as it were. *Popularity-bias* refers to the individual attributes of nodes, so that when one speaks of large cities, big corporations, and rich people, they are said to be "popular" in that they are more likely to come into contact with other nodes. Brown and Moore (1969) have listed other types of biases such as acquaintance circle, reciprocity, and so on. Of course, in a geographic study, we are particularly interested in the *distance bias*.

The Role of Time in Diffusion

In an attempt to understand the diffusion process, it is necessary to mesh space and time simultaneously, since the spread of an innovation over an area is neither geographically uniform nor temporally instantaneous. The spatial diffusion of any item can be conceptualized as a growth process in which the number of units and areas adopting the innovation increases through time. Many growth processes can be modeled as a logistic (S-shaped) function whose key characteristics are a slow beginning, a sharp inflection, a steep ascent, and a plateau.

The form of the logistic curve is

$$P = \frac{U}{1 + e^{a-bt}}$$

where $P =$ the proportion of adopters at time t

$U =$ the upper bound or the saturation level

$a, b =$ empirically derived parameters [they are constants in this expression which determine the way in which the two variables (P and t) change together]

$e = 2.7183$

The logistic expression therefore relates the proportion of adopters to all potential adopters at any given time, in a diffusion process, to the length of time that has elapsed from the origin of the process. The value of U depends on both the spatial context and the nature of the item being diffused. Specifically, the value of U is a function of (1) the size of the spatial entity within which diffusion will occur and (2) the proportion of the population which is susceptible to the particular item being diffused. For example, in the diffusion of the intrauterine contraceptive device, the appropriate target population would be women between the ages of 15 and 45. Thus, the value of U (the saturation level) could be specified.

The shape of the logistic curve depends upon the values of a and b. When the respective values are $a = 3.0$, $b = 1.0$, and $t = 0$, the expression becomes

$$P = \frac{100}{1 + 2.7183^{[3.0-(1.0\times 0)]}}$$

$$= \frac{100}{21} \approx 5 \text{ percent}$$

This figure means that early adopters amount to 5 percent of the total population and are now passing information about the innovation to others. At the third generation or time period ($t = 3.0$), the proportion of the total population knowing or adopting is

$$P = \frac{100}{1 + 2.7183^{[3.0-(1.0\times 3.0)]}}$$

$$= \frac{100}{1 + 2.7183^{0}} = \frac{100}{1+1} = 50 \text{ percent}$$

(Note that any number raised to its zeroth power equals 1.)

If the initial adopted rate is slow, the value of a is large. Thus, if $a = 10.0$, $b = 4.0$, and $t = 0$, then

$$P = \frac{100}{1 + 2.7183^{[10.0-(4.0\times 0)]}}$$

$$= \frac{100}{22{,}026} \approx 0$$

In this case, when the value of t becomes about 2.5, the innovation catches on suddenly, and there is a rapid adoption as the curve quickly approaches the 100 percent limit. The two situations with different values of the parameters are graphed in Figure 11-10. Curve *A* starts off with a 5 percent adoption rate at time 0 and moves slowly upward. Curve *B* begins with 0 proportion of adopters, and until the second time period nothing much happens; but from then on there is a steep, nearly vertical escalation. This escalation is due to the fact that when the constant e is raised to its tenth power, the value of the denominator is made very large, and therefore the resulting proportion of very early innovators is virtually 0. In this way, it can readily be seen that the differences between the two curves arise from the different values of the parameters a and b.

The diffusion of color television sets, as a temporal process, is perhaps best described by curve *A*. The initial group of adopters (buyers) consisted of affluent individuals. The relatively high costs of sets kept the rate of diffusion relatively slow. At some point, however, when people became more affluent or prices were lowered, the spread of the innovation picked up speed. In contrast, curve *B* may describe the diffusion of a fad. For example, flower decals were an ephemeral innovation as were "smiley faces," the hula hoop, and the frisbee. The initial dissemination proceeded at a snail's pace, and hardly anyone had heard of this innovation in the initial stage. Subsequently, an alert and aggressive entrepreneur bought the rights to the innovation, and he became an influential salesman through his advertising and marketing strategy. Almost overnight the innovation blanketed the entire nation, as evidenced by the flower decals on cars and garbage cans.

Figure 11-10
Two logistic curves

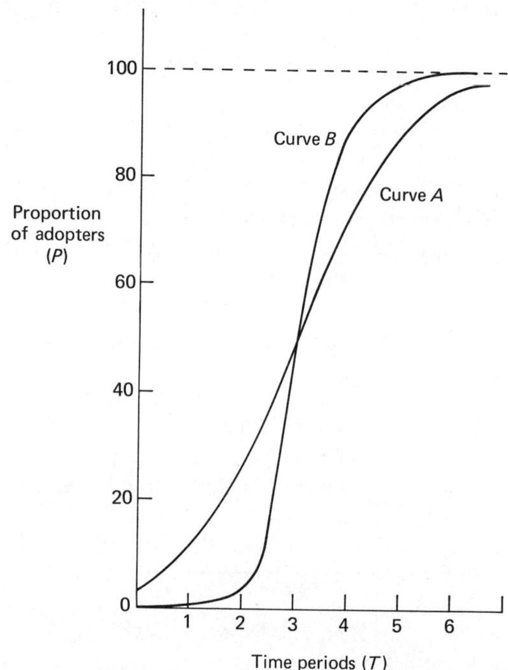

The logistic curve or the logistic model is only one among a number of curves that could be fitted to data on diffusion through time. Compared to the alternatives, the logistic curve is easy to compute, and generally it yields a good fit. In addition, Casetti (1969) has shown that in terms of process the logistic is an adequate description since it incorporates the following notions: (1) potential users become adopters after personal contacts with prior adopters; (2) each potential adopter has a different degree of resistance; (3) this resistance may be breached by multiple tellings, that is, there is some threshold of "sales resistance" that can eventually be overcome.

In spite of its many valuable characteristics in describing the diffusion process through time, the logistic and other such curves are nonspatial. The number of adopters may be 5 percent of 5000, but these 250 adopters may be located in widely separated places. Moreover, there is a finite upper limit, so that 100 percent in a small area may represent only 3 percent of the larger area containing it. The adoption rate of color television in an affluent suburb may reach 100 percent in 2 years, but at the end of the 2-year period, the adoption rate in the entire metropolitan area may be only 5 percent, while it may be only 1 percent in the entire nation. Consequently, the notion of diffusion rates depends heavily upon the specification of the area.

One way to avoid being constrained by a finite population and a bounded area at the same time is to incorporate space and time within one conceptual schema and to think of the diffusion process as wave movement. One of Hägerstrand's early papers, entitled *The Propagation of Innovation Waves* (1952), inspired Morrill (1968) to use the theories of wave mechanics to study spatial diffusion.

The standard wind-generated ocean wave is known as a progressive oscillatory wave. The waveform is the result of a certain amount of energy (wind) traveling over water and causing an oscillatory movement. Its form is of the well-known trough, vertical displacement, crest, vertical displacement, and back to the trough. A bobbing cork would experience all these characteristics. If we follow a wave in the ocean through time, we may observe a build-up, with increasing vertical displacement or wave height, up to some point in time, followed by a decrease in height until the wave dissipates.

The process of diffusion of innovations has some direct analogies to the spatial and temporal sequence of ocean waves sketched above. As a diffusion wave enters an area, there are a small number of initial adopters. This process is followed by a rapid acceleration, and, as suggested by the logistic curve, saturation is reached eventually. As the wave passes on, two or three time periods later it will be cresting in an adjacent area. The analogy to the movement of weather fronts is an obvious one also. Heavy rain occurring now in a particular area will probably fall 3 hours from now in another area located 20 miles to the southeast if that is the direction in which the cold front is moving. Similarly, in hydrology it is possible to predict the cresting of rivers during flooding, at particular locations and times. Thus, if we know that the Mississippi is at flood stage in West Alton, Missouri, now and if we know the river's velocity, it is possible to predict that flood stage will occur or reach Vicksburg, Mississippi, in 12 days.

The foregoing notions are summarized in Figure 11-11. Note that time and distance are equated along both axes. Thus, if the five curves of a single wave

Figure 11-11 Waves of spatial diffusion

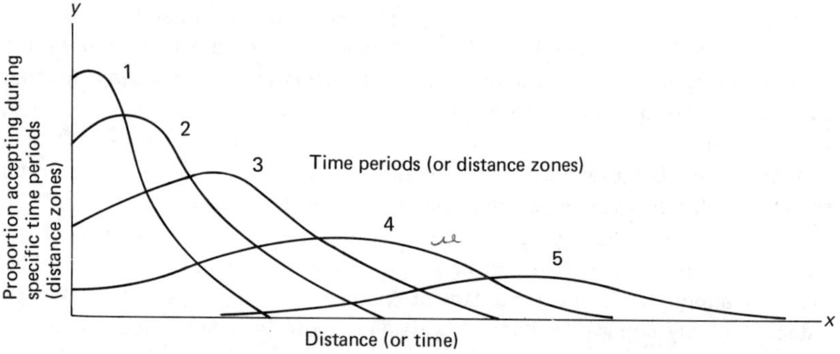

refer to five time periods and if the horizontal axis is distance, then we know that the greatest proportion of adopters is close to the origin (the initial center of adoption) and then decreases outward. If, on the other hand, the curves refer to distance bands and the horizontal axis is time, then Figure 11-11 suggests that, at any given distance zone, the strength of the wave (its height) decreases through time.

Figure 11-12 is an attempt to blend the logistic curve and the wave concept of diffusion of innovations. There are three axes in this diagram: the *x* axis represents distance, the *y* axis is the proportion of adopters, and the *z* axis is time. At time 1 in distance band 1, diffusion is in the early stages of gradual upswing (the first point of inflection in the logistic curve). Simultaneously, in distance band 2, the diffusion process is just getting under way (there are some early adopters), but the wave has not yet reached distance band 3 or 4. By time 3, in distance band 1, the innovation has reached saturation levels (the *U* of the logistic curve has been approached), in distance

Figure 11-12 A progression of logistic curves of spatial diffusion varying with distance

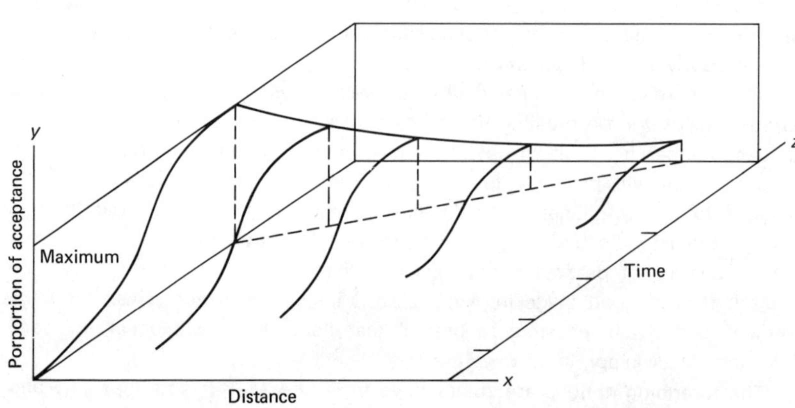

band 3 the wave is cresting, and in distance band 4 the diffusion process is in the early acceptance stage. Nothing has happened in distance band 5, as yet.

One reason why the logistic curve has been used so much in diffusion studies is that data are easy to obtain. The historical statistics of the United States provide ready information about the number of tractors on farms, the number of automobiles, televisions, and so on, in various time intervals without, however, specifying the location of these items. Spatial patterns of diffusion cannot readily be compiled from such data. Consequently, the wave notion of innovation diffusion, interesting and intuitively appealing as it may be, has seldom been tested with real-world data. An early exception was the study by Blumenfeld (1954) entitled *The Tidal Wave of Metropolitan Expansion.* It is possible to conceptualize the built-up area of a metropolis as an innovation (urbanism) moving or spreading in rural geographic space, in much the same way as Morrill (1965) conceptualized ghetto expansion in an urban area as a diffusion process.

The preceding paragraphs suggest two different, although partially reconcilable, approaches to the conceptualization of the role of time in the process of spatial diffusion. The logistic curve, despite being aspatial, permits an overview of the entire diffusion from the earliest adopters to the final laggards in a given area. Further, it is highly descriptive of the rate at which any specific innovation has diffused through an area. In contrast, the wave conceptualization allows for only a limited consideration of the diffusion process because only a slice of time, or of space, may be perceived at any one moment. However, the significance of this particular framework is that it does incorporate space explicitly making it possible to visualize the neighborhood effect and the physical advance or spread of an innovation in space. Thus, although neither conceptualization is holistic with regard to spatial diffusion as a process, together they provide insightful perspectives.

We are now in a position to consider spatial diffusion from the vantage point of knowing something about the nature of contact systems through which all information transfers must occur. We know that these contact systems can be conceptualized as networks, more specifically as random networks with some built-in, but not necessarily apparent, biases. In addition, we know that through time a diffusion process is akin to a growth process in that its rate of expansion varies by stages. Thus, its spatial advance is one of cyclical, not continuous, intensity. With these notions in mind, we can now attempt to derive certain generalizations about spatial diffusion. One way to generalize is to replicate or simulate the diffusion of an innovation and thereby gain some understanding of the process.

Monte Carlo simulation has been a fruitful mode of approach in recent years, and, consequently, we devote the remainder of this chapter largely to the work of Torsten Hägerstrand, a modern pioneer in diffusion studies.

Modeling Spatial Diffusion

With some expenditure of effort, it is not difficult to obtain the basic facts of spatial diffusion and to depict them graphically as was done earlier in this chapter. Frequently, an examination of a chronological series of maps suggests a neighborhood effect in which the innovation originates in one or more centers and, from there, spreads outward through time. These findings prompt the question, Can the pattern of spread of an innovation be modeled or replicated *without* explicit recourse to the initial data upon which the maps were based? (Naturally, we need some preliminary understanding of what happened and from where something diffused.) But, is it possible to generate a process that is totally independent of either the data or the segment of the real world from which the data were collected?

As a preface to a series of attempts at answering these questions, Hägerstrand (1967a) mapped the diffusion of six innovations (state-subsidized pastures, control of bovine TB, soil-mapping, postal checking service, the automobile, and the telephone) through a small area of Sweden. These innovations originated outside the Kinda-Ydre study area. A prodigious amount of minute data collection went into this effort, yielding information concerning the date of adoption of a particular innovation by a particular farmer.

As an example of these analyses, let us consider the diffusion of the idea of soil mapping. The innovation was introduced into the study area in 1939. It was given its original impetus as a result of a grant from the state to the Östergötland Rural Economy Association, which functioned as the change agent. A charge was paid by each farmer who wanted the soils on his farm mapped, and therefore a conscious decision to adopt or not to adopt this innovation had to be made by each farmer. Hägerstrand's basic data came from the Rural Economy Association's maps of completed soil mapping which show the location of each farm mapped as well as the date of mapping. Figure 11-13*a* shows the diffusion pattern. The isopleth values are based on the ratios of acceptances in each cell to the total number of eligible farms in that cell. In 1939, there was a single adopter, located in cell T8*j* (Kättilstad), which may be regarded as the origin of the innovation. By 1940, the innovation had diffused to the northern end of Lake Åsunden (T8*i*), and a secondary origin arose in Sund (T2*d*). Even at an early stage in the diffusion process, regional differentiation emerged, and Figure 11-13*b* shows two subregions with a high level of acceptances located in the east and the west.

The innovation diffused, not uniformly throughout the area, but rather in a pattern of decreasing intensity centered on Kättilstad and Sund. Further, new subregional, secondary concentrations emerged in cells T4*b*, T4*c*, and T5*b*. By 1950, the innovation had not fully caught on, and if one were to relate it to a logistic curve, it might be said that soil mapping had not yet reached the first inflection point.

In this way, Hägerstrand mapped each of the selected indicators. Cartographic analysis showed three repetitive themes about the diffusion process: (1) the existence of an initial agglomeration, i.e., the local concentration of early adopters; (2) the radial dissemination from the initial centers accompanied by the rise of secondary centers, while the original centers continue an intensification of the adoption level (a greater proportion of adopters occurs in these cells); and (3) eventual saturation (although this result is not apparent from Figure 11-13 since the diffusion of soil mapping was in its early stages as of 1950).

These three generalizations were incorporated in the models designed by

Figure 11-13 Diffusion of soil-mapping in Kinda-Ydre, Sweden: (*a*) 1940–1945; (*b*) 1940–1950.

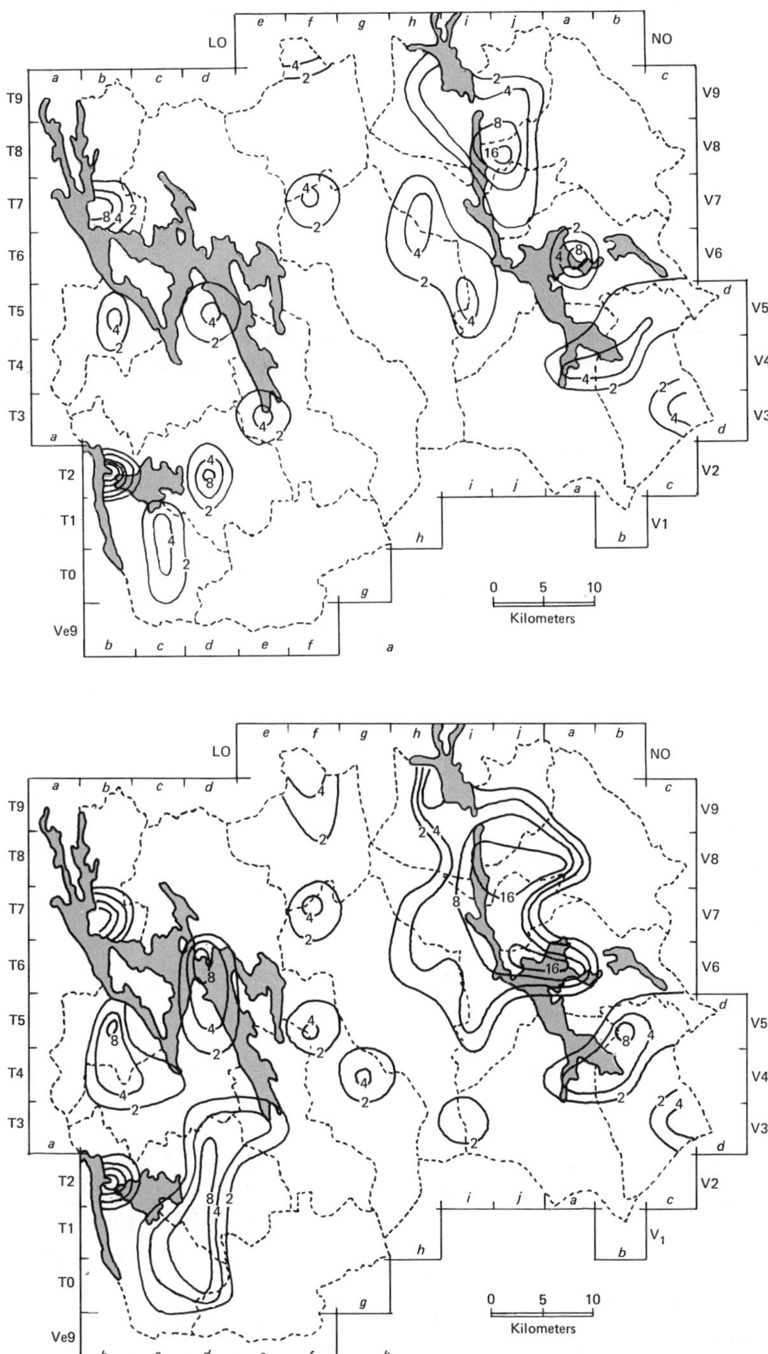

Hägerstrand to simulate diffusion. The models were inspired by Von Thünen and referred to an *imaginary* area, not to the real-world area of Kinda-Ydre, which was intensively studied. This imaginary area was assumed to be completely homogeneous even though topographic irregularities, several large lakes, and an uneven distribution of population were known to exist in the real-world study area. The model area was a square whose side was equal to 45 kilometers. It was divided into 81 cells, each of which measured 5 kilometers on a side and contained 30 persons. The resulting total population of 2430 was approximately that of the real-world study area. This model area was used in each of the various simulations.

A Purely Random Simulation

The basic assumptions underlying this model were as follows. (1) At time t_1 the entire population is informed about the innovation. The implication of this assumption is that there is no word-of-mouth or other transmission of information within the region. Instead, the availability of information is uniform; it is as if everyone had a television and had simultaneously tuned in to the same program. (2) The acceptance pattern is purely random. (3) No saturation limit is hypothesized.

The simulation procedure was as follows. Each one of the 81 cells was assigned a range of 30 consecutive numbers so that cell I10 (Figure 11-14) was assigned the numbers 1 to 30 and cell Q18 was allocated the numbers 2401

Figure 11-14 Purely random simulation

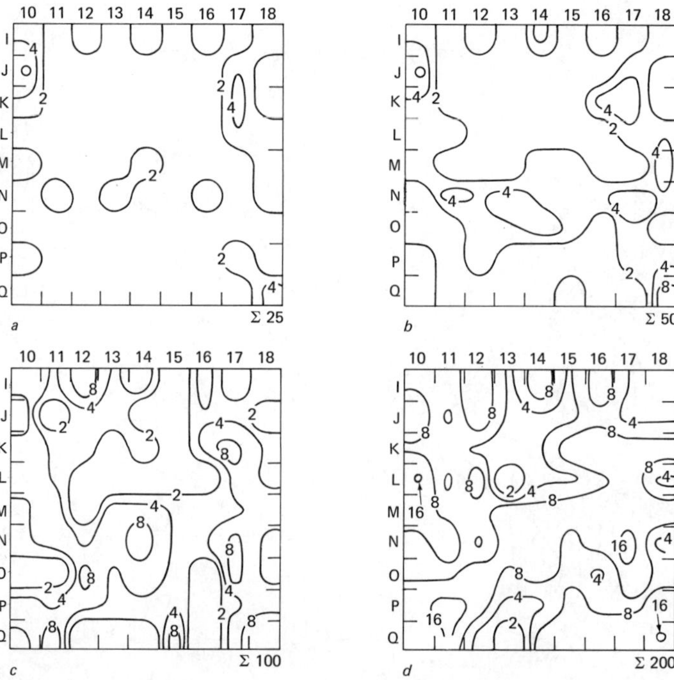

to 2430. Then, four-digit numbers were drawn from a table of random digits. If, for example, the first number picked was 0222, which corresponded to cell I17, then a "hit" was recorded there.

The first 25 "hits" are shown in Figure 11-14*a*. The isopleths, as before, represent the ratio of acceptances in a particular cell to the number of potential, eligible acceptors in that cell. Geometric intervals (1, 2, 4, 8, 16, . . .) were used in order not to clutter up the map with too many lines.

Figure 11-14*b* to *d* shows the results of the purely random Monte Carlo simulation with respect to 50, 100, and 200 acceptances, respectively. One of the major findings emerging from the operation of this model is that in spite of the use of random numbers, regional differentiation in the pattern of acceptances emerged; that is, localization or geographical concentration can occur purely from the operation of chance processes. Thus, although Hägerstrand did not publish alternative maps in his work, the procedures outlined above were repeated using different sets of random digits, and in each case, a pronounced regional differentiation emerged in the simulation.

By comparing the patterns of empirically derived maps with the simulated ones, Hägerstrand concluded that the first stage in the diffusion process was somewhat similar. However, in later stages, the correspondence between reality and simulation disappeared. This result may be interpreted by suggesting that the assumptions are unrealistic. In particular, the absence of a spatial bias is inherent in the initial assumptions. In order to correct these deficiencies in subsequent models, the following two assumptions were incorporated: (1) there is an uneven receptiveness to innovations; (2) there is an uneven geographic distribution of information.

A Distance-biased Random Simulation

Whereas in the preceding model everyone knew about the innovation and had an equal probability of adopting it, in this one the only person who knows about the innovation at the beginning is located in the center of the hypothetical area in cell M14 (Figure 11-15*a*). As in the previous model, the possession of information immediately results in its acceptance. However, the receipt of information is conditioned by a distance bias. After acceptance, an individual adopter tells others about it, causing them in turn to accept the innovation. There are no public sources of information with regard to this innovation, and we rely upon the notion of personal-contact systems. Recall that, according to Hägerstrand, "we are still very neolithic" in the sense that most of our information still comes from private sources. Also, we are more likely to be influenced by information that originates from a private source than from a public one.

In order to operationalize the notion of contact systems, it is necessary at this juncture to make use of the mean information field (MIF). It was introduced in Chapter 7 as being representative of an individual's probable and standardized field of contact. In addition, it was shown that the intensity or volume of contact declines outward from the individual as a function of distance. The computation of an MIF is a relatively simple process which we elaborate upon now.

Figure 11-15 Distance-biased random simulation

Table 11-1
Observed Local Migration in the Asby Area, Sweden

Distance (kilometers)	Zonal area (kilometer²)	Number of migrants	Number of migratory units	Number of migratory units per kilometer²
0–0.5	0.79	13	9	11.39
0.5–1.5	6.28	69	45	7.17
1.5–2.5	12.57	72	45	3.58
2.5–3.5	18.85	44	26	1.38
3.5–4.5	25.14	37	28	1.11
4.5–5.5	31.42	34	25	0.80
5.5–6.5	37.70	33	20	0.53
6.5–7.5	43.99	45	23	0.52
7.5–8.5	50.27	36	18	0.36
8.5–9.5	56.56	18	10	0.18
9.5–10.5	62.82	28	17	0.27
10.5–11.5	69.12	9	7	0.10
11.5–12.5	75.41	14	11	0.15
12.5–13.5	81.69	8	6	0.07
13.5–14.5	87.98	2	2	0.02
14.5–15.5	94.26	8	5	0.05
		Σ 470	Σ 297	

Source: Hägerstrand, 1967a, p. 186, Table 24.

Table 11-1, the starting point for the construction of the MIF, shows the number (Y) of migrating units (households) in the Asby area per square kilometer. A pareto function (see Chapter 7) was fitted to these data and yielded the following:

$$Y = 6.26d^{-1.6}$$

or

$$\log Y = 0.7966 - 1.58 \log d$$

where d is distance from a common origin.

These empirically estimated parameters are then used to construct an expected migration or contact grid which contains an odd number of rows and columns (5×5, 7×7, 9×9, . . .) in order to provide for one central cell. In the Hägerstrand model, a 5×5 grid was used in which each cell was 5 kilometers on a side. Since, as was suggested earlier, the pareto equation overestimates close-in migrants, the actual number of migrating households at very small distances (110.0 in Asby) was entered in the central cell of Figure 11-16. Every cell outside the central cell was further subdivided into 25 1-kilometer² cells. The distance from the center of the central cell to that of each of these small cells was inserted as d in the logged equation above. Twenty-five Y values (expected migrants) were thus estimated for each of the 5-kilometer² cells and then summed. For the cells immediately to the north, east, south, and west of the central cell, the resulting value was 13.57. Since the matrix in Figure 11-16 is square, distances are symmetrical, and therefore the expected number of migrants is also symmetrical. Consequently, cells 1*a*, 1*e*, 5*a*, and 5*e* have identical values just as do cells 1*b*, 1*d*, 2*a*, 2*e*, 4*a*, 4*e*, 5*b*, and 5*d*.

Figure 11-16
Observed local migration in the Asby area, Sweden, standardized by symmetrical cells

	a	*b*	*c*	*d*	*e*
1	2.38	3.48	4.17	3.48	2.38
2	3.48	7.48	13.57	7.48	3.48
3	4.17	13.57	110.00	13.57	4.17
4	3.48	7.48	13.57	7.48	3.48
5	2.38	3.48	4.17	3.48	2.38

In order to convert this grid to the MIF, the cell entries in Figure 11-16 were summed and the value of each cell was divided by that sum. The result is a cell proportion or probability of contact. This new matrix is also symmetrical, and Figure 11-17, according to Hägerstrand, "is the mean field for private information which issues from one farmer and is directed toward other farmers" (1967a, 245).

What is the operational meaning of the numbers in each of the cells? Since the total of the cell values is 9999, while that of the central cell is 4431, the probability that an individual (teller) located in the central cell will communicate with another (receiver) located in the same cell is very high. Specifically, there are 4431 chances out of 9999 that the origin and destination nodes will be in the same cell; i.e., we have manufactured a regulated accident. On the other hand, there are only 96 chances out of 9999 that a message originating in the central cell will be received by an individual in cells 1*a*, 1*e*,

Figure 11-17
Mean information field, Asby area, Sweden

	a	*b*	*c*	*d*	*e*
1	0.0096	0.0140	0.0168	0.0140	0.0096
2	0.0140	0.0301	0.0547	0.0301	0.0140
3	0.0168	0.0547	0.4431	0.0547	0.0168
4	0.0140	0.0301	0.0547	0.0301	0.0140
5	0.0096	0.0140	0.0168	0.0140	0.0096
				Σ	0.9999

5*a*, or 5*e*. In this way, the MIF represents a contact field in which probabilities are assigned to each cell. In the context of Sweden, the MIF represents a maximum area of 625 kilometers^2 within which most migration occurred.

The specific operation of this distance-biased model required the conversion of each of the cells in the MIF to a range of numbers such that the number of digits assigned to each cell was equal to the cell probability in Figure 11-17. For example, the central cell (3*c*) had a value of 0.4431, and therefore, in Figure 11-18, it is assigned that many consecutive numbers (2785 to 7215). Since each of the four corner cells had a probability of 0.0096, cell 1*a* was assigned the range 0001 to 0096 while cell 5*e* was assigned the numbers 9904 to 9999.

It should be reiterated, at this point, that chance is being controlled here by loading the dice, as it were, with distance. More specifically, in Hägerstrand's study, the number of numbers assigned to each cell decreases symmetrically from over 4000 in the central cell to under 100 in each corner cell. The symmetrical nature of the MIF precludes an explicit incorporation of directional effects; therefore, the distance-biased MIF is directionally neutral.

The actual number of numbers varies according to the parameters of the distance-decay function, and Morrill and Pitts (1967) have constructed a number of different MIFs based upon data concerning marriage distances in Seattle, migrating households in Cleveland, and other kinds of person-movements (see Chapter 7). The chance of making a "hit" at or in the vicinity of the center is greater than for other cells, since in drawing random numbers there are over 4000 possibilities of drawing a number assigned to that cell.

Let us now proceed to the simulation of innovation diffusion using the MIF. Since a 9 × 9 grid has been constructed for the model area, while the MIF is only a 5 × 5 grid, the latter can be referred to as a "floating" MIF. Its center can be superimposed upon any cell. Thus, at the beginning of the simulation, since the original innovator was located in cell M14 (Figure 11-15), the MIF is centered on that cell. A four-digit random number is selected: assume that it is 3023. In that case, an acceptance (the second adopter) is

Figure 11-18
Grid to simulate the role of distance in the simulation model (floating MIF)

	a	*b*	*c*	*d*	*e*
1	0001 –0096	0097 –0236	0237 –0404	0405 –0544	0545 –0640
2	0641 –0780	0781 –1081	1082 –1628	1629 –1929	1930 –2069
3	2070 –2237	2238 –2784	2785 –7215	7216 –7762	7763 –7930
4	7931 –8070	8071 –8371	8372 –8918	8919 –9219	9220 –9359
5	9360 –9455	9456 –9595	9596 –9763	9764 –9903	9904 –9999

recorded in the same (central) cell because 3023 falls within the range of 2785 to 7215. Since there are 30 individuals in M14, as in each of the other cells, the selection of the *specific* individual contacted requires the drawing of another random number. Each of the 30 individuals is assigned a number serially from 01 to 30, and the selection of a two-digit random number locates the specific individual in the cell.

If the first four-digit number to be drawn happens to be 1450, then a hit is recorded in cell L14, which is located immediately north of the central cell. The specific individual who accepts the innovation is again identified with the selection of another two-digit random number. Cell L14 then becomes a secondary origin, and therefore the MIF is shifted and centered upon it. If the next number picked is 7749, we record an acceptance in L15, select a specific individual, recenter the MIF on L15, and continue. Meanwhile, of course, the adopters in cells M14 and L14 continue to be tellers. The simulation or game proceeds in this way until an arbitrary number of acceptances are simulated through a number of "generational intervals."

The results of Hägerstrand's original simulation are shown in Figure 11-15. The progression of the number of tellings is a geometric one: 1, 2, 4, . . . , 256, so that 256 tellings can be registered in 8 time intervals or generations. The simulated number of acceptances was actually only 1, 2, 4, 8, 16, 31, 60, 114, and 215. The discrepancy from the sixth generation onward is due to a "blockage effect" in which information was given an individual who had already adopted the innovation ("carrying coal to Newcastle"). Operationally, the same individual in a particular cell is selected twice during the second step In the simulation (the two-digit random number selection routine).

In comparing the results of the distance-biased simulation with the empirical studies, Hägerstrand concluded that it replicated reality with respect to process, at least insofar as the major elements were concerned. Whereas the purely random simulation did not yield adequate results with respect to the cumulative number of acceptors through time, this approach did. The contrasting result is largely due to the assumptions made which yielded the growth curve shown in Figure 11-19. Note that up to the fourth or fifth generation, there is a slow increase in the rate of acceptances, and thereafter, there is a very rapid escalation. Had the simulation been continued beyond 215 adopters, it would probably have yielded a logistic curve.

A further analysis of the spatial pattern of the diffusion of innovations resulting from this simulation revealed that it was not very concentrated around the initial origin. This suggested that "playing" with random numbers may, on occasion, result in an erratic pattern instead of the smooth ripplelike one expected in contagious expansion. Thus, isolated adopters, located at great distances from the original center, begin to generate their own secondary cores of innovation concentration. Finally, the assumption that adoption immediately follows the receipt of information is manifestly unrealistic in light of our knowledge that some people respond sluggishly to new ideas.

A Distance-biased Random Simulation with Built-in Barriers

This model was designed to minimize some of the weaknesses inherent in the immediately preceding one. First, it is reasonable to assume that a person is more likely to adopt an innovation after finding out more about it from an in-

Figure 11-19
Growth curve for the distance-biased random simulation

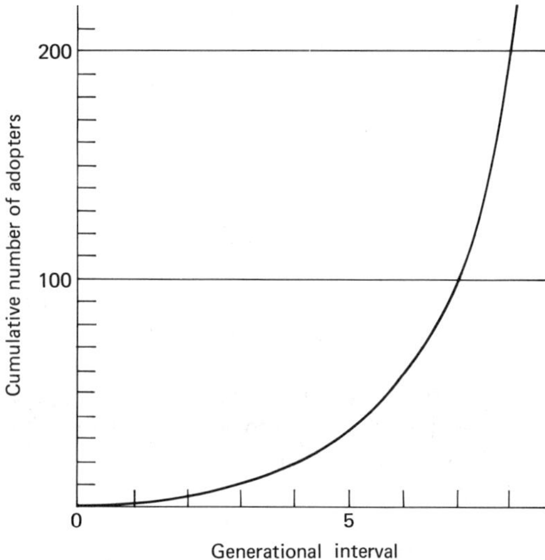

creasing number of contacts with others who have already adopted it. Second, it may be assumed that there are different resistance levels to new ideas among individuals in a society. These differences may be ascribed to such socioeconomic and demographic attributes as age, ethnic origin, farm size, income, education, and so on. With these assumptions in mind, it may be possible to divide all individuals in a society into an arbitrary number of resistance classes. Conventionally, students of diffusion have used a fivefold typology of adopters, and Rogers and Shoemaker (1971) have labeled these as innovators, early adopters, early majority, late adopters, and laggards. Among these categories, the laggards are, of course, the most resistant who need to be told repeatedly about an innovation before they are convinced of its value.

In order to incorporate individual resistance into the model, Hägerstrand stipulated that resistance to new ideas is equal to the "sum of direct contacts concerning the innovation made with already accepting individuals" prior to the acceptance (Hägerstrand, 1967a, 265). Operationally, this stipulation requires that multiple tellings or repeated hits of the same individual occur before adoption can be recorded. The number of tellings required is thus a surrogate measure of an individual's resistance level. Each of the 30 individuals in each of the 81 cells was placed in a particular resistance class. More specifically, a normal frequency distribution was assumed so that there were 2, 7, 12, 7, 2 individuals ($n = 30$) in classes 1 to 5, respectively. Further, in order to specify each individual's resistance class, a new two-digit random number selection process was instituted. In this way, each individual in each cell was assigned to a resistance class, which suggested simultaneously how many tellings were required to make each individual an adopter. Thus, an individual placed in resistance class 1 required only one telling, whereupon he or she adopted the innovation; an individual in class 2 needed to be told twice in order to break down resistance; and so on.

The other procedural details of this particular model are identical to those used in the preceding one. The results of this simulation are shown in

Figure 11-20. The process started with person 18 in cell M14 who contacted person 29 (resistance class 3) in cell M13. Therefore, the innovation was not adopted, and indeed "Mr. 29" did not become an adopter of the innovation, even though he resided in the adjacent cell, until the 61st generation, since it required 61 generations until he could be told 3 times.

In contrast to the simulations generated by the preceding model, the diffusion of innovations shown in Figure 11-20 was very slow because of the impact of distance and resistance upon communication and adoption. Indeed, the original innovator ("Mr. 18" in cell M14) was the only adopter until the eighth generation, as he was unable to convince anybody else to adopt the innovation. The map for the 39th generation (Figure 11-20*a*) shows only eight adopters, although a total of 110 contacts had occurred by then. Thereafter, the innovation caught on, and it can be seen that from the 52nd generation onward (Figure 11-20*d*) the rate of diffusion became relatively rapid. Altogether, 1141 tellings were required over 61 generations to produce 219 acceptances (Figure 11-20*f*).

Figure 11-20*f* was regarded by Hägerstrand as the most realistic of the various simulated patterns. It represents a clear symmetrical outward expansion of acceptances centered on the original innovator. There was a long period of incipient growth and a great concentration of acceptances in the center of the region so that the isopleth value in the vicinity of cell M14 was 64. Subsequently, Hägerstrand compared the simulated pattern with the empirical maps and correlated the rank order of acceptances. He found that in the case of TB control, for example, resistance to its adoption was inversely related to farm size. Thus, operators of the largest farms were the innovators while those of the smallest were the laggards. It is well known that there is a great difference between U.S. agribusinesses on the one hand and marginal sharecroppers on the other in their propensity to adopt innovations.

A Distance-biased Random Simulation with Built-in Barriers on an Anisotropic Surface

In a subsequent study, Hägerstrand (1967b) simulated the diffusion of an innovation on a model plane that incorporated the following. (1) The actual number of farmers (potential adopters) within each cell in the real world study area (Kinda-Ydre). Figure 11-21 is a map of the population distribution of the study area in which the values refer to the number of farmers per cell who owned less than 20 acres of tilled land. (2) Real world contact barriers. These were introduced into the model on the basis of "more than expected" and "less than expected" numbers of telephone calls. The bars on Figure 11-22 indicate more than the number of calls expected while the lines indicate less than the number expected. These data were then used to estimate and locate barriers on the model plane along cell boundaries.

A solid line in Figure 11-21 is referred to as a zero-contact boundary, and if a contact was made from a particular cell to another located across a zero-contact boundary, then the telling was canceled. Such cancellations result in the prolongation of the diffusion process. When a cell is blockaded by a zero-contact boundary on more than one side, the number of directions from which information can reach it is sharply reduced, and therefore the probability of

Figure 11-20 Distance-biased random simulation with built-in barriers

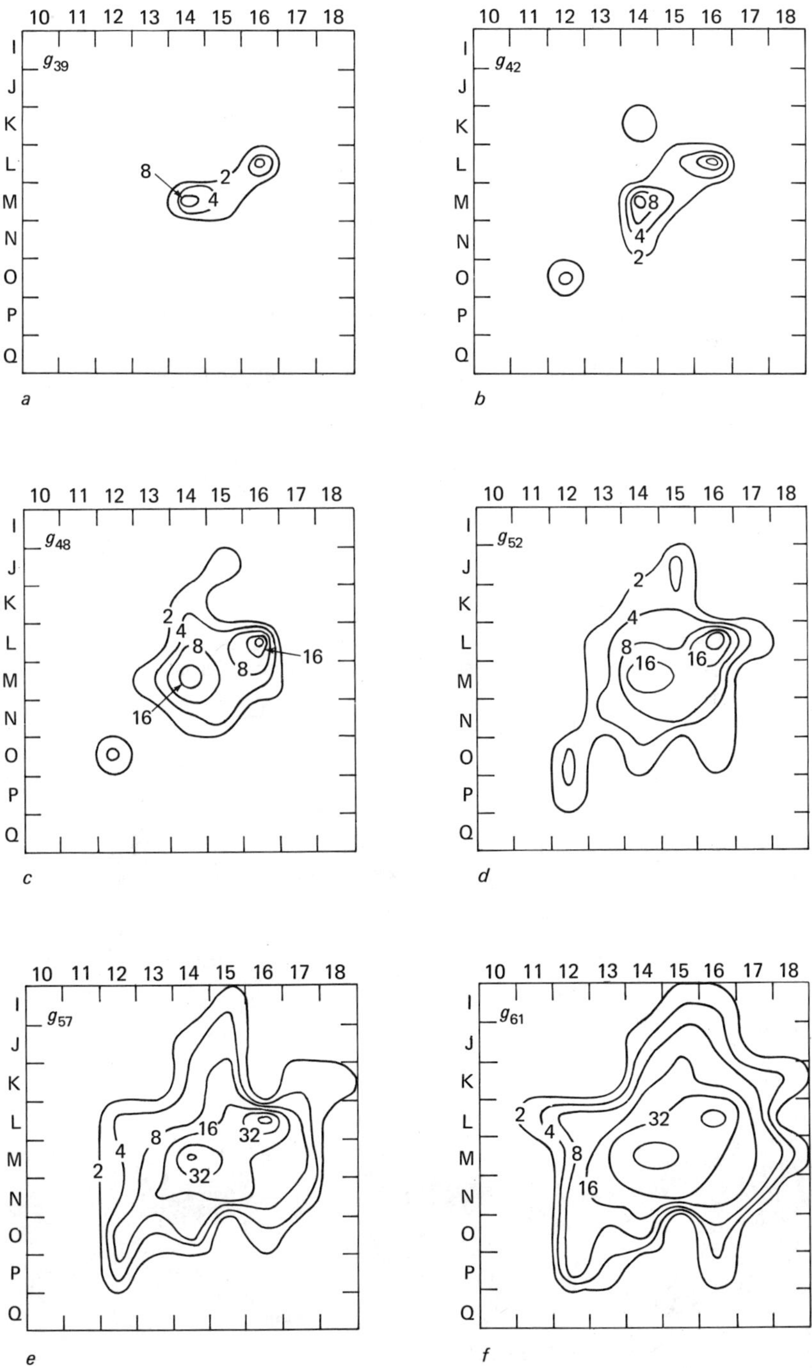

Figure 11-21 Model plane with real world population distribution and contact boundaries

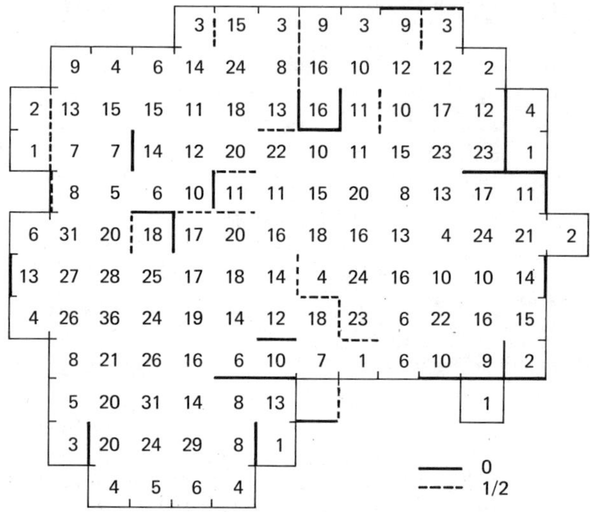

Figure 11-22 Deviations from expected number of telephone calls. Irregularities in the number of telephone calls between neighboring settlements over a census week in 1950. For each pair, an expected number of calls were estimated, depending on the number of subscribers and distance. Bars indicate 2, 4, 6, . . . times the expected number; ridges, 0.6, 0.4, 0.2, . . . times the expected number; black ridges, no calls.

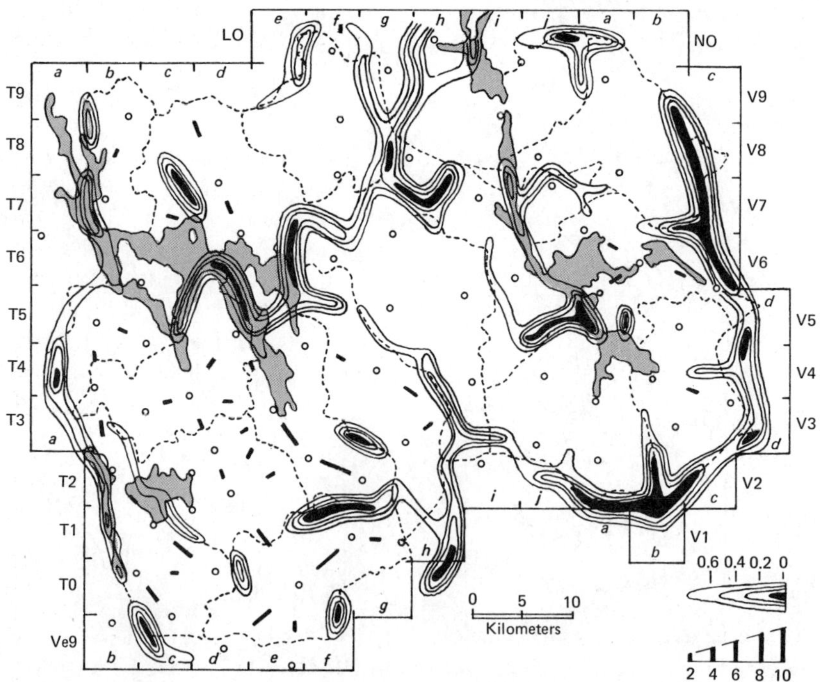

its receiving information is low. Consequently, the generational interval when the innovation will be accepted by an individual located in such a blockaded cell will occur far into the diffusion process. In this way, isolation is built into the model. On a worldwide scale, Tibet is isolated by topographic barriers while the Amish are isolated by cultural barriers which enable them to use horses for plowing with blithe unconcern for the progress of technology in American agriculture. Dotted lines in Figure 11-22 represent "half-contact barriers" which cancel tellings across them every second time, on the average.

The nature of barriers and their influence on spatial diffusion have been considered in some detail by Yuill (1965). According to their functional effects, he classified them into (1) *absorbing barriers* which stop the diffusion of an innovation completely in a direction; (2) *reflecting barriers* which change the direction of the wave of innovation, and (3) *permeable barriers* which may act as either filters, which modify the innovation, or screens, which slow down the spread of the innovation.

Whereas in the earlier studies only one simulation was carried out, three such simulations were made in this study. Obviously, a Monte Carlo random-type simulation can be repeated, and different sequences of random digits will be selected in each run. Since the use of these numbers incorporates chance, varied spatial and temporal patterns will emerge from these successive trials. For a number of simulations, the mean number of adopters as well as the variance and other moments can be computed for each cell. For example, after 1000 runs, it may be found that cell G17 had 0 adopters in 100 runs, 1 adopter in 114 runs, and so on. For this particular cell, the mean number of adopters may be 6. Further, with respect to any one cell, the frequency distribution of the number of adopters will tend to approach normality. Therefore, the mean number of adopters in a cell (computed on the basis of a large number of runs) may be considered to be representative of that cell.

Hägerstrand's original work was published in Swedish in 1953, and for a number of years it was accessible to only the small number of geographers who understood Swedish. At the 1960 Symposium in Quantitative Geography, held at Northwestern University, Hägerstrand read a paper on Monte Carlo diffusion models in English which received wide readership and introduced the technique to a large number of adopters. One of the earliest adoptions is that presented in Bowden's study of the diffusion of the decision to irrigate in northern Colorado (1965). Long-distance telephone-call data as well as attendance at a local barbecue were used to compute a circular or azimuthal MIF. Irrigation wells were assigned to 6 $\times$ 6-mile townships. The adopters of wells became tellers, and as was the case in Hägerstrand's studies, the probability of adoption or information transmission was a function of distance. Sixteen wells or adopters of the innovation per township was assumed to be a saturation level since this seemed to be the maximum ground-water recharge potential in the study area. The object of the simulation was to project the number of wells per township to the year 1990. In order to make this projection, Bowden fitted a logistic curve to data on well installations and, by extrapolation, concluded that there would be 1644 wells by 1990. Figure 11-23 shows the actual patterns of well adopters for 1948 and 1962, as well as the simulated one for 1962 and that projected for the year 1990. The correspondence between the

Figure 11-23 Comparison of simulated and actual patterns of well adoption, and projection to 1990, in the Colorado high plains

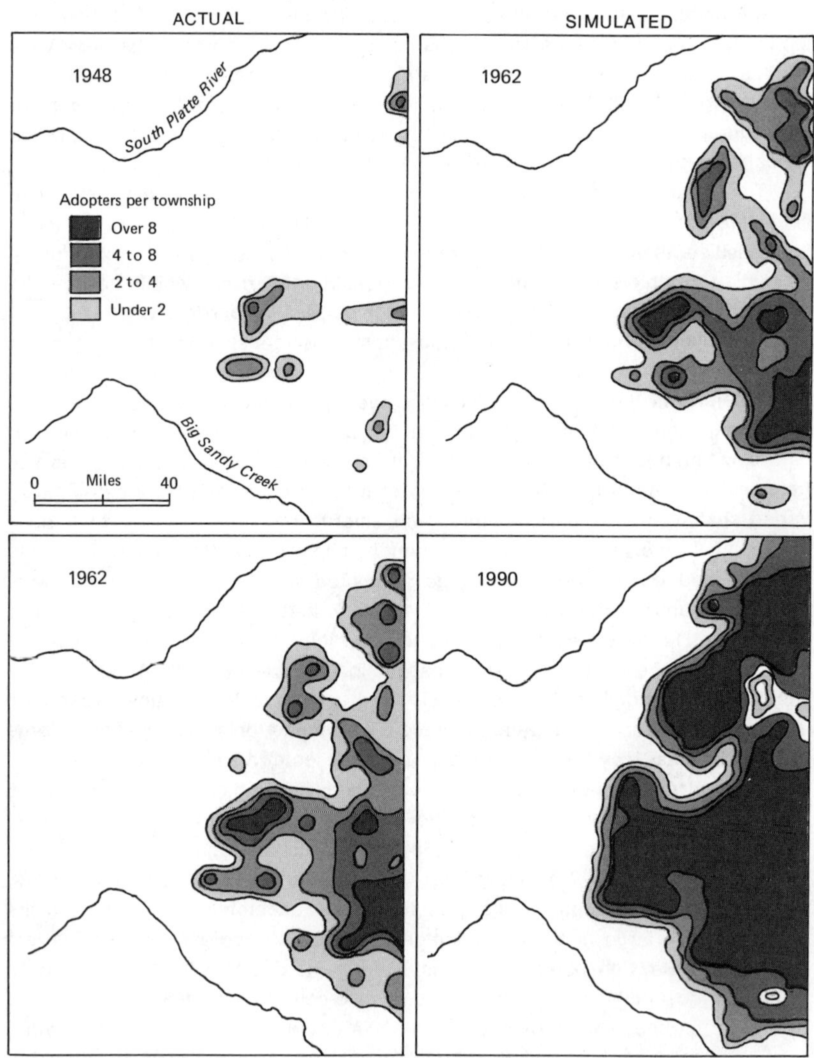

two patterns in 1962 is close but may be spurious, since there is, as yet, no test of significance which allows for the consideration of relative cell location without introducing a cell bias. (For further details concerning this point, see Brown and Moore, 1969, 129.)

The diffusion of agricultural cooperatives in an area of Mysore state in India was studied by Misra (1968), using the Monte Carlo simulation technique. He corrected for the uneven population density and also took into account the actual layout of the transport network and thus of information transfer. If the population of a cell was zero, tellings were canceled; if the density of population was 0 to 250, the probability of a message reaching it was one-half that of a cell whose population density exceeded 250. Similarly, if the transport network in a cell was inefficient, the probability of information reaching it was 0.5.

These various attempts to simulate the spatial diffusion of innovations by utilizing the Monte Carlo technique have shown increasingly higher levels of fidelity in their ability to reproduce the changing patterns. Moreover, certain insights were gained, at each stage, about the process of spatial diffusion itself. The Monte Carlo technique, of course, represents only one approach, and alternative modeling strategies have been exhaustively reviewed by Brown (1968a) and Brown and Moore (1969). With the exception of the distance-biased random net model, none of these approaches has been used in an empirical context in geography, although they have been used in sociology, mathematical biology, epidemiology, and other disciplines. Therefore, only a brief treatment of these other models is warranted in this text.

Epidemiology Models

Epidemiology models are deterministic models that are usually expressed in differential equations. In considering the spread of disease, epidemiologists typically pay more attention to time rather than to space; i.e., they are more interested in answering the question of how fast, rather than of where?

An important characteristic of epidemiology models is that they specify rates not only of infection (adoption) but also of removals (former tellers). The specification of removal rates operationalizes the notion of a threshold, which, in the geographic context, implies that an innovation has spread over the maximum possible area and has been adopted by the maximum number of persons.

The relative removal rate is the ratio of removal rate to infection rate, and in Kendall's model (Brown and Moore, 1969, 136) if the average population density exceeds the relative removal rate, then the infection diffuses over the whole surface under consideration. Removals are analogous to passive adopters who accept an innovation but do not pass information about it to others. Such individuals retard the spread of an innovation in much the same way as does a potential adopter with a high level of resistance. However, there is an important difference between passive adopters and resistant individuals. Given enough time, even fairly high levels of resistance may be breached. Passiveness, on the other hand, may be a more permanent condition. The geographical implication of this distinction is that in the core area from which an innovation diffused initially, there are a number of individuals who stop telling after some time. For example, if everyone on the block has a color TV, the novelty is lost; individuals become blasé about it, and it stops being an object of conversation. "Keeping up with the Joneses" is an important reason for innovation diffusion, but if one has everything that the Joneses have, there is no need to emulate them further. In this way, if an innovation blankets the core or origin area, the individuals within it become passive while, at the same time, toward the outer boundaries the rate of tellings is rapid and the diffusion wave advances.

Random and Biased Nets

In this class of models, each particular model allows for the specification of a different kind of bias. Some of these biases, such as reciprocity, acquaintanceship, and so on, have been defined earlier. A modification of the distance-biased net model has been used by Brown (1968b) to study the diffusion of television receivers in central Skåne (southern Sweden).

A random biased net consists of a set of nodes connected by one-way edges. Given a network of nodes, additional nodes are connected to it by means of the development of subsequent edges. Whether an edge develops between a particular node and another is a matter of chance; consequently, these models are stochastic ones. In a distance-biased net model, the probability of the existence of an edge between a pair of nodes is a function of the distance between them. The nodes may be individuals or places. Those nodes that are linked together by the net have effectively adopted the innovation, while unlinked ones are potential adopters. Information is transmitted by the nodes already in the net to other nodes not in the net in a random fashion.

The modus operandi of the random and biased net model has been summarized as follows (Brown and Moore 1969, 137):

1. Each node issues one or more edges (messages) in the time period immediately following that in which the node first joins the net.
2. Issued edges connect to target nodes according to some probability.
3. Nodes emit edges only in the time period immediately succeeding that in which it was first connected into the net.

Rules 1 and 3 imply that the "action frontier" is on the borders of the net. As in epidemiology models, recent adopters are the most zealous ones who are enthusiastically telling others about the innovation. In a purely random net, the destination nodes are selected with an equal probability from any origin node which is already linked by the net.

The form of the purely random net model is

$$P(t+1) = \left[1 - \sum_{j=0}^{t} P(j) \right] (1 - e^{-aP(t)})$$

where $P(t+1)$ = the probability that a randomly selected node will be connected to the net first at time $t+1$

j = a particular time ($j = 0, 1, 2, 3, \ldots, t$)

a = average number of edges issued from each node

Thus, the probability of a node being connected for the first time in time $t+1$ is the product of the probability that it was not connected before $t+1$ and the probability that the initial connection is established during time $t+1$.

Such a purely random model may be inappropriate in most geographic situations, and indeed, it yielded very poor results when Brown (1968b) applied it to the diffusion of television sets in Sweden. Recall that Hägerstrand's purely random simulation model was also found to be unsatisfactory. Human beings are tethered to geographic space, and distance-decay functions are a near universal regularity. Therefore, conceptualizing the diffusion process as a distance-biased net is more realistic.

In a biased net, each adopter discriminates and is more likely or willing to contact one individual over another. The distance-biased net model takes the form

$$P(x_0, t+1) = [1 - z(x_0, t)]p(x_0, t+1)$$

where $P(x_0, t+1) =$ the probability that the x_0 node will first be connected to the net in the period $t+1$

$z(x_0, t) =$ the probability that a node x_0 is connected to the net by the time t. It is $z(x_0, t) = \sum_{j=0}^{t} P(x_0, j)$

$p(x_0, t+1) =$ the probability that node x_0 is contacted at least once during time $t+1$. This is the equivalent of the second element in the random net equation.

The definition of z assumes that the states $P(x_0,j)$ are mutually exclusive. That is to say, there is a discrete probability for each specific time interval. A node x_0 can be contacted before $t+1$ or during time $t+1$; and from this assumption, the probability that the node will be contacted *by* time $t+1$ is as stipulated above: $z(x_0,t)$.

The major difference between the random net model and the distance-biased net model is that in the former $P(t+1)$ is the same for all nodes, but different for each time period. Therefore, the equation in the random net model must be computed only once for each time period. In the distance-biased model, on the other hand, the $P(x_4,t)$ is different from $P(x_{15},t)$; that is, the probability of an innovation's reaching Austin, Texas (x_4), is different from that of the innovation's reaching Des Moines, Iowa (x_{15}), at time t. Therefore, the distance-biased equation must be recomputed not only for each time period but also for each node at each time period.

In operating the model, one starts with a particular destination node and searches for the most probable origin from among those nodes that were most recently connected to the net. The most likely one is the nearest, although this is not a certainty. The procedure continues, by iteration, until each node has been separately considered as the destination of an innovation. In each case, the question to be answered is, Which is the most likely origin? According to some stipulated number of tellings on the part of each of the origin nodes, those target nodes with the highest computed probabilities are then connected to the system.

AN OVERVIEW OF THE SPATIAL DIFFUSION PROCESS

Throughout this chapter we have presented elements of the spatial diffusion process. We have seen how modeling strategies, specifically the Monte Carlo technique, can be used to illuminate certain aspects of the process itself. Simulation, of course, is not an end in itself, nor should it be. As Garrison (1960b, 100) has commented, "Given enough resources, a researcher may succeed in programming his own ignorance" by constructing a large-scale simulation that bears only a tenuous relationship to real life processes although it may reproduce spatial patterns faithfully. Two ways of avoiding this trap are: (1) a firm theoretical orientation, although, as we have stated before, geographers have as yet to formulate a general theory of movement; (2) a thorough knowledge of both the study area and the phenomenon being diffused.

We may now summarize and synthesize some of the more significant elements of the spatial diffusion process. Clearly, the materials presented do suggest that ideas, as much as things and people, move in geographic space. This movement of ideas follows the already stated sequence of origin, path, destination. Further, the movement, or diffusion, of ideas is characterized by some fundamental regularities which seem to transcend place, culture, and item. These regularities and certain notions that modify them can be stated as follows:

1. Most innovations tend to originate in a large city, in a major national corporation, or with an influential individual. Further, diffusion tends to filter down the settlement hierarchy.

2. As the diffusion of an innovation proceeds through time, it tends to spread outward, with increasing intensity, from the place of origin.

3. This process of outward spread operates through a contact system or network of interpersonal communications whose structure and complexity depend upon the area.

4. The nature of contact systems and the distance-decay characteristic of individual communication patterns force a neighborhood effect upon the spatial diffusion of an innovation. In other words, from the origin, nearer individuals are more likely to adopt an innovation (and at an earlier time) than those located farther out. However, despite the formidable impact of distance, the location of the next specific individual who will adopt an innovation cannot be known with certainty, although it may be expected that the individual will be relatively close to an adopter. Therefore, "degrees of likelihood" can be ascribed to each individual and/or location.

In addition, there are many types of contact systems which operate simultaneously in a society, so that the movement of information about one innovation may be entirely different from that about another. The particular contact system that comes into play at any one time is, of course, dependent upon the nature of the item being diffused.

In spite of these regularities and generalizations, the outward spread of an innovation through a contact system does not result in a smooth spatial expansion, owing to the existence of a number of barriers.

5. Each individual in a contact system exhibits a somewhat different level of resistance to new ideas and certainly to their adoption and implementation. To simplify this notion, individuals can and have been grouped into classes of adopters according to some resistance function.

6. In addition to variations among individuals with respect to their susceptibility to innovations, there are also distinct external barriers standing in the way of the movement of ideas which inhibit and mold the structure of contact systems. Thus, physical barriers such as mountains and lakes, po-

litical boundaries, and cultural systems all play a role in impeding the spatial spread of innovations.

7. Finally, the general uneven distribution of population varies the opportunities for contacts. In other words, the potential for information transfer is spatially biased by areas of high population density through which information can travel rather quickly, in contrast to low-density areas through which information transfer and innovation adoption can occur only slowly.

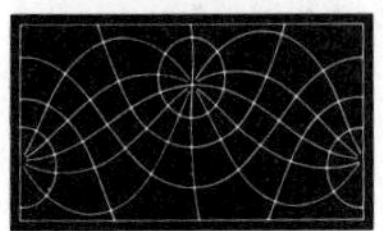

12 Efficiency of Routes and Flows

In this chapter, we consider explicitly notions of "optimization" or spatial efficiency. More specifically, we entertain questions like the following: Given a network, what is the shortest path between two nodes? Given a set of nodes, how can these be connected so as to minimize overall distance? Given a set of specific demand and supply locations, how can the flows be organized so that there is aggregate efficiency of flows? These are "normative" questions in the sense that something is being maximized while something else is being minimized.

It will be readily appreciated that these are practical questions also. Indeed, in the business world such questions are asked and answered routinely. Consequently, a vast literature on these topics has accumulated in the fields of business logistics, management science, operations research, military planning, and so on. We limit ourselves here largely, though not entirely, to a consideration of the relevant geographical literature, more out of convenience than out of any sense of parochialism.

A HIERARCHY OF PROBLEMS IN ECONOMIC GEOGRAPHY

A report prepared by an ad hoc committee of geographers for the National Academy of Sciences and the National Research Council (NAS-NRC, 1965) describes the following four problem areas in "location theory studies," including materials in economic, urban, and transportation geography:

1. Static spatial structure in which the focus is upon the systematic patterning that may be observed in geographic space.

Certain repetitive themes and empirical regularities have been observed, of which the distance-decay relationship (Chapter 7) provides one of the clearest examples. In our earlier consideration of nodes and routes, as well as of point patterns, we were basically analyzing simple spatial structures and considering them as patterned regularities.

2. Spatial systems in which the focus is upon linkages between specific places (accessibility, connectivity, and flows).

Network studies (e.g., the connectivity of the Argentinean airline network) represent significant contributions to the study of spatial systems in that they synthesize transport networks and the spatial distribution of nodes. In addition, descriptive models such as the gravity model and a more theory-based one like the entropy-maximizing model make it possible to study the nature of flows.

3. Deterministic and probabilistic approaches to the temporal development of spatial systems (Chapters 6 and 11).

Deterministic approaches have been used largely in the historical study of spatial structure and organization. Using comparative statics, it has been possible to show how networks develop through time and affect land uses and levels of business activity.

In the probabilistic studies of diffusion processes, it was possible, explicitly, to mesh space and time. By using simple notions of distance decay and specifying certain procedural rules, simulations of the geographic spread of innovations in space as hierarchical and contagious processes were shown to be possible.

4. Efficiency solutions to the location problem which focus on where something *ought* to be located in order to meet some stated objective, rather than where it *is* located.

Early formulations of location-theory models dealt with these normative questions, although it may be argued that they are, after all, studies of simple spatial structures. More recently, the availability of modern mathematical techniques, such as linear programing, has made it possible to develop manipulable models and to test out a variety of alternative solutions to the same problem.

The optimal location of nodes and the selection of the most appropriate (least-cost or most profitable) activity at a point or in an area were hinted at in Chapter 3. There, we used transport cost as an independent or explanatory variable that leads to both the location of a specific manufacturing activity at a certain point (the Weber problem) and the location of varied agricultural activities in particular distance zones surrounding a central city (the Thünen problem). Routes, networks, and flows, however, were ignored in our concern to optimize the selection of nodes. Consequently, this chapter is devoted entirely to the determination of route and flow efficiency, which are treated not as givens, but as solutions or goals to be achieved.

MINIMUM-DISTANCE PATHS

In order to obtain the flavor of optimization problems, let us first consider the Königsberg Bridge problem which was introduced by the Swiss mathematician Euler in 1736 (Ore, 1963, 23–24). Figure 12-1 is a map of a portion of the city of Königsberg (now Kaliningrad) in East Prussia, which, because of its location on the banks and on two islands of the river Pregel, has seven bridges.

It was the custom of the burghers to take a Sunday stroll through town, and the question was asked, Is it possible to plan a promenade so that, starting

Figure 12-1 Four nodes and seven bridges of Königsberg: (*a*) map; (*b*) graph.

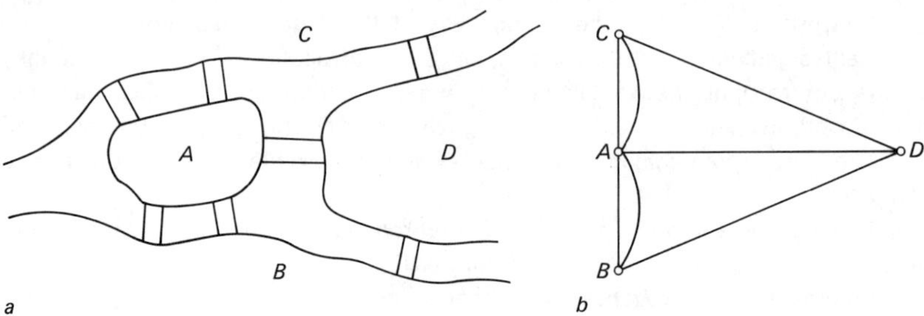

from an origin, one can return there after having crossed each of the seven bridges only once? Since we are not concerned with the width of the bridges or the distance between them, we may, as Euler did, convert the map to a graph, as is shown in Figure 12-1*b*. The four parts of the city are now the vertices, and the edges represent the bridges.

Euler showed that this graph cannot be traversed in a simple circular path without backtracking because a single circular path would have to enter each vertex as many times as it departs from it; i.e., *each* node must have an even number of edges. We see in Figure 12-1*b* that this condition is not fulfilled.

Subsequently, Euler was able to specify completely and prove the sufficient and necessary conditions for a graph that allows a cyclic path (called a Euler line) running through all edges just once. The two conditions are: (1) the graph must be fully connected; (2) the path must enter and exit the same number of times at each vertex (i.e., all local degrees must be even). In this way, Euler established the foundations for a rigorous consideration of a variety of shortest-route problems.

Although Euler's puzzle may seem trivial, minimum-distance-path problems are basically combinatorial, a fact which makes them complex and tedious in most real-world situations, especially when a large number of links are involved and when the distances between pairs of nodes in the network vary greatly and backtracking is allowed. In commodity and passenger movements, of course, backtracking engenders unnecessary costs. We present, initially, the nature of a solution to the "traveling salesman" problem, without going into the modus operandi of the solution.

Consider how a traveling salesman might complete a circuit starting from, say, Charleston, West Virginia, visiting one specified city in each of the remaining 47 conterminous states in the United States, and returning to the origin, so that the overall distance is minimized. From the origin, there are 47 choices; once this choice is made, there are 46 remaining choices; and so on. Altogether, the total number of alternative circuits, forced by the constraint that the journey must end at the starting point, is equal to 47!. It will be recalled that in Chapter 9 we showed that factorial numbers escalate very rapidly in value; thus, $47! = 2.5862^{59}$, which involves several million alternative routes. However, there is only *one* optimal (shortest) route, whose solution, derived by Flood (1956, 70), is presented in Figure 12-2.

Figure 12-2 Solution to the traveling-salesman problem

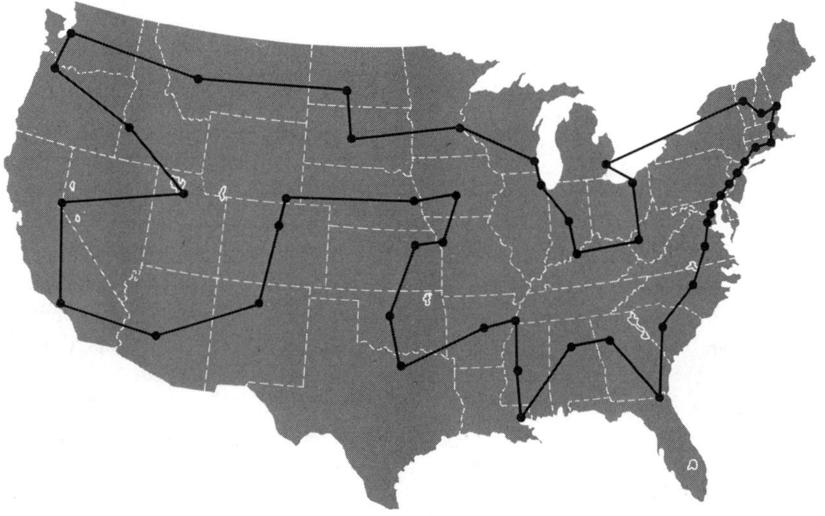

Minimal Trees

We have referred in Chapter 5 to trees and Hamiltonian circuits. It is evident that the traveling-salesman problem is a manifestation of the latter. We shall come back to this situation subsequently. For now, consider how one may link a given set of nodes by means of what is termed a "minimal spanning tree." The end result must obey two conditions: (1) intersections may occur only at the specified vertices; (2) a path must connect each vertex to another. Obviously, this class of problem is most relevant to the planning of communication networks.

A simple graphic algorithm (computational solution) exists to compute the minimal tree. Figure 12-3*a* shows the location of nodes to be connected. The first step is to connect each vertex to its nearest neighbor. This process results in a series of subgraphs (Figure 12-3*b*). The second step involves the connection of each subgraph to its nearest neighboring subgraph. The final solution is presented in Figure 12-3*c*, with all the subgraphs connected to make up a full tree structure.

Figure 12-3 Building a minimal tree, constrained by existing location of nodes: (*a*) set of nodes; (*b*) subgraphs; (*c*) minimal tree.

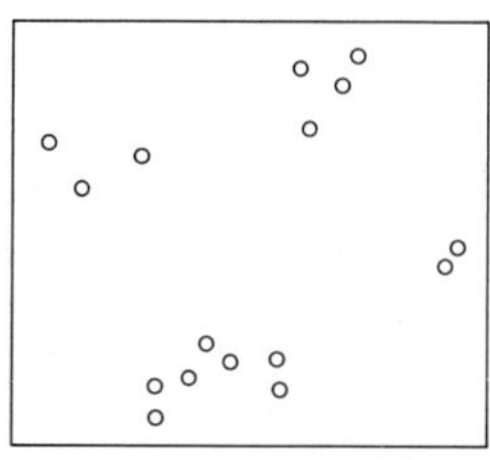

a

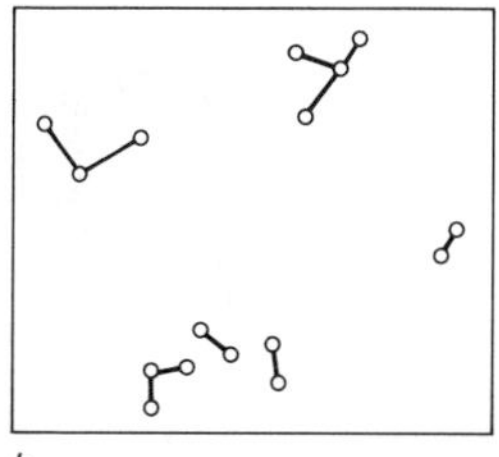

b

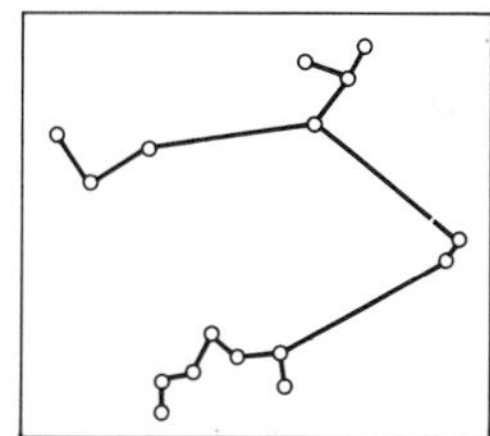

c

This solution, however, immediately leads to another problem: it is an optimum one only if we are constrained by the predefined vertices. We have already seen, in Chapter 6, that the shortest connection between three points is not a triangle but a Y-shaped figure (the delta-wye transformation). With this in mind, let us reconsider Figure 12-3*c*. In the literature, the relaxation of this constraint is known as the "Steiner problem," in which a *Steiner point* is a node whose location was not given initially. Two theorems were presented by Steiner: (1) in a Steiner minimal tree, two arcs which intersect, whether at a previously known vertex or a Steiner point, form an angle $\geqslant 120°$; (2) the number of Steiner points is m, $m \leqslant n - 2$, where $n =$ number of vertices. These two theorems imply that there are certain cases where a Steiner point cannot be located. Consequently, given the state of the art, it appears that alternative topologies for the Steiner minimal-tree problem can be obtained only by means of trial and error. Scott (1917a) has presented two such topologies (Figure 12-4*a* and *b*). The former is 3.1 percent shorter than that in Figure 12-3*c*, while the latter is 7.8 percent shorter.

Shortest-path Solutions

Path between One Node and All Others

Suppose there is a set of links between a set of nodes, as in Figure 12-5*a*. The operators of a trucking line may obviously be interested in the shortest path between pairs of nodes in this network with a view to minimizing flow costs (as opposed to construction costs of the links). The solution to this problem has been formalized by Dantzig's algorithm, among others. Table 12-1 is the relevant distance matrix in which zeros indicate the absence of a direct connection.

Let us now determine the path from vertex 1 that will minimize the total distance to all the other vertices. Step 1 consists of identifying the shortest edge issuing out of vertex 1 and assigning it to the solution set. This edge is, of course, e_{12}, as may be seen in Table 12-1. Step 2 involves the identification of the next edge to be incorporated in the solution set, linking either vertex 1 or vertex 2 with one of the others. This identification is made by comparing the appropriate distances. Specifically, by recourse to Table 12-1, the following

Table 12-1
Distance Matrix for the Network in Figure 12-5*a*

From \ To	1	2	3	4	5	6
1	0	2	0	0	5	0
2	2	0	2	0	6	0
3	0	2	0	1	4	3
4	0	0	1	0	0	3
5	5	6	4	0	0	4
6	0	0	3	3	4	0

Source: A. Scott, 1971, p. 80, Table 5.3.

Figure 12-4
A pair of Steiner minimal trees

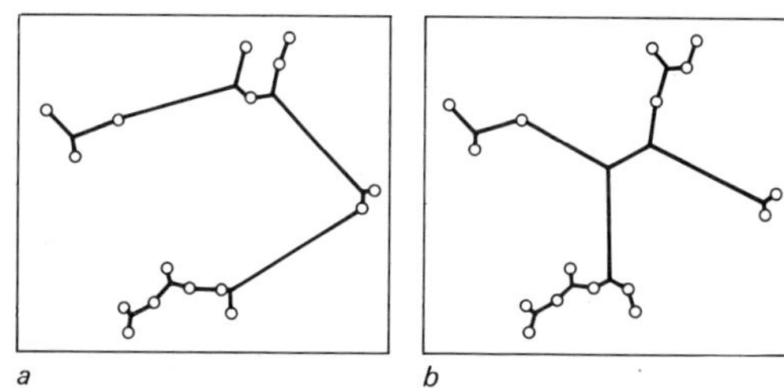

function is evaluated, which measures the minimum distance from vertex 1 to other vertices that are linked directly to some vertex already included in the solution set, even though these other vertices may only be linked indirectly to vertex 1.

$$\min \{d_{15}, d_{12} + d_{23}, d_{12} + d_{25}\} = \min \{5, 4, 8\}$$

d_{15} can be read off directly from the distance matrix (Table 12-1); $d_{12} + d_{23}$ is $2 + 2$, and $d_{12} + d_{25}$ is $2 + 6$. The edge e_{23} is the shortest and is now incorporated in the solution set, which at this step consists of e_{12} and e_{23}.

We then proceed to step 3 to identify the next edge to be added to the shortest-path graph. This next edge will be one emanating from 1 or 2 or 3. The function to be evaluated is the following:

$$\min \{d_{15}, d_{12} + d_{25}, d_{12} + d_{23} + d_{35}, d_{12} + d_{23} + d_{34}, d_{12} + d_{23} + d_{36}\} = \min \{5, 8, 8, 5, 7\}$$

There are now two minimal elements for which $d = 5$. The choice of the next edge to be included is arbitrary, but convenience dictates the selection of e_{15}. We have now incorporated e_{12}, e_{23}, and e_{15} and, therefore, proceed to step 4:

$$\min \{d_{12} + d_{23} + d_{34}, d_{12} + d_{23} + d_{36}, d_{15} + d_{56}\} = \min \{5, 7, 9\}$$

This equation indicates the inclusion of e_{34}, since the minimum is made up of $d_{12} + d_{23} + d_{34}$ and since e_{12} and e_{23} have already been included in previous steps.

Finally, at step 5 we find

$$\min \{d_{12} + d_{23} + d_{36}, d_{12} + d_{23} + d_{34} + d_{46}, d_{15} + d_{56}\} = \min \{7, 8, 9\}$$

Figure 12-5
Shortest path between one node and all others: (*a*) the network as given; (*b*) shortest path from vertex 1 to all others.

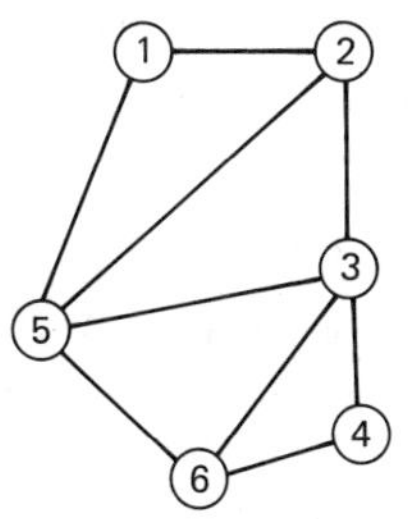

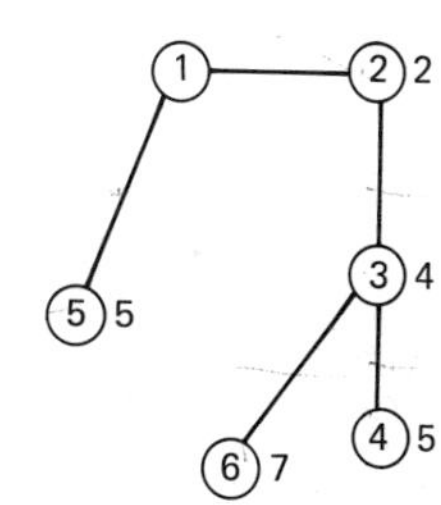

The minimum-distance path between vertices 1 and 6 is 1–2–3–6. The paths are shown in Figure 12-5*b*, and it will be seen that the number of edges has been reduced from 9 to 5. From this figure, we can determine that the shortest path from vertex 1 to vertex 4 (since there is no direct connection) is via vertices 2 and 3, and so on. If we are interested in the shortest paths to all other vertices from, say, vertex 4, we would have to reevaluate the functions, using the procedures outlined above.

It may be useful to recapitulate two essential procedural elements in the Danzig algorithm. (1) Evaluation consists of comparing the distance of links between the selected vertex — in this case vertex 1 — and those vertices which are linked directly to it (2 and 5). (2) For those vertices that do not have a direct connection, we sum distances along intervening links, provided these links connect a vertex that has been incorporated into the solution set at some stage (e.g., compare 1–2–3–6 versus 1–5–6).

An important practical problem arises from the fact that many people may be using the shortest paths and these may become severely congested. Alternatively, a flood, a blizzard, or a traffic accident may dictate the use of the second, third, . . . , or the *K*th shortest path. Confronted with such possible situations, it is useful to have a contingency plan. Bellman and Kalaba (1960) have approached this question and have proposed suitable optimizing solutions.

Path between Pairs of Nodes

The currently available methods for the solution of the shortest-path problem fall into two basic categories: (1) those procedures which, separately, identify the shortest distances from one given vertex to all others; the Dantzig algorithm presented above falls in this category and may be referred to as a "tree-building" method; (2) methods which identify all shortest paths in a network together; these are "matrix" methods, a well-known example of which is the "cascade" algorithm (Farbey, Land, and Murchland, 1967).

In comparison with other matrix methods, the virtue of the cascade algorithm is that it requires substantially fewer operations to find all the shortest distances in a graph. The name "cascade" is suggestive of the cumulative way in which the shortest distances are identified. There are two basic operations that are involved in this algorithm: (1) "the selection of the minimum of two elements when these represent distances between the same pair of vertices by different paths" (Farbey et al., 1967, 20); this process corresponds to elementary addition of the two appropriate elements of the matrix; and (2) the selection of a longer path by adding two consecutive shortest paths between three or more vertices; this process corresponds to matrix multiplication.

Now if A^* is the matrix of shortest distances by paths of any number of edges, we can write

$$A^* = A + A^2 + A^3 + \cdots + A^n$$

where n is the order of A or the number of vertices in the graph. This matrix, however, contains the shortest circuits from a vertex to itself. It will be recalled that in Chapter 5, in connection with the Russian river network, we powered a binary connectivity matrix which resulted in the identification of multistep connections, including the specification of the number of ways of leaving any vertex along the main diagonal and coming back to it. In order to eliminate this situation, Farbey et al. (1967) recommend the use of a unit matrix for multiplication U, which has 0 elements along the main diagonal and ∞ elements elsewhere.

They then demonstrate that the shortest-path matrix S can be obtained as

$$S = U + A^*$$

This equation means that

$$S = U + A + A^2 + \cdots + A^{n-1}$$

or simply

$$S = (U + A)^{n-1}$$

The simplest way to compute this matrix is

1. Impose 0 elements along the main diagonal; insert 1s in the appropriate cells if there is a direct connection and ∞ elsewhere. This matrix is $U + A$.
2. Square this matrix, replacing elements as soon as they are calculated.
3. Utilizing first the forward cascade process, calculate the elements in the first squaring in the order $a_{11}, a_{12}, \ldots, a_{1n}; a_{21}, \ldots, a_{2n}; a_{n1}, \ldots, a_{nn}$; that is to say, work first left to right in each row and downward by row. At the culmination of this operation, there will still be some ∞'s left in the matrix. To eliminate these, the backward cascading process is used; it involves a squaring to calculate elements in the order $a_{nn}, \ldots, a_{n1}, a_{n-1,n}, \ldots, a_{n-1,1}, \ldots, a_{1n}, \ldots, a_{11}$, that is, right to left in each row and upward by row. Therefore, the cascade method requires only two squarings, whatever the size of n may be, instead of the repeated powerings that are required by alternative methods.

Using the cascade algorithm, it is easily possible simultaneously to find all shortest paths between 500 vertices ($n^2 = 250{,}000$ numbers), which is well within the capability of currently available computers. Furthermore, by using this procedure it is feasible to compute not only the shortest-distance paths but also time paths, cost paths, etc., between nodes in complex networks. The practical advantages in planning truck, bus, railroad, airline, and other routes highlight the algorithm's great value.

LINK ADDITION

The United States in recent years has been spending $4 to $5 billion at the federal level for highway construction. Additional highway expenditures at the state and local levels represent an equivalent sum. Many Third World nations are also building new highways and railroads. Since money is scarce in those countries and the demands on available developmental funds are heavy, the critical decision to build or not to build some particular link depends upon accurate evaluation. The cost of mistakes is prohibitive.

The "branch-and-bound" algorithm is a useful one in this context. Basically, this algorithm involves a comparison of each of the combinatorial possibilities of link addition with every other one. Consider Figure 12-6, in which

Figure 12-6 Possible combinations of link additions to a hypothetical urban highway network

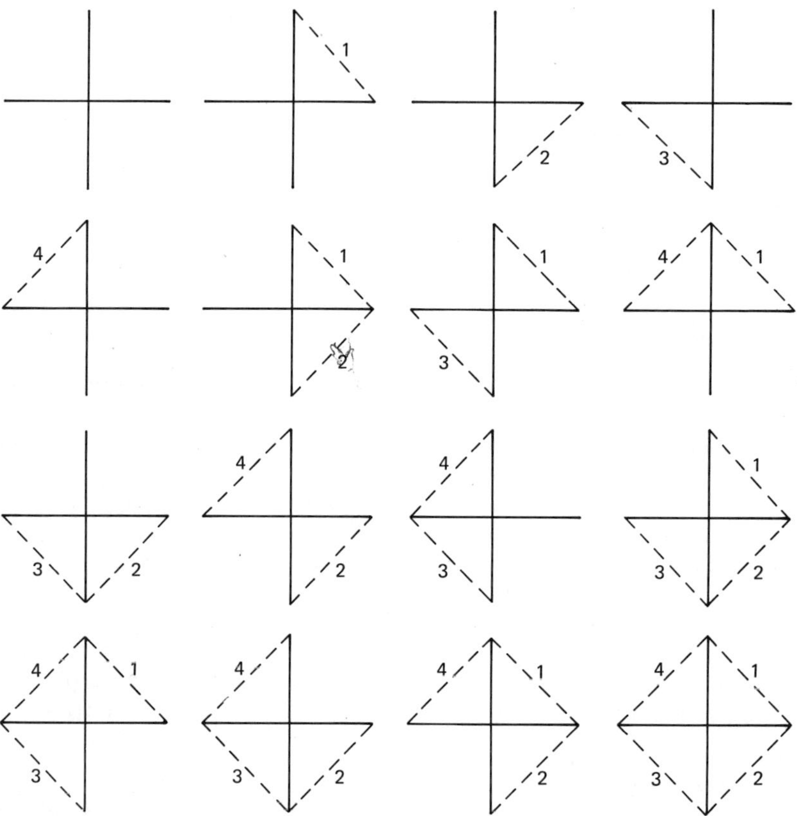

the first diagram represents the freeway network in a hypothetical urban area. Perhaps the network was constructed before businesses moved out to the outskirts of the city and peripheral commuting started. The network is focused on the central business district.

Suppose there is now a need to complete the network. Evidently, four additional links would satisfy this objective if cost were not a constraint. As can be seen in Figure 12-6, there are fifteen combinatorial possibilities plus, of course, the option of not building any link at all. If all four were built (the last diagram), the resulting addition would constitute a beltway. The sixth diagram, for example, shows the addition of links 1 and 2 and so on. Three criteria are relevant to the decisionmaking process: (1) unit cost of travel in each of the proposed links, (2) the proposed capacity of each link, and (3) the construction cost of each link. Among urban freeway construction costs, land acquisition is frequently very expensive. An extreme recent example is the cost of land in Philadelphia: $70 million per mile! Consequently, detailed economic analysis is required in order to accumulate the data necessary for the evaluation of various criteria. The addition of links would, of course, decrease travel costs (by providing direct connections) but would increase construction costs.

Assuming that the types of data specified above were available, it would be possible to compute the trade-off between construction costs and travel costs. In a study of the Houston metropolitan area, Roberts and Funk (1964) evaluated such a trade-off in a case where the four links that were to be added also yielded fifteen combinatorial possibilities. They concluded that the option of building two specific links [links 2 and 3 in their example; see also Haggett and Chorley (1969, 199)] was optimal since it was the only option which enabled a reduction of total transport costs. Specifically, by spending six units of capital expenditures, the total cost could be reduced by one unit (in comparison to the no-building option).

Clearly, the spatial configuration of networks (i.e., the geometry) changes through time. Each addition (or removal) is the result of a conscious decision, which can be facilitated by the utilization of the branch-and-bound algorithm and other such optimization techniques.

FLOW OPTIMIZATION

In developing minimal networks — the shortest path from one vertex to all others or between all pairs of vertices — we are not concerned with capacities of particular link segments, the over-the-road cost of transportation, or supply and demand at different vertices. However, in an attempt to optimize flows, these considerations must be kept in mind, and they, in turn, lead us to a different set of problems.

Capacitated Networks

We are all aware that certain routes are more congested than others. Some routes are used to full capacity, and as a result, traffic is slowed down or stalled. Capacity may be measured by using a number of criteria such as minimum distance between adjacent vehicles, number of vehicles crossing a particular point in a specified time interval, etc. Over-the-road costs (for gasoline, tolls, etc.) vary also. If the costs are low, many individuals will make use of particular route segments and will soon saturate them. The term "cost" is interpreted here broadly to include time and also safety. Savings in time are of crucial importance in such cases as shipment of medicines and military material, as well as in school busing. Therefore, certain questions arise. Between two points what is the optimal route? How much can be shipped over particular route segments?

The nature of the problem is laid out in Figure 12-7, which is a graph of the primary road network linking the fifteen largest cities in eastern Kansas. The values in Figure 12-7 represent mileages in units of 10. Since Kansas is a "flatland" area, we may assume that over-the-road transport costs are a linear function of distance.

The optimal or least-cost path between any pair of cities can be easily determined by visual examination of the graph. Consider some alternative

Figure 12-7 Graph of the road network of eastern Kansas. (Values are distances or costs.)

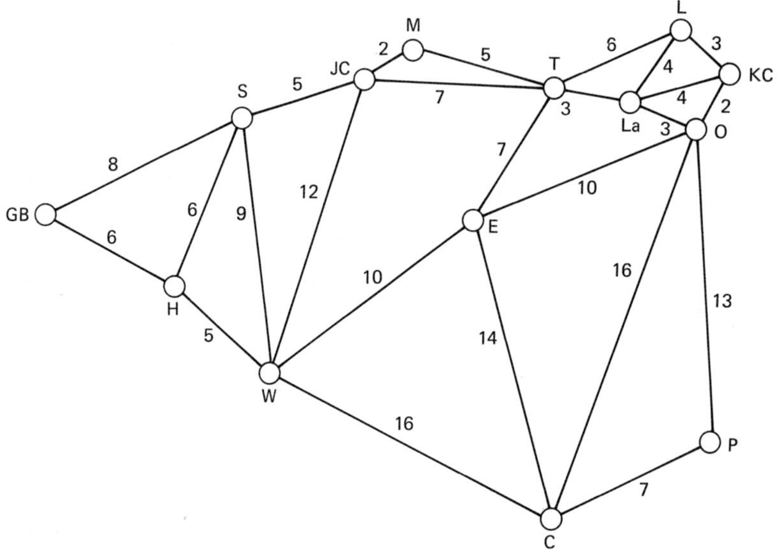

paths between H (Hutchinson) and KC (Kansas City). Three feasible alternatives are

$$H \rightarrow S \rightarrow JC \rightarrow T \rightarrow La \rightarrow KC = 25$$
$$H \rightarrow W \rightarrow E \rightarrow O \rightarrow KC = 27$$
$$H \rightarrow W \rightarrow E \rightarrow T \rightarrow La \rightarrow KC = 29$$

The first route shown above is the least-cost path. To ship three units along this path, the total cost is 75.

However, we know from personal experience that certain route segments tend to become congested or saturated. Figure 12-8 shows the capacities. The Kansas turnpike has the largest capacity (15) owing to its high speed limit, a larger number of lanes, and limited access. Interstate and U.S. highways have a capacity of 10 units, while state roads have a capacity of 5, owing mainly to their lower speeds, traffic signs, etc. This means that the least-cost route (shown in Figure 12-8) can be used only if the volume of shipments is under 5 units. If the volume is over 5 units, there is one bottleneck, and if the volume is over 10, there are three bottlenecks. Therefore, with a shipment of 10 units from H to KC we are compelled to suboptimize in that we must route our shipment so that the unit cost would be 27. For a large shipment of 15 units, it would be necessary to split the shipment two ways into 5 and 10 units, respectively, and to send them via the least-cost and second-least-cost routes, respectively.

The preceding is a trial-and-error search procedure for alternative paths in the face of capacity constraints, which involves keeping track of existing total capacity, used and unused capacities, and travel costs. The search routine can be rather easily accomplished by inspecting a map and comparing alternative routings. However, for any reasonably large problem, the computational and accounting task (concerning the level of capacities, feasible alternatives, and the attendant costs) requires more efficient techniques. Ford and Fulkerson (1962) have described a large number of operational procedures that are useful in determining optimal flow paths in networks. Two alternative techniques that are particularly valuable in this context are the out-of-kilter algorithm and linear programing.

Linear programing presupposes that relationships in the problem are linear. A set of simultaneous equations represents the conditions of the problem, including constraints. The objective to be satisfied is also a linear function. Multiple combinations of alternatives can thereby be evaluated.

The Transportation Problem

A systematic introduction to the use of linear programing in a spatial context is provided by Scott (1971b), and we follow him closely here. The problem is to allocate supplies which originate at given locations to certain specific demand locations. This is known as the transportation problem. The cost of transportation is a linear function of distance. The constraints are manifested in the available supplies and the quantities demanded. On a systemwide basis, all the demands must be satisfied and all the supplies must be used up. The resulting spatial allocation must ensure optimization (minimum transport cost). Figure 12-9 shows the location of four suppliers (origin nodes) and five demand locations (destinations). Table 12-2*a* shows the transport costs.

Figure 12-8 Graph of the road network of eastern Kansas. (Values are capacities.)

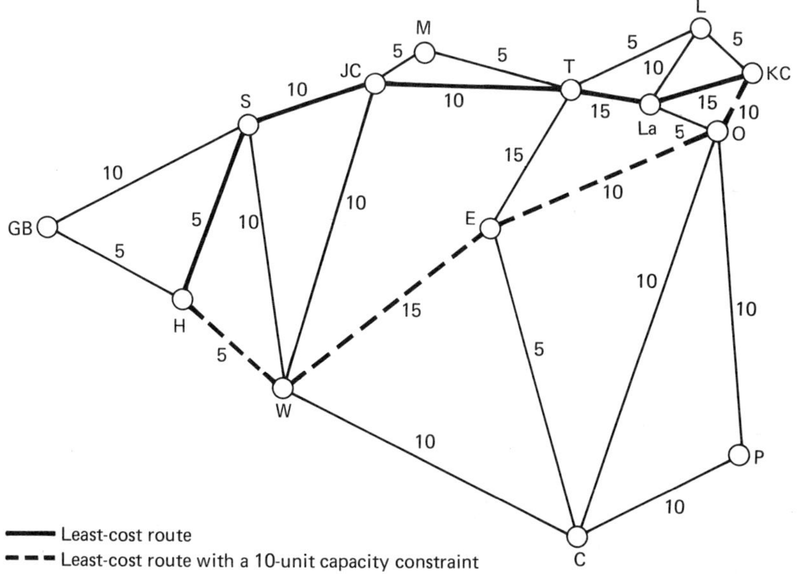

The volumes of supply and demand are shown along the right-hand and bottom margins. The total system generates 30 units of supply and demand. The flow between an origin i and a destination j is x_{ij}, and the problem is to find a solution (flow pattern) in which the sum of all x_{ij} (in the face of constraints) is minimized. Of course, one way to minimize transport costs would be to eliminate all flows. Since flows are needed to keep the system functioning, we seek to allocate flows to links in such a way that supplies are cleared, demands are satisfied, and transport costs are minimized.

We have to start somewhere, and the initial selection in the computational routine involves the so-called "northwest corner" rule. Thus, we start with the upper left-hand corner and work our way to the lower right-hand corner of the matrix, assigning the largest possible shipment to each cell. The first *feasible* (not optimum) shipment is shown in Table 12-2*b*. The value in the corner of each cell is the transport cost per unit (taken from Table 12-2*a*). For cell_{11}, for example, the destination requires one unit of commodity. This is the largest possible assignment from supply location S_1 which can supply as much as 7 units. There is a balance of 6 units, which are assigned to destination D_2, thus exhausting the supply available in S_1. D_2 requires 8 units, of which S_1 has sent 6. The balance of 2 units is supplied from S_2 which can supply 3 units. The balance of 1 unit in S_2 is, in turn, allocated to D_3, exhausting the capacity of S_2. In this way, we proceed to the lower right-hand corner, allocating the maximum demands and using the balance in the next cell. The

Table 12-2

(*a*) Transport Cost Matrix with Respect to the Nodal System in Figure 12-9

	To 1	2	3	4	5	Supply
From 1	9	4	3	7	5	7
2	4	2	7	2	5	3
3	3	7	12	4	9	5
4	9	4	3	5	1	15
Demand	1	8	8	9	4	30

(*b*) The First Feasible Solution to the Transportation Problem ($Z =$ total transport costs)

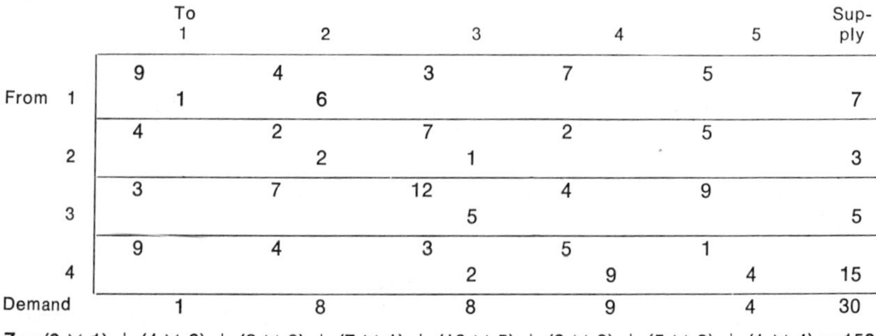

	To 1	2	3	4	5	Supply
From 1	9 / 1	4 / 6	3	7	5	7
2	4	2 / 2	7 / 1	2	5	3
3	3	7	12 / 5	4	9	5
4	9	4	3 / 2	5 / 9	1 / 4	15
Demand	1	8	8	9	4	30

$Z = (9 \times 1) + (4 \times 6) + (2 \times 2) + (7 \times 1) + (12 \times 5) + (3 \times 2) + (5 \times 9) + (1 \times 4) = 159$

Source: A. Scott, 1971b, p. 6, Tables 2 and 3.

Figure 12-9 Location of four supply sources (*S*) and five demand areas (*D*)

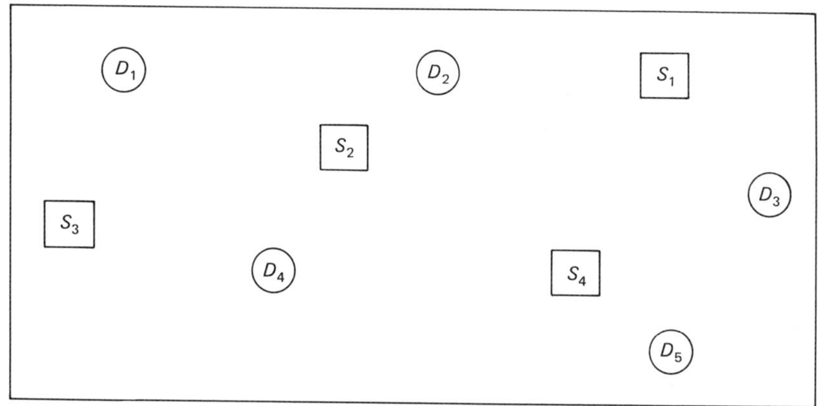

solution shown in Table 12-2*b* is feasible because all supplies are exhausted and all demands have been satisfied. The total movement costs z (found by multiplying the assigned volume of shipments by the unit cost of transportation and then summing) is 159. This value is not necessarily the minimum, but it may be used as the starting point for further computation. The mechanics concerning the detailed operations necessary for the refinements are described fully in Scott (1971b). It will be seen that the final solution, which has been achieved by a systematic process known as the "stepping stone" algorithm, results in a minimum cost of 95 units, a significant improvement compared with the first feasible solution. Figure 12-10 shows the optimal spatial allocation of flows in this constrained system of four origin and five destination nodes.

The step-by-step routine detailed in Scott (1971b) starts with a feasible solution and by means of iteration culminates in the optimal solution, all the while comparing costs of transportation and seeing to it that constraints are not violated. Algebraic solutions and appropriate computer programs are widely available to perform the tedious computations. Examples of the use of linear programing in the geography literature include Morrill and Garrison's (1960) study of optimal patterns of shipments of wheat and flour among regions in the United States, Casetti's (1966) analysis of the movement of iron ore among Great Lakes ports, Gould and Leinbach's (1966) assignment of patients to hospitals, Morrill's (1967) assignment of patients to physicians, and Yeates's (1965) study of the costs of school busing.

School busing is a current issue, and therefore we conclude this chapter with a brief discussion of Yeates's work. It should be noted that linear programing is very flexible and that its effectiveness depends only on the availability of data and the ability of the analyst to specify mathematically the relevant constraints. Although Yeates was concerned primarily with busing costs, one can conceive of a problem in which the objective is to "maximize racial integration." Thus, the specification of the objective is entirely up to the analyst, although it must be realized that "maximizing racial integration"

Figure 12-10 Optimal allocation of shipments after four iterations

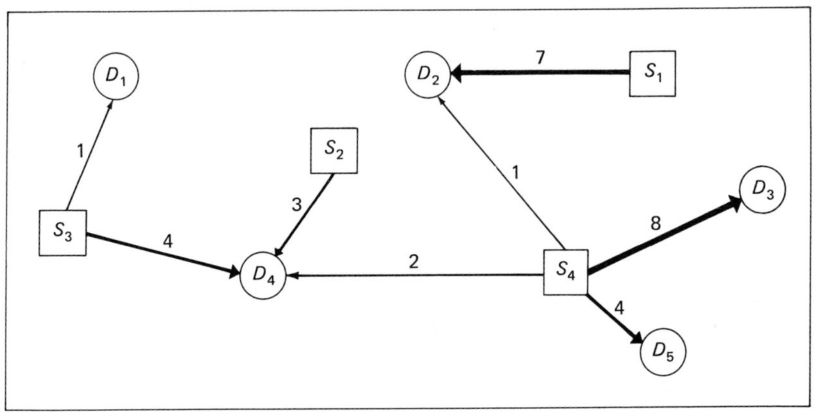

is a rather complex goal for linear programing. Many supply-demand patterns (schools' capacities, supply of black students and demand for them, supply of white pupils and demand for them) must be solved simultaneously and not just one after the other.

In Grant County, Wisconsin, each one of the 1160 mile-square sections represents an origin for high school pupils. The 13 high schools represent the specific destinations. Yeates made a number of obvious assignments visually with the help of a map of population distribution and a map of high school locations. However, 293 sections could not be assigned visually with any degree of certainty. The question thus arose as to which was the optimal allocation.

The objective function is stated as

$$\sum_{i=1}^{293} \sum_{j=1}^{13} S_{ij}C_{ij} = \text{min} \qquad \begin{array}{l} i = 1, 2, 3, \ldots, 293 \text{ (sections)} \\ j = 1, 2, 3, \ldots, 13 \text{ (high schools)} \end{array}$$

where S_{ij} is one student to be transported from the ith origin to the jth destination and C_{ij} is the cost of transporting him or her (in this case, the airline mileage). This equation means that the total transport cost (or distance traveled) should be minimized.

However, schools have varying capacities (supply factor) and mile-square sections have varying populations of high school age (demand factor). These are known and are specified as constraints. The first constraint is

$$\sum_{j=1}^{13} S_{ij} = a_i \qquad i = 1, 2, 3, \ldots, 293 \tag{12.1}$$

where a_i is the number of students at each origin. This constraint says specifically, Do not assign to any one of the 13 high schools or to any combination of the 13 from the ith origin more than the number of available students in that origin. This is the supply constraint and in another context might refer to the prohibition of sending from any origin more beef or autos than are produced there. The second constraint is

$$\sum_{i=1}^{293} S_{ij} = b_j \qquad j = 1, 2, 3, \ldots, 13 \tag{12.2}$$

where b_j is the designed capacity of the jth high school. This constraint states, Do not assign to any one of the 13 high schools or to any combination of the 13 (jth destination) from any one of the 293 mile-square sections more than the capacity of that school. This is the demand constraint. In another problem, the constraint may mean the prohibition of sending to any city from any origin more than the volume of food or automobiles that it is capable of consuming. The third constraint is

$$\sum_{i=1}^{293} a_i = \sum_{j=1}^{13} b_j \tag{12.3}$$

This constraint establishes an equality between available demand and supply and is derived directly from constraints 1 and 2. It means also that the capacity of the schools cannot be expanded nor can the population be redistributed.

Finally, the fourth constraint is

$$S_{ij} \geqslant 0 \tag{12.4}$$

or the nonnegativity (or side) constraint which says, Do not assign a negative number of students (for example, —105 students, in this case, or —13 million tons of coal) from any origin. This negative number is a real world impossibility, but mathematics being what it is, the computer can make such negative assignments unless it is explicitly told not to do so.

Yeates's results are shown in Figure 12-11. The existing school boundaries show the assignments of pupils to schools and the resulting school district boundaries. The shaded areas indicate the needed adjustments together with arrows to the "new" schools. Yeates concluded that 209 mile-square sections (out of 1160) required reassignment; that is, the original assignment was 82 percent efficient. If the school board and the local citizenry conclude that an "inefficiency quotient" of 18 percent is tolerable and does not justify the disruption of existing flow patterns and attachment to particular schools, the situation need not be changed. If, on the other hand, the inefficiency is "sufficiently great" (a subjective matter), then reassignment would be called for. In any event, the linear programing procedures provide a tool for rational decisionmaking.

The optimization solutions that we have referred to in this chapter result in a certain practical rationality. However, given the tendency toward irrational or nonrational behavior on the part of individuals and institutions, group-think and nonoptimizing behavior may be more normal. In affluent societies and in normal times, the price of nonoptimal behavior may be tolerable. However, when a corporate or a national emergency exists, efforts are launched with a view to promoting efficiency and curtailing needless expenditures. Thus, it is no accident that the important innovation of linear programing was developed

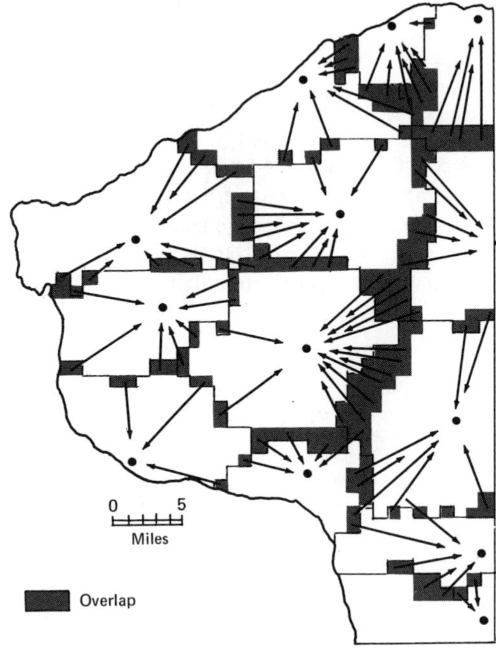

Figure 12-11
Toward spatial efficiency: rationalization of pupil assignment to high schools, Grant County, Wisconsin; movement-minimization solution

in the context of military aircraft production during World War II. The manufacture of more than 50,000 aircraft required detailed planning regarding the location of production facilities and amounts of flow from each of the hundreds of suppliers of materials.

When economic conditions are rosy, corporations can obtain good profits without necessarily being very efficient in their operations. One of the major American can-manufacturing companies for a long time was shipping bulky empty cans to breweries and to other consumers of cans. Recently, following a downward turn in the business cycle, the company reorganized its locational pattern and shipped metal plates to the vicinity of the consumers, fabricating the cans at the market locations. This change resulted in a savings of $20 million/year which, perhaps, may not be very great for a large corporation, but in times of trouble, every saving counts.

One of the difficulties standing in the way of achieving optimization is that in many societies decisionmaking is diffused. During World War II, the United States came close to being a controlled and fully mobilized society, and therefore optimization was possible in that kind of crisis situation. In corporations, the power to make decisions is tightly controlled by a small number of individuals in the executive board room. These are exceptions, however, and in the more normal case, there are goal conflicts, group pressures, and a pervasive inability to recognize what is the optimal course of decisionmaking. One man's optimum may be another man's disaster. Especially in public decisionmaking in government at whatever level, compromises and suboptimization may be more characteristic than strictly defined optimization solutions. The centrally planned economies in Eastern Europe, denied the opportunity for perfect competition, have apparently chosen the opportunity of perfect computation, and it is in such countries that the problems of the space-economy are given the most thorough attention by central planners. Elsewhere, the space-economy is organized and reorganized by a painful process of adjustment in which economic costs are balanced against social costs so that there is probably no such thing as a grand "optimum optimorum" which simultaneously yields the most desirable solutions in the economic, political, and other realms.

13 The Geographical Consequences of Circulation: A Systems Perspective

The French term "circulation" has no exact translation in the English language, but it connotes the manifold kinds of spatial interaction that we have presented throughout this book. Specifically, *circulation* is a comprehensive term including the many modes of transportation, human migrations, diffusion of innovations, money, and information flows, etc. By now, it should be apparent that continued circulation is quite literally vital to the maintenance of human activities and institutions. These activities and institutions are organized in geographic space. They are subject to growth and development and undergo a process of periodic reorganization.

Flows will occur on networks whether we plan them or not, and nodes will develop at certain locations, expand through time, and perhaps subsequently decay, again with or without the benefit of planning. But as we saw in the last chapter, there is a variety of methods available to us that can bring about an optimum situation, whether it be maximizing flows or minimizing the length of networks or the cost of links. If we are able to specify what goals we want to achieve, for example, economic efficiency or maximum social welfare or some combination of them, it is not impossible to achieve them. However, two prerequisites are needed. First, an optimum condition will not automatically develop; it requires conscious planning. Whether the planning is done by corporations (market planning) or governments (public planning) is really irrelevant in our context. The second prerequisite is more difficult to obtain, since planning without understanding the way in which spatial systems function and change may lead to dangerous tinkering and unsought for or unexpected consequences.

ON COMPLEX SYSTEMS

The spatial system, to the extent that human beings are the actors in it, may be called a "social system," as opposed to a "physical system" such as the solar system or the automobile. A social system is always more complex than a physical system, especially because it contains "multiple feedback loops" and behaves in a perverse manner.

Forrester (1970, 252–253) identifies six general characteristics of complex systems that we must recognize if we wish to correct the system that misbehaves:

1. Complex systems are "counterintuitive"; that is to say, they behave in almost exactly the opposite manner from that which our intuition tells us to expect. We should not trust our intuition because it is a result of observations of simple systems; hence we are constantly misled in dealing with complex systems.
2. Complex systems are strongly resistant to most policy changes. Through the mechanism of feedback loops, the system adjusts itself to nullify new policies so that no matter what we do, the intended result does not occur.
3. But there is a silver lining to this cloud in that the converse is also true. There are critical points in complex systems that are responsive to externally induced change. Such points tend to radiate new impulses in ways that produce a new and more desirable result. In our context, the circulatory subsystem may well be just such a critical lever and may enable the creation of, if not Utopia, at least a better world.
4. Complex systems counteract many active programs aimed at alleviating symptoms. These symptoms are conditions of a system, and the system relaxes some of its internal processes if only the symptoms are attacked.
5. The short-term response to a new policy is often likely to be in exactly the opposite direction from the long-term effect. For example, in a developing country, heavy investments in transportation (roads, railroads, ports, broadcasting, telephone systems, and so on) may be necessary in a short period of time. This investment involves foregoing consumption and reducing the standard of living in the short run, which may be any length of time up to a generation. In the long run, however, these sacrifices will pay off for future generations. There is thus a reversal in effects between the short and the long run.
6. Complex systems contain internal dynamic mechanisms that produce observed undesirable behavior. The causes of trouble are deeply entrenched and may persist despite our efforts which seem to attack only symptoms. We have to understand the system sufficiently well in order to ask the right questions and formulate appropriate policies. For example, if traffic jams in central cities are viewed as a problem and if the solution is a high parking tax, then businesses that depend on commuters may move out of the central city, thus decreasing employment opportunities and the tax base of the city. If there is a radial subway system in a metropolitan area, it will facilitate reverse commuting rather than revitalize the central city by bringing suburbanites into it.

Forrester holds that since complex systems are counterintuitive, the computer is a more trusty guide than the human brain in our efforts to deal with urban and regional systems. We would not go that far, if only because the computer programs and the system of equations in his *Urban Dynamics* (1969) model depend on human input. Hence, in the rest of this chapter, we shall attempt to convey an understanding of the functioning of the spatial system, of the way in which it changes, and of the role of circulation.

GROWTH PROCESSES AND THE ROLE OF CIRCULATION

In a classic paper on growth, Boulding (1953) suggests that, generically, there are three types of growth processes:

1. *Simple growth*, in which there is a net accretion to the phenomenon; e.g., a road is extended by 25 miles.
2. *Populational growth*, in which the phenomenon being considered is not viewed as a homogeneous entity, but rather as made up of separate parts whose changes, in the aggregate, result in growth. Thus, a human population increase is a function of the positive difference between births and deaths, which are themselves a function of age and sex distribution. In the transport component of the cultural landscape, *populational growth* might be viewed as the process according to which certain pedestrian trails are eventually abandoned in favor of two-lane country roads which can channel both a larger volume and a larger number of modes of movement. The result of this populational growth process is an increase in route capacity.
3. *Structural growth* is by far the most abstract of the three in that it involves changes in the elements and in the interrelationships among them. Although Boulding notes that all three growth processes are strongly interrelated, it is with the last that we are most directly concerned here, since it is the one which provides us greater insights into changes in the equilibrium of a cultural landscape. Such changes may, indeed, be considered to be a normal state of events.

Structural growth of a settlement system suggests two things: (1) The existence of thresholds (in the language of central place theory) with respect to the elements. Thus, a small town grows into a city which is the focus of a region. (2) In addition, the introduction of innovations is crucial. Thus, the discovery of resources allows a locality to grow quite rapidly, or the introduction of a rail line or other form of transportation refocuses the linkages between urban centers, as was pointed out in Chapter 4. In this context, Burghardt's (1969) study of the development of routes in the Niagara peninsula of Ontario Province demonstrates clearly how the primary focus and directional orientation of the Indian trails were first adopted by the European settlers. However, with the introduction of urban centers, cadastral surveys, resource exploitation, etc., the main directional lines were altered significantly from a northwest-southeast direction to an east-west one.

Thus, structural growth, besides benefiting from simple growth and from populational growth, can be seen as a process in which different levels of equilibrium result as the nature of a system changes. In the case of the

Niagara Peninsula, the area functioned as a transport corridor in the Indian era, and with the entry of European settlers, it became an agricultural area which, subsequently, focused upon a number of urban centers and generated strong internal and external linkages.

The processes of structural growth are complex, and Boulding advances five fundamental principles: (1) nucleation, (2) nonproportional change, (3) growth and form relationships, (4) the "carpenter principle," and (5) equal advantage. Although he defines these processes in terms of the physical, biological, and social sciences, it is possible to couch some of them in terms of the spatial system.

The principle of nucleation can be likened to the formation of the basic elements, the nodes. How nodes come about at a particular place has been the subject of much inquiry under the rubric of location theory as well as voluminous chronicling. In spite of all this analysis, the genesis of an individual node can still be considered to be very much of a mystery.

The principle of nonproportional (or unequal) change suggests that, despite a general growth, the elements of a system cannot grow proportionately. An adult is more than just a heavier and taller baby. Similarly, a metropolis is more than just a big village. A region that contains 5 million people distributed in 40 urban centers is likely to look different from the way it looked when it had only 500,000 persons distributed among 400 villages. It is probable that in the intervening time span, individual villages will have not kept their respective size ranking within the urban hierarchy. In other words, as a result of varying locational advantages, resource bases, transport innovations, entrepreneurial capability, and the like, certain urban centers have surged forward, while others have lagged significantly behind. Thus, nonproportional changes suggest that the largest village did not necessarily absorb the largest share of populational growth in the region, any more than that the largest route segment of the regional network received the largest proportion of the increase in traffic generated by many more activities. Pred (1966) has made a careful empirical analysis of differential urban growth in the United States during its most revolutionary period, 1860–1910. This period represented a "relaxation time" during which the structural relationships in the space-economy were drastically transformed and a new equilibrium emerged.

Equally significant is the fact that, in a region in which there has been a tenfold population growth, the basic character of the area probably changes. Such a change may transform an agricultural way of life with many small villages to a complex urban-industrialized space-economy, or an industrialized space-economy into a postindustrial one.

In the movement context, one of the most relevant aspects of nonproportional change is that as a system grows increasingly larger and becomes more complex, there emerges by necessity a complex system of transportation and communications. Thus, just as colonial America may be considered to have been made up of self-sufficient entities, today's space-economy can function only as long as radio, telephone, television, trucking, and other modes of movement are kept intact and operating as a system.

The carpenter principle refers to the ability of the growth process to "mesh" the individual parts into a recognizable entity. It is almost as if a "grand design" were the underlying basis for all growth. On a more tangible note, however, we may consider the impact of planning upon a city, region, or country. The plan is made up of interlocking parts which have been consciously aggregated. Even in the absence of a deliberate plan, the activities of decisionmakers, be it in the platting of city lots, the location of factories, or the grand schema of a rail net, provide an overall plan or goal which other decisionmakers in other times may follow more or less consciously. Thus, the spatial system develops in what may be considered to be a more or less orderly fashion, although not always the most efficient one.

Every system produces an output. The level of output is partly a function of its structural characteristics which change through time. The output of simple societies, as we saw in Chapter 1, is much less than that of complex societies. With respect to complex systems, the relationship between time and system level is distinctly nonlinear. There are critical thresholds which result in a drastic transformation of the characteristics of a system, and in some cases, there may be a metamorphism, so that a thread of continuity between the old and the new is not easily recognizable. Major transport revolutions, such as those denoted by the canal era, railway period, and the jet age, are examples of metamorphic changes. The occurrence of revolutions that bring about new production functions and new relationships among elements in a system has led some writers to model growth processes in terms of stages of growth.

One of the most widely known attempts at such model conceptualization is that of Rostow (1960). He recognized five stages of growth in a national economy. At first, there is the *traditional society*, characterized by prenewtonian attitudes toward the physical environment. Outputs are low and there is a low celling on the level of attainable output per head. Agriculture is the dominant occupation. Communities are largely self-sufficient. Most of the movement is within small regions, and the transportation network is small in size and is made up of a large number of subgraphs. Information diffuses very slowly, and most places are remote.

The next stage is the *precondition for take-off.* According to Rostow, in general in modern history, the precondition stage arises from some external intrusion by more advanced societies. In other words, there is the introduction of a fundamental change-inducing innovation from elsewhere. The introduction of communism into China is an example of a "parametric shock" administered to a society that, for long, had remained at the traditional stage.

The most crucial stage is the *take-off.* Rostow ascribes a leading role to railroads as being the initiator of take-offs in the United States, France, Germany, Canada, and Russia. The railroad had three impacts on economic growth: (1) It lowered internal transportation costs, brought new areas into production, and enlarged the size of market areas. (2) It aided in the development of export sectors which, in turn, generated new capital for internal development. (3) Via input-output relationships, the development of railroads encouraged expanded production in the coal, iron, and metal-fabricating industries.

This view of Rostow is severely criticized by Fogel (1964). Careful empirical analysis of the relevant period in American economic history enabled Fogel to demonstrate that in 1890 the absence of railroads would have kept in use all but 4 percent of the agricultural land area. That is, the building of the railroads did not materially contribute to the enlargement of the settled area. He also denies that the period from 1843 to 1860 or any other 18-year period was one of unique structural change. But this is not to deny that there was a revolution, only that "one should not expect a revolution to have the swiftness of a coup d'état" (Fogel, 1964, 229). Fogel's conclusion is that American economic growth was a consequence of scientific knowledge acquired in the course of three centuries and diffused to a large number of adopters. Cheap inland transportation, indeed, was required for economic growth as a condition, but the satisfaction of this condition did not entail any specific mode of transportation. Canals would have done just as well as railroads. Furthermore, "the fact that the condition of cheap transportation was satisfied by one innovation rather than another determined, not whether growth would take place, but which of many possible growth paths would be followed" (Fogel, 1964, 237). From our point of view, the important thing to realize is that facilities to increase the volume and intensity of spatial interaction are needed to produce a take-off.

The fourth stage in Rostow's schema is the *drive to maturity.* The volume of international trade increases, and there is a rapid rate of industrialization and urbanization. The diffusion of technological innovations is important at this stage. The transportation network is enlarged and intensified, and mass media of communications develop. High levels of regional and occupational specialization develop, which lead to complementarity.

Finally, there is the *age of high mass consumption*, characterized by a widespread diffusion of a variety of gadgets from refrigerators to electric carving knives. The diffusion of the private automobile is an important characteristic of this stage. The building of numerous and redundant links and multiple connections, the lengthening journeys to work, and the decentralization of manufacturing and retail activities are further characteristics of this stage.

Nations, of course, develop not only in terms of their economies, but there is also a concomitant process of cultural and political development. Meinig's (1972) hypothetical "spatial development" model incorporates within four stages of growth, aspects of change in circulation, population, culture, and political organization. His model is broader in scope than the Taaffe, Morrill, and Gould (1963) model of transport expansion (Chapter 6), but it shares some of the weaknesses of stages-of-growth models in general.

Table 13-1 presents a summary of the major generalizations garnered by Meinig on the basis of a study of what he calls the "American Wests," and note the plural. Specifically, his study area included New Mexico, the Mormon region, the Oregon country, Colorado, northern California, and southern California. While the so-called stages may be a bit artificial, or contrived, the correspondence of certain characteristic elements in each of the four subsystems in each of the stages underscores the close interrelationships among these subsystems. In the ensuing discussion, we shall concern ourselves with population and circulation (settlement nodes and routes), although culture and the development of political areas are by no means irrelevant to the overall process of regional change.

Table 13-1
Correspondence among Key Spatial Subsystems

	Circulation	Population	Culture	Political organization
Stage 1	Isolation	Implantation of a nucleus of settlement	Transplant of selected cultural traits from elsewhere	Nuclear county
Stage 3	Regional tree-like system of networks	Expansion of settlement	Emergence of distinct regional culture	Development of concordance between political territory and functional area
Stage 2	Interregional network, hierarchy of nodes	Competition for development from other people along bordering zones	Diffusion of national cultural elements	Statehood
Stage 4	Intermetropolitan national networks	Metropolitanization	Dissolution of traditional regional culture	Administrative, multilayered superstructures

Source: Adopted from Meinig (1972, 162–163); reproduced by permission from the *Annals* of the Association of American Geographers, vol. 62, 1972.

In this schema (Figure 13-1), stage 1 pertains to the entry of people into an hitherto uninhabited area. Simultaneously, it represents the initial nucleation in the area, a nucleation whose origin and raison d'être are largely unknowable, according to Boulding. Nucleation, however, continues to occur through stages 2 and 3. Increasing numbers of newcomers to the area contribute to the spread of settlement (populational growth) as well as to the expansion of nucleation. This process is facilitated by a primitive, treelike transportation network shown in stage 2.

By stage 2, growth of population and continued nucleation have made it possible for competition to occur between various centers. A number of nodes have taken on a primary importance (due to their locational or other advantages) which has been manifested in differential growth rates. As a result, in stage 3, we see that a definite hierarchy of centers has developed, with one large center which happens, in this case, to be the oldest and may have benefited from initial advantage, four intermediate-size centers, and fourteen small ones. This hierarchical development is a manifestation of nonproportional change.

The transportation network in stage 3 has become a complex one in which there are a number of loops and a certain differentiation has occurred between the routes. In addition, for the first time the region is linked to the "outside" world.

Through these first three stages, there has been a constant interplay between nucleation and circulation. Further, the configuration of the pattern in stage 3 is an extension of the pattern existing in stage 2, that is, there is more

Figure 13-1 Concomitant stages model: population growth and circulation growth

Stage	Population	Circulation	Stage
1	 Implantation of a nucleus of settlement by migrants attracted by special environmental qualities (resources, refuge, exploitable indigenes)	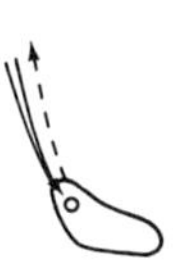 Isolation; seasonal inflow of people; outflow only of high-valued, low bulk, or self-propelled products; pack trains, wagons, stages; interregional communications infrequent	1
2	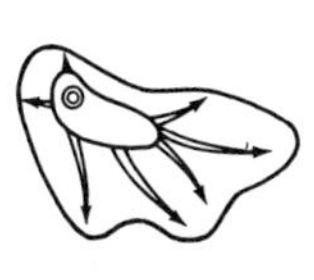 Expansion of settlement to the limit of land exploitable with available technology; the completion of the "frontier" phase of "free" land readily available	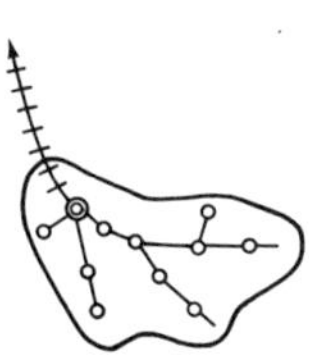 Regional system; emergence of central places linked to regional capital; export of a few primary products; first railroads, improved roads, riverboats, first transcontinental railroad and telegraph connections	2
3	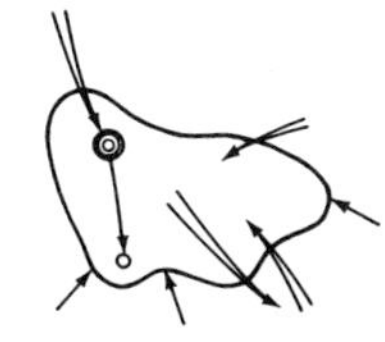 Competition for development from other peoples along bordering zones; influx of new migrants, especially into new industrial and commercial districts	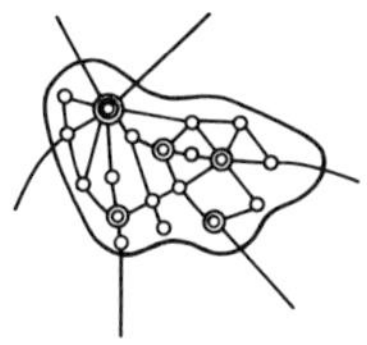 Interregional network; elaboration of central place system and regional linkages; integral part of nationwide systems; variety of transport and communication systems; railroads, interurban electrics, paved highways, buses, trucks, first airlines, telephones, radio	3
4	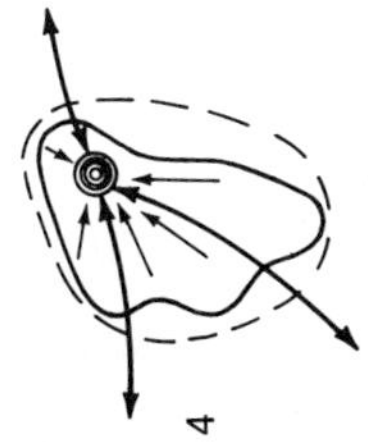 Metropolitanization; population largely urban and suburban; commuting range brings most of the area within close contact of center; high mobility of population, much interregional contact and movement	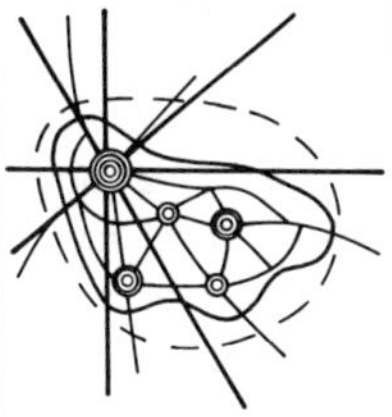 Intermetropolitan national network; elaborate metropolitan freeway system; nonstop air service to national and international centers; superhighways, unit trains, products pipelines; television	4

of the same. Thus, the main north-south route and its tributaries have become the major focus upon which additions have been made by stage 3.

By stage 4, the pattern of urbanization has changed radically. Metropolitan fields have emerged with intense functional linkages within them. Moreover, the internally focused orientation up to that time has shifted as it becomes a part of a much larger functional system. A regional system which was an entity unto itself up to the end of stage 3 has now become a subsystem of a larger system. As a result, there emerges a system of interregional routes, focused upon the largest and the oldest nucleation in the region. An additional event that occurs during this stage is a simplification of the overall transport network with an accompanying regional reorientation. This simplification has its tolls, of course, as some of the smaller nucleations and route segments disappear and certain other nucleations benefit. This latter group has accommodated much of the new growth because of the newly found locational advantages, while the loss of the other small centers was due to their sudden locational isolation, among other reasons.

It is possible to summarize the regional growth process represented in Figure 13-1 as one in which the early amplification of settlement and road development was followed by a structuring based upon differentiation through the growth of a hierarchy. Subsequently, as functional reorientation occurred, the entire regional settlement and transport structure underwent a distinct amplification from intraregional to interregional. Throughout these stages, the nature of the spatial system, including the circulation pattern, has changed. A dominant theme in the model presented above is that of spatial reorganization.

SPATIAL INTERACTION, TRANSPORT INNOVATION, AND SPATIAL REORGANIZATION

Spatial reorganization may be defined as the process according to which individual locations adapt their functional (social, economic, and political) roles in a system of places as a function of their changing relative connectivity or accessibility to the system as a whole. Undoubtedly, the most significant forces in changing accessibility within a space-economy arise from changes in the structure of transport networks and from radical improvements in transport technology. It is only fitting that we should conclude the last chapter of a book on movement by reiterating the importance of movement in shaping the spatial system.

Janelle (1969) has modeled the process of spatial reorganization in six steps by recourse to the concept of "locational utility" (Figure 13-2). In this figure, step 1 represents a time interval in which one place — or a number of places — requires a greater level of accessibility to accommodate the greater volume of shipments generated by a new plant or the development of a regional complex of processing plants. A search procedure (step 2) is undertaken for technological innovations which stimulates the discovery and subsequent implementation of that innovation (step 3). This transport innovation reduces transport time or cost between the various places, and time-space convergence ensues in which all these places are now "closer together" (step 4).

Figure 13-2 A process model of spatial reorganization: a simple schema

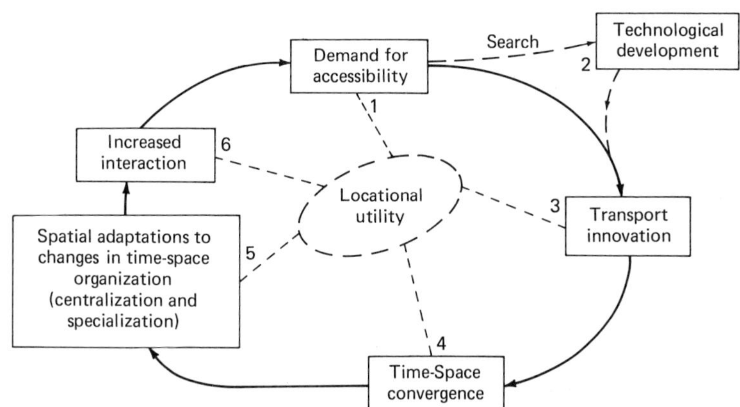

The greater accessibility to larger tributary areas for a small number of centers makes them good places in which to "do business," and, consequently, they attract a large number of new activities. The first aspect of spatial reorganization is thus one of centralization or spatial concentration of activities. In the first chapter of this book, we referred to agglomeration economies as one of the reasons for centralization, and at this juncture it may be realized that spatial reorganization also leads to agglomeration economies. Depending upon the particular nature of the agglomeration, it will be possible to realize internal scale economies (advantages of large-scale production) and/or external scale economies (advantages accruing from interindustry linkages). Frequently, as a result of comparative advantage, there are relative levels of industrial specialization as certain activities are concentrated in specific places. Thus, a second aspect of spatial reorganization is specialization (step 5).

The combined effect of greater concentrations of activities and of increased specialization is, of course, an increased amount of interaction. Thus, one can conclude that movement begets movement as increased interaction forces the various places to look for new transport innovations that will enable them to accommodate the increased traffic and thus maintain their newly found preeminence in the spatial system (steps 6 and 1). The process is clearly a circular one that tends to continue only as long as transport innovations are forthcoming. During specific times in this spatial reorganization process, undoubtedly lags occur. There is a simultaneous decline in the locational utility of certain places while others, perhaps more fortunate in their implementation of transport innovations, may emerge as new focal points.

This process of spatial reorganization was also implicit in Figure 13-1 concerning the growth of a hypothetical area in which new routes allowed certain nucleations to grow very rapidly while other nucleations disappeared.

Recognizing that locational utility probably varies with individual activities (e.g., the desirable or optimal national locational pattern of soft-drink plants is obviously different from that for automoblle assembly plants), Janelle suggests that there may be, at any one point in time, a number of utility surfaces. On this basis, he poses two significant questions:

1. Do transport improvements and certain agglomerative forces lead to increasing spatial variance in locational utility and, thus, toward greater place concentration of human enterprise?

2. Are these innovations (transport) and certain distributive forces leading toward a more homogeneous distribution of man's socioeconomic activities? (Janelle, 1969, 350–351)

The answer to both of these questions is a resounding yes, in that both processes of centralization and decentralization are occurring simultaneously in industrialized nations in general and certainly in the United States today. The process of spatial reorganization modeled in Figure 13-2 if allowed to continue more or less indefinitely would result in strong regional concentrations of activities such as in the U.S. Manufacturing Belt, the Wheat Belt, the petrochemical Southwest, and other regions with other specialties.

In an expanded version of his original conceptualization, Janelle has also modeled the process of spatial reorganization that results in decentralization of activities (Figure 13-3). In this model, two constraints that were implicit in the basic one are relaxed. Economic rationality, the continuous and explicit goal of maximizing locational utility, is assumed not to be an integral characteristic of the modus operandi of individuals and places. In addition, centralization of activities creates a continuous demand for land which, subsequently, entails a number of complications. The expanded model contains the basic model plus an additional loop which branches off from both the "centralization" and the "increased interaction" steps.

Thus, following the loop from step 5 (spatial centralization), we find that there is a simultaneous demand for space to contain these various new activities. At the same time, the increased interaction in a given spatial system results in some form of congestion whose end result is time-space as well as cost-space *divergence*. In other words, internal movement is no longer as ef-

Figure 13-3 A process model of spatial reorganization: an articulated schema

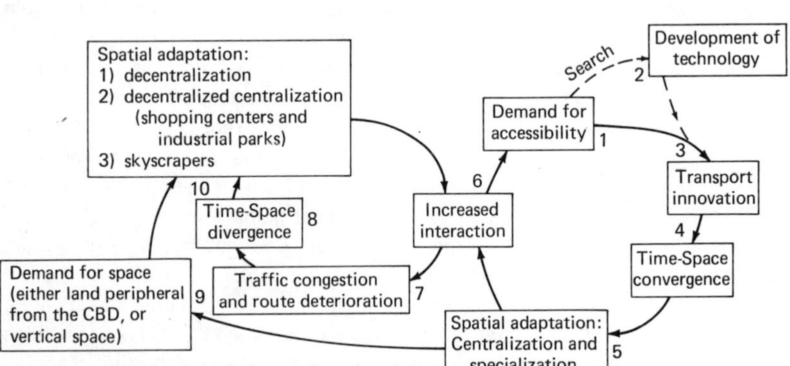

ficient as it was when the innovation was first put into effect, and activities are now relatively farther apart from one another in an individual agglomeration.

The combined effect of the demand for land and spatial divergence results in a new form of spatial adaptation in which there is a distinct decentralization in the form of new towns, industrial parks, office parks, and shopping centers, as well as vertical growth in the form of skyscrapers.

While there is time-space and cost-space divergence in the intraurban realm, convergence occurs among locations in a large region or a nation. In addition, there is a secular equalization in incomes among regions. Increased mobility decreases contrasts in wage rates. Transport innovations (e.g., pipelines and piggyback carriers) decrease the unit cost of commodity movement. Consumer preferences and tastes also equalize, partly as a result of the elaborate communication networks, especially the mass media. The cumulative impact of these changes is the emergence in the United States of what Friedmann and Miller (1965) call a "homogeneous coast-to-coast cost surface."

In this manner, we see a national space-economy that is continuously reorganizing itself spatially as a result of the operation of two forces simultaneously: concentration and decentralization. Growth begets growth as large urban regions are able to attract increasingly more activities, partly as a function of their highly developed system of interregional transport. This centralization occurs, of course, at the expense of the interstitial areas. By the term "centralization" we refer to an aggregative phenomenon, in which large urban centers are increasingly becoming the locales for a number of different types of activities. However, if we consider any specific activity, e.g., the steel industry, it may well be undergoing a process of decentralization in the sense that the traditional centers are losing their relative importance. Indeed, this is the way in which homogeneity and the blurring of interregional contrasts occur. Simultaneously, within these large urban regions, increasing time-space divergence, in the absence of new transport innovations, is rapidly leading to the decentralized urban form of the contemporary American scene.

POSTSCRIPT

Finally, it should be reiterated that a system is not a real thing, but a conceptual apparatus that enables us to make some sense out of the confusing real world. If the interrelationships are ill-defined and haphazard, then we will find it difficult to detect any order. Alternatively, we can say that a slice of reality lacks a coherent structure, but this lack may be due more to our lack of understanding than to any fault of reality. Also, when reality is changing quickly and when new structural interrelationships are being fabricated, the real world is not at rest, so to speak, and hence it is difficult to observe. It is easiest to recognize a portion of the real world as a system when it is in a condition of stable equilibrium. Systems exist in the context of an environment from which external forces emerge, and in order to retain its original structure and equilibrium, a system must have the capability of assimilating such external forces. An important external force that is operative in the world, as this book goes to press, is the "energy crisis." The shortages of gasoline may not have devastating consequences for the model of spatial reorganization outlined above, but we must recognize that the model may have to be modified somewhat.

Oil shortages and very expensive gasoline constitute major externally imposed "parametric shocks" to which the system must adjust itself. Any shortage (time, money, natural resources) is a constraint, but a gasoline shortage is a severe constraint to spatial interaction, especially in the American context. Dependent as we are on the private automobile and lacking as we are in public transportation facilities, the locations of residences, work places, stores, drive-in churches, and drive-in movies have adjusted themselves to a mass gasoline-consuming society over a period of three or four decades. Cheap gasoline has reduced the friction of distance and, as we saw in Figure 9-7 (income/people), the energy supply available to individuals in affluent nations is high, with few individuals being at "ground stage." This situation has allowed wasteful travel and a high level of system entropy. With an energy shortage, we can ill afford such high levels of entropy, and we need to concern ourselves with how to achieve some level of negative entropy with the minimum amount of economic and social hardship.

The transition to a new equilibrium requires both short-run and long-run adjustments. There may be a period of temporary chaos, while we make an effort to create a new equilibrium (an efficient set of structural interrelationships). The time required before a new equilibrium is created is known as "relaxation time." In social systems, such as urban and regional ones, relaxation times are long in comparison to those in physical systems. Some examples of short-run adjustments include the reduction of speed limits on highways and the elimination of some scheduled air carrier services. These are Band-Aid type or cosmetic adjustments.

In the long run, the basic spatial structure or organization of the system may need to be changed. Life-styles and attitudes, travel patterns, the location of activities, the low-density residential structure of the American city, the reliance on the private automobile, and much else may have to change before the system relaxes. New relationships between nodes and new flow patterns have to be established.

As of this writing, the price of imported crude oil is $10.75/barrel in the United States, and further increases are projected; the price of a gallon of gasoline is $2.07 in Poland and is equivalent to 3 percent of per capita annual income in India. All these factors increase the cost of movement, and consequently individuals will ask, Is this trip really necessary? The volume of interaction at particular distances may be expected to conform even more closely to distance-decay functions and gravity-model predictions. Indeed, distance *will* begin to matter even in affluent societies, and jet-setters will "jest set." Members of the human race will be even more tethered to geographic space. In Bunge's words, movement and space may be the most convenient primatives for geography. "Space will tell" (Bunge, 1966, 248), only louder and clearer than in the recent past.

Bibliography

Abler, Ronald (1971). "Distance, Intercommunications and Geography," *Proceedings* of the Association of American Geographers, **3**: 1–4.

Akers, S. B. (1960). "The Use of Wye-Delta Transformation in Network Simplification," *Journal of Operations Research,* **8**(3): 311–323.

Alao, N. A. (1970). "A Note on the Solution Matrix of a Network," *Geographical Analysis,* **2**: 83–88.

Alcaly, Roger (1967). "Aggregation and Gravity Models: Some Empirical Evidence," *Journal of Regional Science,* **7**(1): 61–73.

Aleksandrov, A. D., A. N. Kolmogorov, and M. A. Lavrentief (eds.) (1963), trans. by K. Hirsch. *Mathematics, Its Contents, Methods and Meaning,* vol. 3. Cambridge, Mass.: The M.I.T. Press.

Avondo-Bodino, G. (1962). *Economic Application of the Theory of Graphs,* New York: Gordon & Breach, Science Publishers, Inc.

Bachi, Roberto (1963). "Standard Distance Measures and Related Methods for Spatial Analysis," *Papers* of the Regional Science Association, **10**: 83–132.

Bagrow, Leo (1964). *History of Cartography,* Cambridge, Mass.: Harvard University Press.

Bellman, R., and R. Kalaba (1960). "On the *k*th Best Policies," *Journal of the Society for Industrial and Applied Mathematics,* **8**: 582–588.

Berge, C. (1962). *The Theory of Graphs and Its Applications,* New York: John Wiley & Sons, Inc.

Berry, Brian J. L. (1960). "An Inductive Approach to the Regionalization of Economic Development," in N. Ginsburg (ed.), *Essays on Geography and Economic Development,* Chicago: University of Chicago, Department of Geography, Research Paper no. 62, pp. 78–107.

——— (1964). "Approaches to Regional Analysis: A Synthesis," *Annals of the Association of American Geographers,* **54**: 2–11.

——— (1966). *Essays on Commodity Flows and the Spatial Structure of the*

Indian Economy, Chicago: University of Chicago, Department of Geography, Research Paper no. 111.

——— (1971). "Hierarchical Diffusion: The Basis of Developmental Filtering and Spread in a System of Growth Centers," in Niles M. Hansen (ed.), *Growth Centers in Regional Economic Development,* New York: The Free Press, pp. 108–138.

——— and W. L. Garrison (1958). "Alternate Explanations of Urban-Rank-Size Relationships," *Annals of the Association of American Geographers,* **48**: 83–91.

——— and Frank Horton (1970). *Geographical Perspectives on Urban Systems,* Englewood Cliffs, N.J.: Prentice-Hall, Inc.

Birdsall, Stephen S. (1971). "The Development and Cost of Location Stability," *Tidjschrift Voor Economische en Sociale Geografie,* **72**: 35–44.

Black, William R. (1971a). "An Iterative Model for Generating Transportation Networks," *Geographical Analysis,* **3**: 283–288.

——— (1971b). *Substitution and Concentration: An Examination of the Distance Exponent in Gravity Model Commodity Flow Studies,* Bloomington, Ind.: Department of Geography, Discussion Paper series no. 1.

——— (1973). "Toward a Factorial Ecology of Flows," *Economic Geography,* **49**: 59–67.

Blumenfeld, Hans (1954). "The Tidal Wave of Metropolitan Expansion," *Journal of the American Institute of Planners,* **20**: 3–14.

Boulding, Kenneth (1953). "Toward a General Theory of Growth," *Canadian Journal of Economic and Political Science,* **19**: 326–340.

Bowden, Leonard (1965). *Diffusion of the Decision to Irrigate: Simulation of the Spread of a New Resource Management Practice in the Colorado Northern High Plains,* Chicago: University of Chicago, Department of Geography, Research Paper no. 97.

Breese, G. (1966). *Urbanization in Newly Developing Countries,* Englewood Cliffs, N.J.: Prentice-Hall, Inc.

Britton, John N. H. (1971). "Methodology in Flow Analysis," *The East Lakes Geographer,* **7**: 22–36.

Broek, Jan O., and John W. Webb (1973). *A Geography of Mankind,* 2d ed., New York: McGraw-Hill Book Company.

Brown, Lawrence A. (1968a). *Diffusion Process and Location, A Conceptual Framework and Bibliography,* Philadelphia: Regional Science Research Institute, Bibliography Series no. 4.

——— (1968b). *Diffusion Dynamics, A Review of the Quantitative Theory of the Spatial Diffusion of Innovation,* Lund Studies in Geography, Series B, Human Geography no. 29, Lund: C. W. K. Gleerup.

——— (1970). "On the Use of Markov Chains in Movement Research," *Economic Geography,* **46**(Supplement): 393–403.

——— and Frank E. Horton (1970). "Functional Distance: An Operational Approach," *Geographical Analysis,* **2**: 76–83.

——— and David B. Longbrake (1970). "Migration Flows in Intraurban Space: Place Utility Considerations," *Annals of the Association of American Geographers,* **60**: 368–384.

——— and E. G. Moore (1969). "Diffusion Research in Geography: A Perspective," in Christopher Board, R. J. Chorley, P. Haggett, and D. R. Stoddart (eds.), *Progress in Geography,* vol. 1, London: Edward Arnold (Publishers) Ltd., pp. 119–157.

———, John Odland, and Reginald Golledge (1970). "Migration, Functional Distance and the Urban Hierarchy," *Economic Geography,* **46**: 472–485.

Bunge, William (1966). *Theoretical Geography,* Lund Studies in Geography, Series C, General and Mathematical Geography no. 1, Lund: C. W. K. Gleerup.

Burch, James S. (1961). "Traffic Interactance between Cities," in *Forecasting Highway Trips,* Washington, D.C. Highway Research Board Bulletin no. 297, pp. 14–17.

Burghardt, Andrew (1969). "The Origin and Development of the Road Network of the Niagara Peninsula, Ontario, 1770–1851," *Annals of the Association of American Geographers,* **59**: 417–440.

Capot-Rey, R. (1946). *Geographie de la Circulation sur les Continents,* Paris: Gallimard.

Carey, H. C. (1858). *Principles of Social Science,* Philadelphia: J. B. Lippincott Company.

Carroll, J. Douglas, and Howard W. Bevis (1957). "Predicting Local Travel in Urban Regions," *Papers and Proceedings* of the Regional Science Association, **3**: 183–197.

Carrothers, Gerald A. P. (1956). "An Historical Review of the Gravity and Potential Concepts of Human Interaction," *Journal of the American Institute of Planners,* **22**: 94–102.

Casetti, Emilio (1966). "Optimal Location of Steel Mills Serving the Quebec and Southern Ontario Steel Market," *The Canadian Geographer,* **10**: 27–39.

——— (1969). "Why Do Diffusion Processes Conform to Logistic Trends?" *Geographical Analysis,* **1**: 101–105.

Chisholm, Michael (1966). *Geography and Economics,* New York: Frederick A. Praeger, Inc.

——— (1967). *Rural Settlement and Land Use, An Essay on Location,* New York: John Wiley & Sons, Inc.

——— and Patrick O'Sullivan (1973). *Freight Flows and Spatial Aspects of the British Economy,* Cambridge, Mass.: Cambridge University Press.

Chombart de Lauwe, Paul-Henry (1952). *Paris et L'Agglomération Parisienne,* vol. 1, Paris: Presses Universitaires de France.

Chorley, Richard J. (1964). "Geography and Analogue Theory," *Annals of the Association of American Geographers,* **54**: 127–137.

——— and Peter Haggett (1967). *Models in Geography,* London: Methuen & Co., Ltd.

Clark, P. J., and F. C. Evans (1954). "Distance to Nearest Neighbor as a Measure of Spatial Relationships in Populations," *Ecology,* **35**: 445–453.

Clawson, Marion (1972). *America's Land and Its Uses,* Baltimore: The Johns Hopkins Press.

Clozier, R. (1963). *Geographie de la Circulation,* Paris: M. Th. Génin.

Conmy, Judy (1973). *A Comparison of Inter-State Economic Area Migration Flows, 1955–1960 and 1965–1970,* Washington: George Washington University, Department of Geography, unpublished paper.

Creighton, R. L. (1970). *Urban Transportation Planning,* Urbana, Ill.: University of Illinois Press.

Curry, Leslie (1964). "The Random Spatial Economy: An Exploration in Settlement Theory," *Annals of the Association of American Geographers,* **54**: 138–146.

——— (1966). "Chance and Landscape," in J. W. House (ed.), *Northern Geographical Essays in Honour of G. H. J. Daysh,* Newcastle-on-Tyne, Oriel Press, pp. 40–55.

Davis, Kingsley (1970). *World Urbanization 1950–1970, Volume I: Basic Data for Cities, Countries and Regions,* University of California, Berkeley: Institute of International Studies, Population Monograph Series no. 4.

District of Columbia (1969). *Taxicab Zone Map,* Public Service Commission of the District of Columbia.

Dixon, W. J. (ed.) (1971). *BMD Biomedical Computer Programs,* University of California Publications in Automatic Computation, no. 2, Berkeley: University of California Press.

Dodd, Stuart C. (1950). "The Interactance Hypothesis: A Gravity Model Fitting Physical Masses and Human Groups," *American Sociological Review,* **15**: 245–256.

Duncan, Otis Dudley, et al. (1960). *Metropolis and Region,* Baltimore: The Johns Hopkins Press.

Dyos, H. J., and D. H. Aldcraft (1969). *British Transport,* Leicester University Press.

Eighmy, T. H. (1972). "Rural Periodic Markets and the Extension of an Urban System: A Western Nigeria Example," *Economic Geography,* **48**: 299–315.

Ekström, A., and M. Williamson (1971). "Transportation and Urbanization," in A. G. Wilson (ed.), *Urban and Regional Planning,* London: Pion, Papers in Regional Science no. 3, pp. 37–46.

Farbey, B. A., A. H. Land, and J. D. Murchland (1967). "The Cascade Algorithm for Finding All Shortest Distances in a Directed Graph," *Management Science,* **14**: 19–28.

Flood, Merrill M. (1956). "The Travelling Salesman Problem," *Operations Research,* **4**: 61–75.

Fogel, Robert (1964). *Railroads and American Economic Growth,* Baltimore: The Johns Hopkins Press.

Ford, L. R., and D. R. Fulkerson (1962). *Flows in Networks,* Princeton, N.J.: Princeton University Press.

Forrester, Jay (1969). *Urban Dynamics,* Cambridge, Mass.: The M.I.T. Press.

——— (1970). "Systems Analysis as a Tool for Urban Planning," in *Industrial Location Policy,* Hearings before the Ad Hoc Subcommittee on Urban Growth, Committee on Banking and Currency, House of Representatives, Ninety-first Congress, Second Session, Washington, D.C.: U.S. Government Printing Office, pp. 239–265.

Fox, Karl A., and T. Krishna Kumar (1965). "The Functional Economic Area:

Delineation and Implications for Economic Analysis and Policy," *Papers* of the Regional Science Association, **15**: 57–85.

Friedmann, John, and John Miller (1965). "Urban Fields," *Journal of the American Institute of Planners,* **31**: 312–320.

Galt, John E. (1968). *The Residential Distribution of the Employees of Argonne National Laboratory. Patterns and Implications,* Unpublished Master's thesis, University of Chicago.

Garrison, William (1960a). "Connectivity of the Interstate Highway System," *Papers* of the Regional Science Association, **6**: 121–137.

——— (1960b). "Toward Simulation Models of Urban Growth and Development," *Proceedings of the IGU Symposium in Urban Geography, Lund 1960,* Lund Studies in Geography, Series B, Human Geography no. 24, Lund: C. W. K. Gleerup, pp. 91–108.

———, Brian J. L. Berry, D. F. Marble, J. D. Nystuen, and R. L. Morrill (1959). *Studies of Highway Development and Geographic Change,* Seattle: University of Washington Press.

——— and Duane Marble (1962). *The Structure of Transportation Networks,* Evanston, Ill.: Northwestern University, The Transportation Center for U.S. Department of Defense, Transportation Command.

Gauthier, H. L. (1970). "Geography, Transportation, and Regional Development," *Economic Geography,* **46**: 612–619.

Getis, Arthur (1963). "The Determination of the Location of Retail Activities with the Use of Map Transformations," *Economic Geography,* **39**: 14–22.

Goddard, J. B. (1970). "Functional Regions within the City Centre: A Study of Factor Analysis of Taxi Flows in Central London," *Transactions* of the Institute of British Geographers, **49**: 161–182.

Golledge, Reginald, R. Briggs, and D. Demko (1969). "The Configuration of Distances in Intra-Urban Space," *Proceedings* of the Association of American Geographers, **1**: 60–65.

Gottman, Jean (1961). *Megalopolis, the Urbanized Northeastern Seaboard of the United States,* New York: The Twentieth Century Fund.

Gould, Peter (1966). *On Mental Maps,* Ann Arbor, Mich.: Inter-University Community of Mathematical Geographers, Discussion Paper no. 9.

——— (1967). "Structuring Information on Spacio-Temporal Preferences," *Journal of Regional Science,* **7**(2, Supplement): 259–274.

——— (1969a). "Problems of Space Preferences Measures and Relationships," *Geographical Analysis,* **1**: 31–44.

——— (1969b). *Spatial Diffusion,* Washington, D.C.: Association of American Geographers, Commission on College Geography, Resource Paper no. 4.

——— (1972). "Pedagogic Review," *Annals of the Association of American Geographers,* **62**: 689–700.

——— and T. R. Leinbach (1966). "An Approach to the Geographical Assignment of Hospital Services," *Tijdschrift voor Economische en Sociale Geografie,* **57**: 203–206.

Hägerstrand, Torsten (1952). *The Propagation of Innovation Waves,* Lund Studies in Geography, Series B, Human Geography no. 4, Lund: C. W. K. Gleerup.

——— (1957). "Migration and Area," in David Hannerberg, Torsten Hägerstrand, and Bruno Odeving (eds.), *Migration in Sweden: A Symposium,* Lund Studies in Geography, Series B, Human Geography no. 13, Lund: C. W. K. Gleerup, pp. 27–158.

——— (1965). "Quantitative Techniques for Analysis of the Spread of Information and Technology," in C. A. Anderson and M. J. Bowman (eds.), *Education and Economic Development,* Chicago: University of Chicago Press, pp. 244–280.

——— (1966). "Aspects of the Spatial Structure of Social Communication and the Diffusion of Information," *Papers* of the Regional Science Association, **16**: 27–42.

——— (1967a). *Innovation Diffusion as a Spatial Process,* trans. by Alan Pred, Chicago: University of Chicago Press.

——— (1967b). "On Monte Carlo Simulation of Diffusion," in W. L. Garrison and D. F. Marble (eds.), *Quantitative Geography, Part 1: Economic and Cultural Topics,* Northwestern University, Studies in Geography no. 13, 1–32.

Haggett, Peter (1966). *Locational Analysis in Human Geography,* New York: St. Martin's Press, and London: Arnold.

——— (1967). "Network Models in Geography," in R. J. Chorley and Peter Haggett (eds.), *Models in Geography,* London: Methuen & Co., Ltd., pp. 609–668.

——— and Richard Chorley (1969). *Network Analysis in Geography,* New York: St. Martin's Press, and London: Arnold.

Hammer, Carl, and F. C. Iklé (1957). "Intercity Telephone and Airline Traffic Related to Distance and the 'Propensity to Interact,'" *Sociometry,* **20**: 306–316.

Harris, Chauncy D. (1954). "The Market as a Factor in the Localization of Industry in the United States," *Annals of the Association of American Geographers,* **44**: 315–348.

Harvey, David (1966). "Geographic Processes and the Analysis of Point Patterns: Testing a Diffusion Model by Quadrat Sampling," *Transactions* of the Institute of British Geographers, **40:** 81–95.

——— (1967). "Models of Spatial Patterns in Human Geography," in Richard Chorley and Peter Haggett (eds.), *Models in Geography,* London: Methuen & Co., Ltd., pp. 549–608.

——— (1969). *Explanation in Geography,* London: Edward Arnold (Publishers) Ltd.

Hay, Alan, and Robert H. Smith (1970). *Interregional Trade and Money Flows in Nigeria 1964,* Ibadan, Nigeria: Oxford University Press.

Hempel, C. G., and P. Oppenheim (1948). "Studies in the Logic of Explanation," *Philosophy of Science,* **15**: 135–175.

Hilbert, D., and S. Cohn-Vossen (1952). *Geometry and the Imagination,* New York: Chelsea Publishing Company.

Hodder, B. W. (1961). "Rural Periodic Day Markets in Part of Yorubaland," *Transactions* of the Institute of British Geographers, **29**: 149–159.

——— (1965). "Distribution of Markets in Yorubaland," *Scottish Geographical Magazine,* **81**: 48–58.

Hodge, Gerald (1965). "The Prediction of Trade Center Viability in the Great Plains," *Papers* of the Regional Science Association, **15**: 87–115.

Hoover, Edgar M. (1948). *The Location of Economic Activity,* New York: McGraw-Hill Book Company.

Horton, Frank E., and Paul W. Shuldiner (1967). "The Analysis of Land-Use Linkages," *Highway Research Record* no. 165, Washington, D.C.: National Research Council, Highway Research Board, pp. 96–107.

Hudson, John C. (1969). "Diffusion in a Central Place System," *Geographical Analysis,* **1**: 45–58.

——— (1972). *Geographical Diffusion Theory,* Northwestern University, Studies in Geography no. 19.

Huff, David (1960). "A Topographical (sic) Model of Consumer Space Preference," *Papers* of the Regional Science Association, **6**: 159–173.

Huntington, Ellsworth (1952). "Geography and Aviation," in Griffith Taylor (ed.), *Geography in the Twentieth Century,* London: Methuen & Co., Ltd., 1957, pp. 528–542.

Iklé, F. C. (1954). Sociological Relationship of Traffic to Population and Distance," *Traffic Quarterly,* **8**: 123–136.

Inose, Hiroshi (1972). "Communications Networks," *Scientific American,* **227**(3): 117–128.

Isard, Walter (1956). *Location and Space Economy,* Cambridge, Mass.: The M.I.T. Press.

——— et al. (1960). *Methods of Regional Analysis: An Introduction to Regional Science,* Cambridge, Mass.: The M.I.T. Press.

Jackman, W. (1916). *Development of Transportation in Modern England,* 2 vols., Cambridge, Mass.: Cambridge University Press.

James, G. A., A. D. Cliff, P. Haggett, and J. K. Ord (1970). "Some Discrete Distributions for Graphs with Applications to Regional Transport Networks," *Geografiska Annaler,* **52B**: 14–21.

Janelle, Donald G. (1968). "Central Place Development in a Time-Space Framework," *The Professional Geographer,* **20**(1): 5–10.

——— (1969). "Spatial Reorganization: A Model and Concept," *Annals of the Association of American Geographers,* **59**: 348–364.

Kansky, K. (1963). *The Structure of Transportation Networks,* Chicago: Department of Geography, Research Paper no. 84.

Kenyon, James B. (1970). "Elements of Inter-Port Competition in the United States," *Economic Geography,* **46**: 1–24.

King, Leslie (1969). *Statistical Analysis in Geography,* Englewood Cliffs, N.J.: Prentice-Hall, Inc.

Klein, Hans-Joachim (1967). "The Delimitation of the Town-Center in the Image of Its Citizens," in *Urban Core and Inner City, Proceedings of the International Study Week,* Amsterdam, Sept. 1966, Leiden: E. J. Brill, pp. 11–17.

Kniffen, Fred (1949). "The American Agricultural Fair: The Pattern," *Annals of the Association of American Geographers,* **39**: 264–279.

——— (1951). "The American Covered Bridge," *The Geographical Review,* **41**: 114–123.

——— (1965). "Folk Housing: Key to Diffusion," *Annals of the Association of American Geographers,* **55**: 549–577.

Knorst, William J. (1949). *Transportation and Traffic Management,* Chicago: College of Advanced Traffic.

Kolars, J. F., and H. J. Malin (1970). "Population and Accessibility: An Analysis of Turkish Railroads," *The Geographical Review,* **60**: 229–246.

Kulldorf, Gunnar (1955). *Migration Probabilities,* Lund Studies in Geography, Series B, Human Geography no. 14, Lund: C. W. K. Gleerup.

Lachene, R. (1965). "Networks and the Location of Economic Activities," *Papers* of the Regional Science Association, **14**: 183–196.

Lakshmanan, T. R., and Walter G. Hansen (1965a). "Market Potential Model and Its Application to a Regional Planning Problem," *Highway Research Record,* (102): 19–41.

——— and ——— (1965b). "A Retail Market Potential Model," *Journal of the American Institute of Planners,* **31**: 134–143.

Lösch, August (1954). *The Economics of Location,* New Haven: Yale University Press.

Luce, R. Duncan, and Albert D. Perry (1949). "Matrix Analysis of Group Structure," *Psychometrika,* **14**(1): 95–116.

Lynch, Kevin (1960). *The Image of the City,* Cambridge, Mass.: The M.I.T. Press.

——— (1972). *What Time Is This Place?,* Cambridge, Mass.: The M.I.T. Press.

Mackay, J. Ross (1958). "The Interactance Hypothesis and Boundaries in Canada: A Preliminary Study," *The Canadian Geographer,* **11**: 1–8.

Marble, Duane (1959). "Transport Inputs at Urban Residential Sites," *Papers* of the Regional Science Association, **5**: 253–266.

——— and M. Bowlby (1968). "Shopping Alternatives and Recurrent Travel Patterns," in Frank Horton (ed.), *Geographic Studies of Urban Transportation and Network Analysis,* Evanston, Ill.: Northwestern University, Studies in Geography no. 16, pp. 42–75.

Marschner, F. J. (1959). *Land Use and Its Patterns in the United States,* Washington: United States Department of Agriculture, Agricultural Research Service, Agricultural Handbook no. 153.

Marshall, Alfred (1930). *Principles of Economics,* London: Macmillan & Co., Ltd.

Meinig, Donald (1962). "A Comparative Historical Geography of Two Railnets: Columbia Basin and South Australia," *Annals of the Association of American Geographers,* **52**: 394–413.

——— (1972). "American Wests: Preface to a Geographical Interpretation," *Annals of the Association of American Geographers,* **62**: 159–184.

Mera, K. (1971). "An Evaluation of Gravity and Linear Programming Models for Predicting Interregional Commodity Flows," in J. Meyer (ed.), *Techniques of Transport Planning,* vol. 1, Washington, D.C.: Brookings Institute, pp. 297–303.

Misra, R. P. (1968). *Diffusion of Agricultural Innovations,* Mysore.

Morrill, Richard L. (1963a). "The Distribution of Migration Distances," *Papers* of the Regional Science Association, **11**: 75–84.

——— (1963b). "The Development of Spatial Distributions of Towns in Sweden: An Historical-Predictive Approach," *Annals of the Association of American Geographers,* **53**: 1–14.

——— (1965). "The Negro Ghetto: Problems and Alternatives," *The Geographical Review,* **55**: 339–361.

——— (1967). "The Movement of Persons and the Transportation Problem," in W. L. Garrison and D. F. Marble (eds.), *Quantitative Geography, Part I: Economic and Cultural Topics,* Evanston, Ill.: Northwestern University, Studies in Geography, no. 13, pp. 84–94.

——— (1968). "Waves of Spatial Diffusion," *Journal of Regional Science,* **8**(1): 1–18.

——— (1970). *The Spatial Organization of Society,* Belmont, Calif.: Wadsworth Publishing Company, Inc.

——— and William L. Garrison (1960). "Projections of Interregional Patterns of Trade in Wheat and Flour," *Economic Geography,* **36**: 116–126.

——— and Forrest Pitts. (1967). "Marriage, Migration and the Mean Information Field: A Study in Uniqueness and Generality," *Annals of the Association of American Geographers,* **57**: 401–422.

Muhsham, H. V. (1963). "Internal Migration in Open Populations," in J. Sutter (ed.), *Human Displacements,* Monaco: Entretiens de Monaco.

Murdie, Robert A. (1965). "Cultural Differences in Consumer Travel," *Economic Geography,* **41**: 211–233.

Mylroie, Willa (1956). "Evaluation of Intercity Travel Desire," in *Factors Influencing Travel Patterns,* Highway Research Board Bulletin 119, Washington, D.C., pp. 69–92.

Myrdal, Gunnar (1957). *Rich Lands and Poor,* New York: Harper & Row, Publishers, Incorporated.

National Academy of Sciences-National Research Council (NAS-NRC) (1965). *The Science of Geography,* Publication 1277.

Nordbeck, Stig (1964). "Computing Distances in Road Nets," *Papers* of the Regional Science Association, **12**: 207–220.

Nystuen, John D. (1963). "Identification of Some Fundamental Spatial Concepts," *Papers of the Michigan Academy of Science, Arts and Letters,* **48**: 373–384.

——— and Michael F. Dacey (1961). "A Graph Theory Interpretation of Nodal Regions," *Papers* of the Regional Science Association, **7**: 29–42.

Official Airline Guide (1971). Oakbrook, Ill.: The Reuben H. Donnelley Corp.

Olsson, Gunnar (1965). *Distance and Human Interaction: A Review and Bibliography,* Philadelphia: Regional Science Research Institute, Bibliography Series, no. 2.

——— (1967). "Central Place Systems, Spatial Interaction, and Stochastic Processes," *Papers* of the Regional Science Association, **18**: 13–45.

——— (1970). "Explanation, Prediction and Meaning Variance: An Assessment of Distance Models," *Economic Geography,* **46**(Supplement): 223–233.

Ore, O. (1963). *Graphs and Their Uses.* New York: Random House, Inc.

Patton, Donald J. (1958). "General Cargo Hinterlands of New York, Philadelphia, Baltimore and New Orleans," *Annals of the Association of American Geographers,* **48**: 436–455.

Paullin, C. O. (1932). *Atlas of the Historical Geography of the United States,* New York: American Geographical Society.

Pitts, F. (1965). "A Graph-Theoretic Approach to Historical Geography," *The Professional Geographer,* **17**: 15–20.

Pred, Allan (1964). "Toward a Typology of Manufacturing Flows," *The Geographical Review,* **54**: 65–84.

——— (1966). *The Spatial Dynamics of U.S. Urban-Industrial Growth, 1800–1914,* Cambridge, Mass.: The M.I.T. Press.

——— (1967). *Behavior and Location: Foundations for a Geographic and Dynamic Location Theory,* Part I, Lund Studies in Geography, Series B, Human Geography no. 27, Lund: C. W. K. Gleerup.

——— (1971). "Large-city Interdependence and the Pre-electronic Diffusion of Innovations in the U.S.," *Geographical Analysis,* **3**: 165–181.

Raisz, Erwin (1948). *General Cartography,* New York: McGraw-Hill Book Company.

Ratzel, Friedrich (1882). *Anthropogeographie,* 2 vols., Stuttgart: J. Engelhorn.

Ravenstein, E. G. (1885). "The Laws of Migration," *Journal of the Royal Statistical Society,* **48**, Part 2: 167–235.

Ray, D. Michael (1967). "Cultural Differences in Consumer Travel Behavior in Eastern Ontario," *The Canadian Geographer,* **11**: 143–156.

Reed, Wallace E. (1967). *Areal Interaction in India: Commodity Flows of the Bengal-Bihar Area,* Chicago: University of Chicago, Department of Geography, Research Paper no. 110.

Reilly, William J. (1929). *Methods for the Study of Retail Relationships.* University of Texas, Bulletin no. 294.

——— (1931). *The Law of Retail Gravitation,* New York: Knickerbocker Press.

Rimmer, Peter (1967). "The Changing Status of New Zealand Seaports," *Annals of the Association of American Geographers,* **57**: 88–100.

Roberts, P. O., and M. L. Funk (1964). *Toward Optimum Methods of Link Addition in Transportation Networks,* Cambridge, Mass.: Massachusetts Institute of Technology, Department of Civil Engineering.

Rodgers, Allan A. (1952). "Industrial Inertia — A Major Factor in the Location of the Steel Industry in the United States," *The Geographical Review,* **42**: 56–66.

Rogers, Everett M., and F. Floyd Shoemaker (1971). *Communications of Innovations, A Cross-Cultural Approach,* New York: The Free Press.

Rostow, Walt W. (1960). *The Stages of Economic Growth,* Cambridge, Mass.: Cambridge University Press.

Rushton, Gerard, Reginald Golledge, and W. A. V. Clark (1967). "Formulation and Test of a Normative Model for the Spatial Allocation of Grocery Expenditures by a Dispersed Population," *Annals of the Association of American Geographers,* **57**: 389–400.

Sauer, Carl O. (1952). *Agricultural Origins and Dispersals, The Domestication of Animals and Foodstuffs,* New York: American Geographical Society.

Scott, Allen J. (1971a). *Combinatorial Programming, Spatial Analysis and Planning,* London: Methuen & Co., Ltd.

——— (1971b). *An Introduction to Spatial Allocation Analysis,* Washington, D.C.: Association of American Geographers, Commission on College Geography, Resource Paper no. 9.

Siegel, S. (1956). *Nonparametric Statistics for the Behavioral Sciences,* New York: McGraw-Hill Book Company.

Smith, Adam (1909). *An Inquiry into the Nature and Causes of the Wealth of Nations,* New York: Collier.

Smith, Robert H. T. (1964). "Toward a Measure of Complementarity," *Economic Geography,* **40**: 1–8.

——— (1970). "Concepts and Methods in Commodity Flow Analysis," *Economic Geography,* **46**(Supplement): 404–416.

Smith, William, and Associates (1966). *Transportation and Parking for Tomorrow's Cities,* New Haven, Conn.: Wilbur Smith and Associates.

Snyder, David (1962). "Commercial Passenger Linkages and the Metropolitan Nodality of Montevideo," *Economic Geography,* **38**: 95–121.

Soja, Edward W. (1968). "Communications and Territorial Integration in East Africa: An Introduction to Transaction Flow Analysis," *The East Lakes Geographer,* **4**: 39–57.

Sorre, Max (1954). *Les Fondements de la Geographie Humaine,* vol. II, Les Fondements Techniques, Paris: Armand Colin.

Stea, David (1969). "The Measurement of Mental Maps: An Experimental Model for Studying Conceptual Space," in Kevin R. Cox and Reginald Golledge (eds.), *Behavioral Problems in Geography: A Symposium,* Evanston, Ill.: Northwestern University Studies in Geography, no. 17, pp. 228–253.

Stewart, John Q. (1941). "An Inverse Distance Variation for Certain Social Influences," *Science,* **93**: 89–90.

——— (1947). "Empirical Mathematical Rules concerning the Distribution of Equilibrium of Population," *The Geographical Review,* **37**: 461–485.

Taaffe, Edward J. (1956). "Air Transportation and the United States Urban Distribution," *The Geographical Review,* **46**: 219–239.

——— (1958). "A Map Analysis of United States Airline Competition — Part 1. The Development of Competition," *The Journal of Air Law and Commerce,* Spring, pp. 121–147, "Part 2 — Competition and Growth," Autumn, pp. 402–427.

——— (1962). "The Urban Hierarchy: An Air Passenger Definition," *Economic Geography,* **38**: 1–14.

———, B. J. Garner, and M. Yeates (1963). *The Peripheral Journey to Work,* Evanston, Ill.: Northwestern University Press.

———, R. Morrill, and P. Gould (1963). "Transport Expansion in Underdeveloped Countries: A Comparative Analysis," *The Geographical Review,* **53**: 503–529.

Taylor, George R. (1951). *The Transportation Revolution, 1815–1860,* New York: Harper & Row, Publishers, Incorporated.

Thrower, N. J. W. (1966). *Original Survey and Land Subdivision,* Chicago: Rand McNally & Company.

Timbers, J. A. (1967). "Route Factors in Road Networks," *Traffic Engineering and Control,* **9**: 392–401.

Tobler, Waldo (1961). *Map Transformation of Geographic Space,* Ph.D. thesis. University of Washington, Seattle.

——— (1963). Geographic Area and Map Projections," *The Geographical Review,* **53**: 59–78.

Travers, Jeffrey, and Stanley Milgram (1969). "An Experimental Study of the Small World Problem," *Sociometry,* **32**(4): 425–443.

Ullman, Edward L. (1949). "The Railroad Pattern of the United States," *The Geographical Review,* **39**: 242–256.

——— (1954). "Amenities as a Factor in Regional Growth," *The Geographical Review,* **44**: 119–132.

——— (1956). "The Role of Transportation and the Bases for Interaction," in William L. Thomas (ed.), *Man's Role in Changing the Face of the Earth,* Chicago: University of Chicago Press, pp. 862–880.

——— (1957). *American Commodity Flow, A Geographical Interpretation of Rail and Water Traffic Based on Principles of Spatial Interchange,* Seattle: University of Washington Press.

——— (1958). "Regional Development and the Geography of Concentration," *Papers and Proceedings* of the Regional Science Association, **4:** 179–198.

U.S. Census of Population (1970). *Number of Inhabitants,* U.S. Summary, Department of Commerce, Bureau of the Census, Census of Population, PC (1) A1.

U.S. Department of Commerce (1965). "The Transactions Table of the 1958 Input-Output Study and Revised Direct and Total Requirements Data," *Survey of Current Business,* **45**(9): 33–49, Washington, D.C.: U.S. Government Printing Office.

——— (1969). Office of Business Economics, *Input-Output Structure of the U.S. Economy:* 1963, vol. II, Direct Requirements for Detailed Industries, Washington, D.C.: Government Printing Office.

U.S. Department of Labor (1950). U.S. Bureau of Labor Statistics, *Interindustry Flow of Goods and Services by Industry, of Origin and Destination,* Washington, D.C.

Van Royen, William, and Nels A. Bengtson (1964). *Fundamentals of Economic Geography,* Englewood Cliffs, N.J.: Prentice-Hall, Inc.

Vidal de la Blache, P. (1926). *Principles of Human Geography,* New York: Holt, Rinehart and Winston, Inc.

Warntz, William (1961). "Trans-Atlantic Paths and Pressure Patterns," *The Geographical Review,* **51**: 187–212.

——— (1964). "A New Map of the Surface of Population Potentials for the United States," *The Geographical Review,* **54**: 170–184.

——— (1965). *A Note on Surfaces and Paths and Applications to Geographical Problems,* Ann Arbor, Mich.: Michigan Inter-University Community of Mathematical Geographers, Discussion Paper no. 6.

——— (1966). "The Topology of Socio-Economic Terrain and Spatial Flows," *Papers* of the Regional Science Association, **17**: 47–61.

——— (1967). "Global Science and the Tyranny of Space," *Papers* of the Regional Science Association, **19**: 7–19.

Webber, M. (1964). "Culture, Territoriality and the Elastic Mile," *Papers* of the Regional Science Association, **13**: 59–69.

Weber, Alfred (1929). *Theory of the Location of Industries,* trans. by C. J. Friedrich, Chicago: University of Chicago Press.

Werner, C. (1968). "A Research Seminar in Theoretical Transportation Geography," in F. Horton (ed.), *Geographical Studies of Urban Transportation and Network Analysis,* Evanston, Ill.: Northwestern University, Department of Geography, Studies in Geography no. 16, pp. 128–170.

Wheeler, James O. (1972). "Trip Purposes and Urban Activity Linkage," *Annals of the Association of American Geographers,* **62**: 641–654.

Wilson, A. G. (1970). *Entropy in Urban and Regional Modelling,* London: Pion.

Wilson, G. L. (1954). *Transportation and Communications,* New York: Appleton-Century Crofts, Inc.

Wolpert, Julian (1965). "Behavioral Aspects of the Decision to Migrate," *Papers* of the Regional Science Association, **15**: 159–169.

Yeates, Maurice H. (1965). "Hinterland Delimination: A Distance Minimizing Approach," *The Professional Geographer,* **15**(6): 7–10.

——— (1974). *An Introduction to Quantitative Analysis in Human Geography,* New York: McGraw-Hill Book Company.

Young, E. C. (1924). "The Movement of Farm Population," *Cornell Agricultural Experiment Station Bulletin,* no. 426, Ithaca, N.Y.

Yuill, Robert S. (1965). *A Simulation Study of Barrier Effects in Spatial Diffusion Problems,* Ann Arbor, Mich.: Michigan Inter-University Community of Mathematical Geographers, no. 5.

Zipf, G. K. (1949). *Human Behavior and the Principle of Least Effort,* Cambridge, Mass.: Addison-Wesley Press, Inc.

Index

Credits

Figure 2-4 Adapted from William Warntz, *A Note on Surfaces and Paths and Applications to Geographical Problems,* Michigan Inter-University Community of Mathematical Geographers, Discussion Paper no. 6, 1965, p. 16, Fig. 4; by permission of the editor.

Figure 2-8 Adapted from Torsten Hägerstrand, "Migration and Area," in D. Hannerberg, T. Hägerstrand, B. Odeving (eds.), *Migration in Sweden: A Symposium,* Lund Studies in Geography, Series B, Human Geography no. 13, 1957, Fig. 38, Lund: C. W. K. Gleerup; by permission of the publisher.

Figure 2-10 Adapted from William Bunge, *Theoretical Geography,* Lund Studies in Geography, Series C, General and Mathematical Geography no. 1, 1966, p. 180, Fig. 7.1, Lund: C. W. K. Gleerup; by permission of the author and the publisher.

Figure 2-11 From *General Cartography* by Erwin Raisz, copyright 1938, 1948 by the McGraw-Hill Book Company, p. 4, Fig. 2; used with permission.

Figure 3-2 From *The Location of Economic Activity* by Edgar M. Hoover, copyright 1948 by McGraw-Hill, Inc.; used with permission of McGraw-Hill Book Company; adapted from p. 24, Table 2.2.

Figure 3-3 From William J. Knorst, *Transportation and Traffic Management,* vol. 1, 1949, Chicago: College of Advanced Traffic, figure on p. 269; used with permission.

Figure 3-4 From David E. Snyder, "Commercial Passenger Linkages and the Metropolitan Nodality of Montevideo," *Economic Geography,* 1962, p. 110, Fig. 5; used with permission of the editor.

Figure 3-6 *Official Airline Guide,* 1971.

Figure 3-7 C & P Telephone Company.

Figure 3-10 From *America's Land and Its Uses,* by Marion Clawson, copyright by the Johns Hopkins University Press, 1972, published for Resources for the Future by The Johns Hopkins University Press, Fig. 2, p. 13; used with permission.

Figure 3-11 Janelle (1968: 6, Fig. 1); reproduced by permission from *The Professional Geographer* of the Association of American Geographers, vol. 20, 1968.

Figure 4-1 From Peter Haggett, *Locational Analysis in Human Geography,* St. Martin's Press, Inc., and Edward Arnold, Ltd., 1966, p. 18; used with permission of the author and the publisher.

Figure 4-2 Patton (1958: 440, Fig. 3); reproduced by permission from the *Annals of the Association of American Geographers,* vol. 48, 1958.

Figure 4-3 From *Geographie de la Circulation,* by R. Clozier, Paris: M. Th. Génin, 1963, p. 125; used with permission of the publisher.

Figure 4-7 Warntz (1961: 205, Fig. 7), adapted from *The Geographical Review,* vol. 51, 1961, copyright by the American Geographical Society of New York; used with permission.

Figure 5-3 Pitts (1965: 17, Fig. 2); reproduced by permission from *The Professional Geographer* of Association of American Geographers, vol. 17, 1965.

Figure 5-8 Garrison and Marble (1962: 59, 63, 64, Figs. 14 to 17).

Figure 5-9 Adapted from William Bunge, *Theoretical Geography,* Lund Studies in Geography, Series C, General and Mathematical Geography no. 1, 1966, pp. 187–188, Lund: C. W. K. Gleerup; used with permission of the author and the publisher.

Figure 5-10 Garrison and Marble (1962; 5, Fig. 1).

Figure 5-11 From Peter Haggett, *Locational Analysis in Human Geography,* St. Martin's Press, Inc., and Edward Arnold, Ltd., 1966, p. 82. Fig. 3.15; used with permission of the author and the publisher.

Figure 5-12 Reproduced from Richard Chorley and Peter Haggett (eds.), *Models in Geography,* London: Methuen & Co., Ltd., 1967, Fig. 15.11B, p. 626, with permission of the publisher.

Figure 5-13 Reproduced from Richard Chorley and Peter Haggett (eds.), *Models in Geography,* London: Methuen & Co., Ltd., 1967, Fig. 15-12A, B, C, E, p. 627, with permission of the publisher.

Figure 5-14 Adapted from Peter Haggett, *Locational Analysis in Human Geography,* St. Martin's Press, Inc., and Edward Arnold, Ltd., p. 82, Fig. 3.15; used with permission of the author and the publisher.

Figure 6-1 Adapted from C. O. Paullin, *Atlas of the Historical Geography of the United States,* C. I. W. Publication no. 401, 1932, published for the Carnegie Institution of Washington by the American Geographical Society, Plates 140A, 141A, and 141B, courtesy of the Carnegie Institution of Washington.

Figure 6-2 Gottman (1961: 649).

Figure 6-3 Taaffe, Morrill, and Gould (1963: 504, Fig. 1); adapted from *The Geographical Review,* vol. 53, 1963, copyright by the American Geographical Society of New York.

Figure 6-4 Lachene (1965: 194, Fig. 4); reprinted with permission of the Regional Science Association.

Figure 6-5 Meinig (1962: 413, Fig. 3); reproduced by permission from the *Annals of the Association of American Geographers,* vol. 52, 1962.

Figure 6-6 Reprinted from "An Iterative Model for Generating Transportation Networks," by William R. Black, in *Geographical Analysis,* vol. 3 (July 1971), p. 287. Copyright © 1971 by the Ohio State University Press. All rights reserved.

Figure 6-7 Adapted from Karel Kansky, *The Structure of Transportation Networks,* University of Chicago, Department of Geography, Research Paper no. 84, pp. 143, 146, Figs. 30, 31; used with permission of Professor Kansky and the University of Chicago.

Figure 6-8 Kolars and Malin (1970: 234–236, Figs. 3 to 7); adapted from *The Geographical Review,* vol. 60, 1970; copyright by the American Geographical Society of New York.

Figure 7-1 Adapted from Peter Gould, *On Mental Maps,* Michigan Inter-University Community of Mathematical Geographers, Discussion Paper no. 9, 1966, Figs. 2, 5; with permission of the editor.

Figure 7-2 Lynch (1960: 147, Fig. 38); reprinted from *The Image of the City* by Kevin Lynch, by permission of The M.I.T. Press, Cambridge, Mass.

Figure 7-4 Marble and Bowlby (1968: 43, 44, Figs. 1, 2); adapted from *Northwestern University Studies in Geography* no. 16, with permission of the editor.

Figure 7-6 Murdie (1965: 221, Figs. 14, 15); reprinted from *Economic Geography,* vol. 41, 1965, with permission of the editor.

Figure 7-7 Morrill and Pitts (1967: 404, Fig. 1); reproduced by permission from the *Annals of the Association of American Geographers,* vol. 57, 1967.

Figure 7-8 Adapted from Morrill and Pitts (1967: 403, Table 1; 407, Table 2; 408, Table 3; 409, Tables 4, 5); by permission from the *Annals of the Association of American Geographers,* vol. 57, 1967.

Figure 7-9 Morrill and Pitts (1967: 414, Fig. 10); reproduced by permission from the *Annals of the Association of American Geographers,* vol. 57, 1967.

Figure 8-1 William Van Royen and Nels A. Bengtson, *Fundamentals of Economic Geography,* 4th ed., © 1956, p. 278; reprinted by permission of Prentice-Hall, Inc., Englewood Cliffs, N.J.

Figure 8-3 Morrill (1967: 91); adapted from *Northwestern University Studies in Geography* no. 13, with permission of the editor.

Figure 8-4 Adapted from John E. Galt, *The Residential Distribution of the Employees of Argonne National Laboratory*, 1968, unpublished master's thesis, University of Chicago, with permission of the author.

Figure 8-5 Pred (1964: 68, Fig. 1); adapted from *The Geographical Review,* vol. 54, 1964; copyright by the American Geographical Society of New York.

Figure 9-1 Reprinted from *Methods of Regional Analysis,* by Walter Isard et al., 1960, by permission of The M.I.T. Press, Cambridge, Mass., p. 496, Fig. 1.

Figure 9-4 Mackay (1958: 4, Fig. 2); adapted from *The Canadian Geographer,* vol. 11, with permission of the editor.

Figure 9-5 Adapted from Torsten Hägerstrand, "Migration and Area," in D. Hannerberg, T. Hägerstrand, and B. Odeving (eds.), *Migration in Sweden: A Symposium,* Lund Studies in Geography, Series B, Human Geography no. 13, 1957, p. 114, Figs. 68, 69, Lund: C. W. K. Gleerup; by permission of the publisher.

Figure 10-2 Nystuen and Dacey (1961: 35, Fig. 1); reprinted with permission of the Regional Science Association.

Figure 10-3 Nystuen and Dacey (1961: 39, Fig. 2); reprinted with permission of the Regional Science Association.

Figure 10-4 Hay and Smith (1970: 133, Fig. 4.2); reprinted with permission of Oxford University Press.

Figure 10-5 Soja (1968: 48, Fig. 1); reprinted with permission of the editor of the *East Lakes Geographer.*

Figure 10-6 Reprinted from Brian J. L. Berry, *Essays on Commodity Flows and the Spatial Structure of the Indian Economy,* University of Chicago, Department of Geography, Research Paper no. 111, 1966, Figs. 92, 94, 96, 98, 100; with permission of the author and the University of Chicago.

Figure 10-7 Reprinted from J. B. Goddard, "Functional Regions within the City Centre: A Study of Factor Analysis of Taxi Flows in Central London," *Transactions of the Institute of British Geographers,* 49, 1970, p. 164; with permission of the Institute of British Geographers.

Figure 10-8 Reprinted from J. B. Goddard, "Functional Regions within the City Centre: A Study of Factor Analysis of Taxi Flows in Central London," *Transactions of the Institute of British Geographers,* 49, 1970, pp. 163, 170, 171, 172, 173, 174; with permission of the Institute of British Geographers.

Figure 11-1 Hägerstrand (1966: 35–37, 39); adapted with permission of the Regional Science Association.

Figure 11-3 Hudson (1972: 116), from *Northwestern University Studies in Geography* no. 19; with permission of the editor.

Figure 11-4 Reprinted from "Large-City Interdependence and the Pre-electronic Diffusion of Innovations in the U.S.," by Allan R. Pred, from *Geographical Analysis,* vol. 3 (April 1971), p. 176. Copyright © 1971 by the Ohio State University Press. All rights reserved.

Figure 11-5 Sauer (1952, plate I); reprinted with permission from a map copyrighted by the American Geographical Society of New York.

Figure 11-6 Marschner (1959: 29).

Figure 11-7 Gould (1969b: 63, Fig. 68); reproduced by permission from the Commission on College Geography, Resource Paper no. 4, *Spatial Diffusion,* by P. Gould, of the Association of American Geographers, and by permission of the author.

Figure 11-9 Reproduced from Jeffrey Travers and Stanley Milgram, "An Experimental Study of the Small World Problem," *Sociometry,* vol. 32, no. 4, December 1969, p. 439, Fig. 3; with permission of the authors and the editor.

Figure 11-10 Gould (1969b: 20, Fig. 26); reproduced by permission from the Commission on College Geography, Resource Paper no. 4, *Spatial Diffusion,* by P. Gould, of the Association of American Geographers, and with permission of the author.

Figure 11-11 Morrill (1968: 7, Fig. 10); reprinted with permission of the Regional Science Association.

Figure 11-12 Morrill (1968: 4, Fig. 8); reprinted with permission of the Regional Science Association.

Figure 11-13 *Innovation Diffusion as a Spatial Process,* by Torsten Hägerstrand, trans. A. Pred, The University of Chicago Press, 1967; English translation and Postscript © 1967 by Torsten Hägerstrand, pp. 102, 103, Figs. 49, 50.

Figure 11-14 *Innovation Diffusion as a Spatial Process,* by Torsten Hägerstrand, trans. A. Pred, The University of Chicago Press, 1967; English translation and Postscript © 1967 by Torsten Hägerstrand, p. 142, map I (four figures).

Figure 11-15 *Innovation Diffusion as a Spatial Process,* by Torsten Hägerstrand, trans. A. Pred, The University of Chicago Press, 1967; English translation and Postscript © 1967 by Torsten Hägerstrand, p. 254, map III (six figures).

Figure 11-16 *Innovation Diffusion as a Spatial Process,* by Torsten Hägerstrand, trans. A. Pred, The University of Chicago Press, 1967; English translation and Postscript © 1967 by Torsten Hägerstrand, p. 244, Table 24.

Figure 11-17 *Innovation Diffusion as a Spatial Process,* by Torsten Hägerstrand, trans. by A. Pred, The University of Chicago Press, 1967; English translation and Postscript © 1967 by Torsten Hägerstrand, p. 245, Table 38.

Figure 11-18 *Innovation Diffusion as a Spatial Process,* by Torsten Hägerstrand, trans. A. Pred, The University of Chicago Press, 1967; English translation and Postscript © 1967 by Torsten Hägerstrand, p. 254, Table 45.

Figure 11-19 *Innovation Diffusion as a Spatial Process,* by Torsten Hägerstrand, trans. A. Pred, The University of Chicago Press, 1967; English translation and Postscript © 1967 by Torsten Hägerstrand, p. 257, Fig. 98.

Figure 11-20 *Innovation Diffusion as a Spatial Process,* by Torsten Hägerstrand, trans. A. Pred, The University of Chicago Press, 1967; English translation and Postscript © 1967 by Torsten Hägerstrand, p. 268, map IV (six figures).

Figure 11-21 Hägerstrand (1967b: 19, Fig. 7); adapted from *Northwestern University Studies in Geography* no. 13, with permission of the editor.

Figure 11-22 Hägerstrand (1967b: 21, Fig. 8); adapted from *Northwestern University Studies in Geography* no. 13, with permission of the editor.

Figure 11-23 Adapted from L. Bowden, *The Diffusion of the Decision to Irrigate,* University of Chicago, Department of Geography, Research Paper no. 97, 1965, Figs. 15, 21, 24, 28; with permission of the author and the University of Chicago.

Figure 12-1 Adapted from Oystein Ore, *Graphs and Their Uses*; © copyright 1963 by Yale University and Random House, Inc., pp. 23–24, Figs. 2.21 and 2.22; used with permission.

Figure 12-2 Flood (1956: 70); adapted with permission; copyright 1956, Operations Research of America.

Figure 12-3 Adapted from A. Scott, *Combinatorial Programming, Spatial Analysis and Planning,* London: Methuen and Co., Ltd., 1971, p. 69, Fig. 5.1*a*; p. 70, Fig. 5.1*b*; p. 71, Fig. 5.1*d*; used with permission of the author and the publisher.

Figure 12-4 Adapted from A. Scott, *Combinatorial Programming, Spatial Analysis and Planning,* London: Methuen and Co., Ltd., 1971, p. 76, Fig. 5.4*a*; p. 77, Fig. 5.4*b*; used with permission of the author and the publisher.

Figure 12-5 Adapted from A. Scott, *Combinatorial Programming, Spatial Analysis and Planning,* London: Methuen and Co., Ltd., 1971, p. 80, Fig. 5.5; p. 82, Fig. 5.6; used with permission of the author and the publisher.

Figure 12-9 Reproduced by permission from the Commission on College Geography, Resource Paper no. 9, *An Introduction to Spatial Allocation Analysis* by Allen Scott, of the Association of American Geographers, 1971, and with the permission of the author, p. 5, Fig. 1.

Figure 12-10 Reproduced by permission from the Commission on College Geography, Resource Paper no. 9, *An Introduction to Spatial Allocation Analysis,* by Allen Scott, of the Association of American Geographers, 1971, and with the permission of the author, p. 12, Fig. 2.

Figure 12-11 Yeates (1965: 9, Fig. 5); reproduced by permission from the *Professional Geographer* of the Association of American Geographers, vol. 15, 1963.

Figure 13-1 Meinig (1972: 162, Fig. 1); reproduced with permission from the *Annals of the Association of American Geographers,* vol. 62, 1972.

Figure 13-2 Janelle (1969: 350, Fig. 3); reproduced by permission from the *Annals of the Association of American Geographers,* vol. 59, 1969.

Figure 13-3 Janelle (1969: 353, Fig. 5); reproduced by permission from the *Annals of the Association of American Geographers,* vol. 59, 1969.

ABCDEFGHIJ–H–798765

LIBRARY
MAR 2 0 1976
UNIVERSITY OF TORONTO